MW00343026

Mastering Private Equity

Mastering Private Equity

Transformation via Venture Capital, Minority Investments & Buyouts

Claudia Zeisberger
Michael Prahl
Bowen White

WILEY

This edition first published 2017
© 2017 Claudia Zeisberger, Michael Prahl and Bowen White

Registered office
John Wiley & Sons Ltd, The Atrium, Southern Gate, Chichester, West Sussex, PO19 8SQ, United Kingdom

For details of our global editorial offices, for customer services and for information about how to apply for permission to reuse the copyright material in this book please see our website at www.wiley.com.

All rights reserved. No part of this publication may be reproduced, stored in a retrieval system, or transmitted, in any form or by any means, electronic, mechanical, photocopying, recording or otherwise, except as permitted by the UK Copyright, Designs and Patents Act 1988, without the prior permission of the publisher.

Wiley publishes in a variety of print and electronic formats and by print-on-demand. Some material included with standard print versions of this book may not be included in e-books or in print-on-demand. If this book refers to media such as a CD or DVD that is not included in the version you purchased, you may download this material at http://booksupport.wiley.com. For more information about Wiley products, visit www.wiley.com.

Designations used by companies to distinguish their products are often claimed as trademarks. All brand names and product names used in this book are trade names, service marks, trademarks or registered trademarks of their respective owners. The publisher is not associated with any product or vendor mentioned in this book.

Limit of Liability/Disclaimer of Warranty: While the publisher and author have used their best efforts in preparing this book, they make no representations or warranties with respect to the accuracy or completeness of the contents of this book and specifically disclaim any implied warranties of merchantability or fitness for a particular purpose. It is sold on the understanding that the publisher is not engaged in rendering professional services and neither the publisher nor the author shall be liable for damages arising herefrom. If professional advice or other expert assistance is required, the services of a competent professional should be sought.

Library of Congress Cataloging-in-Publication Data

Names: Zeisberger, Claudia, author. | Prahl, Michael, author. | White, Bowen, author.
Title: Mastering private equity : transformation via venture capital, minority investments
    & buyouts / Claudia Zeisberger, Michael Prahl, Bowen White.
Description: Hoboken : Wiley, 2017. | Includes index. |
Identifiers: LCCN 2017013988 (print) | LCCN 2017014649 (ebook) | ISBN 9781119327943 (pdf) |
    ISBN 9781119327981 (epub) | ISBN 9781119327974 (paperback) | ISBN 9781119327943 (ebk) |
    ISBN 9781119327981 (ebk)
Subjects: LCSH: Private equity. | Venture capital. | Capital investments. |
    Consolidation and merger of corporations. | BISAC: BUSINESS & ECONOMICS / Finance.
Classification: LCC HG4751 (ebook) | LCC HG4751 .Z42 2017 (print) | DDC
    658.15/224—dc23
LC record available at https://lccn.loc.gov/2017013988

ISBN 978-1-119-32797-4 (hardback) ISBN 978-1-119-32794-3 (epdf)
ISBN 978-1-119-32798-1 (epub)

10 9 8 7 6 5 4 3 2

Cover design: Wiley
Cover image: (c) jps/Shutterstock

Set in is 10/12pt Helvetica LT Std by Aptara, New Delhi, India
Printed in Great Britain by Bell & Bain Ltd, Glasgow

CONTENTS

LIST OF CONTRIBUTORS

Our distinguished Guest Authors made time to share their experiences and at times critical comments, thereby adding a practical perspective to our writing. We are grateful for their support and list them in order of appearance.

Henry R. Kravis, Co-Chairman & Co-CEO of **KKR** kindly agreed to write the foreword for this book and we appreciate his thoughtful contribution on the evolution of private equity over the years.

The views expressed in the guest comments are the opinion of the respective author and not necessarily that of their firms and organizations.

FOREWORD

Henry R. Kravis, Co-Chairman and Co-CEO of KKR

What is private equity? Given you're reading this book, I'm certain this is a question you'd like to have answered.

To define the asset class properly is not as simple as looking it up in a dictionary or conducting a quick search on the internet. To do so would give you some version of private equity is capital that is invested privately. Not on a public exchange. The capital typically comes from institutional or high-net worth investors who can contribute substantially and are able to withstand an average holding period of seven years.

But private equity is so much more than its literal definition.

The way I would describe private equity, or PE, today is an asset class delivering market-beating investment returns that has grown college endowments and enhanced the retirement security of millions of pension beneficiaries, including teachers, firefighters, police and other public workers. Just as important, private equity does this by helping companies grow and improve, starting from day one of an investment.

Different firms approach this in different ways, but consistent among them is the first enduring principle of private equity: alignment of interest. This refers to alignment between a company's management and the firm investing in it, but it also means alignment between the firm investing and its own investors.

At KKR, once we make an investment, we work with a company's management team to improve the balance sheet, margins, operations, and, importantly, their topline. These actions may seem obvious steps in how to create successful companies today, but when George Roberts, Jerry Kohlberg and I co-founded KKR a little over 40 years ago, they were not.

In the '70s and '80s, companies were less concerned with these efficiencies, perhaps because management was focused on other things. To help solve for this, when we were getting started, we instituted management ownership programs, a concept that was not typical in those days. Running a company as an owner unlocks value and this alignment of interest impacts company profitability substantially. I remember a board meeting at one of our investments in the '80s, a business in the oil and gas industry, where management recommended a $100 million oil exploration budget. Our first reaction was that they must be quite optimistic about their prospects to risk that much of the shareholders' capital. We pointed out to them that as shareholders who owned 10% of the company, they were putting $10 million of their own capital at risk. Moments later, management decided to reconsider the budget. One month later, the exploration budget had been cut in half, and they were acutely more focused on the results of each and every drilling site.

The opportunity to improve companies, the ability to have an alignment of interest with management and us being the shareholders with long-term, patient capital—to me, these are the hallmarks of private equity.

And while we have been focused on delivering exceptional long-term investment returns from the outset, private equity has evolved quite a bit since we started out four decades ago.

After leaving Bear Stearns to start our own firm, we had $120,000 between the three of us—$10,000 each from George and me, which was about all we had at the time, and $100,000 from Jerry who was 20 years our senior. With $120,000 in the bank, we went to raise our first fund, a $25 million private equity fund. Keep in mind there were no such funds in those days and there was no one doing what is now considered private equity. Given this environment, we had a difficult time raising the $25 million on terms that we felt made sense. So we had a thought: Why don't we go to eight individuals and ask them to put up $50,000 each for a five-year commitment and in return, we'd give them the ability to come into any of our deals. And if they did invest, we'd take 20 percent of the profits—what is known today as carried interest.

How did this happen? George's father and my father were in the oil-and-gas business where, in those days, there was something called "a third for a quarter." If you had a lease and wanted to drill, you put up 25 percent of the cost and found someone to put up the remaining 75 percent of the cost. Consequently, that person gets a two-thirds interest for what they put down and you get a one-third interest. When applying this concept to our own business, we thought 20 percent was close enough to third for a quarter, and that's still the standard today.

When we first started doing deals, private equity transactions, better known as leveraged buyouts at the time, were in their infancy. The PE industry as we know it was not yet born. In fact, we never imagined we'd ever use the term "industry" when talking about what we do.

Private equity deals looked very different than they do today. The asset class was new, and so too was its level of sophistication. As PE explored elaborate capital structures, new sources of funding, larger pools of equity capital and did so through variable economic conditions, we did not properly explain these complexities—or our mission— to the public. As a result, PE deals became associated with hostile takeovers at the time. Referring to PE as "corporate raiders" or "barbarians," the public's reaction to the very same question I asked you—what is private equity?—was simply: an investment vehicle to acquire, strip and sell an asset for profit. We never thought of it this way; we were always focused on the opportunity at hand to create value at the companies in which we invested. Nonetheless, we and others did not pay enough attention to communicating this with our various stakeholders.

Looking back 40 years later, this is one of the many lessons, perhaps the hardest, that we've learned along the way. These lessons—and the headlines referencing barbarians that came with them—are not exclusive to KKR. The experiences of the early days of PE served as a catalyst for transformation of the entire PE industry.

I think it is safe for me to speak on the industry's behalf when I say we have learned there is so much more to investing than buying low and selling high. As my colleague Bill Cornog will expand upon in Chapter 13, we've learned to think of ourselves as industrialists. When we buy a company, we ask ourselves: what can we do to make it better? How can we create value? What constituents should we be mindful of and will factor into a good outcome for everyone?

At KKR, key to answering these questions is the development of what we call 100-Day Plans. These plans are put into place as soon as we make an investment. That means we hit the ground running from the day a transaction closes. Our goal is to focus, with a sense of urgency, on the creation of value. As part of this process, we establish upfront operating metrics. These can often reveal underlying problems with a business before those problems can be seen in the financial data. In this way, we can make difficult operational and personnel decisions as early as possible in the process. Recognizing, acknowledging and addressing problems up front are part and parcel of the successful ownership model.

This value creation process involves not only understanding a company's balance sheet and financial statements, but also its employees, their impact on the world around them and being good participants in community life. This all contributes to value creation—or destruction.

As an industry, we've learned that we can make a difference by integrating our performance-focused investment philosophy with environmental, social and governance (ESG) initiatives. It is our responsibility—not only to serve our investors through great investor returns—but also to support them by investing in the communities of the corporations in which we invest. Over the years, I think the PE industry has picked up on this quite a bit.

And while that doesn't mean every company we invest in is advancing an ecological solution, I believe PE-backed companies can help solve challenges—economic or otherwise—in their communities. Whether it's improving municipal water treatment facilities, funding sustainable economic initiatives in underprivileged communities or reducing waste and promoting eco-efficiency in plants and factories, incorporating ESG practices has become a focal point throughout the lifecycle of an investment.

As I mentioned earlier, one of the key principles to making this work is the alignment of the interests of all parties—managers, investors and employees alike.

Investing alongside one's investors, or our limited partners (LPs), is the best demonstration of partnership. While the principle of alignment has not changed from four decades ago, it has definitely been emphasized more greatly in recent years. We, and others, have continued to make larger firm and employee commitments to our funds, further incentivizing our employees to do well for our investors.

With the addition of new technologies and important groups like the Institutional Limited Partners Association, there is also a focus on making sure LPs have greater visibility into the underlying details of the companies in which they are invested. This enhanced transparency is not limited to the PE industry alone, and our world is better off for it. Information is at our fingertips. This is a good thing and promotes efficiency, integrity, and accountability. In my opinion, these are the mainstays to being a trusted partner in private equity, not just to LPs but to all of our stakeholders.

Today, success in PE involves many more facets and many more faces related to a deal. Our constituents include our limited partners and their beneficiaries but also the employees of our portfolio companies, stockholders, regulators and government officials as well as the media. As the collection of stakeholders has evolved quite significantly, so has the industry's approach to engaging with them.

To succeed in PE, communication and transparency are key. As we work to build strong relationships with our stakeholders, we remember: people do business with people they like and trust.

As far as the mainstays to being a good investor? I'd say curiosity and a sense of history. To me, people who are curious are going to be far better stewards of others' money. Why? If there's no curiosity, you're basically doing something that's already been done by someone else. Moreover, being knowledgeable of the past means you can learn from past mistakes and, hopefully, not repeat them. Without these two attributes, one will miss out on opportunities, or experience slip-ups, by not seeing the whole picture.

Now I know this has been a long answer to what is private equity? In my mind, at the forefront of this lengthy explanation has been one of my favorite quotes from General Eric Shinseki: "If you don't like change, you will like irrelevance even less." The industry has gone through many changes, but by doing so, private equity continues to attract some of the most sophisticated investors in the world.

While we will have to wait and see how the asset class continues to evolve, I anticipate that private equity of the future will need to prioritize diversity to remain germane.

Too many of the same people means too much of the same thinking—an element of today's industry that I feel greatly needs to be addressed. As we discussed earlier, more of the same is a stepping stone to irrelevance. We need to value having more diverse groups of people—diversity of gender, race and ethnicity, and especially diversity of experiences and thinking. There is no doubt that diverse groups drive better outcomes—it has been proven time and again—it creates a better work environment, more creative ideas and is a critical focus area of our investors. I think this is a lesson we are in the middle of and hope the industry will heed this important message in order to succeed in the future.

So what is private equity?

You will hear many answers to this question from industry leaders in the chapters ahead, but what I hope I've made clear is that private equity is so much more than its literal definition. For me, private equity always has been and always will be about building value over the long-term.

PREFACE

Gone are the days when "being in PE"[1] meant buying assets with steady cash flows in heavily leveraged transactions and riding the investments out to a successful exit. Despite the evolution, growth and increasing diversity of PE, this dated image persists, but no longer does the industry justice.

So, what does modern PE look like? The main difference from the activities of the '70s and '80s is that PE firms have developed into transformation agents that impact businesses at critical junctures of their development. PE funds are no longer just hands-off financial investors seeking to profit through changes to the capital structure or by selling off parts of a business; as the industry has matured, PE firms increasingly engage via active ownership to drive value creation in their portfolio companies. Indeed, a partnership with PE can provide portfolio companies with the edge to remain relevant in the hypercompetitive age of globalized markets.

Although PE has become synonymous with exceptional growth and wealth generation, the industry has endured its share of challenges. In particular, each financial crisis has opened the door to controversy. The spotlight focused on the performance of leveraged buyouts in times of highly visible defaults and then switched to venture investors' ambitious start-up valuations when valuations slipped and follow-on transactions took on a distinct pass-the-parcel flavour. There are ongoing debates about the fairness of profit-sharing between limited partners and general partners (and taxation of the latter) as well as the industry's impact on its investee companies and on the economy at large.

Will the value-added focus of the PE industry become a model for the financial markets of tomorrow? Will the limited partnership model itself require dramatic changes to survive? How can we better communicate the benefits professional PE can bring to companies and not only to investors? These are some of the relevant questions being asked by senior industry players as we set out to write this book.

As PE works its way into the economies of the 21st century, board members, senior executives, finance professionals and entrepreneurs are well advised to follow the industry's development carefully. After all, whether venture funds, super angels, growth equity funds, turnaround investors or buyout funds, we are talking about gatekeepers and agents who are entrusted with the capital of their investors to find the best entrepreneurial opportunities possible, whether in developed, emerging or frontier markets.

As for students of the industry and junior PE professionals, developing a solid understanding of the overall business model of PE will enable them to develop new ways to differentiate their firms in the eyes of investors. Attractive target companies in search of funding can choose from more than 8,000 professional PE firms worldwide to find those who meet their expectations and can deliver worthwhile partnerships.

---

1. In the context of this book, PE is defined broadly and includes venture capital (VC), growth equity and buyout funds. More about this later in the book.

A NOTE FROM CLAUDIA ZEISBERGER

As a professor at INSEAD, one of the leading global business schools, I am fortunate to be part of a diverse, young, dynamic and entrepreneurial community. As the academic director of the school's Global Private Equity Initiative, I am often the first port of call for students, alumni, senior executives and entrepreneurs for a multitude of PE related issues, including career transitions, start-up ideas, fundraising and access to industry professionals.

For years I have been asked for a resource that would enable them to deepen their knowledge on a specific topic of PE or VC. Every class has a group of students keen to dive deeper into a variety of niche topics that cannot be addressed within the time constraints of an MBA course. To satisfy those questions and to complement my classes, I started to write "Private Equity Primers"—short, concise class notes that focused on topics that deserved more detailed coverage.

The book you are about to explore started as a collection of those primers, often written in response to conversations with industry players at conferences to shed light on areas of PE that are, by their nature, not easy to understand. The notes have been fine-tuned over many years of class use.

Supporting this book with a selection of INSEAD case studies (published in *Private Equity in Action—Case Studies from Developed and Emerging Markets*) was an easy decision. They add context to the theoretical concepts, and allow the reader to consider the potential conflicts, controversies and challenges those PE funds face when deploying capital to deserving firms in both developed and emerging markets.

News coverage of the PE industry, often embellished for dramatic effect, does a good job of fueling the imagination of anyone from laymen to seasoned financial professionals. PE, with its wide variety of colorful characters and at times unconventional strategies, is often portrayed as the boogeyman of the financial services industry—deservedly or not—depending on whom you ask. To my frustration, much of the criticism of these private investment vehicles shows a lack of understanding of the basic principles of PE and VC. Admittedly, this is a function of a traditionally opaque industry that could have done a much better job of educating the broader public on the mechanics of and benefits behind its investment activities.

This book aims to create clarity, increase the level of understanding of PE and help interested professionals not only to connect the dots, but also to support them in the process of executing that first deal, whether as a PE professional or as a board member courting the first external investor.

Two INSEAD alumni join me as co-authors for this book. Over the years, we have collaborated on various research projects at INSEAD's PE center and, through their work in the alternative investing space globally, they add another perspective to the industry.

Asking senior professionals in our network to add their thoughts to each chapter in brief guest comments and also to review our writing, was a natural extension of this principle of marrying academic rigor with the real-life challenges facing PE professionals. Our guest authors provide a candid counterpoint to our arm's length discussion and raise critical points.

The authors' views and biases of course play into the reflections; they shape the lens through which we view the world. In my case, more than 20 years in the now fully emerged markets of Asia have certainly given me a vantage point away from the standard western PE model. I have had the opportunity to observe PE firms professionalize and improve young businesses, revamp their operations and allow them to launch into an accelerated growth phase, despite owning a minority equity stake. Overall I have seen PE effect real change in the fast-growing markets of Asia and Latin America. My co-authors balance this out through their experience.

Writing this book was a fascinating journey that brought several points to light:

- PE and VC, while popular topics, are rarely, if ever, examined in the context of the broader economy.
- Industry players are often frustrated by the lack of understanding of their craft within the business community, which leads to misinterpretation and misrepresentation and at times to a backlash or unfair accusations.
- Research papers—both of the applied and academic kind—more often than not take a closer look at narrow and specific areas of PE, thereby ignoring the contextual issues. Resources to help one understand the big picture, covering the spectrum from venture to growth equity to buyouts, are few and far between.

There was room for a book to step in and fill some of the gaps to prepare all parties for an informed discussion.

HOW TO USE THIS BOOK

This book was written with a professional audience in mind and carefully structured to accommodate both graduate students and experienced professionals. It makes a solid attempt at reflecting on its central themes without judgment, by relating the facts and ensuring that readers are well prepared to participate in an intelligent discussion about the pros and cons of private equity (PE).

Used together with the case book *Private Equity in Action — Case Studies from Developed and Emerging Markets*, which complements the text, this book brings the learning points to life and offers readers a ringside seat to the day-to-day challenges facing partners in PE and venture funds.

- For novices to the field of PE, our book provides clear insights into the workings of the industry. While the book assumes a sound understanding of basic finance, accounting techniques and risk–return concepts, it offers links to literature and research to ensure clarity for those rusty in the theoretical concepts behind today's financial markets.

- Graduate and postgraduate students will find the book an invaluable companion for their PE, venture capital and entrepreneurship courses; it will allow them to connect the dots and ensure that an understanding of the dynamics in the industry is maintained as they explore the respective chapters in greater detail.

- For seasoned financial professionals, the book includes guest comments from industry experts and links to advanced literature that provides a nuanced view of the industry and will allow them to engage with other professionals, be they lawyers, bankers, consultants or partners of PE firms, in a meaningful way.

Ensuring that our readers develop a sound understanding of PE before diving into more controversial aspects of the industry was a clear goal from the outset; it defined the flow and the logic of the chapters. The book's structure allows the expert reader to use the book as a quick reference with easily retrievable highlights of the best practices employed in the industry; it also allows observers of the industry and students to work through the topics step by step and take advantage of the many resources and cross-references to other finance topics.

Overall the chapters are grouped into five sections:

SECTION I offers a high-level introduction to PE to ensure that we speak the same language and use appropriate industry terms and definitions throughout the book. It puts venture capital, growth equity and leveraged buyouts into context and describes several alternative PE investment strategies such as distressed investing and real estate.

SECTION II looks in greater detail at PE investment processes, starting with deal sourcing, due diligence and target valuation before exploring deal pricing considerations and the actual structuring of PE deals. It also includes a thorough coverage of transaction documentation.

SECTION III asks: What do PE and venture funds do with their portfolio companies during the holding period? How will they transform these businesses and prepare them for exit?

SECTION IV describes the key dynamics involved in raising a PE fund. We step into the shoes of global institutional investors in PE to examine their demands with regard to reporting and portfolio customization.

SECTION V builds on the understanding gained in the previous chapters and takes a closer look at recent developments in the industry, from direct and co-investment programs to the fast-growing secondaries markets and the recent rise of listed PE funds. In the closing chapter the authors comment on the industry's development and explore key themes that will shape private equity and venture capital in the years ahead.

Additional material to complement this book and connect it to the case book *Private Equity in Action — Case Studies from Developed and Emerging Markets* can be found on the companion website:

www.masteringprivateequity.com

SECTION I
Private Equity Overview

The first section of the book provides readers with a high-level introduction to the institutional private equity (PE) market—from early-stage venture capital to growth equity and buyouts, plus a brief description of several alternative PE strategies. While buyouts have historically accounted for the vast majority of global PE capital deployed,[1] venture capital and growth equity investment activity has steadily increased as the industry matured over the past decades (see Exhibit A).

Section I is by far the least technical part of this book, intended to familiarize newcomers with the asset class and the concept of investing institutional capital in private companies in return for equity stakes. While crucial for readers new to PE, professionals familiar with the industry may choose to move directly to later sections of the book.

Exhibit A: Total PE Industry Capital Deployed by Strategy

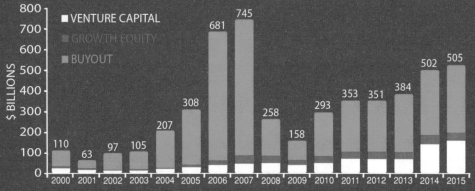

Source: Preqin

---

1. Buyouts have accounted for more than three-quarters of industry capital deployed between 1980 and 2015. Source: Preqin.

Section Overview

Chapter 1. Private Equity Essentials: This chapter defines the traditional limited partnership fund model, specifically the players involved, a fund's investment lifecycle, and typical fund economics and fee structures. To be clear, our work refers to the organized PE market, i.e., professionally-managed equity investments by specialized intermediaries (PE firms) and their institutional backers; it excludes other forms of "informal" private capital investments.

Chapter 2. Venture Capital: Venture capital (VC) generally flows into early-stage companies—start-ups—that offer high risk/high return investment opportunities. We introduce the different types of venture investors (business angels, start-up incubators and accelerators, VC funds, and corporate VCs) and explain the use of VC at different points in a company's development, from proof-of-concept to commercialization and scaling up. Both aspiring entrepreneurs as well as future venture investors will find this chapter useful.

Chapter 3. Growth Equity: Acquiring minority equity stakes in fast-growing companies is the focus of growth equity funds. Managing multiple stakeholders without a control position is a key challenge for these funds; establishing a productive working relationship with existing managers and owners is therefore a key determinant of success. This chapter is particularly relevant for readers interested in PE in emerging markets.

Chapter 4. Buyouts: Buyout funds acquire controlling equity stakes in mature and sometimes listed target companies, often employing ample amounts of debt in leveraged buyouts (LBOs). The skillset required to execute large LBOs and drive value post-investment differs from that needed for growth equity or VC: it requires both financial and process management skills, combined with the ability to create operational value in the portfolio firms.

Chapter 5. Alternative Strategies: In the final chapter of this section, we explore alternative PE strategies focused on investing in distressed businesses and real assets. The former requires unique skills to restructure and improve a company's operations (turnaround) or its balance sheet (distressed debt), while the latter describes a range of strategies (investing in real estate, infrastructure, and natural resources) that use a PE operating model and adapt it to distinct industry verticals.

At some point in their development, all companies will need either a helping hand or a shot in the arm. A fresh injection of capital or external managerial expertise is often necessary to help organizations overcome developmental challenges, realize their full potential and seize the opportunities that lie ahead. Start-ups hunt for the visionary capital that will enable them to turn a concept into a launched product. Mature companies are increasingly subject to market disruption, increased competition or pressure to update manufacturing processes and corporate governance structures. Companies that have been performing poorly for a prolonged period of time need to identify and then rectify the problems that confront them. Family businesses must honestly address succession planning ("it is only but three generations from shirtsleeves to shirtsleeves"[2]).

The needs and demands of businesses at such critical inflection points often exceed the capabilities and services provided by the established financial institutions and consulting firms. Capital markets, for instance, are unlikely to offer a solution for small and medium-sized enterprises (SMEs). Into this void steps private equity (PE) in the form of venture, growth, and buyout funds, at its best offering patient and long-term capital, dedicated expert advice and hands-on operational support.

In the last four decades PE has emerged as the transformation agent of choice for companies seeking change; at times, it is the only choice for a business in need of capital and a risk-sharing partner to facilitate future growth. The PE ecosystem has grown dramatically during that time; as of 2015 the industry (including its alternative strategies and co-investments) has over US$4.5 trillion in assets under management, of which US$2.3 trillion are deployed through core PE strategies. This capital is being invested and managed by over 8,000 professional funds globally. Understanding this industry—its drivers and its dynamics—is a must for entrepreneurs, owners of family businesses, board members of multinationals and senior managers.

So what exactly is PE? PE funds invest long-term capital in private (or, at times, public) companies in return for an equity stake that is not freely tradable on a public market.[3] Our definition of PE includes so-called "take-privates" (i.e., delistings of public companies) and private investment in public equity that come with specific governance rights. This book focuses strictly on the activity of professionally managed PE funds advised by highly specialized intermediaries (PE firms) and excludes "informal" private capital, such as investments made by business angels or families who typically draw on their own private wealth.

This first chapter gives our readers a high-level overview of PE funds, by defining their structure and the motivation of the key players involved. We then explain how PE funds go about their business, both from the general partner's (GP's) and limited partner's (LP's) perspective and shed light on the often complex economics and fee structures in PE.

---

2. Origin unknown but the quote is often attributed to Andrew Carnegie.

3. In our context, PE takes on a broad definition that includes VC, growth capital, and buyout funds. It should be mentioned that other sources might restrict the definition of PE to buyout activities and consider VC to be a separate asset class. Further, PE is frequently defined as investments in private companies but buyout activities extend to investments in and the privatization of public companies. For the sake of clarity, our definition of "private" equity refers to the status of the equity stake held by the PE fund post-investment.

PRIVATE EQUITY FUNDS DEFINED

A PE fund is a stand-alone investment vehicle managed by a PE firm on behalf of a group of investors. The capital is raised with a clear mandate to acquire equity stakes in private companies and divest them over time.

Most PE funds globally are set up as closed-end limited partnerships and operate as "blind pool" vehicles. Closed-end funds have a finite lifespan and require investors to commit capital for the fund's entire term—typically 10 years—without early redemption (or withdrawal) rights.[4] While investors in a PE fund have a clear idea of its broad mandate (for example, mid-market European buyouts), they have no say in the choice of the individual companies that a fund will invest in, hence the term "blind pool." Certain jurisdictions use limited liability companies or corporate structures as the vehicle of choice for a PE fund, but they are the exception.

We will start with a closer look at the parties involved in a limited partnership PE fund structure, as shown in Exhibit 1.1.

Exhibit 1.1 Limited Partnership PE Fund Structure

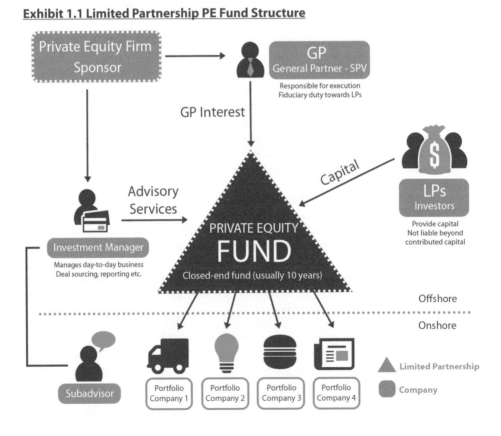

4. The PE secondaries market can provide liquidity for an LP wishing to sell its interest in a PE fund. This market has developed rapidly over the last decade with dedicated funds raised for the express purpose of acquiring secondary fund stakes. See Chapter 24 Private Equity Secondaries for more information.

PE FIRM: A PE firm is a company with expertise in executing a venture, growth or buyout investment strategy. It raises and advises a fund—and, if successful, over time a family of funds—generally through two separate yet affiliated legal entities: the GP and the investment manager. Members of a PE firm typically hold all the key directorships and other decision-making positions of both the GP and the investment manager for every fund raised by the firm. Establishing these separate legal entities insulates the PE firm from liabilities related to and its principals from any claims on the PE fund. Examples of notable PE firms are buyout firms Kohlberg Kravis Roberts (KKR) and APAX Partners as well as venture firms Sequoia Capital and Kleiner Perkins Caufield Byers.

LIMITED PARTNERS: Investors or LPs contribute by far the largest share of capital to any PE fund raised. LPs participate merely as passive investors, with an individual LP's liability limited to the capital committed to the fund. Investors active in PE include private and public pension funds, endowments, insurance companies, banks, corporations, family offices, and fund of funds.[5] LPs are purely financial investors and cannot be involved in the day-to-day operation or management of the fund or its investee companies without running the risk of forfeiting their limited liability rights. LPs legally commit to provide capital for investment when it is drawn down (or "called") by the PE fund and they receive distributions of capital—including a share of profits—upon successful exit of the fund's investments.

GENERAL PARTNER: A fund's GP is wholly responsible for all aspects related to managing the fund and has a fiduciary duty to act solely in the interest of the fund's investors. It will issue capital calls to LPs and make all investment and divestment decisions for the fund in line with the mandate set out in its Limited Partnership Agreement (LPA). The GP may delegate some of the management functions to the investment manager or a PE firm's investment committee (IC),[6] but remains fully and personally liable for all debts and liabilities of the fund and is contractually obligated to invest the fund's capital in line with its mandate.[7] A GP—and in turn a PE firm's partners and senior professionals—will also commit capital to the fund to align its interest with that of the fund's LPs by ensuring that the firm's partners have "skin in the game"; the GP stake typically ranges from 1 to 5% and rarely exceeds 10% of a fund's total capital raised.

INVESTMENT MANAGER: In practice, the investment manager[8] conducts the day-to-day activities of a PE fund; it evaluates potential investment opportunities, provides advisory services to the fund's portfolio companies, and manages the fund's audit and reporting processes. The manager is paid a management fee by the fund for providing these services, some of which may be passed on to a subadvisor. The management fee is typically set at around 1.5–2% of committed capital during the investment period of the fund; after the end of the investment period, it is calculated

---

5. A fund of PE funds (fund of funds) is a vehicle that invests in a portfolio of individual investment funds. A fund of funds offers clients diversified exposure to the PE asset class without the need for deep investment expertise or lengthy due diligence on the individual funds. An additional layer of fees applies.

6. The IC is typically a committee of the GP and makes the binding investment and divestment decisions for the fund under delegated authority from the GP ("binding" in the sense that once the IC votes, there is no other vote needed or taken).

7. GPs are usually set up as distinct special purpose vehicles (SPVs) for each fund; these SPVs serve as the GP for only one fund to avoid cross-liabilities between related funds of the PE firm. Please refer to Chapter 16 for further details on fund formation.

8. Investment managers will also be referred to as advisors or simply managers.

Exhibit 1.2 Key Relationships GPs Must Manage

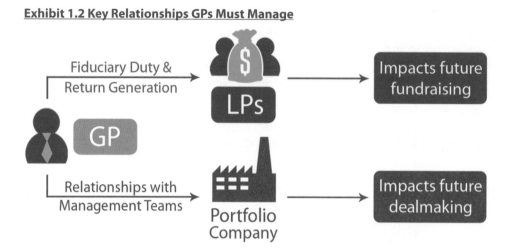

on invested capital and may step down to a lower rate. More information on fee structures can be found later in this chapter.

PORTFOLIO COMPANY: Over its lifecycle, a PE fund will invest in a limited number of companies, 10–15 on average, which represent its investment portfolio. These companies are also referred to as investee companies or (during the due diligence process) as target companies. A PE firm's ability to sell its stakes in these companies at a profit after a three- to seven-year holding period will determine the success or failure of the fund.

From the perspective of the PE firm and its affiliated entities, the business of PE comes down to two simple yet distinct relationships: on the one hand, the firm's fiduciary duty towards its LPs and on the other hand its engagement with entrepreneurs, business owners and management teams in its portfolio companies (Exhibit 1.2). Establishing a reputation of professional conduct and value-add will ensure access to both future fundraising and investment opportunities.

THE GP PERSPECTIVE
LIFECYCLE OF A PE FUND

A traditional PE firm's business model relies on success in both raising funds and meeting its target return by effectively deploying and harvesting fund capital. PE funds structured as limited partnerships are typically raised for a 10-year term plus two one-year extensions, commonly referred to as the "10+2" model. Generally speaking, a GP will deploy capital during the first four to five years of a fund's life and harvest capital during the remaining years. The two optional years allow the GP to extend a fund's lifespan at its discretion if and when additional time is needed to prudently exit all investments.

Exhibit 1.3 shows the overlapping timelines for the fundraising, investment, holding, and divestment periods of a closed-end fund.

Exhibit 1.3 Lifecycle of a PE Fund

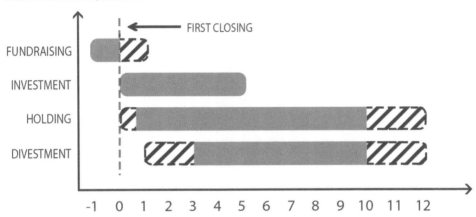

FUNDRAISING: PE firms raise capital for a fund by securing capital commitments from investors (LPs) through a series of fund closings.[9] A PE firm will establish a target fund size from the outset—at times defining a "hard cap" to limit the total amount raised in case of excess investor demand. Once an initial threshold of capital commitments has been reached, the fund's GP will hold a first closing, at which time an initial group of LPs will subscribe to the fund and the GP can start to deploy capital. A fund holding its first closing in 2016 is referred to as a "vintage 2016 fund," a fund with a first closing in 2017 will be known as a "vintage 2017 fund," and so on. Fundraising will typically continue for a defined period—12 to 18 months—from the date of the first closing until the fund reaches its target fund size and a "final closing" is held. The total amount raised by a PE firm is known as a fund's committed capital.

INVESTMENT PERIOD: Rather than receiving the committed capital on day one, a GP draws down LP commitments over the course of a fund's investment period. The length of the investment period is defined in a fund's governing documents and typically lasts four to five years from the date of its first closing; a GP may at times extend the investment period by a year or two, with approval from its LPs. Once the investment period expires, the fund can no longer invest in new companies; however, follow-on investments in existing portfolio companies or add-on acquisitions are permitted throughout the holding period. A fund's LPA may also permit its GP to finance new investments from a portion of fund realizations within a certain limited period after divestment (this is known as the recycling of capital), thus increasing a fund's total investable capital.

GPs draw down investor capital by making "capital calls" to fund suitable investment opportunities or to pay fund fees and expenses. LPs must meet capital calls within a short period, typically 10 business days. If an LP fails to meet a capital call, various remedies are available to the GP. These include the right to charge high interest rates on late payments, the right to force a sale of the defaulting LP's interest on the secondaries[10] market and the right to continue to charge losses and expenses to the

---

9. Please refer to Chapter 17 for more details on the fundraising process and its dynamics.
10. Please refer to Chapter 24 Private Equity Secondaries for further details on the mechanics behind the transfer of such LP stakes.

Exhibit 1.4 PE Industry Dry Powder

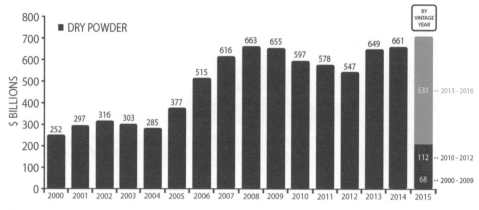

Source: Preqin

defaulting LP while cutting off their interest in future fund profits. The portion of LPs' committed capital that has been called and invested is referred to as contributed capital. A fund's uninvested committed capital is referred to as its "dry powder"; by extension, the total amount of uninvested committed capital across the industry is referred to as the industry's "dry powder." Exhibit 1.4 shows the increase of the industry's dry powder since 2000; the 2015 data adds perspective on its origin by grouping dry powder according to vintage year.[11]

HOLDING PERIOD: Holding periods for individual portfolio companies typically range from three to seven years following investment, but may be significantly shorter in the case of successful companies or longer in the case of under-performing firms. During this time, a fund's GP works closely with portfolio companies' management teams to create value and prepare the company for exit.[12]

DIVESTMENT PERIOD: A key measure of success in PE is a GP's ability to exit its investments profitably and within a fund's term; as a result, exit strategies form an important part of the investment rationale from the start.[13] Following a full or partial exit, invested capital and profits are distributed to a fund's LPs and its GP. With the exception of a few well-defined reinvestment provisions,[14] proceeds from exits are not available for reinvestment. When a fund remains invested in a company at the end of a fund's life, the GP has the option to extend the fund's term by one or two years to avoid a forced liquidation.[15]

---

11. Dry powder in Exhibit 1.4 is for venture, growth and buyout investment strategies. Source: Preqin.
12. Please refer to Chapter 13 Operational Value Creation for more background.
13. Please refer to Chapter 15 for a detailed description of exit considerations and the related processes.
14. The capital invested in a deal and returned without any profits achieved, may be reinvested under the following conditions: (a) a so-called "quick flip" where an exit was achieved within 13–18 months of investing during the investment period; or (b) to match the amount of capital drawn down to pay fees, with the target to put 100% of the fund's committed capital to work. These rules are defined in a "remaining dry powder" test.
15. Please refer to Chapter 20 Winding Down a Fund for additional information on end-of-fund life options.

Box 1.1

RAISING A SUCCESSOR FUND

Established PE firms will raise successor funds every three to four years and ask existing LPs to "re-up"—or reinvest—in their new vehicle. PE firms will typically begin raising a successor fund as soon as permitted by the LPA, usually once 75% of the current fund's capital is invested or has been reserved for fees and future deals.

PE firms see their business as a going concern, meaning they continuously work on a deal pipeline of potential investee companies, make investments and divestments. To efficiently capitalize on opportunities in the market, it is crucial for PE firms to have access to capital, ready to be drawn down and deployed, at all times. This also allows a firm to maintain stable operations, employ an investment team and maximize the efficiency of its resources.

Exhibit 1.5 shows the lifecycle of a successful PE firm with a family of four funds.

Exhibit 1.5 Lifecycle of a Successful PE Firm

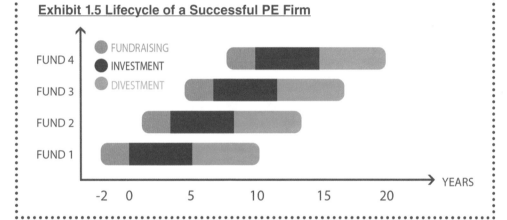

THE LP PERSPECTIVE
COMMITTING CAPITAL AND EARNING RETURNS

Investors have traditionally allocated capital to PE due to its historical outperformance of more traditional asset classes such as public equity and fixed income.[16] However, this outperformance comes with higher (or rather different) risks first and foremost due to the illiquid nature of PE investments. Given its lack of liquidity and the long investment horizon of a PE fund, hitting a target allocation to PE is a far more challenging task than maintaining a stable allocation to any of the liquid asset classes.[17] In addition, PE funds' multiyear lock-up and 10-day notice period for capital calls introduce complex liquidity management questions.

16. Please refer to Chapter 19 Performance Reporting for a detailed comparison of PE and public market performance.
17. Our Chapter 18 LP Portfolio Management takes a closer look at the challenges of deploying assets under management into PE and VC; Chapter 23 Risk Management complements the discussion.

Effectively managing portfolio cash flows is among the key challenges faced by investors in the PE asset class. LPs starting a PE investment program from scratch must prepare for years of negative cumulative cash flows before a positive net return will eventually be generated by their PE portfolios. Seasoned investors with a well-diversified exposure to PE, on the other hand, will often have commitments to well over 100 funds and a complex set of cash flows to manage. A PE fund's "J-curve" provides a way to visualize the expected cash flow characteristics of an LP's stake in an individual PE fund and the challenges related to managing a PE portfolio.

THE J-CURVE

A PE J-curve represents an LP's cumulative net cash flow position—the total capital invested along with fees paid to the PE firm minus the capital returned to the LP by the GP—in a single fund over time. Exhibit 1.6 illustrates the characteristic cash flow for an LP (with a US$10 million commitment to a $100 million fund) over the fund's 10-year life. For simplicity's sake we assume both consistent drawdowns from the GP and exits split evenly across the years. It should be noted that capital calls and distributions are difficult to forecast with any degree of accuracy, requiring LPs to develop a flexible approach to cash management.[18]

Exhibit 1.6 PE Fund Cash Flow J-curve

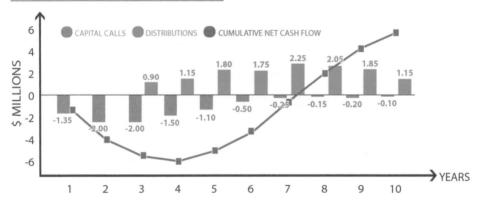

Early in the investment period, the J-curve has a steep negative slope, as a fund's initial investments and management fees (paid on committed capital) result in large cash outflows for its LPs. As the fund begins to exit its portfolio company holdings, distributions of capital slow the J-curve's descent; some funds may in fact show a positive slope before the end of the investment period. While the low point of a J-curve is theoretically defined as the fund's total committed capital, J-curves rarely dip below 80% of committed capital due to the time required to deploy capital and early divestment activity. In fact, many funds do not even reach a net drawdown of more than 50%.

Following the start of the divestment period, the J-curve turns upward as exit activity picks up and invested capital plus a share of profits are returned to LPs. Capital called for follow-on investments and management fees continue to generate small LP outflows during the divestment period. As soon as the J-curve crosses the x-axis, the fund has reached breakeven; the final point on the J-curve represents an LP's total net profit generated by the fund.

18. Please refer to Chapter 18 for further insight into the cash management challenges LPs face when starting a PE investment program or when managing multiple funds in a PE portfolio.

While LPs will attempt to optimize their portfolio allocation, modeling cash flows as well as net asset values remains challenging, given the blind pool nature of the funds and the overall scarcity of data in PE. The secondaries market nowadays offers a realistic avenue to add liquidity, shorten the J-curve and manage a PE portfolio proactively.

THE FEE STRUCTURE AND ECONOMICS OF PE
OR WHO EARNS WHAT?

The typical fee structure of a PE fund is designed to align the economic interest of the PE firm and its fund investors. The fee structure in PE is commonly referred to as "2 and 20" and defines how a fund's investment manager and GP—and in turn its PE professionals—are compensated: the "2%" refers to the management fee paid by the LPs per annum to a fund's investment manager while the "20" represents the percentage of net fund profits—referred to as carried interest or "carry"—paid to its GP. The clear majority of profits, 80%, generated by a fund is distributed pro rata to a fund's LPs. As long as carried interest remains the main economic incentive for PE professionals, their focus will continue to be on maximizing returns, which in turn benefits the LPs. Exhibit 1.7 visualizes the flow of fees and share of net profits to the entities involved in a PE fund.

Exhibit 1.7 PE Fees and Carried Interest

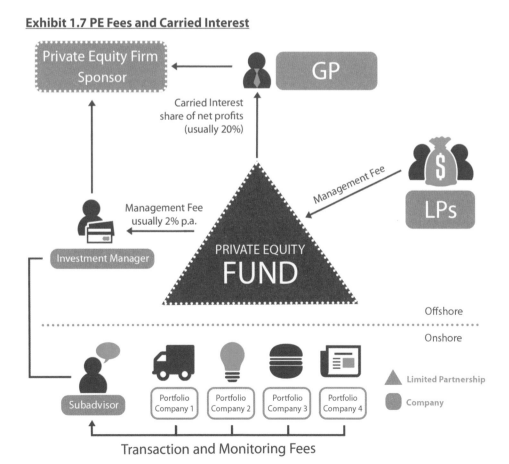

Returns in PE are typically measured in both internal rate of return and multiples of money invested.[19] Given a fund's cost structure, its net return—that is, the return on capital generated by the fund net of management fees and carried interest—is the relevant metric for its investors and LPs will ultimately define success on that basis at the end of the fund's life.

We take a detailed look at fees and carried interest below.

MANAGEMENT FEES: A PE fund's investment manager charges the fund—and ultimately its LPs—an annual management fee to cover all day-to-day expenses of the fund, including salaries, office rent and costs related to deal sourcing and monitoring portfolio investments. In the early days of PE, the management fee charged was an almost consistent 2% per annum, yet currently it ranges from 1.3 to 2.5% depending on the size and strategy of a fund and the bargaining power of the PE firm during fundraising. For example, it is accepted that smaller, first-time funds will charge higher fees to cover their fixed costs, while large funds and mezzanine funds often charge lower fees. Since the global financial crisis of 2008 management fees have come under pressure, sometimes in an indirect way, through a sizable increase in free or discounted co-investment opportunities for LPs.[20]

Management fees accrue from a fund's first closing onwards and are usually paid either quarterly or semi-annually in advance. Management fees are charged on committed capital during the investment period, and on net invested capital after the investment period; the rate charged on invested capital may step down from the initial percentage.[21] This fee structure causes fee revenue to drop over the lifetime of a PE fund as capital is deployed and exits occur. Early in a fund's life, management fees are typically drawn directly from investors' committed capital, while proceeds from profitable exits may be used to offset management fees later in a fund's life.

OTHER FEES: An investment manager may charge additional fees to the fund, particularly in the context of a control buyout. The main fee categories are transaction fees linked to a fund's investment in and exit from a portfolio company and monitoring fees for advisory and consulting services provided to portfolio companies during the holding period. Other fees also include but are not limited to broken deal fees, directors' fees, and other fees for services rendered at the fund or portfolio company level. Over the last decade, management fee offsets have increasingly been included in LPAs; when these offsets are in place, management fees charged to the LPs are reduced by a percentage of "other" fees collected by the fund—historically between 50 and 100%, now trending towards 100%. These offsets reduce the fee burden for LPs and shift a portion of the fee-based compensation from the GP to the limited partnership as a whole.

CARRIED INTEREST: Proceeds from successful exits are distributed to a fund's LPs and its GP in line with a distribution "waterfall" set out in a fund's LPA.[22] Carried interest is the share of a fund's net profits paid to its GP—typically 20%—and serves as the main incentive for a PE firm's principals. In a typical distribution waterfall, PE funds will return all invested capital and provide a minimum return to investors—a fund's hurdle rate[23] or

---

19. See Chapter 19 Performance Reporting for additional detail on fund performance measurement.
20. See Chapter 21 for further details on this co-investment trend.
21. Net invested capital consists of contributed capital minus capital returned from exits and any write downs of investment value.
22. Please refer to Chapter 16 Fund Formation for a detailed description of distribution waterfalls and examples of carried interest calculations.
23. The hurdle rate, typically set at 8%, will be negotiated during fundraising. A fund is only "in the carry" (i.e., performance incentives for the GP kick in) once it has reached an annual return of 8%.

preferred return—before any carried interest is paid out to the GP. After the hurdle rate has been reached, PE funds will typically include a "catch-up" mechanism that provides distributions to the GP until it has received 20% of all net profits paid out up to this point. Thereafter, all remaining profits are split at the agreed-upon carried interest percentage (80–20). Should a GP for any reason receive more than its fair share of profits, a clawback provision included in a fund's LPA requires GPs to return excess distributions to the fund's LPs. Exhibit 1.8 shows the basic steps common to all distribution waterfalls.

Exhibit 1.8 PE Fund Distribution Waterfall

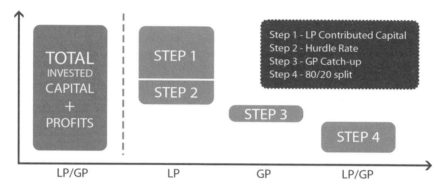

The industry uses two standard models to calculate distributions to LPs:

- *All capital first:* Also known as a *European-style waterfall*, this structure entitles a GP to carried interest only after all capital contributed by investors over a fund's life has been returned and any capital required to satisfy a hurdle rate or preferred return has been distributed.

- *Deal-by-deal carry (with loss carry-forward):* Also known as an *American-style waterfall*, this structure entitles a GP to carried interest after each profitable exit from a portfolio investment during the fund's life, but only after investors have received their invested capital from the deal in question, a preferred return and a "make whole" payment for any losses incurred on prior deals.

A detailed description of distribution waterfalls together with examples of carried interest calculations can be found in Chapter 16. Fund Formation.

A Look Back at the Last 45 Years
By T. Bondurant French, Executive Chairman, Adams Street Partners

In reflecting on the changes in the private equity industry over the last 45 years, fundraising trends were one of the first things that stood out. Looking at fundraising data for the private equity industry, I was a little taken aback to see that 1960 through 1983 were barely visible on my bar graph, compared to the funds being raised today. In 1972, $225 million was raised for venture funds in the US; buyout funds didn't exist and Kleiner Perkins was a first time fund. Venture fundraising bottomed in 1975 at $60 million.

By 1979, the economy was better, capital gains tax rates had been lowered from 50% to 28%, venture-backed companies were bounding (Intel, Microsoft, Apple, and Genentech), and $800 million was raised for venture funds. In the early 1980s, venture funding really took off on the back of excellent returns and a rising stock market. In 1983, $3.7 billion was raised and for the first time the term "mega fund" was used.

It is hard to imagine today, but we had no real data to evaluate the managers with and there were very few realized deals. Almost everyone was a first time fund and there were virtually no formal standards in place. Benchmarks, quartile rankings, written valuation guidelines, and placement agents did not exist. Neither did industry conferences and newsletters, with the exceptions of the National Venture Capital Association's annual meeting and the Venture Capital Journal. The fax machine hadn't yet been invented, but a new venture-backed company, Federal Express, helped us with overnight documents.

Back then, fundraising was exceptionally difficult. Most pension consultants did not follow or cover the asset class. We spent a lot of time doing educational presentations for trustees and their consultants at offsite retreats, board meetings and pension conferences. During the 1980s, our hard work finally began to pay off. As we had actual data going back to 1972, we became pension funds' source of information on expected returns, standard deviations and correlation coefficients for the private equity "asset class." The new term "asset class" implied a transition from a niche activity to something that was becoming institutional. We took the lead in establishing the first industry performance benchmarks, chaired the committee that established the private equity valuation guidelines, and worked with the CFA Institute to establish the guidelines for private equity performance reporting.

Throughout the 1970s and for most of the 1980s, we had lived in a US and venture-centric world. Now, the buyout business was emerging as a new practice within the world of private equity. Pioneered by KKR, CD&R and a handful of other firms, the use of leverage to buy and manage a company was a new idea. The development of the high yield bond market, led by Michael Milken of Drexel Burnham Lambert, made this practically possible on a much wider scale than previously thought. Heretofore, "junk bonds" were formerly high grade bonds of companies that got into trouble and were in or likely to be in default. The idea of a new issue "junk bond" was a new concept.

In 1980 only $180 million was raised for buyout funds in the US. This grew to $2.7 billion in three years, and $13.9 billion by 1987. As with many things in the financial and investment markets, this was a good idea carried to an extreme, culminating in the takeover of RJR Nabisco in 1989 by KKR (as told in a book and a movie, both called *Barbarians at the Gate*).

During the second half of the 1980s, managers in Europe and Asia began to adopt "American style" venture capital and buyout practices. Many of these managers made fundraising trips to the US as, relatively speaking, there were more willing investors there. Along with pension funds and endowments, nearly all of the private equity funds of funds were based in the US.

By 1990, the US was in a recession and a savings and loan crisis. Buyout fundraising dropped dramatically, with only $6 billion raised in 1991. Fortunately, lessons were learned by all parties and the buyout business grew steadily and more rationally throughout the 1990s. What were originally highly leveraged transactions morphed over time to become today's private equity industry, which provides a variety of equity capital, including growth capital, to a broad range of industries and businesses.

By the mid-1990s, the globalization of the private equity market was on the horizon. A number of venture and private equity managers were becoming established in emerging markets. By the mid-2000s, institutional investors were interested in global exposures enhancing their diversification and return potential by accessing rapidly growing economies. Significant money was raised by Asian general partners, particularly in China. Fast forward to today, the private equity industry has expanded to nearly every corner of the globe.

While many things about the private equity industry have changed over the last 45 years, several things remain the same. Private equity remains a people business and, at Adams Street, we understand that the people we invest with are of paramount importance. Spending time with them is an important part of developing real relationships based on trust and mutual respect. Nothing has changed in that regard and these relationships are a critical part of our investment process. The characteristics of successful private equity firms are the same today as they were decades ago. It takes mutual respect, independent thinking, and an optimal mix of experience and energy. At the heart of all enduring firms are good investors who have time to work with their companies, an international awareness and network, and a differentiated deal flow edge.

I am very proud of what the private equity industry does. We generate above average returns for our investors while also providing capital to finance business growth. This financing cuts across a wide spectrum of company stages, industries, and geographies. The end result is greater growth in job creation, wealth, and GDP than would otherwise be possible.

CLOSING

PE as an asset class continues to grow and evolve, both in developed and emerging markets. Business operators the world over—from entrepreneurs looking for start-up funding, to SME business owners with global ambitions, to management teams interested in buying out a corporate division—often find the right partner in PE funds to invest in their ambitions. As a result, PE is deeply entrenched in the economic model and will remain an important driver of business transformation globally.

KEY LEARNING POINTS

• PE is a simple business—buy a stake in a company (minority or majority), improve the business and sell it after a (limited) holding period.

• The preferred method employed by PE firms is to raise and invest individual funds, which they manage on behalf of investors (LPs). PE funds are typically structured as closed-end limited partnerships that require investors to commit capital for a period of 10 years or more.

• PE funds differ from traditional asset classes due to their illiquidity and the unpredictable cash flows generated from their investments.

• Both the fee structure and profit sharing arrangements in PE ensure alignment of interest; incentives change as the funds mature.

RELEVANT CASE SUDIES

from *Private Equity in Action—Case Studies from Developed and Emerging Markets*

Case #1: Beroni Group: Managing GP–LP Relationships

Case #3: Pro-invest Group: How to Launch a Private Equity Real Estate Fund

Case #6: Adara Venture Partners: Building a Venture Capital Firm

REFERENCES AND ADDITIONAL READING

Gompers P., Kaplan S. and Mukharlyamov V. (2015) What do Private Equity Firms Say they Do? HBS and NBER, April.

Guide on Private Equity and Venture Capital for Entrepreneurs (2007) An EVCA Special Paper. European Venture Capital Association.

InvestEurope (2016) *European Private Equity Activity—Statistics on Fundraising, Investments and Divestments,* May, http://www.investeurope.eu/media/476271/2015-european-private-equity-activity.pdf.

Private Equity Principles, Institutional Limited Partners Association (ILPA).

Topping, M. (2014) Evergreen Alternatives to the 2/20 Term-Limited Fund, White & Case LLP, Emerging Markets Private Equity Association.

Vild, J. and Zeisberger, C. (2014) Strategic Buyers vs Private Equity Buyers in an Investment Process, INSEAD Working Paper No. 2014/39/DSC/EFE (SSRN), May 21.

From iconic brands, such as Google, Facebook, Uber and Alibaba to blockbuster biotech or renewable energy companies, venture capital (VC) has funded and nurtured some of the most influential companies in today's global economy. Along with these runaway successes, however, VC has also been center-stage for some of the more spectacular flameouts in modern finance, from the bursting of the tech-bubble at the turn of the millennium to the storybook valuations of numerous billion-dollar "unicorns"[1] a decade and a half later. This "hit-or-miss," "all-or-nothing" character of venture investing drives both the mystique of the industry and on-the-ground decision-making bias of VC investors.

This chapter explores the dynamics of the VC industry, starting with the defining characteristics of VC investing and the unique elements differentiating it from growth equity and buyouts.[2] We then turn to the other side of the table and briefly touch on fundraising for early-stage firms and start-ups; first-time entrepreneurs preparing to raise funds will find this chapter useful to understand the dynamics inside a VC firm before entering into discussions with one of its partners.

VENTURE CAPITAL DEFINED

VC funds are minority investors betting on the future growth of early-stage companies—defined as pre-profit, often pre-revenue and at times even pre-product start-ups. Despite the lack of a controlling stake, VCs are among the most active investors in the PE industry and use their capital, experience, knowledge and personal networks to nurture and grow young companies. VCs may invest in specific verticals, technologies, and geographies, and often specialize in a distinct substage of investment, referred to as early-stage, mid-stage or late-stage VC funding. While every VC firm is unique, a few defining attributes apply to most, as detailed in Exhibit 2.1.

Exhibit 2.1 Defining Characteristics of Venture Capital

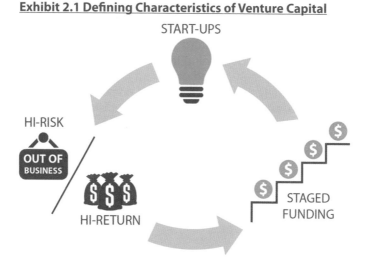

START-UPS

HI-RISK

OUT OF BUSINESS

HI-RETURN

STAGED FUNDING

---

1. "Unicorns" is an industry term for private companies with valuations above US$1 billion.
2. Please refer to Chapter 3 Growth Equity and Chapter 4 Buyouts for in-depth discussions.

START-UP COMPANIES: VC funds invest in start-ups and guide them through their early years of development, as they seek to establish defensible market positions in rapidly expanding industries by disrupting existing products and services through innovation. A start-up can range from an early-stage company with a limited operating history—i.e., an entrepreneur, an idea, and a PowerPoint presentation—to a late-stage company with a fast-growing business. As a result, the capital requirements of start-ups vary widely, from a few thousand dollars to facilitate the development of an early prototype to significant injections in the tens or sometimes hundreds of millions of dollars to drive revenue growth at companies with billion dollar valuations.

Start-ups all face one common challenge: reaching the next stage of development and raising fresh capital before running out of cash. A negative monthly cash flow and high burn rates are the order of the day at a start-up, and regular injections of capital are needed to maintain and expand operations. This requires a management team that can carefully balance aggressive growth targets with the reality of a company at the pre-revenue stage. As such, venture capitalists carefully assess the founding team as much as the business concept of a start-up and prefer backing experienced entrepreneurs. A VC firm's knowledge in a given vertical and its ability to add value through mentorship and active engagement can be critical elements of success for the start-up; for entrepreneurs, this expertise is a differentiating factor when choosing from a group of potential investors.

HIGH RETURNS AND HIGH RISKS: Research shows that on average two-thirds of the investments made by a VC fund lose money and one-third of VC-backed companies eventually fail. For VC funds to achieve their fund-level target return,[3] low-performing and failed investments must be offset by at least one or two highly successful—and highly visible—investee companies that generate a return of 10 times (10×), 100 times (100×) or more on the VC's invested capital. These "home runs" often return 100% or more of a single fund's committed capital and determine the success of an entire fund. This tail-heavy, feast-or-famine return profile underscores both the riskiness of VC investing and the significant risk appetite required from limited partners (LPs) to include VC funds in their private equity (PE) programs.[4]

The high risk of VC investments has a distinct impact on venture capitalists' investment decisions and their portfolio management style. Reflecting on the risk of failure, VCs require high deal-level target returns when exploring the next investment: a 40–80% target internal rate of return is not unusual and feeds directly into the valuation and equity stake underpinning the investment.[5] VC funds typically invest in more companies per fund than growth or buyout funds to increase the chances of a "home run" and to diversify their risk. The larger number of portfolio companies and the high rate of failure require VCs to make tough decisions and (potentially) write off underperforming investments quickly to focus their time and resources on the most promising companies. Entrepreneurs are well advised to be aware of these dynamics before presenting their business plans to a VC fund.

The risk–return dynamics of VC investing are a concern for its investors. While limited partners remain intrigued by the industry's well-publicized winners and

---

3. Chapter 19 Performance Reporting explains the dynamics of fund-level returns in greater detail.
4. Chapter 18 LP Portfolio Management discusses the decision-making process when allocating to PE in detail.
5. Please refer to Chapter 7 Target Valuation for a worked-out example on VC valuation.

its fabled returns, a landmark report by the Kauffman Foundation published in 2012[6] raised doubts on the return contributions from venture to an institutional portfolio, implying that the risks may outweigh the strategy's return and that LPs make decisions based on "seductive narratives like vintage year and quartile performance." It suggested that the LP investment process may be broken, and that LPs have themselves "created the conditions for the chronic misallocation of capital."

FUNDING IN STAGES: VC funding is raised via discrete rounds of investments. Each round will fund a start-up's operations for a specific period of time and enable the company to reach a predefined operating milestone.

Deploying funding in stages allows a VC fund to assess the progress of the company against milestones and allocate follow-on capital to the best performing companies in its portfolio. By spreading its capital out, the fund can invest in more companies thereby "buying an option" in more potential blockbusters. It also enables individual VC firms to specialize in a specific phase of company development, from early stage to late stage, and offer stage-appropriate expertise.

Successful VC-backed companies are typically funded through progressively larger rounds of preferred equity.[7] Each subsequent VC investor will look for positive momentum (as proof of the company's value proposition) and for signs of successful execution. The preferred shareholding structure establishes a hierarchy of claims on future proceeds in the event of an exit…or liquidation.

In each financing round, entrepreneurs and existing investors give up a share of their equity in exchange for additional capital, with the percentage largely depending on the amount to be raised and the new investor's return expectations, which take into account the company's riskiness and its forecasted value at exit.

In the case of a successful start-up, raising capital step by step allows an entrepreneur to benefit from progressively higher valuations and give up less equity per dollar raised as the business matures.

START-UP DEVELOPMENT
VENTURE CAPITAL TARGETS

A start-up will navigate several stages of development before reaching profitability and a steady state of operation. Along the way, the company draws capital and expertise from different types of investors in the VC ecosystem. While each start-up follows a unique path, three distinct stages of development can be defined: proof-of-concept, commercialization, and scaling up. It should be noted that the vast majority of start-ups will never reach this final phase of accelerated growth.

---

6. Kauffman Foundation; 'We have met the enemy – and he is us'; (2012).
7. Please refer to Chapter 9 Deal Structuring and to the Glossary in the back of the book for more details on the different share classes used in VC.

Exhibit 2.2 Start-up Development and Funding

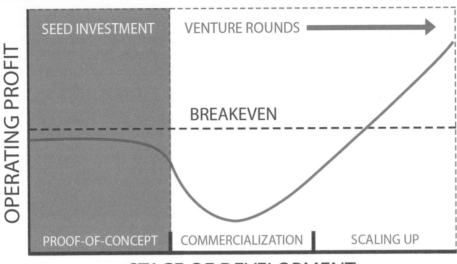

Exhibit 2.2 highlights the type of investment required at the respective stage to successfully grow and scale a business.

PROOF-OF-CONCEPT: Companies at this stage have little or no track record and only a concept of a product, technology or service. Small amounts of funding are required to conduct product feasibility studies, define relevant markets, formulate a business plan, and develop a prototype. Once the product or service is developed, engaging with and securing a user base to show that the idea has the potential to translate into a successful long-term business is a critical step to achieving proof-of-concept and attracting further funding; it also shows that the founding team has the ability to execute. During the proof-of-concept stage, company development is funded by seed investment often provided by the entrepreneur, friends and family, business angels or seed-stage VC investors.

COMMERCIALIZATION: After a company's value proposition has been validated by a group of core customers the focus shifts to translating the idea into an operating business and growing the top line. Companies at this stage of development focus on refining the product or service offering, expanding the sales and marketing functions, filling out missing capabilities in the core management team, and targeting large-scale customer acquisitions. They start to generate revenue but are far from cash flow positive; building up operations naturally increases operating cost, which combined with the initial working capital and capital expenditure needed in a growing business results in a high burn rate. In many cases, funding raised from VCs to drive commercialization are the first injections of institutional capital.

SCALING UP: This stage is all about expansion and market penetration. By now, companies are typically growing exponentially and are on their way to profit or even operating cash flow breakeven. However, profits generated from operations are reinvested in the company and may need to be supplemented by additional VC funding to meet market demand. In addition to rapidly growing a start-up's core offering, funding is needed to expand product and service offerings to differentiate the company from competitors and to balance product-specific sales fluctuations. Mid- and late-stage VC investors, along with growth equity funds, are the main investors at this stage.

Box 2.1

VENTURE CAPITAL REMAINS US FOCUSED

Geographic location is crucial for VC as an asset class, given the importance of networks when growing early-stage companies. The deepest, most "developed" VC ecosystems can be found in the United States—Silicon Valley in particular—but other geographies such as China, India, Europe and Israel have seen active clusters emerging. Successful VC communities not only have complementary funding vehicles that support early-stage growth with angel investors, crowdfunding platforms, corporate venture capital, and government funding vehicles, but provide ready access to follow-on rounds and serve as magnets to attract the talent needed to scale quickly. Exhibit 2.3 shows the total amount of venture capital invested by geography over three consecutive five-year periods starting in 2001.

Exhibit 2.3 Global VC Investment by Geography

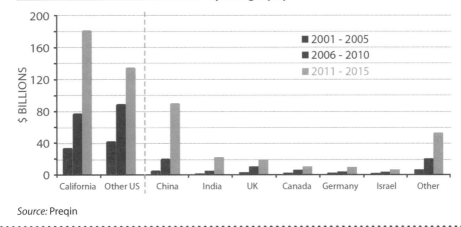

Source: Preqin

THE VENTURE CAPITAL INVESTMENT PROCESS
UNIQUE ELEMENTS

The immaturity of companies targeted by VC funds introduces a range of unique elements into the VC investment process. Identifying future unicorns is an art, while structuring an investment to mitigate the investment risk involved is rather a science. We explore these elements in the section that follows.

DEAL SOURCING: Deal sourcing in venture is closely related to the reputation of the VC firm and the partners involved; established and well-known firms will have a regular stream of calls, pitch books and ideas flowing their way. Partners will also attend the various demo days of accelerators or industry conferences to scout for potential targets. When screening investment opportunities, VC investors' gut-feel about a start-up and its team is a crucial component and often drives the decision to pursue a specific deal. Nevertheless, questions revolving around the entrepreneur, the team's experience and motivation and the uniqueness, defensibility and scalability of the business model tend to feature prominently in those early discussions.

VALUATION: Determining the valuation of an early-stage investment is a highly subjective process.[8] While a company's current operations and future cash flow forecasts are a key component in establishing its value, so too are the robustness of its team, the strength of the business model and the size of the addressable market. As early-stage companies are typically unprofitable, investors employ multiples of revenue and other key performance indicators to arrive at a "post-money valuation,"[9] which also determines the equity split following an investment round. The expected number of future fundraising rounds will also impact valuation, as they will lead to dilution of the equity stakes for both entrepreneurs and past VC investors.

HANDS-ON SUPPORT: Many successful entrepreneurs join VC firms to become early-stage investors themselves. The best VC funds will therefore draw on a strong bench of partners, who not only have an intimate understanding of the challenges faced by their portfolio companies, but also come with their own hard-earned experience to give credible advice. Venture partners mentor management teams, help develop the marketability of a start-up's product or service, identify and fill holes in its team, and facilitate the development of business processes required to scale up. Venture capitalists are also a key resource for start-ups when raising new rounds of capital, both in shaping the fundraising message and identifying potential investors in their network.

SYNDICATED DEALS: While "club deals"[10] are rare in growth equity and buyouts, venture rounds are quite often funded by multiple VCs. Typically, a lead investor will engage with the entrepreneur and founder, conduct due diligence, arrive at a valuation, negotiate terms and commit to funding a portion of the round. Once the lead investor establishes the commercial terms, a group of "followers" will join the round.[11] The lead investor will typically invest the largest amount of capital in a round, and will be the one to engage with the start-up post-investment. This type of club investment allows VC funds to diversify their risk and gain access to a wider range of investment opportunities.

---

8. See Chapter 7 Target Valuation for further details on VC valuation techniques and a worked example.

9. Subtracting invested capital from a post-money valuation establishes the "pre-money" valuation.

10. Club deals are PE investments made by two or three PE funds; they were particularly fashionable for large buyouts during the years leading up to the global financial crisis in 2008.

11. Existing investors often participate in subsequent rounds to maintain their ownership percentage in the business and to signal both their continued support and overall health of the business.

Box 2.2

VENTURE CAPITAL TERM SHEETS

Term sheets serve as the main negotiation tool in VC fundraising and, once agreed upon, set out the rights and obligations of investors in a round's newly created preferred share class. The provisions of the term sheet are then formalized in a share subscription agreement, and in an amended or redrafted shareholders' agreement plus articles of association of the target company.[12]

First-time entrepreneurs are well advised to carefully review the terms under negotiation before signing a term sheet, especially as earlier investment rounds set the ground rules for future fundraising, potentially complicating that process. Guidance from an experienced entrepreneur or a friendly venture partner can help overcome the knowledge gap between start-up founders and seasoned VC investors.

The provisions in a term sheet can be divided into economic terms and control terms.

Economic Terms

Economic terms set out the price of shares, the investment amount and the rights and obligations of the newly created preferred share class.

SHARE PRICE AND VALUATION: The first part of the term sheet defines the offer made by the VC in a given round, including the valuation of the company (pre-money), amount of invested capital, number of shares to be issued and price per share. The type of securities to be issued for this round, for example "series B preferred stock," is clearly defined.

LIQUIDATION PREFERENCE: This clause gives preferred shareholders preference over any distributions received in case of a defined liquidity event, be it an acquisition by a strategic buyer, a merger, an initial public offering (IPO) or the liquidation of the company. Preferred shareholders receive their invested capital back first (and at times a multiple thereof) before any distributions are made to common shareholders. In the case of "participating preferred shares," preferred shareholders will share the balance of the exit proceeds after the liquidation preference has been satisfied pro rata with common shareholders, on an as-converted basis.

EMPLOYEE STOCK OWNERSHIP PLAN (ESOP): An ESOP sets aside a percentage of shares in the start-up that can be granted to non-founding employees in the form of stock options to attract, reward and retain first-rate talent. A term sheet will stipulate a vesting schedule for these options—a clearly defined timeline for the options to convert into shares—it will also allow the board to force a forfeit of these options under certain circumstances. In addition, the term sheet will

12. More information on deal documentation can be found in Chapter 10.

clearly define the number of shares reserved for the ESOP, and the strike price, timing and expiration date of the options. Given that ESOPs are a source of dilution for all existing shareholders, both the size and timing of an ESOP need to be carefully considered when planning to raise external funding. Many VCs will require an ESOP of 20% of the outstanding shares before closing a round.

ANTI-DILUTION: This provision protects earlier investors in the event of a "down-round" (i.e., a round of funding raised at a lower valuation than the previous round). With anti-dilution provision in place, the conversion price of the preferred share class will be adjusted downwards to the level of the new valuation; as a result, shareholders who invested at a higher valuation in earlier rounds will receive additional shares to maintain their ownership stake in the start-up and avoid dilution.

Common shareholders do not have such protective provisions and will be diluted. Anti-dilution clauses come in various degrees of severity, and founders are well advised to be aware of their impact.

CONVERSION RIGHTS: Preferred shareholders may convert at any time to common stock at their sole discretion; the conversion rate—at the outset usually 1:1 of preferred to common—is clearly defined in this clause. Investors will generally be converted from preferred to common shareholders at clearly defined trigger events, typically just prior to a sale or merger. In the event of an IPO, conversion of the preferred stock is usually automatic.

Control Terms

Despite being minority shareholders, venture investors typically request certain control rights to monitor the development of the start-up and influence important decisions.

BOARD REPRESENTATION: VCs will expect to be represented on the board of directors of the investee company. Whether it is one or two board seats with the respective votes or merely an "observer right" depends very much on the dynamics during negotiations. (An in-demand company courted by several venture investors may be able to negotiate lesser representation as a condition of investment.) Founders are well advised to have a clear board plan—defining the number of seats available to venture investors and those assigned to independent directors—before raising their first external round.

PROTECTIVE PROVISIONS: Venture investors usually receive voting rights on an "as-converted" basis equal to that of common shareholders. In addition certain actions may require the consent of the VC or approval of at least 50% of the preferred shareholders. These actions may include alterations of the certificate of incorporation, which would adversely change the rights, privileges and powers of the preferred shareholder, or approval of any sale of assets or mergers, or any changes to the number of preferred shares issued. Veto rights may apply with regards to specific events such as an IPO, new equity financing or increase in the ESOP and can extend to governance matters such as the right to approve the appointment of senior executives.

DRAG-ALONG/TAG-ALONG PROVISIONS: A drag-along provision gives the majority shareholder the right to force other shareholders to sell their shares in a third-party transaction. This provision enables the majority shareholder to sell out and achieve a clean break at exit. A tag-along provision provides minority shareholders with the right to sell their shares in conjunction with the majority shareholder in a third-party transaction, participating in any liquidity event pro rata.

TRANSFER RIGHTS AND NEW ISSUE RESTRICTIONS: The term sheet typically includes preemptive rights for share transfers and new issues, stating that the existing shareholders shall be offered any shares first in the case of an existing shareholder wanting to sell out.

INFORMATION RIGHTS: This provision clearly states which operational and financial information must be provided to preferred shareholders and when; the requested information usually includes at a minimum unaudited monthly and annual financial statements.

FOR THE FIRST-TIME ENTREPRENEUR
RAISING MONEY FROM VCs

First-time entrepreneurs often think that all VCs invest in great ideas and innovative companies across industries and at any time in their lifecycle. This is far from the truth; every venture firm has a very specific focus on verticals, technologies, geographies, and most important investment amounts or funding rounds. They are likely to pass on a great idea if it doesn't fit their focus or sweet spot; thus, entrepreneurs should carefully select those funds worthwhile approaching. Due diligence is crucial for both parties, and entrepreneurs should ask for references from past investee companies before selecting a VC fund. Speaking with those founders will give them a clear idea of the day-to-day reality of working with and accepting funding from the respective VC.

Beyond focusing on how to fund their start-up, founders also need to decide on the timing and size of the various rounds. Entrepreneurs must balance the need for raising capital from external investors with the requirement of giving up equity in the process.

Consider the hypothetical financing of a start-up shown in Exhibit 2.4 in which an entrepreneur raises four rounds of external funding, at progressively higher valuations, over a three-and-a-half-year period.

The above example brings up a number of issues for entrepreneurs to consider. First, as the valuation of the start-up increases, the entrepreneur is able to raise larger sums of capital in exchange for lower equity stakes in the company. The burn rate allows an entrepreneur to plan the amount of funding needed to achieve the next development milestone and to optimize the time between rounds. Finally, the entrepreneur's

Exhibit 2.4 Fundraising Considerations for Entrepreneurs

	CHARACTERISTICS OF ROUNDS			CONSIDERATIONS FOR ENTREPRENEURS			
ROUND	POST-MONEY VALUATION (USD)	CAPITAL RAISED (USD)	EQUITY STAKE OF THE ROUND	BURN RATE (USD/MONTH)	FUNDING (MONTHS)	ENTREPRENEUR'S EQUITY STAKE	USD PER 1% EQUITY STAKE
SEED	2m	150k	7.5%	15k	10	92.5%	20k
SERIES A	12m	2m	16.7%	150k	13	77.1%	120k
SERIES B	25m	3m	12.0%	300k	10	67.8%	250k
SERIES C	75m	6m	8.0%	CASH FLOW POSITIVE	N/A	62.4%	750k

declining equity stake following each round of investment shows clearly the impact of dilution when raising external funding.[13]

Some founders question the merit of giving up substantial amounts of equity in return for venture funding. They often consider an alternative: growing the company organically without external funding by conservatively managing the early stage with their own capital and trying to quickly grow revenue. With the rise of the "lean start-up"[14] model (and the availability of low-cost funding sources, i.e., crowd funding), this alternative path has become a realistic option for certain business models.[15]

What Is a Venture Capitalist?
By Brad Feld, Managing Director, Foundry Group

One of the biggest mistakes entrepreneurs make is to assume that all VCs are the same. Over and over again I hear questions like "how do I raise venture capital?," or "how do I approach a VC?," or "what does a VC want to see in the first meeting?," or "now that I'm going to pitch a VC, what should I show them?" The answer—generically—is "I have no idea—WHO are you meeting with?" This usually gets the person's attention, at least a little.

There is no single archetype for a VC, or for a VC firm. Instead, each VC, and firm, is different. Consider the game Dungeons & Dragons (or, if you don't know D&D, contemplate one of the *Lord of the Rings* movies.) Some VCs are elves, some are orcs, others are wizards, or mages, or trolls. Each character has a different set of skills, weapons, money, and experience points, which change, increase, and evolve over time.

---

13. Note that not only the entrepreneur gets diluted by subsequent financing rounds but also previous investors.
14. Reis, E. (2008).
15. Wasserman, Nazeeri, and Anderson (2012).

There are dozens of archetypes of VCs. Each individual VC has a different set of skills. Their styles, beliefs, and personalities vary widely. Their approaches and ideas are influenced by the individual's historical experiences. Behavior—both in the moment and over time—varies widely.

A VC firm is a collection of individual VCs with differing archetypes. Firms vary widely in shapes and sizes. My firm, Foundry Group, consists of equal partners and no additional professionals. Other firms have many layers of investment professionals, including partners, principals, associates, analysts, entrepreneurs-in-residence, and operating partners. Some VC firms are small—there are even single partner firms—while others have dozens of investment partners. Some firms are operator heavy (partners with operating backgrounds), others are financial heavy (MBAs and bankers), while others are a mix.

The entry points of VC firms vary widely. Some VCs invest early. Others invest late. You have firms that label themselves as pre-seed, while others call themselves seed and early-stage investors. Other firms wait until a company is in the market with a product that is starting to scale. Other VCs, often called growth investors, prefer to engage when a company is clearly succeeding and is now scaling. Still others like to be the last round investor prior to an IPO and are consequently called late-stage investors. And yes, there are firms that cut across multiples of these categories.

The categories that firms invest in, and how they describe them, also vary widely. Foundry Group uses a thematic approach that we pioneered in 2007. Other firms use a sector approach, which has been around for many years. Some firms invest only in software and Internet-related companies, while others invest in clean tech or life sciences. Once again, the configuration of the approaches can be combined in many different, and occasionally unique, ways within a VC firm.

Once you realize you are dealing with many different archetypes of individual VCs with widely varying skills and experience levels, and the configuration of these archetypes into a firm is similar to how characters combine and interact in a battle in D&D, you realize that there is no generic VC or VC firm.

As an entrepreneur, you should do your research on the person and firm you are approaching or talking to. It's easy to do today using the web and the power of all the network connections between people. If you understand who you are talking to, what motivates them, and what they care about, you can both target them better as well as have a much more effective conversation with them.

Box 2.3

BEYOND VENTURE CAPITAL
ALTERNATIVE PATHS TO FUNDING

VC funds are not the only source of capital for start-ups. A variety of players provide capital and expertise to these businesses, each with a different set of value propositions. Early-stage companies may work with several of these players and VC investors to get their business off to a successful start.

BUSINESS ANGELS: Angel investors are affluent individuals who invest their personal funds at a very early or "idea" stage of development. They are often experienced professionals from the industry in which the start-up operates and may be closely involved in shaping and developing the company's first business plan.[16]

START-UP INCUBATORS AND ACCELERATORS: These vehicles help start-ups develop and grow their businesses.[17] Particularly first-time entrepreneurs may find the structure, support and mentorship offered by these programs attractive. Admittance into the best programs is highly competitive, with some accepting no more than 10 candidates per 1,000 applicants. Incubators and accelerators are often mentioned in the same vein—but there are differences:

- Incubators: Incubators guide entrepreneurs through the first steps of idea generation and help them develop a business model on the basis of that idea. These programs have no set duration and typically provide office or co-working space, administrative support and networking opportunities to entrepreneurs in exchange for rent or—in some instances—an equity stake in the start-up. Incubators are often sponsored by a government entity or university and generally do not provide capital.

- Accelerators: Accelerators offer short, intense courses and access to industry mentors for entrepreneurs that have a proven concept and are ready to consider raising VC financing. Accelerators admit start-ups in cohorts and each program culminates in a "demo day" when participants pitch their investment idea to a group of potential investors. Most accelerators are privately owned and often provide a small amount of seed funding in exchange for an equity stake in a participating company.

CORPORATE VENTURE CAPITAL: Corporations have emerged as a fast-growing source of funding for start-ups and compete head-on with independent VC funds. Corporate venture capital (CVC) is created by business entities not usually engaged in financing and investing; INTEL Capital, Unilever Ventures and Google Ventures are among the most prominent. These investors often

---

16. Please refer to the links and references at the end of this chapter for additional material on angel investors.
17. Readers will find a list of incubators and accelerators on our website (www.masteringprivateequity.com).

leverage the expertise of their parent organizations and invest in industries where the parent is active. The main incentive to start a CVC program is to gain early access to disruptive innovations that may help (or hinder) the strategic goals of the parent company, with financial returns often a secondary consideration.

CLOSING

Fast-growing companies, incubated around a creative idea on how to solve a problem or explore an opportunity, are not a coincidence. Big successes require a meeting of minds between a skilled founding team and investors providing funding and mentorship to offer advice if and when needed. This chapter offered perspectives from both sides of the table, considering investors and entrepreneurs alike. The magic in the form of big disruptions and extraordinary returns happens when talented entrepreneurs meet the best-suited venture partners.

KEY LEARNING POINTS

• **VC funds invest minority stakes in start-ups seeking to develop defensible, fast-growing businesses by disrupting existing products and services through innovation.**

• **VC investing is characterized by tail-end returns, with one or two home runs typically offsetting the failed investments in a successful fund.**

• **VC funds invest in specific industry verticals and stages of company development, from seed to early to late stage.**

• **Entrepreneurs must be aware of the trade-offs between accepting external funding and giving up equity when raising capital from VC funds.**

• **Understanding the future impact of the terms negotiated during fundraising is key, especially for first-time entrepreneurs.**

RELEVANT CASE STUDIES

from *Private Equity in Action—Case Studies from Developed and Emerging Markets*

Case #5: Sula Vineyards: Indian Wine?—Ce n'est pas possible!

Case #6: Adara Venture Partners: Building a Venture Capital Firm

Case #7: Siraj Capital: Investing in SMEs in the Middle East

REFERENCES AND ADDITIONAL READING

Babson (2013) Term Sheets in Early Stage Venture Capital Financing (BAB710C).

Chemmanur, T.J., Krishnan, K. and Nandy, D.K. (2011) How Does Venture Capital Financing Improve; Efficiency in Private Firms? A Look Beneath the Surface, *Review of Financial Studies*, 24(12): 4037–90.

Damodaran, Aswan, VC is About Pricing—Not Valuation, http://aswathdamodaran.blogspot.com.ar/2016/10/venture-capital-it-is-pricing-not-value.html.

Gompers, P., Gornall, W., Kaplan, S.N., and Strebulaev, I.A. (2016) How Do Venture Capitalists Make Decisions? (No. w22587), National Bureau of Economic Research.

Gompers, Paul A. (1995) Optimal Investment, Monitoring and the Staging of Venture Capital, *Journal of Finance*, 50(5), December, available at SSRN https://ssrn.com/abstract=6971.

Kaplan, S.N. and Lerner, J. (2010) It Ain't Broke: The Past, Present, and Future of Venture Capital, *Journal of Applied Corporate Finance*, 22: 36–47.

Kauffman Foundation (2012) We Have Met the Enemy—and He is Us, http://www.kauffman.org/~/media/kauffman_org/research%20reports%20and%20covers/2012/05/we_have_met_the_enemy_and_he_is_us.pdf.

Reis, E. (2008) The Lean Startup.

Wasserman, Naom, Nazeeri, Furqan and Anderson, Kyle (2012) *A "Rich-vs.-King" Approach to Term Sheet Negotiations*, HBS.

For detailed discussion on term sheets please refer to:

Feld, Brad, Venture Deals and his related blog http://www.askthevc.com/ .

Further reading on angel investing, incubators and accelerators:

Accelerators vs. Incubators, http://www.techrepublic.com/article/accelerators-vs-incubators-what-startups-need-to-know/.

Cohen, S, What Do Accelerators Do? Insights from Incubators and Angels, http://www.mitpressjournals.org/doi/pdf/10.1162/INOV_a_00184.

Growth equity funds occupy the space between (and thus complement) venture and buyout investing, providing fast-growing but established businesses with funds and support for a transformational leap in their development. Growth equity accounts for the largest number of private equity (PE) deals executed in emerging markets. In addition, following the global financial crisis, growth equity investments have gained fresh momentum in developed markets, as they provided an avenue to deploy capital at a time when debt markets were closed.

This chapter explores the strategy's defining traits, describes the attributes of its target companies and the unique characteristics of the growth equity investment process. We conclude with a closer look at some of the minority shareholder rights sought by growth equity investors.

GROWTH EQUITY DEFINED

Growth equity funds invest in fast-growing businesses (which have moved beyond the start-up stage) in exchange for a minority equity stake. Given the lack of control, a strong working relationship and trust-based partnership between the investors, existing owners, and management are required to achieve the desired outcome: advancing the company to a new stage of development. These dynamics are shown in Exhibit 3.1.

Exhibit 3.1 Defining Characteristics of Growth Equity

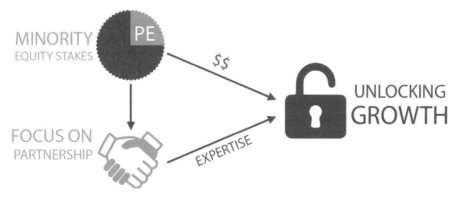

MINORITY EQUITY STAKES: Growth equity investments are usually made in exchange for a minority equity stake; strategic and operational control of the company will remain with its existing business owners. A growth equity fund's stake in a business typically consists predominantly of newly issued shares, although a portion of funding may be used to provide an exit for existing business owners. Only a small subset of growth equity deals results in the PE firm acquiring more than 50% of a company's equity and benefiting from the ensuing majority shareholder rights. In these instances, the key aspect differentiating growth equity from control buyouts is the active role both founders and management teams retain in the company.

The minority equity position of an incoming PE investor shapes all aspects of the investment process, from deal structuring and operational decision-making during the holding period, to the course of action at exit. From the outset, it is important for minority investors to understand the motivations of the majority shareholders and ensure they are aligned with the fund's investment thesis, its base case scenario for expansion and its plans for change. Still, focusing on an agreed-upon plan and executing the necessary changes can prove quite challenging from a minority position, even with a good working relationship and appropriate minority shareholder rights in place.

FOCUS ON PARTNERSHIP: In an ideal scenario, owners, existing management and new investors will form a successful partnership contributing complementary skills that help obtain superior operating results at the portfolio company. Growth equity investors bring financial acumen to the table, in particular experience in optimizing capital structures, in buying and selling businesses, and familiarity with capital markets and the initial public offering (IPO) process. In addition, they often have a broad network in both commercial and financial circles and experience in creating corporate governance structures in line with global best practices. Overall, their skillset can be an effective complement to the operating knowledge and local networks developed by owners and management.

As growth equity does not primarily provide liquidity to the owners, the economic interests of both parties are well aligned. Furthermore, it may be in the PE firm's best interest to keep the existing management in place and in control, as they have a working knowledge of the operating business and its markets. A growth equity investment will therefore often be minimally disruptive to the operating dynamics of a business, since existing relationships between owners, management, suppliers, customers and other stakeholders are maintained.

To ensure a smooth working relationship, both parties need to agree on growth and development targets and align their interests from the start. A clear understanding of the culture and approach to business at both the PE firm and the target company can help manage expectations and set realistic rules of engagement for both parties. PE investors and existing company owners must each carefully select partners that complement their individual investment and management styles. For example, a hands-on active investor may be best advised to avoid investing in a "closed" family business, and a passive investor might not be the right partner for a business with urgent restructuring needs.

UNLOCKING GROWTH: Growth equity funds invest in established businesses with proven business models and attractive future prospects for expansion. Portfolio companies often operate in expanding economies, in sectors exceeding a country's average national growth, or in industries ripe for disruption. A growth equity fund's capital, its industry and operational know-how can provide a company with the resources to unlock latent potential, improve profitability and enable accelerated growth.

The capital invested by a growth equity fund is typically used for two purposes:

- To fund specific, value-accretive projects at the portfolio company. Growth equity firms often employ a bench of operating partners who can help define these projects and drive the value creation process. Incoming funds may be used, for example, to realize international expansion plans, develop a new product line, fund working capital to reach scale, expand existing facilities, or consolidate a fragmented industry through roll-up acquisitions. Companies should select their preferred growth equity partner from a group of suitors based on their experience in driving the specific initiatives needed to maximize value creation.

- To provide liquidity to the current owners and founders and help simplify its shareholding structure. The latter can help reduce the complexity of economic claims on a company and significantly simplify the governance process. The new investor may, for example, replace a number of venture capital (VC) investors from earlier investment rounds in a successful start-up or step into the shoes of a group of family members in a family-owned business.

Creating Value through Genuine Partnerships
By J. Frank Brown, Managing Director and Chief Operating Officer, General Atlantic

Partnership is a frequently overlooked cornerstone of successful growth equity investing. Many fast-growing businesses are at an inflection point in their development, in need of a candid, patient, and strategic partner to help them manage and accelerate their growth by seizing new opportunities, mitigating risks, and preparing to scale their business models. The most important aspect of any partnership is the alignment of interests; if an investor and investee work together to build a successful company that is designed to scale and grow—the holy grail of growth investing—both will be successful.

In order to unlock maximum value and drive superior returns, an investor needs to build a genuine partnership with entrepreneurs by using a relationship-focused approach founded on an alignment of interests. But what makes a partnership genuine? What components are needed to maximize the success of a growth investment?

- Transparency and mutual understanding. With fast-growing companies, there needs to be agreement on a host of factors related to a company's current and potential future growth trajectory, including: how fast the company can grow, how it will expand, what capital is needed for that to happen, who is the optimal management team to lead that growth, and much more. In our experience, people are the most important factor determining a company's success, which means having the right leadership and employees in place as quickly as possible is critical.

- A short- and long-term plan. The investor and company management team also need to agree on a plan for the first year of the investment, as well as a longer-term plan, including how to prepare the company for its next phase of growth in the coming decade. Is the company going to expand to other markets, and to other products or services? How will the business need to grow in terms of its employees and management team? What capabilities are needed that don't currently exist at the company and does it have the right in-house talent to lead those capabilities effectively?

- Ongoing engagement. An investor needs to remain engaged over the lifecycle of the investment, with the investment team continuing to work hand in hand with the portfolio company over the entire period of ownership, instead of passing off responsibility once the deal has closed. They should connect the portfolio company to the impactful advice, relationships, and resources it needs to enable and sustain growth. One of the most important roles of a growth investor is serving as a sounding board to entrepreneurs, offering guidance and best practices in all aspects of the business, including human capital, revenue generation, and operational excellence. To do this effectively, an investor needs to build and leverage a global network of relationships to help growing companies draw from best practices across industries and regions, and build a world-class leadership team and board that will help them scale.

- A structure-reinforcing partnership. A growth equity firm's investing structure should be geared toward alignment with its portfolio companies. For example, we generally invest in common stock with a simple liquidation preference that provides protection without overly structured provisions. To engrain an ethos of partnership and collaboration in a firm, investment teams need to be incentivized to add value and harvest gains, not put money in the ground. For example, our collective team represents the single largest commitment in our capital base. Our team members put their own money into every deal that we do, creating the ultimate alignment of interests. This motivates everyone to help build a successful enterprise from the time we finalize negotiations with a company and fund the capital until the time we exit the investment.

- Engagement across geographies. If a growth equity firm has a global footprint, the optimal incentive structure will rally team members around the globe to help a company unlock value and drive growth across geographies—critical for the many growth companies that rank global expansion as one of their chief objectives. While many global private equity firms have separate geographic funds with separate economics, motivating their investment teams to focus solely on deals within their region, at General Atlantic, we channel our communal focus on global growth equity. We have a unique global carry pool so team members benefit—and thus are ready and willing to help a portfolio company succeed—regardless of where a deal is done and who does it.

By building a transparent, aligned, and enduring partnership with a rapidly growing business, a growth equity investor is in a unique position to serve as a steady co-pilot, helping it stay on course and rise to new heights—and, by doing so, generate value and maximize returns.

GROWTH EQUITY TARGETS

Growth equity funds invest predominantly in three types of businesses: late-stage venture capital-backed companies, mature small and medium-sized enterprises (SMEs), and spin-offs from large corporations. These companies typically have high capital expenditure and increased working capital requirements to sustain their growth trajectory. Their investment requirements leave little free cash flow to service debt and the scale of company operations often inhibits their ability to tap public equity markets. As a result, an infusion of PE growth equity can be an attractive way to fund incremental growth. We explore the three types of target companies below.

LATE-STAGE VENTURE-BACKED: Growth equity is a crucial ingredient for VC-backed companies that have established a successful business model, claimed a defensible market position and reached profitability in their steady-state operations. Having arrived at this stage, these post-revenue and post-profit companies require access to deeper pools of capital to scale their activities and execute secondary or tertiary growth strategies. Thus, engaging with a growth equity fund clearly marks the transition from a start-up to a robust, sustainable business. Like VC funds, growth equity funds may continue to deploy capital into these companies over several rounds of investment and may over time establish a path to a controlling stake.

MATURE SMEs: Mature businesses with a unique competitive advantage and attractive development prospects offer perfect opportunities for growth equity investment. These companies often possess a strong market position with a well-recognized brand and a solid network. Investments from a growth equity fund frequently represent the firm's first and only engagement with a financial investor. As SMEs are in many cases family businesses or entrepreneur owned and controlled, a minority investment allows these owner/managers to maintain control of the board and the company's day-to-day operations. This differs from a successful late-stage VC-backed company, where founding entrepreneurs have typically given up significant equity and governance rights in earlier fundraising rounds.

SPIN-OFFs: Growth equity investors at times target divisions of large corporations that are well positioned for divestment or spinoff. In these instances, a corporation will typically retain control of the division initially but add capital and know-how from the PE investor to spark growth and pave the way for a smooth handover to a new investor (including public market) when the corporation eventually decides to step out. These targets are often inadequately resourced from a funding and talent perspective and thus offer greater upside under a new ownership and governance structure outside the parent entity.

Box 3.1

GROWTH EQUITY IN EMERGING MARKETS

As mentioned earlier, one aspect of growth equity investment is its prevalence in emerging markets. Observers of PE are often surprised to note that more than three-quarters of the PE deals in emerging markets are minority investments into mature SMEs. The reason: the majority of attractive companies that have thrived during the rapid economic development in these markets are family-owned businesses, still managed and controlled by the first or second generation of families. These founders are often reluctant to give up control of their company. Yet, after decades of rapid growth the foundations of these businesses are often lacking and governance structures are in need of a revamp. An experienced growth equity fund can help reform and professionalize the board, bring in experienced senior and middle management and help the firm think through suitable levers to ensure success for future generations.

THE GROWTH EQUITY INVESTMENT PROCESS
UNIQUE ELEMENTS

The typical growth equity investment process is distinct from other forms of PE investing. From deal sourcing to value creation to exit, understanding the needs of a growth company requires a specific skillset.

DEAL SOURCING AND DUE DILIGENCE

Identifying targets for growth equity funds can be a challenge: minority investment opportunities in mature SMEs are less intermediated than control deals and the most attractive target companies rarely seek an infusion of capital from external investors. Sourcing growth equity deals therefore requires a strong proprietary network; it can take years to build a relationship with company owners, argue the case for investment and eventually consummate a deal. Often these businesses do not explicitly need capital to maintain their current operating model, shifting the onus to the growth equity investor to open doors and convince company owners of the opportunities that an infusion of external capital can unlock.

Once a suitable target is identified, the lack of robust monitoring and reporting structures at many growth equity targets can introduce a significant information gap between existing owners and new investors, placing PE firms at a disadvantage during due diligence, valuation and negotiations. For investments in highly visible late-stage VC-backed companies, the challenge is slightly different: competition from multiple growth equity funds can accelerate the capital-raising process, but require investors to make decisions quickly with incomplete information, and accept valuations or terms driven by competitive dynamics or market momentum.

Negotiating growth equity deals can be particularly challenging given the presence of strong entrepreneurs and founders, as decisions often hinge on non-economic interests that may be difficult to identify for an outside party. The pre-investment phase is nevertheless the time when PE investors have the best chance of shaping a company's strategy by convincing management of its expertise and influencing shareholding terms given their position as prospective new capital providers.

Finalizing and executing growth equity deals is typically easier than in more complex buyout transactions; the lack of leverage and the smaller number of parties involved makes negotiation, information gathering, vetting of documentation, and closing the deal significantly easier.

VALUE CREATION

Whether a mature SME, a VC-backed company or a corporate spin-off, growth equity portfolio companies share similar levers for value creation. As growth equity investors rarely employ debt to magnify returns on their equity stake, their focus will be on driving change at the operating company (through strategic, operational and

Exhibit 3.2 Value Creation in Growth Equity

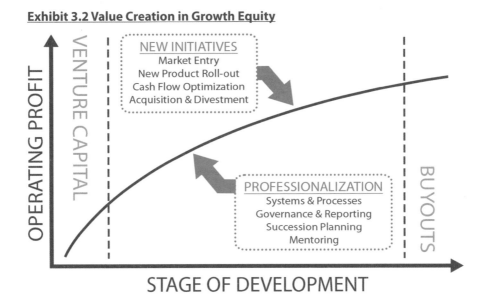

financial initiatives), or professionalization and governance optimization, as shown in Exhibit 3.2[1]

Professionalizing governance and business processes provides the necessary backbone to execute value creation initiatives. Given the initially lean set-up of VC-backed companies and the resource constraints in SMEs, many of the structures and processes governing their business operations and decision-making have previously been implemented in an ad-hoc fashion. Therefore, improving reporting structures and information flow, and professionalizing the management of both human resources and capital is essential for these companies to consolidate their advantage and enable the next stage of growth. PE investors can add value by mentoring current management and identifying blue-chip talent to help with succession planning. In addition to the PE firm's network, the presence of a new and committed shareholder sends a strong signal to the market, which may attract talent to the company.

When working with owner-operators, PE investors must be realistic about the number of changes they can implement during the holding period. While contractual rights can reassure and protect the investor's interests, the ability to execute controversial restructuring and cost-cutting plans will likely be constrained by the fund's minority equity position.

EXIT

Similar to most PE investors, growth equity funds will target to exit their investments within three to seven years. While the company may have grown in line with the business plan, finding a buyer willing to step into the shoes of a minority shareholder can be difficult. At times, the majority owner may exit alongside the growth equity fund, providing a viable acquisition target to strategic investors, who usually require a control stake in a business; however, these cases are the exception rather than the

---

1. Please refer to Chapter 13 Operational Value Creation for further insights into the tools used by PE firms to improve their portfolio companies during the holding period.

rule. More likely, the growth equity stake will be sold on its own, for instance via a secondary sale to another PE fund or a buyback by the entrepreneur.

Large portfolio firms may choose the IPO route, allowing on the one hand the owner to maintain a controlling stake and on the other hand the PE investors to sell down their holdings during or after listing. A similar mechanism applies for private investments in public equity, a common structure for growth equity funds in certain jurisdictions; given the company is already listed, the growth investor can sell into the public market upon exit.

Disagreements between the multiple shareholders can complicate the exit process. A mismatch in valuation expectations or non-economic priorities such as job preservation for family members or the protection of the company heritage can confound the exit process. In addition, a PE firm may be unable to optimally prepare the portfolio company for the sale of its stake from a minority position. Clarifying possible exit avenues early on and drafting the necessary documentation to ensure both parties are aware of and aligned with future plans are important to mitigate these risks and reduce conflicts.

MINORITY SHAREHOLDER RIGHTS

To mitigate the risk associated with minority ownership, growth equity investors negotiate explicit shareholder rights to monitor their investee firms, influence company proceedings, and preempt or mitigate potential conflicts of interest with the majority shareholder. Explicit rights and safeguards are included to ensure that the investor's interests are clearly expressed and aligned with those of the company's owners. Contractual provisions may be included to enable enforcement; they are negotiated as early as the submission of a letter of interest or term sheet and later formalized in an amended company's shareholder agreement post-investment.[2] Exhibit 3.3 shows some of the mitigating contractual safeguards employed by minority investors.

A jurisdiction's regulatory code and its established case law provide an important safety net for minority shareholders to mitigate the risk of unfair treatment, or ensure the enforcement of their rights. The investor may petition a court, stating that majority shareholders have run the company in a manner unfairly prejudicial to the minority shareholder; examples include not sharing financial information in a timely manner, dealing with associated companies on a non-arm's length basis or

Exhibit 3.3 Minority Shareholding Dynamics

CHALLENGES   SAFEGUARDS

Operating Control ⟶ Voting, Approval and Information Rights

Company Culture ⟶ Management Incentives (ESOP)

Exit Timing ⟶ Buyback mechanism, drag-along rights

---

2. For further details on the process and documentation of PE transactions please refer to Chapter 10 Transaction Documentation.

gross incompetence of senior management (or a family member). The court may then ask the controlling shareholder to refrain from certain activities, authorize civil proceedings or order the minority stake to be acquired by the controlling shareholder.

OPERATING CONTROL: The governance terms associated with growth equity investments vary widely, but typically include representation on a portfolio company's board of directors and certain negative control and approval rights. Growth equity investors may also seek voting rights disproportionate to their ownership share to strengthen their ability to execute strategic and operational change and prepare the company for a successful exit. Negative control and approval rights provide growth equity investors with control over decisions related to operating and capital budgets, C-level executive changes, mergers and acquisitions and divestment activity, new borrowing and equity issuance, divergence from strategic plans, and expansion into new business lines. Information rights ensure that accounts and advanced notice of important corporate actions are disseminated in a timely fashion. Overall, these contractual provisions provide growth equity investors only with the means to block company activities detrimental to their interest, underscoring the importance of developing a productive working relationship with business owners to drive value creation.

MANAGEMENT INCENTIVES: Given their limited operating control, growth investors strive to boost alignment with management through financial incentives. A management share or option plan tied to key operating and financial metrics will focus the manager's attention on growing the business in line with investor's goals. Ideally, shares should only vest upon exit of the PE fund to match the investor's time horizon. An incentive plan will often constitute a requirement to attract higher-caliber talent to professionalize management and drive the next phase of growth in the company.

LIQUIDITY: As minority investors, growth equity funds lack the voting rights to force the hand of majority owners at exit time. Some of the contractual provisions that protect their interests include put options that allow a fund to sell its stake back to the controlling shareholders at a predetermined minimum price or, in the case of severely missed performance targets, the ability to initiate a liquidity event such as an IPO. They may also include drag-along rights that enable the investor to force the remaining shareholders to participate in the sale of the business.

CLOSING

Growth equity has developed into a recognized strategy within the PE industry. In many instances and particularly in developing markets, where businesses are often owned and managed by the first or second generation of families, minority investors are much sought after, especially when they come with relevant industry expertise and the ability to open doors to new (overseas) markets. Given their reliance on strong partnerships and cooperation with the founding families, it is no surprise that successful PE firms take specific care to develop lasting relationships and a solid reputation with the business communities at large. In the day and age of ample dry powder, it is no secret that even traditional buyout funds have expanded their investment strategy to include minority investments in order to deploy capital in a timely manner.

KEY LEARNING POINTS

• Growth equity funds invest in fast-growing, established companies in return for a minority equity share and make a concerted effort to establish a solid partnership with all company stakeholders (especially majority owners).

• Beyond capital, growth equity funds offer hands-on involvement with their portfolio companies to assist with business development, professionalization and expansion.

• Minority protection rights are crucial for growth investors especially with regards to achieving a successful future exit.

RELEVANT CASE STUDIES

from *Private Equity in Action—Case Studies from Developed and Emerging Markets*

Case #7: Siraj Capital: Investing in SMEs in the Middle East

Case #8: Private Equity in Emerging Markets: Can Operating Advantage Boost Value in Exits?

REFERENCES AND ADDITIONAL READING

Achleitner, Ann-Kristin, Schraml, Stephanie and Tappeiner, Florian (2008) Private Equity Minority Investments in Large Family Firms: What Influences the Attitude of Family Firm Owners?, https://ssrn.com/abstract=1299573 or http://dx.doi.org/10.2139/ssrn.1299573.

Amess, K., Stiebale, J. and Wright, M. (2015) The Impact of Private Equity on Firms' Innovation Activity, ISSN 2190-9938 (online).

Boucly, Q., Sraer, D. and Thesmar, D. (2011) Growth LBOs, *Journal of Financial Economics*, 102(2): 432–53.

Davis, S.J., Haltiwanger, J., Handley, K., Jarmin, R., Lerner, J. and Miranda, J. (2014) Private Equity, Jobs, and Productivity, *American Economic Review*, 104(12): 3956–90.

Mooradian, P., Auerbach, A. and Quealy, M. (2013) Growth Equity Is All Grown Up, Cambridge Associate US Market Commentary, June.

Schneider, A. and Henrik, C. (2015) Private Equity Minority Investments: Can Less Be More? Boston Consulting Group, accessed here https://www.bcgperspectives.com/content/articles/private_equity_minority_investments_can_less_be_more/.

From the earliest modest takeovers of the 1960s to the mega-deals of recent years, buyouts have accounted for the majority of the capital invested globally by private equity funds. Racking up both spectacular successes and headline-grabbing failures, buyout firms have been viewed with either admiration or trepidation by investors, governments, regulators, and the media.

The public perception of buy-out transactions is cyclic; waxing and waning with the prevailing macroeconomic environment or one's ideological position. However, control transactions undeniably provide the levers to radically re-engineer a business and drive change across all aspects of an investee company. And they can measurably impact the economy at large.

This chapter first defines the three essential components of a buyout and then analyzes a typical funding structure in leveraged buyouts (LBO).[1] It goes on to examine the principal stakeholders in various types of buyouts and concludes with an overview of the common buyout strategies.

BUYOUTS DEFINED

Buyout funds acquire controlling equity stakes in companies that allow them to restructure the targets' financial, governance, and operational characteristics. However, despite this control element, buyout investors must work proactively with a wide range of stakeholders—from management to debt providers—to execute on their investment thesis by driving value creation in their portfolio companies.

Three components define a buyout strategy: equity control, leverage and economic alignment. Each of these levers, shown in Exhibit 4.1, provide buyout funds with ways

Exhibit 4.1 Defining Characteristics of Buyouts

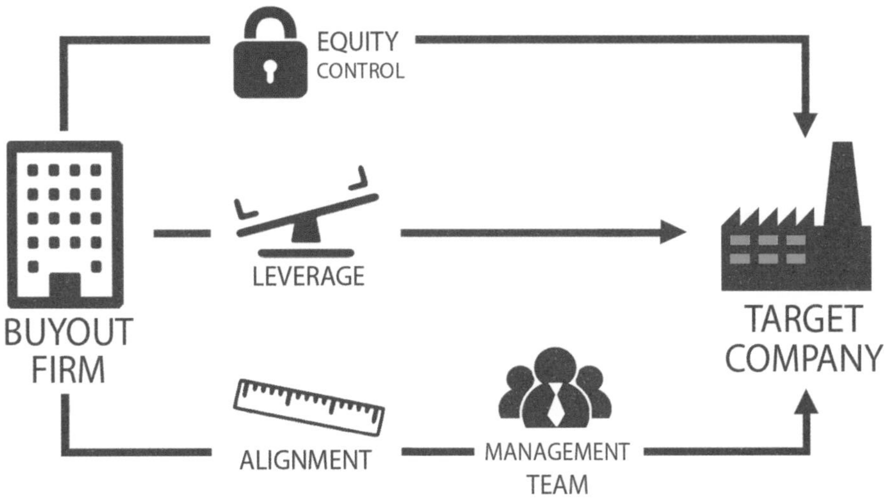

1. For the sake of simplicity, we will use the terms "LBO" and "buyout" interchangeably.

to influence strategic and operational decision-making at the target to maximize their return on investment.

EQUITY CONTROL: In a typical buyout, the PE fund will control a majority of the economic and voting interests in the portfolio company. A controlling interest does not necessarily imply 100% ownership of shares—in fact, in certain circumstances it may even be less than 50%—but rather that the buyout fund has the right to dictate strategic and operational decisions via the board of directors. In the case of a minority stake, de facto control can be obtained through a coalition of like-minded investors or specific provisions in the shareholders' agreement.

Control allows a buyout fund to apply leverage to a company's capital structure, expand or replace a portfolio company's management team, restructure its governance and reporting structures, drive operational improvement, and professionalize the overall business throughout the holding period. Control is crucial when it comes to exit planning, as buyout investors can initiate the necessary governance upgrades, ensure strategic alignment and authorize additional spending if and when required to optimally position the investee company for sale.

Given those advantages, acquiring a controlling interest in a company frequently commands a higher price ("control premium"), especially in the case of take-private transactions of publicly listed companies.[2]

LEVERAGE: Most buyouts are structured as LBOs, with a significant portion of the transaction financed through debt. A portfolio company's capital structure post-buyout will typically consist of 50–75% debt, with equity funding the balance.[3] The debt capacity of a target is a function of several factors, including the stability of cash flows across an industry, the target's ability to generate cash flow from operations (i.e., its cash conversion rate), market conditions and the buyout investor's reputation (i.e., as a borrower in earlier deals). During the investment process, buyout funds analyze a range of operating scenarios to optimize the amount of leverage applied in a transaction, thereby considering various downside scenarios and ways to reduce the risk in an investment.[4]

Assuming a fixed purchase price, the primary benefit of leverage is the ability to achieve higher returns on the buyout fund's equity stake. Leveraged capital structures increase an investor's return on capital by reducing the amount of equity required to fund its transactions. However, due to the competitive nature of most sales processes, the benefit of a leveraged transaction accrues to a large extent to the seller, as it allows the buyer to offer a (higher) purchase price that would be impossible to reach without debt.

So while the benefits (mostly) remain with the seller, the buyer faces the other side of the coin, namely, the increased cost and strong cash flow required to service the debt (both annual interest payments and debt repayment). These obligations make the

---

2. Please refer to Chapter 8 Deal Pricing Dynamics for additional information on deal pricing and public-to-privates.

3. The original buyout transactions in the 1980s employed higher leverage ratios, sometimes as high as 90% or more. As the PE industry matured, the amount of leverage applied in buyout investments dropped and settled at a generally lower level. In some jurisdictions new regulations have made the use of leverage beyond a certain point less economical.

4. Please refer to Chapter 7 Target Valuation for additional information on optimizing the funding structure in a buyout.

portfolio company more susceptible to external shocks, thereby increasing the risk of financial distress or even bankruptcy.

The impact of a highly leveraged capital structure is not entirely negative: the increased risk of financial distress following an LBO has been shown to have a disciplining effect on management. Debt servicing requirements reduce the free cash flow available for capital investment and force management to prioritize high net present value projects.[5]

Finally, the covenants associated with debt financing introduce a monitoring and early warning system to identify lapses in company performance. The breach of a covenant triggers a range of remedies to protect the debt holders' economic claim on a portfolio company, giving them an opportunity to take action before the viability of the business is at risk.[6]

ECONOMIC ALIGNMENT: The ability to align the economic interests of its portfolio company's management team with that of its fund is a key driver of PE's success in buyouts.[7] The management compensation plans used provide senior executives with meaningful equity stakes in the target company and substantial upside in the event of a successful exit. These plans typically require a significant personal co-investment from each participating executive. With managers participating in a buyout as owners, a PE fund's goal of maximizing financial return is thus shared by those in charge of executing the fund's investment plan and managing the day-to-day operations at the portfolio company.

While the structure of these compensation plans magnifies management's potential returns on the upside, it comes with risks. A management team's "sweet equity" and stock options produce a return several multiples of that realized by the PE fund, should an investment perform as planned. However, in the case of a poorly performing business, management's co-investment is at risk of being wiped out, as their equity stake is often subordinated to that of the PE fund. In such a scenario, the PE fund's equity stake will typically retain some value and claim 100% of the proceeds to equity shareholders given its preferred position in the capital structure.

LEVERAGED BUYOUT FUNDING

In an LBO, buyout investors combine their fund's equity capital with debt capital raised from a range of lenders to acquire a target company.[8] While the specific instruments employed vary deal by deal, typical LBO financing consists of senior debt, junior debt and equity capital.

---

5. Debt has been found to make managers risk averse in the face of bankruptcy risk.
6. Please refer to Chapter 9 Deal Structuring and Chapter 10 Transaction Documentation for further details on bank financing and covenants.
7. Please refer to Chapter 12 Securing Management Teams for a detailed example of management incentive structures.
8. Please refer to Chapter 9 Deal Structuring for additional detail on LBO debt instruments.

Exhibit 4.2 Sources and Uses of Funds in a Buyout

SOURCES		USES	
Senior Debt	450.0	Purchase Target Equity	550.0
Junior Debt	200.0	Refinancing Net Debt	430.0
Equity	350.0	Transaction Costs	20.0
Total Sources	1,000.0	Total Uses	1,000.0

The capital is used to fund the acquisition of the target company's equity, repay a target's existing net debt and cover fees and expenses associated with the acquisition. Exhibit 4.2 shows a simplified example of the sources and uses of funds in a buyout.

SENIOR DEBT: Senior debt is typically issued by one or more banks and represents the largest portion of debt raised for an LBO. This class of debt is the least expensive source of long-term financing as it has a priority claim on the company's assets in case of bankruptcy; it is typically "secured" against specific company assets, further strengthening senior debtholders' bankruptcy rights. It typically has the shortest term (five to eight years) among all debt instruments, pays an annual cash coupon and comes with the most stringent debt covenants in the capital structure. Senior debt is often raised in multiple tranches, one of which is amortized through annual repayments (with any balance due at the end of the loan's term); the remaining tranches are repaid in a single bullet payment at maturity.

JUNIOR DEBT: Junior debt accounts for the remaining debt capital in a buyout; the most common forms are mezzanine financing raised in the private institutional market and high-yield bonds raised from the public bond markets. This layer of debt is unsecured and subordinated to senior debt in the event of bankruptcy. Junior debt instruments have longer maturities than senior debt (eight to ten years), pay annual cash interest and may in some cases accrue additional non-cash interest; they are typically repaid via a single bullet payment at the end of the term.

EQUITY CAPITAL: Equity capital typically accounts for 25–50% of LBO funding. The equity portion of a buyout may be sourced from a single buyout fund or a consortium of funds, management team members, and LP co-investors. Equity is the most junior funding instrument, with only a residual claim on operating cash flow and company assets in the event of bankruptcy or restructuring. The equity in a buyout is often divided into a preferred share class or shareholder loan (typically accounting for the majority of equity capital invested), and common equity. A PE fund will usually hold the vast majority or all of the preferred shares, while management will own a significant portion of the common equity.

Box 4.1

BUYOUT VALUATION AND VALUE DRIVERS

This example explains the mechanics of a "standard" LBO and illustrates value creation at both the company and equity level. It shows how returns can be broken down and attributed to the various basic value drivers in a buyout[9] (Exhibit 4.3).

Exhibit 4.3 Buyout Valuation and Return

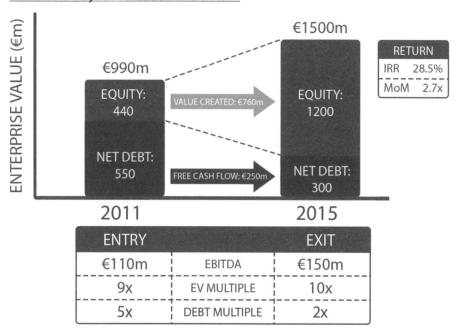

ENTRY		EXIT
€110m	EBITDA	€150m
9x	EV MULTIPLE	10x
5x	DEBT MULTIPLE	2x

Let's assume a PE fund acquires in 2011 a company with €110 million in earnings before interest, tax, depreciation and amortization (EBITDA). The purchase price (enterprise value) has been negotiated and agreed to be €990 million, representing a multiple of 9× EBITDA. As typical in an LBO, a substantial amount of the purchase price is financed by debt, about 5× EBITDA or about 55% of the purchase price, while the remainder is paid for with equity.

Over the next four years, the company grows its EBITDA at an annualized rate of about 8% to €150 million. Crucially, over the same period, the company generates €250 million in free cash flow (after investment and after financing cost) allowing the owners to repay some of the debt.

With a better performing company at hand (and maybe with the benefit of a generally improved economic climate) the PE fund is able to sell the company at a multiple of 10× EBITDA in 2015. After subtracting the remaining debt from the enterprise value of €1.5 billion, the value of the equity amounts to €1.2 billion or 2.73× the invested capital. For a holding period of four years, this equates to an internal rate of return (IRR) of 28.5%.[10]

---

9. Please refer to Chapter 13 Operational Value Creation for more on attributing operational value-add.
10. The simplified calculation does not include transaction cost on entry or exit.

It is worth noting that the enterprise value over this period has "only" grown at about 11% per annum, clearly demonstrating the effect of leverage on the returns in buyout deals. Overall, €760 million in equity value has been created, through the contributions of the value drivers shown in Exhibit 4.4.

Exhibit 4.4 Buyout Value Drivers

CREATED VALUE	=	EBITDA IMPACT	+	MULTIPLE IMPACT	+	NET DEBT IMPACT
€760m	=	€360m	+	€150m	+	€250m
(100%)	=	(47%)	+	(20%)	+	(33%)

In this case, 47% of the equity value came from EBITDA growth (calculated as [Exit EBITDA minus Entry EBITDA] × Entry Multiple), 20% from multiple expansion (calculated as [Exit Multiple minus Entry Multiple] × Exit EBITDA and finally 33% from net debt reduction of €250 million.[11]

A Differentiated Approach—Buying Right and Creating Value Early

By Andrew Sillitoe, Co-CEO, Apax Partners LLP and a Partner in the Tech & Telco team

There are two distinct approaches to LBO investing that can be seen in the market, firstly paying up for sustained growth and secondly an approach that can be referred to as "buying right and creating value early."

The first approach essentially offers only one value creation lever—EBITDA growth. This approach can lead to inflated entry prices, justified by ambitious, high-growth five-year business plans that forecast acceptable IRRs, but that often result in less reliable, back-end loaded returns. The high multiples paid, often when too much capital is chasing too few deals, mean buyers effectively spend the first two years, the most predictable in a buyout, running hard to stay still, having acquired investments at values that have already factored in the profit improvement over this period. This situation can get even worse if markets correct. This undermines the potential to generate returns over the first two years and pushes any return drivers to the, inherently less reliable, later years.

The high multiples paid reduce significantly the chances of multiple expansion and the effects of deleveraging are also likely to be minimal, given the large

---

11. This breakdown does not attribute any of the improvement in multiple and debt paydown to the underlying EBITDA growth.

amounts of equity and debt used to finance the acquisitions. The reliance on one, back-end loaded driver of returns may lead to a significantly higher risk of disappointment and investments skewed to the downside.

The second approach of "buying right and creating value early" involves staying focused on entry multiples, rather than IRR models, buying assets at or below their intrinsic value, and finding opportunities where value creation can be engineered through the operation of multiple levers early in the life of an investment. Executed well, this approach creates an early margin of safety, with the focus on moderate entry multiples providing greater protection if asset valuations show a sustained downward move and, conversely, an opportunity for multiple expansion if conditions are benign.

These opportunities can be found more readily by shunning mainstream assets and by forming differentiated and sometimes contrarian views. This differentiated approach to investing is not easy to execute and can sometimes mean taking other forms of risk, albeit ones that are inherently more controllable. It requires three key conditions to be met:

1. The availability of a rich pipeline of differentiated opportunities
2. The ability to make judgements to avoid the pack
3. A toolkit to transform businesses

Differentiated Opportunities

The strategy requires discipline and the resolve to say "no" frequently. It requires a rich pool of opportunities from which to select and sector expertise to generate a quality and differentiated deal flow. This approach also benefits from a global footprint, which can enhance opportunities for value arbitrage, offer potential for global expansion (either organically or through M&A) and optimize exit opportunities.

Avoiding the Pack

Sector expertise is critical, both at the macro level to enable a focus on subsectors which are underappreciated, and at the micro level to find individual companies that have often been overlooked. This requires a skill to look beyond the obvious to find opportunities which are less "picked over," taking differentiated and, sometimes, contrarian views.

A Toolkit to Transform Businesses

Ensuring a business is led by the most effective senior team is priority one. The operational skills of private equity firms should therefore be designed to help strong management teams maximize a business' potential through specific functional expertise; strong management teams don't require general management advice, they require partners that will help them solve critical business issues. Gaining alignment around the transformation program pre-deal is critical to ensure that this program begins on day one.

In essence, identifying good opportunities to buy right and create value early means being able to differentiate between great assets and great investments.

The industry needs to guard against becoming too price-insensitive for supposedly stable assets, making it ever more critical to source differentiated opportunities, execute robust value creation strategies and unlock hidden value—the keys to generating enduring, absolute returns.

MANAGEMENT TEAMS IN A BUYOUT

A strong management team is a key ingredient to a successful buyout. As controlling shareholders, buyout investors have full discretion to choose the teams they work with. A close cooperation between management and the respective partners at the buyout firm is vital to ensure both a smooth acquisition process as well as productive engagement post-acquisition. Depending on how active the role of the management team is during the acquisition process, one can distinguish several types of buyouts, namely, management buyouts (MBOs), management buy-ins (MBIs), and institutional buyouts (IBOs).[12]

MANAGEMENT BUYOUT (MBO): In an MBO, the incumbent management team initiates the buyout of a company or corporate division with the financial backing of a buyout fund. This arrangement allows PE firms to capitalize on the management team's knowledge of the target company and provides a distinct advantage relative to other interested parties. An MBO can be particularly attractive when management, given its familiarity with the business and established relationships with internal and external company stakeholders, wishes to capitalize on new growth opportunities. The acquisition process is often led by the management team with the buyout fund providing, primarily, capital and some of its structuring expertise as a repeat buyer. While successful MBOs provide management teams the opportunity to work in an entrepreneurial environment with greater rewards, failed MBO attempts may lead to alienation between senior management, existing owners and company staff.

MANAGEMENT BUY-IN (MBI): In an MBI, a buyout fund partners with an external management team to pursue an acquisition of a portfolio company. If successful, new management with an equity stake in the firm will replace the incumbent management team. Typical MBI targets have sound growth potential and the right business model but may lack effective management. Buyout firms often work with successful management teams on multiple MBIs, benefiting from an established working relationship. On the downside, MBIs often require a longer due diligence period as the buyout fund cannot leverage the insights of existing management; in addition, possible conflicts between the new management team and existing employees may need to be addressed.

INSTITUTIONAL BUYOUT (IBO): In an IBO, the buyout is initiated by a PE firm without the support of the incumbent or external management team. Rather, a buyout fund negotiates directly with the seller, with little or no support from any management team until the acquisition terms have been agreed. The buyout fund may decide to retain existing management, replace the management team or selectively augment an existing team with new talent for specific roles once the transaction has been finalized. IBOs are by far the most common form of buyouts in mid-sized to large transactions.

---

12. In addition to the three main types of buyouts discussed in this section, various combinations of the three strategies can be employed. For example, in a 'buy-in management buyout,' the existing management team is bolstered by new team members and partners with the PE sponsor on an acquisition.

TYPES OF BUYOUT TRANSACTIONS

Buyout firms target businesses with diverse forms of current ownership such as privately held, stand-alone businesses, publicly listed companies, divisions of large corporations, and assets sold by government entities. While businesses targeted for an LBO typically generate consistent annual cash flow for debt servicing and have a strong market position, value creation levers available to the buyout fund often vary depending on the target's origin. The following section describes some of the most common strategies employed by buyout funds, the type of businesses targeted and common value creation levers applied.

PUBLIC TO PRIVATE: Publicly listed companies are often acquired in public-to-private (P2P) transactions, also known as take-privates. The principal motivation for taking a company private lies in reduced agency risk—resulting from the often tenuous alignment of interests between public shareholders (the principals) and company management teams (the agent)—under a single owner and the implementation of a governance structure that increases accountability of the management team (Exhibit 4.5). In addition, delisting a business eliminates the costs associated with public reporting and the focus on short-term, quarterly earnings in a publicly listed business, freeing management to focus on long-term value creation. Taking a business private also allows a company to carry more leverage. A PE firm's conviction in the value creation potential is reflected in the (at times large) premiums paid by PE funds to delist businesses.

Exhibit 4.5 PE Value-add: P2P

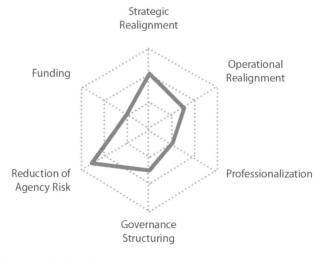

CARVE-OUT: Buyout funds often acquire a corporate division, business unit or subsidiary and set it up as a stand-alone company. It makes for a viable strategy for business units that, for example, are no longer core to a company's strategy or that were unsuccessfully integrated during a corporate merger or acquisition (Exhibit 4.6). These divisions often do not receive adequate attention from top management, appropriate funding or talent relative to other more dynamic business units, and may be structured in a suboptimal way due to a bloated cost structure or inexact allocation of overhead expense. In carve-outs, PE firms principally unlock value by developing a robust strategy for the new, stand-alone company, establishing governance and control systems and providing adequate funding to expand business operations.

Exhibit 4.6 PE Value-add: Carve-out

PRIVATIZATION: Government privatization programs provide a rich source of targets for buyout funds. Significant value can be unlocked in state-owned institutions by updating the company's business model, reducing cost inefficiencies systemic in the public sector, providing fresh resources for growth and focusing management on profit maximization; non-financial goals traditionally pursued by state-owned businesses may be sacrificed in the process (Exhibit 4.7). PE firms can also add value by replacing dated decision-making processes with an updated governance structure that empowers employees throughout the organization.

Exhibit 4.7 PE Value-add: Privatization

FAMILY BUSINESS: Privately owned family businesses[13] are a popular target for buyout funds, as external management teams installed by a fund can rapidly professionalize a business and drive value creation (Exhibit 4.8). As decision-making in family businesses often rests with a single founder or a core group of family members, updated corporate governance measures, including the establishment of a formal advisory board with

---

13. Family businesses often use buyouts as a viable succession option.

independent directors, can help remove biases related to personal relationships and introduce checks and balances at appropriate levels of the business. PE firms can create value by leveraging strong brands and relationships built under family ownership, or by updating legacy strategies and focusing on cost reduction. It is important to note that positive attributes of a family business, such as close networks, a strong company culture or the loyalty of employees to the family, are sometimes diluted under the new ownership.

Exhibit 4.8 PE Value-add: Family Business

SECONDARY BUYOUT: Portfolio companies controlled by another buyout fund are frequent acquisition targets and such transactions are referred to as secondary buyouts. The principal opportunity to add value here is through strategic realignment (Exhibit 4.9). Although the exiting PE firm has likely capitalized on a range of value creation opportunities, the acquiring PE firm may bring a unique combination of skills, knowledge and in-house networks to drive new strategic initiatives at the company. In the case of a prior LBO, these targets have "proven" their ability to service debt, and current management has experience running a levered business; therefore, a larger proportion of debt financing can often be secured for a secondary buyout.

Exhibit 4.9 PE Value-add: Secondary Buyout

CLOSING

Mention PE and audiences will often think of buyouts first. Indeed, buyouts make up the largest (in dollar terms) and often most visible part of all PE transactions and constitute a sizable portion of all mergers and acquisitions. Defined in the early years by their aggressive use of debt, buyout funds have long become smart operators, increasingly driving value creation in their portfolio companies with the help of operating partners. The governance mechanisms that are central to their business model include full equity control and interest alignment with management and will be the focus of distinct chapters later in the book.

KEY LEARNING POINTS

• **In a buyout, PE investors acquire a controlling equity stake in a target allowing them to make all financial, strategic and operational business decisions.**

• **Management teams execute the investment strategy of the fund, making it paramount to create an incentive scheme that aligns the interests of management and PE owners.**

• **Most buyouts are structured as LBOs with debt financing a large portion of the acquisition price.**

RELEVANT CASE STUDIES

from *Private Equity in Action—Case Studies from Developed and Emerging Markets*

Case #11: Chips on the Side (A): The Buyout of Avago Technologies

Case #13: Going Places: The Buyout of Amadeus Global Travel Distribution

REFERENCES AND ADDITIONAL READING

Damodaran, A. (2008) The Anatomy of an LBO: Leverage, Control and Value, http://papers.ssrn.com/sol3/papers.cfm?abstract_id=1162862.

Gottschalg, O. and Berg, A. (February 2005) Understanding Value Generation in Buyouts, article in *Journal of Restructuring Finance*, 2(1), accessed here https://www.researchgate.net/publication/4816134_Understanding_Value_Generation_in_Buyouts.

Guo, S., Hotchkiss, E.S. and Song, W. (2011) Do Buyouts (Still) Create Value, *Journal of Finance*, LXVI(2): 479–517.

Jensen, M. (1986) Agency Costs of Free Cash Flow, Corporate Finance and Takeovers, *American Economic Review*, 76(2): 323–9.

Kaplan, S. and Stroemberg, P. (2008) Leveraged Buyouts and Private Equity, http://faculty.chicagobooth.edu/steven.kaplan/research/ksjep.pdf.

Morris, Peter (2014) Approach Private Equity's "Value Bridge" with Caution, *Financial World*, October/November 2014, https://ssrn.com/abstract=2563532.

Funds that invest in venture capital, growth equity and buyout deals constitute the backbone of the private equity (PE) industry. Yet, as the industry matured and assets under management grew, PE firms started to look further afield – to different markets, assets and previously untapped business situations – to deploy capital and apply their skills.

Our introductory section on PE would not be complete without a closer look at two of these alternative strategies: distressed PE and real asset investing. The evolution and appeal of these strategies has much to do with their different risk–return profiles and the demand from limited partners (LPs) for returns that historically have been uncorrelated with their traditional portfolios. Both areas are composed of several substrategies: distressed PE investing includes corporate turnaround and distressed debt strategies, while real asset investing includes real estate, infrastructure and natural resources.

DISTRESSED PRIVATE EQUITY

Distressed PE funds invest in mature companies in need of substantial restructuring in the face of imminent failure or bankruptcy. While the reasons for distress may be complex, the PE investor will frequently find a business straining under an unsustainable debt burden or struggling to make an inefficient operating model work, or quite often a combination of both. Addressing these issues requires highly specialized teams experienced in turnaround management and financial restructuring under extreme time constraints. Given the poor state of a typical target company, distressed PE investors must act decisively after limited due diligence, gain control of the company and immediately attend to short-term liquidity issues to ensure the firm survives and can be repositioned for recovery: no survival without recovery; no recovery without survival. While the specific circumstances and degree of distress vary from deal to deal, PE funds in this space subscribe to a common approach: gain control of the asset at a discounted valuation and drive the restructuring process quickly and efficiently.

In the section that follows, we take a closer look at the two main distressed PE strategies: turnaround investing and distressed debt investing, and touch in turn on some of the causes of distress.

TURNAROUND INVESTING

Turnaround funds acquire majority equity stakes in mature companies that are in considerable operational distress.

Majority equity stakes are a prerequisite for most turnaround investors. In a situation that requires quick and decisive actions based on a rigorous diagnostic review of the business immediately post-investment and an analysis of the various stakeholder positions, a controlling stake is indispensable.[1] The PE team will need ready access to all aspects of the business, since the often rapidly dwindling cash of the firm may impede even the day-to-day operations of the portfolio firm. Negotiations with banks, creditors and suppliers will commence without delay to ensure their cooperation.

Target companies are typically generating significant operating losses and burning through cash reserves at the time of investment. The modus operandi for a turnaround fund is an immediate maximization of short-term cash flow to stabilize the business and avoid insolvency. To get clarity on the urgency of the situation and the time available to implement improvements, a detailed short-term cash flow analysis—a 13-week cash flow forecast is industry best practice—needs to be performed. "Cash is king" in the world of turnaround investing: finding it, unlocking it, and driving cash flow improvement to remain solvent and operational are crucial.

Turnaround investing requires an investment team that can reliably assess the feasibility of a turnaround opportunity during due diligence, complemented by an operating team adept at rapidly addressing weaknesses in the operating business and affecting change. This task may be complicated by the need to manage not only a financial restructuring program and negotiations with stakeholders, but also the legal challenge of avoiding bankruptcy. Given the lack of a global bankruptcy code, the latter requires having local, country-by-country legal expertise in-house. As maintaining a full team of turnaround professionals entails significant cost, this strategy is clearly a niche undertaking for truly experienced funds and presents a high barrier to entry into this segment of the PE industry.

No turnaround situation is alike, but Exhibit 5.1 shows the typical steps recommended by turnaround experts.

Exhibit 5.1 Typical Turnaround Process

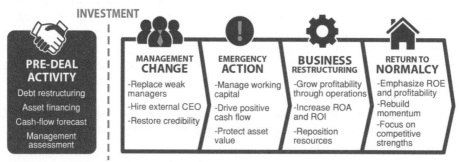

Source: Turnaround Management Association

When dealing with target firms in dire straits, protecting the PE fund's interest (and in turn that of its LPs) is paramount, and turnaround funds will ensure that certain

---

1. Turnaround funds are not always able to acquire a controlling position from the outset, as some equity owners may only be willing to relinquish their stakes in the firm over time. This adds the risk of a prolonged holding period, which may in turn lower internal rates of return.

minimum conditions are in place before investing. Finding a sustainable short-term funding solution with the cooperation of the debt holders is a requisite first step to a turnaround. Depending on the jurisdiction, placing the company into voluntary bankruptcy may be the most efficient way to gain time and restructure the business. A short-term cash flow forecast will have given clarity on the state of the business and shown how long its cash will last; injections of fresh capital are often needed to fund working capital requirements and create the flexibility to execute short- and long-term operating improvements. As turnaround investment opportunities typically result from poor execution, a careful assessment of the existing management team is a must and will start during due diligence.

The situation often requires the existing management to be replaced or at a minimum to be complemented with a few seasoned experts with industry and/or turnaround experience to stabilize the business and reassure debt holders, suppliers and customers of the changes to come. With a clear understanding of the time at its disposal, turnaround investors will look for low hanging fruits to solve the cash flow shortage, improve operating performance and rapidly turn the cash flow positive. Once the company's existing business processes have been stabilized and the threat of immediate failure has been removed, the PE team will shift its sights to improving the productivity of its assets and allocating capital and resources to restore the company back to a sustainable going concern. Ensuring survival in the short term and recovery in the long term is the target.

DISTRESSED DEBT INVESTING

Distressed debt funds acquire stakes in the debt obligations of companies in financial distress to generate returns either through the appreciation of the debt or an eventual restructuring of the target company.

When acquiring short-term stakes or "trading" positions to generate returns from price appreciation, these funds compete head-on with hedge funds or the proprietary trading desks of banks, looking to benefit in the short term from mispriced assets. Yet, most distressed debt funds aim to acquire a significant position across the target company's debt structure to influence or drive the restructuring process. Some funds combine expertise in debt investment and restructuring with turnaround and operational capabilities to execute a "loan-to-own" strategy and aim to gain equity control of a business. This ability to take charge and operate a company via a controlling equity stake post-restructuring is a key differentiating factor from other market participants mentioned above.

In a distressed scenario, the fair value of a target company may fall below the face value of its outstanding debt, in the process erasing the value of the company's equity and impairing even the junior tranches of debt.[2] Distressed debt funds—particularly those looking to build a significant stake in the target—therefore typically invest in senior debt tranches that retain a claim on the economic value of the target company,

---

2. Please refer to Chapter 9 Deal Structuring for an overview of typical debt securities in a PE setting.

allowing the fund to drive the restructuring process and gain equity control post-restructuring.

One would assume that gaining a robust understanding of a distressed company's business activity and building a sound investment case before investing is a given; however, distressed debt investors rarely have access to management or the ability to conduct deep due diligence before beginning to build a stake in a target company. As such, small, initial investments are often made to open the doors and gain access to private company information.[3] Should the initial investment rationale change for the worse following engagement with management, the distressed debt fund will take advantage of the (often) liquid underlying market for corporate debt to sell its stake, if necessary at a loss.

Rarely do the interests of the various stakeholders align in a restructuring. Thus, it is crucial for PE investors to understand who the owners of the remaining debt instruments are; having like-minded parties involved will allow for a focused process and quick exit.

Exhibit 5.2 shows the capital structure and ownership of a distressed company pre- and post-restructuring. Creating the best possible capital structure by converting the appropriate amount of debt to equity is key to enable the company to operate in a sustainable manner post-restructuring.

Note that, while in a senior position to all other instrument holders, even senior debt holders will typically accept a small writedown (or "haircut") to facilitate a smooth restructuring process. Senior debt holders control the process and will be the ones holding a controlling equity stake post-restructuring in the "loan-to-own" model.

Exhibit 5.2 Distressed Debt-to-Control

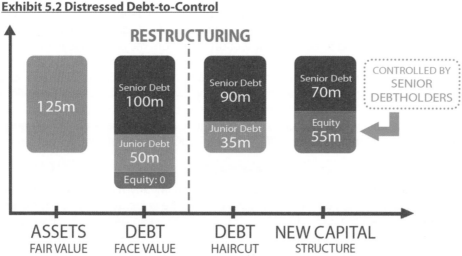

Source: Turnaround Management Association

---

3. Once due diligence can be initiated, PE investors will ensure that the language in the loan documents enables them to take control and drive the restructuring process at a later stage.

Distressed Investing: Why Europe is Different from the US

By Karim Khairallah, Managing Director, European Principal Group, Oaktree Capital Management (UK) LLP

In contrasting the investment environment in Europe and the US, one has to consider that Europe is comprised of a multitude of countries with a myriad of experiences. In this section, I attempt to summarize the differences, acknowledging that it is difficult to do so without significant generalization. It is important to understand that the intricacies of distressed investing in Europe require very specific knowledge and experience. It is markedly different from the US for a number of reasons, outlined here.

Legal Environment

The US bankruptcy code (Chapter 11) is well-tested and allows for the continuation of operations and then an orderly exit as a going concern. Many, if not most, continental European bankruptcy laws are relatively new, untested, with limited precedents and less creditor-friendly. Furthermore, they do not necessarily allow for a business to continue operating as a going concern and, often, lead to significant value destruction through fire sales, liquidations, and the withdrawal of supplier and financing lines. In the US, Chapter 11 can be effectively used by all stakeholders to allow for an orderly business reorganization (balance sheet and operational) to ensure the company's survival. It can also be used by creditors to protect their legal and economic rights, and ultimately take control of a company. In Europe, creditors have less control over the entry into and exit out of a bankruptcy, with management or independent court-appointed administrators being the key decision makers. These differences drive the route that investors will likely pick to protect their investments.

Multiple Stakeholders

Many European countries have multiple stakeholders, who each have an important voice in a distressed situation. These include management, unions, equity holders, debtholders (senior and junior, with differing roles), the courts (pre- and post-bankruptcy filing) and even, in some cases, governments. This requires knowledge of each stakeholder's motivations and objectives, an ability to dialogue with them, and a realization that value will potentially leak to stakeholders whose legal rights would not normally warrant this.

Consensual versus Non-Consensual

Consensual deals are achieved when all relevant parties can agree to an outcome that usually avoids a bankruptcy. Non-consensual deals are those where there is conflict and/or hostility between some or all of the parties resulting in a lack of common ground. As described above, the US system is well tested, has clear precedence and the range of outcomes in a non-consensual deal are far more predictable and therefore manageable. On the other hand, a non-consensual route in Europe is rife with risks and uncertain outcomes so, where possible, it is preferable to target a consensual outcome. Given the multiple stakeholders, this is a highly complicated process necessitating very different interactions than in the US. This therefore requires an investor to have a broad set of skills within its team to undertake this complexity and ensure a consensual outcome.

Financing Structure (Senior and Junior)

Junior debt has fewer *teeth* or enforcement options in a distressed situation in Europe (unlike in US Chapter 11) and the legal process typically does little to protect its economic interests. As a result, in consensual restructuring negotiations, junior creditors can be sidelined and coerced into accepting a deal negotiated by others. For this reason, Europe has a less active junior financing market; debt structures are typically characterized with larger senior debt tranche and comparatively little in the way of junior debt. Trading junior claims is a typical distressed investing activity in the US, but in Europe it is fraught with risk and, as a result, the junior debt market is much more limited.

Debtholders

Compared to the US, Europe has historically had a higher proportion of banks as debtholders and the leveraged loan market has historically been the primary source of financing for private equity-related transactions. Though this has changed since 2009, when the high-yield market became a more developed source of financing in Europe, banks are still very large debtholders. This results in less liquidity in distressed markets because banks, as compared to institutional investors, have tended to be more hesitant to sell down their positions. This creates more complexity in reaching a consensual solution. Therefore, a European distressed strategy needs to encompass a strong relationship with banks to either access the debt they hold or to ensure their support in a restructuring.

In summary, US and European distressed markets are very different animals, as exemplified by the small number of pure-play European distressed investors, as compared to the US. The strategy requires a very localized solution to drive a consensual outcome. Choosing a non-consensual route has been proven to destroy more value than a consensual route could have created. Despite this, a consensual solution is easier said than done given the broader spectrum of stakeholders required at the table and their inherent diverging objectives. This makes splitting the pie an art as opposed to a science.

Box 5.1

PRIVATE DEBT

The wave of regulation and the curtailed lending activity of the international banking system post-global financial crisis presented a new opportunity for traditional PE firms: raising capital to provide debt funding. Historically focused on financing riskier tranches of debt in LBO transactions, capital deployed from private debt funds has expanded rapidly post-2009 on the back of direct lending demand from businesses. Both traditional PE firms and specialist debt investors have raised funds to capitalize on this trend. We include a short summary of direct lending and transaction financing below (Exhibit 5.3).

Exhibit 5.3 Private Debt Substrategies

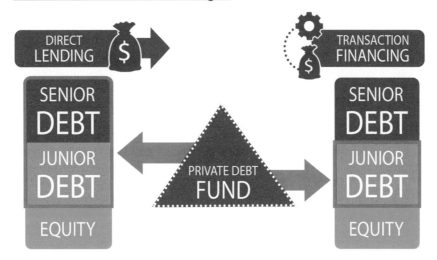

DIRECT LENDING: Direct lending is a form of corporate lending in which debt funds issue loans directly to a business or acquire these loans in the secondary debt market. Borrowers are typically small- and medium-sized enterprises that find it difficult to obtain bank financing or may be looking to diversify their funding base. Direct lending is highly customizable and can take the form of both senior and junior debt with its respective risk profiles. Given the higher predictability of cash flows associated with direct lending relative to PE investments, debt funds often employ leverage at the fund level to boost returns.

TRANSACTION FINANCING: Debt funds may also provide capital to finance LBOs. In this instance, debt funds typically provide junior debt while banks provide the senior debt tranche. The most common transaction financing debt instrument is mezzanine capital.[4]

---

4. Please refer to Chapter 4 Buyouts and Chapter 9 Deal Structuring for further details on debt financing in buyout transactions.

REAL ASSETS

Funds investing in industries such as real estate, infrastructure and natural resources are regularly classified as a subset of the PE asset class and referred to as real asset investors. PE investments in this category span a wide range of activity, from "traditional" equity investment in companies with underlying exposure to real assets, to providing debt and equity directly to real asset projects. The pool of investors active in real assets is deep, ranging from the largest global PE firms (such as Blackstone, KKR and Partners Group), to funds specializing in one specific real asset class, to LPs providing direct investment capital.

PE funds finance the full range of underlying real assets, from the development of greenfield projects to the improvement of existing facilities to the operation of mature assets. The maturity or stage of the development has of course a distinct impact on the risk–return profile of the underlying investment: a pre-completion project requires a higher risk tolerance but offers the greatest potential for price appreciation, while an investment in mature projects provides exposure to stable, long-term cash flows.[5] Leverage is typically employed at all stages of development to enhance returns, with the physical assets themselves serving as collateral. Exhibit 5.4 provides a simple overview of the two project stages (early stage and mature) and the risk–return characteristics of real estate, infrastructure and natural resources projects.

Mature real assets provide not only a steady dividend stream but also diversification benefits to any investment portfolio given their historically uncorrelated returns with other asset classes. This has made them an attractive target for large institutional

Exhibit 5.4 Real Assets Project Stage

COMPLETION

ASSET CLASS	EARLY-STAGE	MATURE
REAL ESTATE	Construction	Operation
INFRASTRUCTURE	Greenfield	Brownfield
NATURAL RESOURCES	Exploration & Development	Production
CASH FLOW	Negative	Positive
RISK	High	Low

5. The duration of investments in real assets may significantly exceed the standard 10-year lifespan of a traditional PE fund. It is therefore not unusual to see real asset PE funds raised with 20-year commitments or more.

investors with a long-term investment horizon and an appetite for cash distributions to offset regular funding demands from their investment programs. Real asset investments also provide an effective hedge against inflation, as the real asset pricing risk is effectively transferred to the consumer.

Sovereign wealth funds and pension plans have also begun to invest directly[6] in mature infrastructure and real estate projects, thereby competing with the general partners at PE firms. It is therefore little surprise that the assets under management in the alternative asset classes listed below have grown steadily in recent years.[7]

REAL ESTATE: Real estate funds employ three main strategies—core-plus, value-add and opportunistic—and invest across the four main subsectors of real estate: residential, office, retail and industrial properties. The core-plus strategy focuses on investments in high-quality, low-risk mature projects that produce stable, predictable cash flows. Core-plus properties typically require minimal—if any—renovation to boost property values, and the strategy generates the majority of its return from rent payments and leases. The value-add strategy focuses on acquiring mature projects that require significant investment and renovation to realize value. This strategy entails more risk than core-plus and relies on asset appreciation rather than cash flows for the majority of its returns. The opportunistic strategy invests in high-risk projects at various stages of maturity, ranging from investment in raw land to pre-construction projects to distressed mature projects. Opportunistic projects require a high degree of operational engagement to bring them to a cash flow producing stage; these improvements and the resulting appreciation in value produces the vast majority of returns in the strategy.

INFRASTRUCTURE: Infrastructure funds invest in projects that develop and operate physical structures and facilities in sectors such as transportation, communication, utilities, conventional energy supply chains, renewable energy, and social infrastructure (hospitals, schools or prisons). PE funds typically invest in three types of projects, in descending order of risk: greenfield, rehabilitation brownfield and core brownfield projects.[8] Funds often invest at specific stages of the development process to leverage in-house expertise. The nature of infrastructure projects frequently requires fund terms of 20 years or more, which aligns well with the long-term duration of certain LPs' liabilities.

Infrastructure funds deploy capital into two main types of investment: public private partnerships (PPPs) and private infrastructure investments. In a PPP, a government organization invests alongside an infrastructure fund to develop and operate greenfield projects or existing brownfield assets. Governments provide access to the greenfield concession while a fund adds both capital and expertise to execute the project. Revenue subsidies and tax concessions offered by governments are often key levers to make a project economically viable for the private sector. Private infrastructure investments, on the other hand, are projects without any government support. The returns in these investments tend to be driven by capital gains rather than current income.

This asset class remains in need of substantial further capital to meet the immense financing needs for new infrastructure in developing countries[9] and to revamp and upgrade the infrastructure in developed countries.

---

6. Please see Chapter 21 for more on LP direct and co-investment strategies.
7. Please see Chapter 25 Evolution of Private Equity for real asset under management data.
8. Rehabilitation brownfield are mature projects that require significant capital for repairs and maintenance.
9. Lin and Lu (2013).

NATURAL RESOURCES: The success of and demand for PE funds investing in natural resources is closely tied to the highly volatile and cyclical price of the underlying commodities. As commodities prices have a direct impact on the profitability profile of a project, natural resource funds present significant risk to LPs. PE investment activity focuses primarily on three subsectors, listed in order of their size and relevance: oil and gas, metals and mining and agriculture or agribusiness. Within these subsectors, activity is divided into exploration, development and production projects. Exploration and development projects involve locating or growing the raw commodity and extracting or harvesting it, while production projects involve transforming the raw commodity into a commercially viable product.

Oil and gas has historically been the most prevalent natural resources strategy, particularly the midstream segment where the predictable cash flows generated by transporting, storage and wholesale marketing provide steady cash flow. Within metals and mining, base metals have historically absorbed the majority of PE capital, followed by precious and ferrous metals. The agriculture and agribusiness sector includes investments across the entire value chain, from investing in land to the operation of farms and plantations to the processing of agricultural goods. Agriculture land investments can be further separated into buy-and-lease or own-and-operate models, the latter of which is popular with PE investors.

CLOSING

As the PE industry evolves, additional strategies are expected to emerge to connect return-seeking investors with attractive investment opportunities, thereby channeling much-needed funds to private enterprises.

This concludes our high-level overview and broad introduction to PE. We defined early- and late-stage strategies, differentiated minority investments from their majority counterparts and explained the dynamics of the industry from the perspective of its various stakeholders. In our next section, we shift our focus to the PE investment process.

KEY LEARNING POINTS

• **Aside from mainstream PE, two alternative strategies, distressed PE and real assets, have gained prominence in recent years.**

• **Distressed investing requires a specific skillset geared either towards operational improvements (turnaround investing) or balance sheet optimization (distressed debt). In all distressed situations, a laser-like focus on cash and stakeholder management is required.**

• **Real asset investments divide into three strategies: real estate, infrastructure and natural resources. Long holding periods, low correlation with traditional asset classes and the stable cash generation of mature projects have made them attractive investments to certain types of institutional investors.**

RELEVANT CASE STUDIES

from *Private Equity in Action—Case Studies from Developed and Emerging Markets*

Case #14: Crisis at the Mill: Weaving an Indian Turnaround

Case #15: Vendex KBB: First Hundred Days in Crisis

Case #17: Rice from Africa for Africa: Rice Farming in Tanzania and Investing in Agriculture

REFERENCES AND ADDITIONAL READING

CAIA, Investing in Distressed Debt, https://www.caia.org/sites/default/files/3investing_in_distressed_debt_caia_aiar_q2_2012.pdf.

CAIA, Risk, Return, and Cash Flow Characteristics of Private Equity Investments in Infrastructure, https://www.caia.org/sites/default/files/2risk_return_cashflow_characteristics_private_equity_investments_caia_aiar_q2_2012.pdf.

Cuny, Charles J. and Talmor, Eli (2006) A Theory of Private Equity Turnarounds, https://ssrn.com/abstract=875823.

Kazimi, H. and Tan, T. (2016) How Private-equity Owners Lean into Turnarounds, *McKinsey Quarterly*, http://www.mckinsey.com/business-functions/strategy-and-corporate-finance/our-insights/how-private-equity-owners-lean-into-turnarounds.

Lin, Justin and Lu, Kevin (2013) To Finance the World's Infrastructure, We Need a New Asset Class, *Huffington Post*, October 10, http://centres.insead.edu/global-private-equity-initiative/research-initiatives/documents/to-finance-the-worlds-infrastructure.pdf.

Preqin Special Report: Institutional Investors in Natural Resources Funds, https://www.preqin.com/docs/reports/Preqin-Special-Report-Natural-Resources-Investors-October-2015.pdf.

Weber, B., Straub-Bisang, M. and Alfen, H.W. (2016) *Infrastructure as an Asset Class*, John Wiley & Sons.

SECTION II
Doing Deals in PE

The second section of our book follows private equity (PE) funds through their investment process. As repeat buyers and sellers, PE firms are among the most experienced players in the mergers and acquisitions (M&A) market. Their investment process is all about evaluating and balancing the risks and return potential presented by different investment opportunities.

The process, from reviewing a business plan to investing in a deal, can take a PE firm several months, and at times more than a year, depending on the experience of the team, the quality of company information provided and the competitive dynamics of the process. Exhibit B shows the main steps in the PE investment process as it moves towards completion.

Exhibit B: PE Value Chain

Crucial initial steps include identifying a target company, assessing its business model and business plan and developing forward-looking business case scenarios. Identifying a target often involves screening hundreds of opportunities and gradually narrowing the choices down to a few select prospects.

Once due diligence has started, the information collected is used to develop an investment thesis and populate a transaction model. In assessing the risks and opportunities, the PE firm will assign a valuation (range) to an investment target.

With an approximate valuation in hand, focus shifts to agreeing on a price with the seller, often in a competitive setting. Venture and growth investors focus on assigning value to the target's equity, while buyout investors must size and structure both debt and equity financing appropriately. However, price is not the only (although an important) determinant in closing a deal and other factors must be taken into account.

Finally, terms agreed upon during negotiations are detailed in a number of key documents that govern the economic and control rights of the investing PE funds, the sellers, and, where involved, debt providers after the transaction is finalized.

Section Overview

The chapters in this section will walk the reader through the deal-making process from sourcing to execution and closing.

Chapter 6. Deal Sourcing & Due Diligence: Finding the best deals and actively creating a steady flow of deal opportunities is crucial in PE. A robust due diligence process is the next step to ensuring that various risks and opportunities are identified and adequately dealt with, e.g., through price adjustments, insurance and indemnities.

Chapter 7. Target Valuation: Getting entry valuations right is as much an art as it is a science. Valuation methods differ between investing in early-stage and mature companies. We explain the main steps of valuing a business and include a discussion of multiple valuation, the core method used in later-stage PE transactions.

Chapter 8. Deal Pricing Dynamics: We look at the dynamics and the competitive process in leveraged buyout (LBO) deal-making, addressing questions around the standard two-stage auction process as well as price adjustment and closing mechanisms. We also take a closer look at the unique elements of public-to-private transactions.

Chapter 9. Deal Structuring: Adding debt to a PE transaction complicates matters. This chapter provides a simple overview of the various debt and equity instruments utilized in PE investments and the capital structures employed by LBO funds to enhance investment returns. We then explain the rationale behind the frequent use of special purpose vehicles in PE investments when executing deals.

Chapter 10. Transaction Documentation: For those planning to step into the shoes of a PE professional, this chapter is vital; after all, getting transactions properly documented is critical and finalizes the commercial terms agreed between PE firms and their counterparties. Indeed, it takes up a significant amount of time during deal execution. We delve into the specific provisions of the key transaction, debt and equity documents used in PE—covering topics such as "reps and warranties," covenants, subordination, and economic and control rights. It is a dense chapter, but very much part and parcel of a PE job.

Section Overview

Being successful in private equity (PE) is as much about doing good deals as it is about avoiding bad deals. Two key areas that can differentiate an average fund from a great fund are deal sourcing and due diligence (DD).

Deal sourcing refers to the process in which PE firms screen investment opportunities and identify attractive targets. In today's competitive and crowded mergers and acquisitions (M&A) environment, PE firms rely on increasingly tailored and sophisticated sourcing strategies that capitalize on a firm's network within the business community and present a differentiated message to target companies. Given the sheer number of potential deals available, PE firms rigorously filter out those that do not match their mandate or appear less attractive to focus on a handful of deals that offer the best upside. For example, as detailed in Exhibit 6.1, a well-established European buyout fund may well review 800 deals in a year but eventually only execute five investments.

For investments that have passed through a fund's initial deal sourcing filter, the next step is thorough DD. During this critical step, PE firms employ both internal and external manpower in an increasingly resource-intensive process, to explore all material aspects related to investing in a target company. While PE firms may explore any aspect of the target, they normally follow a structured process and focus on several standard DD areas. The breadth and depth of this process is limited by the expense of conducting DD and the uncertainty of whether an investment will be closed, particularly when conducted during a competitive process. Findings from DD

Exhibit 6.1 Annual PE Deal Funnel

Opportunities Reviewed in a Year:
800

Preliminary DD:
150

Investment Committee
Review:
35

Formal DD:
20

INVESTMENTS MADE: 5

Source: Bridgepoint

are presented to a firm's investment committee (IC), which decides on whether to submit an offer. In making that decision, the IC will only consider those opportunities with the best risk–return profile and fit for the fund.

This chapter provides an overview of the deal sourcing and DD processes for mature target companies.[1] We first place deal sourcing in the context of proprietary and intermediated deals, before stepping through a typical DD process. We conclude the chapter with an overview of the four main areas of DD: commercial, financial, legal and human resources.

GENERATING DEAL FLOW

Deal sourcing is the first step in a PE firm's investment process, when potential investment opportunities are identified and screened. To maximize the number of quality opportunities in a fund's deal pipeline, PE firms begin sourcing well before a fund's first commitments are secured, and continue to do so throughout the investment period. For established firms, deal sourcing is a continuous process, as follow-on funds provide a constant source of fresh capital.

Deal sourcing is a time-consuming and inefficient process, requiring a thorough review of deals at varying stages of progress. While many investment opportunities are presented to a firm execution-ready, others require patience and monitoring until a set of circumstances—often beyond the PE firm's control—catalyze business owners to seek external investors. To ensure a consistent sourcing process and reduce the demand on deal professionals, PE firms with sufficient resources have established internal business development teams tasked solely with deal sourcing. These teams act both as a first point of contact for intermediaries and as drivers of the firm's proprietary deal flow. However, deal sourcing typically involves the entire firm, as there is no telling where the next quality lead will come from, e.g. former portfolio firms and their owners or entrepreneurs may well add to the deal flow.

There are two main ways to source deals: proprietary deal flow sourced through in-house resources and intermediated deal flow sourced through paid third parties.

PROPRIETARY DEAL FLOW: Proprietary deals are sourced directly by a PE firm without the assistance of financial advisors. The primary sources of proprietary deals are the personal and business relationships of a PE firm's investment professionals. In addition, proprietary deals are also sourced through a PE firm's executive network[2] and existing portfolio companies' management teams

---

1. The processes described below apply to mature target companies with real assets, historical performance data and the intrinsic value of a going concern. Venture funds investing in early-stage companies have to rely on different ways to assess the viability of an investment. Chapter 2 Venture Capital describes the deal dynamics in a venture setting in detail.

2. A PE firm's executive network is an investor-sponsored group of executives with the ability to add value to portfolio companies. These executives are often required to make a token investment in a fund and have various compensation arrangements with PE firms, ranging from fully salaried and carry-entitled operating partner roles to retainer based, and tied to a specific activity (consultant role) with portfolio companies. PE firms may also tap expert networks, i.e., firms that provide access to experienced industry executives.

and advisory boards. Other proactive sourcing techniques include cold calling, reviewing industry regulatory filings and published reports, and attending industry or networking conferences.

PE professionals express a preference for proprietary deals as they are often more tailored to a fund's size and sector requirements, provide a direct link to a target company's management team, and have a higher chance for exclusivity than deals sourced through intermediaries. In addition, proprietary deals are often faster and cheaper to execute once they mature. LPs clearly favor firms with strong proprietary deal flow.

However, proprietary deal flow has certain drawbacks. As proprietary targets are often not in urgent need of capital, it can take a significant amount of time—often years—for a PE firm to build the relationship and make a case for its involvement, with no guarantee that an investment will ultimately materialize. With a minimal, if any, financial commitment to the sales process, business owners in a proprietary deal setting can easily walk away from a transaction. In addition, a deal proactively sourced in-house may still attract attention from other bidders, triggering a more competitive process.

INTERMEDIATED DEAL FLOW: Paid intermediaries—such as integrated investment banks, M&A boutiques and corporate advisory arms of accounting firms—play a key role in deal sourcing for larger growth equity and buyout funds. The bulk of these intermediaries' compensation comes in the form of a success fee contingent on the completion of a transaction, with a retainer fee occasionally covering costs over the course of the engagement. Intermediated deals are predominantly introduced by advisors engaged by the target company (or sell-side advisors) and advisors engaged directly by the PE firm (or buy-side advisors), and—more rarely—by "fund-less" promoters who finance transactions on a deal-by-deal basis in exchange for an equity stake or fee.

When a company engages a sell-side advisor it sends a signal that it is serious about the proposed transaction, is of sufficient quality to attract an advisor and has potentially prepared for the sale. The presence of a sell-side investment bank typically indicates an auction process, where a number of investors will be shown the opportunity and invited to bid.[3] While participation in auctions is a necessary requirement for investments in large companies, PE firms' conversion rate of these opportunities is low given the sheer number of parties involved in the bidding process; it is certainly lower than deals sourced independently.

The size of a PE fund, and thus the average size of its investments, is a key determinant of the type and number of paid intermediaries it will engage to generate deal flow. PE firms managing large and mega-funds predominantly source opportunities from investment banks, as most large target companies will hire an investment bank as a sell-side advisor to maximize transaction value. Firms managing mid-market and smaller funds predominantly source opportunities from the corporate advisory arms of accounting firms and M&A boutiques.

---

3. Please refer to Chapter 8 Deal Pricing Dynamics for an overview of a two-stage auction process.

Box 6.1

DEAL SOURCING STATISTICS

Which deal sourcing channels generate the most opportunities? The answer varies by firm: younger PE firms managing smaller funds or investing in emerging markets tend to source more deals in-house, while firms executing large buyouts derive a smaller percentage from their proprietary networks.[4] It should be added that sourcing deals in emerging markets adds to the complexity, as explained by our guest author below.

In contrast to buyout and growth equity firms, venture capital (VC) firms—particularly those investing in early-stage start-ups—rely far less on paid intermediaries to source deals, drawing rather on proprietary deal flow generated by the firm's reputation and the personal networks of its partners; after all "sourcing" that next up-and-coming entrepreneur is hard to institutionalize.[5] Aside from proprietary deals, VC firms look at times to quasi-intermediated deal flow from incubators, accelerators, angel investors and a whole eco-system of individuals or boutique firms that assist up-and-coming entrepreneurs with their business plans. Early-stage VCs may attend venture competitions at business schools and universities to gain early access to ideas. Venture deal-making is in general more inclusive; one firm may lead a round and invite a small "club" of co-investors, thereby providing deal flow to them.

Beyond anecdotal data, there are few studies providing a breakdown of deal sources in PE; those that do exist should be taken with a grain of salt, as deal sourcing varies from market to market and is typically self-reported. That being said: we show the results of a survey of global buyout and VC firms (Teten, 2010) in Exhibit 6.2.

Exhibit 6.2 PE Deal Sources

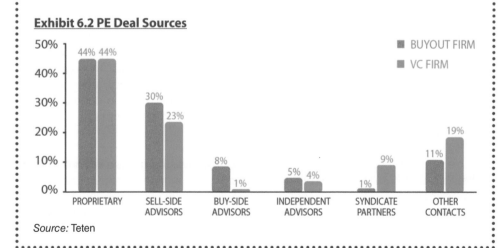

Source: Teten

---

4. Firms executing buyout strategies typically invest in mature, highly intermediated markets with sophisticated sellers and large transaction sizes. Sellers in these markets have the resources to hire a financial advisor.
5. Please refer to Chapter 2 Venture Capital for additional information on VC deal sourcing.

Hunting for Deals in Emerging Markets
By Nicholas Bloy, Founding Partner, NAVIS Capital Partners

Intermediation in emerging markets is immature and inefficient. Investment opportunities are typically smaller and global investment banks don't like to get out of bed for fees of less than 5 million US dollars. This is good for private equity players because where there is inefficiency, there is the opportunity for alpha, that measure of value generation we all seek.

In mature deal environments, sourcing is like waiting for the bus; if you miss it, never mind, there will be another one in a few minutes, driven by an investment banker with a fat information memorandum and perhaps stapled financing. In emerging markets, investment opportunities rarely come in a well-documented form and often they don't come at all. When they do, you might be dealing with a lawyer or accountant friend of an entrepreneur who is considering retirement. Financial statements might be unaudited, perhaps prepared more for tax purposes than performance measurement and may be the unconsolidated addition of a number of legal entities with overlapping activities. There may be no credible validation of the bona fides of the investment opportunity. While frustrating, this creates attractive market inefficiencies. It helps to be sceptical, but it is also important to form a quick opinion on the quality and positioning of the company and of industry attractiveness. If you like what you see (or *feel* because the financial and other information is incomplete), it is critical to make the transaction bilateral before it becomes part of a formally intermediated process where you will either pay a higher price or lose it to someone else.

The dearth of intermediary-prepared, ready-to-close deals in emerging markets means that an effective in-house sourcing model is a great advantage. Building one is easier said than done. Self-generated deals start with a philosophy that opportunities are everywhere and like Michelangelo's angel enclosed in a block of marble, they are waiting to be revealed.

At the supermarket, you may be shopping for items on your list, but you are also shopping for opportunity. Take a look at brands with prominent facings, pick one up and see who makes it. If it says Unilever on the back, return it to the shelf. But if it's a local or regional brand, buy it, try it and contact the owners to see if perhaps they would like help in entering new markets, or acquiring a competitor, or anything that will help you generate a dialogue about how third-party capital and expertise can create value. Opportunity can arise almost anywhere—at an alumni reunion, a wedding, driving around an industrial estate, meeting other parents at school events, the list goes on.

Another approach is top-down and research-driven starting with an observation or idea. In emerging markets, valuable insight can be gained from understanding a country's age and income characteristics combined with knowledge of the level of household or personal income that triggers demand for a particular item. Income distribution curves vary by country but they will typically have bulges of population on the verge of achieving income levels that stimulate consumption of something previously unaffordable. This can highlight products or services where supercharged growth can be anticipated. For example, substitution of a car for a motorcycle doesn't happen at an even pace; auto ownership increases rapidly at the point where a large bulge of the population crosses the threshold level of income for auto ownership. As always in emerging markets, the key for such *revealed opportunities* is to keep the dialogue bilateral.

Happy hunting!

DUE DILIGENCE CONSIDERATIONS

Once an attractive target company has been identified, DD is the next critical step in the investment process. During this process, the PE firm explores all material aspects related to the target with the goal of developing a robust understanding of its underlying strengths and weaknesses to arrive at a go or no-go investment decision and reveal specific areas that require negotiation. DD is a time-consuming, resource-intensive process that places significant demand on the lean teams found at most PE firms. It is therefore important, to initiate DD solely on high potential targets and limit the scope of the initial DD to questions that are material to a go, no-go decision.

Throughout the DD process, PE firms assess the viability of a target's business model relative to their investment thesis. Input from DD is used to build and stress-test an investment's financial forecast, identify and ring-fence material issues at the target, and inform the bidding, negotiation and documentation processes. The degree and scope of market and company-specific risks and opportunities are assessed and built into a company's value creation plan for the expected holding period, to be implemented in particular during the period immediately following the investment (often referred to as the "first 100 days"). DD also provides a PE firm with the opportunity to establish a rapport with a target's management team and form an opinion on whether the team can deliver on the plan. More often than not, a PE firm will choose to forego an attractive deal if the management team is unlikely to execute in line with the firm's base case scenario and a change of those executives is considered as too disruptive.

The characteristics of PE introduce unique elements to the DD process. As a PE fund's mandate often stretches across several sectors, PE firms commonly assess targets in industry segments with which they are not intimately familiar. As a result, PE teams must draw on external advisors, consulting firms or experts from existing portfolio companies to complement existing in-house expertise. The typical 10-year, closed-end PE fund structure also requires firms to consider exit paths and potential acquirers during the DD process; optionality is the key word here and it is preferable to have an investment with a realistic choice of exit paths.[6]

From the seller's perspective, DD signals the beginning of the transfer of legal responsibility regarding the performance and risks of the business to the PE buyer; findings from DD representing the state of the business are later included in transaction documentation.[7] Sellers have an incentive to fully disclose all known and material

---

6. Please refer to Chapter 15 for additional information on Exits.
7. Please refer to Chapter 10 for additional information on Transaction Documentation.

risks related to a business as it mitigates their exposure to post-transaction litigation in the event of poor or unexpected business performance.

THE DUE DILIGENCE PROCESS

The DD process has several distinct phases. While emphasis and execution may differ from deal to deal, certain processes have very much become the expected minimum and can be considered the industry standard. We will walk through a highly structured process for investments in mature companies, as per Exhibit 6.3.[8]

Screening of an investment opportunity begins with information gathered from the earliest meetings and discussions with the target firm. During deal sourcing, the focus is on a high-level assessment of the (potential) investment's fit with the fund's mandate and a review of publicly available information of both the target and industry sector. PE investors will also meet with external parties—such as customers, suppliers and sector specialists—to gain a perspective on the company's reputation and market position, its structure, the industry's supply chain, and the target's competition.

Exhibit 6.3 PE Due Diligence Process

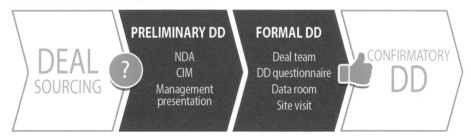

PRELIMINARY DD

The structured DD process typically begins with a review of the target by the PE firm's professionals. Following the execution of a confidentiality or non-disclosure agreement (NDA), the target firm will share a Confidential Information Memorandum (CIM) providing a broad overview of the opportunity. This is followed by a management presentation, which marks the first formal meeting between management and the PE firm. We discuss these elements of the DD process in further detail below.

NON-DISCLOSURE AGREEMENT (NDA): An NDA is executed between the PE firm and a target company so that non-public information can be securely exchanged; these agreements cover all information shared during the DD, negotiation and closing process.[9] An NDA limits the buyer's ability to freely discuss the target with industry

---

8. DD processes for proprietary deals can be more informal and at times highly unstructured, as they involve fewer parties and less time constraints surrounding the transaction.
9. NDAs are rarely a part of the DD process in early-stage VC investment.

players; therefore, the buyer will typically undertake preliminary DD on its own and sign the NDA only when additional input from the seller is needed. Indeed, a PE firm will typically not sign an NDA or enter into a structured DD process unless it has developed an initial feel for the target and is comfortable that it fits the mandate of the fund.

CONFIDENTIAL INFORMATION MEMORANDUM (CIM): A CIM is the first formal document shared by a target and provides an up-to-date overview of its business and the investment opportunity. The CIM, often prepared with the help of a sell-side advisor, includes a detailed description of the business and its industry, historical and projected financials, forward-looking strategy and opportunities, and an overview of the management team and key personnel. The CIM is typically accompanied by a letter detailing key milestones and steps of the sales process, including the projected timeline for closing and bidding procedures.[10]

MANAGEMENT PRESENTATION: The management presentation tends to represent the first face-to-face meeting between a PE firm and the company's management in an intermediated DD process. This presentation expands on the information provided in the CIM, highlights and illustrates key elements of the target's operations, updates relevant business developments and provides a forum for investors to ask questions. The presentation also gives buyers insights into the managers' strategic thinking, business planning, management style and at times team dynamics.

FORMAL DD

The information gained from preliminary DD is organized in a Preliminary Investment Memorandum and submitted to the PE firm's IC. Depending on the PE firm's internal process, approval from the IC may be required to commit additional resources and continue with the DD process. If approval and a corresponding budget are received, the deal team responsible for the transaction engages in a thorough review of all key aspects of the target business, to arrive at a recommendation for the IC as to whether, and under what conditions, to submit a formal bid for the company.

DEAL TEAM: Deal teams typically consist of several professionals from the PE firm responsible for driving the investment process and managing a host of external advisors. These advisors include consultants, lawyers and accountants who add additional firepower and specific expertise to the transaction. External advisors often provide advice and guidance free of charge during deal sourcing and the preliminary DD phase in the hope of securing a formal mandate later in the process.

DD QUESTIONNAIRE: A DD questionnaire is prepared by the deal team and submitted to the target to collect material information related to the investment opportunity. Parts of these questionnaires are standardized to extract information relevant for any transaction; these generic questions are then complemented by those unique to the specific opportunity at hand. A point of contact is established by the selling company or its advisor and the questionnaire is systematically completed, with additional questions added throughout the process.

---

10. Please refer to Chapter 8 Deal Pricing Dynamics for an overview of an auction and the bidding process.

DATA ROOM: The target and its advisors establish and maintain a data room that contains material documentation for the DD process. Documents shared include historical financial statements and financial projections, shareholding agreements and corporate charters, employment contracts and compensation plans, contracts with key suppliers and customers, and other key company agreements. Virtual data rooms, in which copies of all documents are stored electronically, have become the norm, but physical data rooms still exist. Access to a virtual data room can be easily managed and restrictions on the terms of review, forwarding rights, printing and other specific permissions can help increase security of information.

SITE VISIT: Site visits provide deal teams with the opportunity to gain an understanding of a target's operations in person and typically take place at company offices and facilities. These visits are highly structured to maximize the productivity of a deal team's time on the ground and often include inspection of facilities and meetings with management and key line managers. Meetings with non-management team personnel, frequently restricted due to the sensitivity of the process, allow PE professionals to engage directly with employees not involved in the sales process, allowing for a more forthright assessment of a target's day-to-day activity and company culture.

Once a deal team is satisfied with its findings from the DD process, it will present a Final Investment Memorandum to its IC. If the deal team receives approval from their IC, it will submit a binding bid for the target, subject to confirmatory DD. Confirmatory DD is conducted to address any remaining questions before a final bid is made and to gain access to the most commercially sensitive information that will only be shared with the preferred bidder. Additional information that surfaces at this stage of DD can result in adjustments to deal pricing and provisions.[11] In parallel to the confirmatory DD, relevant transaction documentation is drafted and negotiated.

The Due Diligence "Conspiracy"
By Richard Foyston, Founding Partner, NAVIS Capital Partners

To be part of a private equity firm's due diligence exercise is to be part of an extensive conspiracy. From the newly hired, wet-behind-the-ears associate to the senior partner, it behoves every private equity professional to be aware of its dangers.

Almost every deal process participant is a co-conspirator with an interest in getting the deal done. The deal professional who found the lead wants to demonstrate that he or she has a finely tuned sense of detecting attractive prey from a great distance. That same professional is also likely to have a financial interest in seeing the deal completed. For a deal closing partner, perhaps with the pressure of compensation-linked management buyout (MBO), better opportunities may not come along and hopes are always high that one's deal will pass the due diligence test. There are other co-conspirators as well. The seller is highly incentivized to make a sale. Intermediaries working for the buyer and the seller have the motivation of both financial reward and professional pride to "get the deal done." Specialist participants, including accountants, lawyers and consultants should be

---

more circumspect and search doggedly for flaws in the story that is the basis of the deal due diligence chase. But the reality is that they too are financially and professionally rewarded for participating in successful pursuits. There are typically other, more minor players. Secretaries, systems analysts, executive search firms, personnel departments and others are all on board the deal-closing train. Who benefits from being part of an aborted deal? Can you build a career being a pessimist? It may feel risky to be a naysayer. The young deal associate may feel overwhelmed by the momentum of the chase that all parties are engaged in.

Like the hungry lion whose odds of a successful hunt may be only one in three, the private equity firm faces a trade-off. It needs to try its best to make each pursuit successful but can't afford to expend too much energy on deals that don't close. It's better to cut losses early on "bad" deals and move on quickly to those with better chances of success. Chasing poor deals can be very costly. First, you waste your time (and lots of other people's as well) and the longer you chase a "bad" deal the greater the chance of wasting your money as well (or more accurately, that of your investors). The lion who unwisely commits wasted energy to an ultimately unsuccessful chase may be too exhausted to succeed the next time. The PE investor risks similarly dire consequences of chasing a bad deal too far—too committed to be able to dispassionately walk away from a deal even when a detached and unbiased professional would. The result of failing to abandon a "bad" deal can be years of financial pain, expended resources and professional disappointment.

It makes for a delicate game. Engage too timidly and the investment case will be weak and unconvincing. Pursue without sufficient wariness and suspicion and the risk of wasted time and, even worse, wasted money looms large. It is prudent for the young PE professional to be wary. He or she is an inevitable participant in a great conspiracy and is well advised to be a cautious and suspicious sage, always ready to recognize early the folly of a doomed chase.

DUE DILIGENCE AREAS

PE firms focus the DD process on specific aspects of a target company: commercial, financial, legal and human resources. While these areas are often assessed in isolation, they inevitably interact and combine to provide the PE firm with a holistic view of the business. Deal teams will be vigilant and on the lookout for potential red flags—issues that pose a material threat to a successful investment—to ensure that a firm is not committing resources to a flawed opportunity. Exhibit 6.4 provides an overview of these four areas of DD.

COMMERCIAL DD (CDD): The main goal of the commercial DD (CDD) is to better understand the company's business model and explore how the company addresses the needs of its customers, capitalizes on key industry trends and navigates the competitive environment. CDD is typically conducted in conjunction with consultants bringing specific industry expertise; these external experts typically prepare market studies, undertake competitive benchmarking and conduct location studies to provide requisite background information. CDD can also include the analysis of systems and infrastructure supporting a target's operations.

Exhibit 6.4 PE Due Diligence Areas

Examples of CDD red flags that may stop an investment in its tracks include:

- Shrinking market size and/or a declining market share
- Disruptive and commoditization threats
- Dependence on powerful suppliers or a concentrated customer base

FINANCIAL DD (FDD): Financial DD (FDD) includes a detailed examination of a target's historical financial statements and management's financial projections. FDD is typically conducted in conjunction with an accounting firm engaged to thoroughly review audited historical financial statements (generally at least the past three to five years), budgeted versus actual performance, current unaudited financials and management's financial projections. Review of a target's current performance oftentimes centers on establishing a normalized earnings before interest, tax, depreciation and amortization (EBITDA) and target working capital, which form a key input for valuation and negotiation at a later stage in the investment process.[12] Other items assessed include contingent liabilities and employee entitlement provisions and their tax implications. Data points gathered from commercial DD coupled with the company's historical financials are used to prepare a forecast for the target's financial performance.

Examples of FDD red flags include:

- Off-balance sheet financial instruments
- Weakening working capital trends
- Accounting adjustments to obscure actual performance

LEGAL DD (LDD): During legal DD (LDD), deal teams review a target's material legal documentation and assess the legal status of its key stakeholders. Law firms are

---

12. Please refer to Chapter 8 Deal Pricing Dynamics for additional information on EBITDA and working capital adjustments.

typically engaged to conduct a thorough review of corporate records, material corporate agreements, and intellectual property rights. Environmental, social and governance issues, the contractual underpinnings of future liabilities—such as employee pension and benefit programs—and pending litigation are also examined to determine potential cash flow and reputational impacts on the target. Background checks on current owners and top management are conducted to learn more about key counterparties and reveal any history of criminal, commercial or financial misconduct. In addition to company-specific topics, LDD also involves a review of legal and regulatory guidelines governing activity in a company's sector and geographies. The output of LDD flows directly into the negotiation of terms and conditions related to the assumption of risk and exposure when drafting the share purchase agreement.

Examples of LDD red flags include:

- Pending regulatory issues
- Corruption and bribery accusations
- Insufficient protection of intellectual property
- Questionable ownership rights

HUMAN RESOURCES DD (HRDD): Human resources DD (HRDD) involves a thorough review of the capabilities of key employees at a target, starting with the management team. HRDD is typically conducted by PE professionals and external consultants hired to assist in the process. Recruitment agents are often used to provide further details on employees. A strong management team is a crucial driver of both investment performance and value creation post-investment. The cohesion of the team and the impact of each team member on the company's operational performance and success are thus closely evaluated. Analyzing the management team provides a window into the company's culture and core values, and may reveal early on when changes in or additions to the team are required.[13] Beyond senior executives, HRDD extends to line managers and other key employees in the target's talent pool. Other items assessed include recruitment and retention programs, employment contracts, compensation and benefit programs.

Examples of HRDD red flags include:

- Frequent board changes
- The management team deciding to cash out all its equity
- Strong personal loyalty to existing owners

CLOSING

Deal sourcing and DD are the first steps in the deal-making process of PE firms investing in mature companies; the process allows them to develop clear business scenarios for the investment opportunity at hand before pursuing the target company further. All information gathered during this process will flow into the critical discussions of valuation, covered in the next chapter.

---

13. It is not unusual in a PE transaction for parts of the management team to be replaced. This may require a PE firm's operational in-house experts to step in initially, followed by a permanent replacement as soon as possible. Changes can be costly and may have an impact on the effectiveness of the organization during the search for new employees. Please refer to Chapter 12 Securing Management Teams for further discussions on this topic.

KEY LEARNING POINTS

• **Deal sourcing and DD are the first steps of the investment process. A PE fund's IC will rely on the information gathered during the DD process when making an investment decision.**

• **PE firms are keen to develop proprietary deal flow; nevertheless, intermediated deals, referred through investment banks and advisors, make up a significant part of the deals sourced—especially for larger transactions and buyouts.**

• **Once a suitable target company is found and has passed an initial screening during deal sourcing, the deal team will proceed into the formal phase of the DD process.**

• **PE firms conduct DD across four main areas of the target company: commercial, financial, legal and human resources.**

RELEVANT CASE STUDIES

from *Private Equity in Action—Case Studies from Developed and Emerging Markets*

Cases #11 and 12: Chips on the Side (A and B): The Buyout of Avago Technologies

Case #13: Going Places: The Buyout of Amadeus Global Travel Distribution

REFERENCES AND ADDITIONAL READING

Gompers, P. Kaplan, S.N. and Mukharlyamov, V. (2014) What Do Private Equity Firms Do?, https://editorialexpress.com/cgi-bin/conference/download.cgi?paper_id=1475&db_name=AFA2015.

INSEAD White Paper (2014) Strategic Buyers vs. Private Equity Buyers in an Investment Process, https://sites.insead.edu/facultyresearch/research/doc.cfm?did=54372.

Rimmers, S. and San Andres, A. (2012) Human Resources Due Diligence, PricewaterhouseCoopers, https://www.pwc.com/us/en/hr-management/assets/pwc-human-resource-due-diligence.pdf.

Snow, D. (ed.) (2014) Deal Sourcing: Intermediaries, Business Development, and the Future of Private Equity Deal Flow, Privcap, Q3, http://www.privcap.com/wp-content/uploads/2014/09/Special-Report-Intermediaries-3.pdf.

Teten, D. and Farmer, C. (2010) Where are the Deals?, *Journal of Private Equity*, 14, Winter.

Getting valuations right in private equity (PE) is notoriously difficult; it is nevertheless a topic that permeates the entire lifecycle of PE investing. Of particular significance is the value that PE investors assign to a target company during due diligence. This valuation is a key factor in determining whether a PE firm will pursue a deal or not; it links to the price paid for the shares in the company and ultimately the profitability of the investment.

During the valuation process, PE firms employ various tools to arrive at the economic worth—or fair value—of a target company. It should be added that valuation is rarely the starting point for an investment decision; the decision-making process on whether to engage with a company starts long before "valuation" is discussed.[1]

Valuation techniques vary based on a company's stage of development. For venture capital (VC) investments in early-stage companies, valuation is typically used as a tool to determine the equity stake a VC firm requires for a given dollar amount invested, taking into account the VC's target return. For growth capital and buyout investments in mature companies, valuation is typically based on a target's profits, its operating cash flow and valuation multiples of comparable businesses.

This chapter provides an overview of the various valuation techniques employed by venture, growth and buyout investors, and concludes with a section on valuation multiples.

THE VALUATION TOOLKIT

At the core of any valuation process stands a detailed business plan that translates a target's forward-looking risks and opportunities into a multiyear financial forecast. PE investors will typically start with the existing management's strategic vision for the target, break it down according to key value drivers, and rebuild their own business plan based on assumptions around risk and future initiatives that they expect will lead to operational improvements, accelerated growth and ultimately a successful exit. PE investors use knowledge acquired during due diligence to develop a range of possible operating outcomes, including a base case scenario as well as possible downside and upside cases. Macroeconomic assessments will also play a role, especially in highly cyclical industries.

Next, PE investors apply valuation multiples from comparable businesses to operating metrics from the business plan to arrive at a company's enterprise valuation (EV). The operating metric of choice varies from company to company; however, a common key metric in mature companies is earnings before interest, taxes, depreciation and amortization (EBITDA). PE investors then derive a target's equity value by subtracting its net debt—the main components of which are a target's interest-bearing liabilities and cash[2]—from its EV. Exhibit 7.1 shows these simple mechanics using an EBITDA multiple as an example.

---

1. Please refer to Chapter 6 Deal Sourcing & Due Diligence for an overview of the investment process.
2. Please refer to Chapter 8 Deal Pricing Dynamics for a detailed definition of net debt.

Exhibit 7.1 Enterprise and Equity Valuation

EBITDA ❶	Enterprise Value
X EBITDA Multiple ❷	- Net Debt ❶
- - - - - - - - - - - - - - - -	- - - - - - - - - - - - - - - -
Enterprise Value	Equity Value

❶ ⌐ - - - - - - - - - - - - - - - - - - - ¬
  ⌐ Business Plan or Financial Statements ⌐
   ∟ - - - - - - - - - - - - - - - - - - - ⌐

❷ ⌐ - - - - - - - - - - - - - ¬
  ⌐ Industry Comparables ⌐
   ∟ - - - - - - - - - - - - - ⌐

The nature of PE investment, which requires target companies to be both bought and sold within a PE fund's 10-year term, has a distinct impact on how PE investors think about valuation. PE investors calculate a target's EV both at the time of investment—often based on a company's performance over the last 12 months—and at various points in the future that represent potential exit points. Assessing EV and equity value at entry and exit allows a PE investor to determine an expected return for the investment opportunity and assess whether it aligns with the riskiness of the opportunity and the mandate and target return of the fund.

It should be noted that strategic investors employ different valuation methods, as they emphasize the long-term value of acquisitions as well as potential synergies with their existing business. As a result, strategic investors favor the discounted cash flow (DCF) valuation method, which uses future free cash flow projections and discounts them to arrive at an estimate of present value.[3] PE investors mostly consider the output from a DCF valuation—and at times more exotic valuation techniques, such as real option pricing—only in a complementary manner or to assess how other parties may value the target.

We will now show how these techniques are applied to value early-stage companies (VC targets) and mature companies (growth equity and buyout targets).

VENTURE CAPITAL
THE VALUATION OF EARLY-STAGE COMPANIES

VC investors face the greatest uncertainty when it comes to setting a fair and accurate value for their potential target investments—in terms of both entry and exit valuations—since venture funds typically invest in immature start-ups with little or no operating history. Business plans at start-ups project how management will deploy capital raised over multiple rounds of investment to develop the company into a full-fledged, profitable business.

At the time of investment, VC targets are usually pre-profit, often pre-revenue and—when it comes to seed funding—even pre-product. Therefore, any valuation is based

---

3. The many assumptions that DCF valuations rely on, such as terminal value and the calculation of a discount rate, also serve as a deterrent to employing this technique in practice.

on assumptions related to the development of a unique and sustainable business model and the successful execution of a growth business plan.[4]

Because of the associated market and execution risk, VC investors generally set a high target rate of return to allow for the substantial failure rate among early-stage companies. A fund's target internal rate of return (IRR) used to model the pre-money valuation of a VC investee company ranges from 40 to 80%, depending on the maturity of the company.

The starting point for VC investment discussions is the amount of capital a start-up company will need to reach its next stage of development; the money raised is typically sufficient to last the company for 12 to 18 months before new funds will be needed. VC investors work backwards from the required amount—considering the target IRR for the investment, the company's expected future value and the number of years to exit—to determine both a start-up's post-money valuation and the VC fund's equity ownership percentage. As start-up companies are typically funded entirely by equity, the EV and the equity value of these companies are broadly the same.

Exhibit 7.2 steps through an example of a VC valuation. Given the uncertainty related to company profitability in our start-up, we use expected sales and sales multiples to

Exhibit 7.2 Valuing Early-stage Companies

A VC firm is looking at an investment of $2 million in an early-stage opportunity today.

Exit in 5 years at a Revenue multiple of 8x and Yr 5 Revenue of $15m.

➡ Exit Value 8 x $15m = $120m

No debt required; no additional equity to be raised.

Cash flow profile:

YEAR	0	1	2	3	4	5
CF	(2)	0	0	0	0	120

Required IRR 70%.

Post-Money = $120/(1.70)^5 = $8.45m$

What % of the company should the VC ask for?

Equity Percentage = $2m/$8.45m = 23.66%$

Watch out for difference between pre-money ($6.45m) and post-money valuation ($8.45m).

---

4. Please refer to Chapter 2 Venture Capital for more information on what VCs look for when assessing start-ups and investable companies.

estimate the value at exit in five years' time. Our VC investor discounts the expected value at exit by its target IRR of 70% to arrive at the start-up's post-money valuation. The post-money value minus the funds invested is referred to as the pre-money valuation of the firm.

Start-ups will usually require several rounds of fundraising. As the company matures, the target IRR required by late-stage VC investors will drop towards 40% as the operational stability of the business increases and investment risk correspondingly decreases. Valuations at a start-up often increase at a non-linear rate, meaning that founders and existing investors give up a proportionally smaller percentage of equity per dollar of new money raised in later rounds. Nevertheless, the equity stake held by owners will be diluted over time by subsequent rounds of VC funding. The ownership split between founders and external investors must be considered throughout the start-up's fundraising process to ensure that the founding team is engaged and motivated by a meaningful stake in the business.

VC investors are particularly concerned with so-called down rounds (when start-ups raise capital at a lower valuation than that of previous rounds) and regularly include protective provisions in their term sheet to avoid being diluted.[5]

GROWTH EQUITY AND BUYOUTS
THE VALUATION OF MATURE COMPANIES

Growth equity and buyout investors target mature, profitable companies with established operations and a track record of performance; as a result, these investors have access to historical data plus the intrinsic value of a going concern and its assets to determine a target's value. Given the maturity of these businesses, growth and buyout investors focus on profit multiples to value a target; EBIT and EBITDA are preferred over net earnings, as they are not subject to a company's capital and tax structure.

Based on input from management and findings from due diligence, growth equity and buyout investors develop business plans with multiple operating scenarios: the base case financial scenario represents the target's expected operating performance, while downside and upside cases reflect scenarios of underperformance and outperformance, respectively. Although multiple expansion and contraction are considered in the context of broad industry and market cycles, a reasonable starting assumption for the base case is a constant multiple for both entry and exit valuation.

In the context of an LBO, the ability to finance a portion of the target's EV with debt is a key driver of investment returns. When determining a target's valuation, buyout investors estimate the level of debt financing that banks are likely to extend to the transaction. The estimate is initially based on industry debt multiples (i.e., the

---

5. Please refer to Chapter 2 Venture Capital for details on the provisions included in VC term sheets, in particular antidilution provisions.

amount of interest-bearing debt per unit of operating cash flow) and then later in the process on the debt capacity of the specific target company as well as preliminary discussions with financing banks (in our Exhibit 7.3 below, debt capacity equals 4x a company's EBITDA). The minimum amount of equity that banks require as a buffer for a company to secure financing at this debt multiple provides an aggressive case for the transaction's financing structure. Buyout investors consider a range of capital structures, debt instruments and debt servicing requirements when determining the optimal capital structure for a buyout.[6]

Exhibit 7.3 shows a simplified valuation for a buyout investment. Buyout funds value a company's EV at acquisition and exit based on current and forecast EBITDA and its comparable EBITDA multiple; they then use a market-based debt multiple to determine an acquisition financing structure and to forecast a debt repayment schedule. Based on this analysis, the equity required for the company's purchase, and the expected return to equity at exit, can be calculated. Given these values and assumptions on intermediate cash flows, a PE investor arrives at a target return, expressed as an IRR and a multiple of money invested (MoM).[7]

Armed with this information plus the findings from due diligence, buyout investors form a view on whether the return on investment is appropriate for the combined operational and financial risk (from leverage). Buyout funds use scenario analysis— in some cases a Monte Carlo simulation—to better understand an investment's

Exhibit 7.3 Valuing Mature Companies

A PE firm has developed a Base Case business plan for an LBO arriving at a moderate (but steady) profit growth profile.

Comparable/competitive pricing indicates:
- Entry Enterprise Value multiple of about 7x EBITDA (LTM)
- Debt multiple of 4x EBITDA (LTM)

Exit in 4 years at a 7x EBITDA multiple.

YEAR	2010	2011	2012	2013	2014	CAGR
EBITDA	180	195	210	252	240	7.5%
Multiple	7				7	
EV	1260				1680	

Debt Multiple	4					
Debt Paydown		55	70	85	100	
DEBT	720	665	595	510	410	
EQUITY	-540	0	0	0	1270	

IRR	24%
MoM	2.4

Model gives expected return as 24% IRR or 2.4x MoM after 4 years.

---

6. See Chapter 9 Deal Structuring for further details of the capital structure in leveraged buyouts (LBOs).
7. See Chapter 19 Performance Reporting for additional information on an investment and fund's IRR and MoM.

downside and upside risk profile, and will adjust the financing structure accordingly. Ultimately, a PE firm's investment committee will decide whether the target's risk–return profile is in line with the fund's strategy, its mandate and overall target return.

Understanding Enterprise Value
By Graham Oldroyd, former Partner, Bridgepoint Private Equity

Assuming a normalized working capital position, Enterprise Value, or EV, can be thought of as the value a buyer might place on 100% of the shares of a business having no borrowings and zero cash at bank, i.e. for the purchase of a business "debt-free, cash-free."

Offers to acquire unquoted companies will commonly be expressed in terms of EV, as opposed to price per share and market capitalization seen in the quoted arena. The typical unquoted company will have both borrowings and a cash balance, and in this case the net-debt position (debt minus cash) will be deducted from EV to derive an eventual share purchase consideration. PE firms nevertheless consistently work in terms of EV when valuing companies. This facilitates valuation comparison across companies in the same sector irrespective of debt structure. Also, where a PE investment involves a change of ownership, as in most LBOs, the change of control will usually trigger mandatory repayment of existing senior debt. The PE buyer's funding requirement, to be met by equity from the PE fund and any new bank borrowings, will then be the share purchase consideration plus the target's existing senior debt, i.e. target EV.

It might be concluded that by applying enough mathematical analysis a single Enterprise Value number can be calculated for any company. Different metrics and underlying assumptions will, however, provide a range of possible values. These are often represented on a valuation "football field," as shown in Exhibit 7.4, so called because the mean can be seen as a half-way line with values ranging either side. Ultimately, these calculated values are merely points of reference. They may be used for half-yearly valuation purposes in reporting portfolio company values to PE fund investors. In a transaction, however, the true market value is determined by the price actually agreed between a willing buyer and a willing seller.

This is not to say that EV calculations are unimportant in actual transactions. They form the basis from which PE buyers will formulate their offer, justify proposed pricing internally and to PE fund investors, and estimate their likely possible investment returns. If the seller is using professional advisers, similar calculations are also likely to underpin the seller's price expectations. The final price paid will, however, be a matter for negotiation. Here, non-financial considerations can have a significant impact on price paid, and thence the retrospectively derived transaction valuation.

Exhibit 7.4 Valuation Football Field

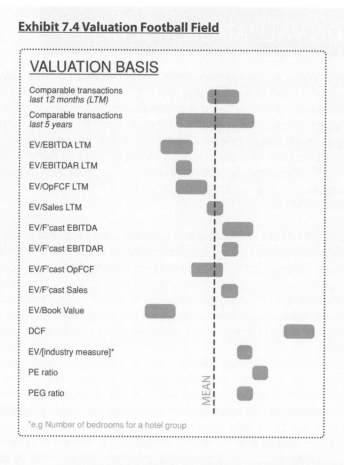

PE firms who are adept at understanding these non-financial considerations benefit, overall, by being able to buy more cheaply and have a higher proportion of transactions successfully completing. A common example is a seller's wish for speed and transaction certainty. In this case a seller may prefer a fair offer delivered quickly over a higher competing offer which was, however, subject to multiple conditions and uncertain timing.

Sellers are also rightly wary of "price chipping." Where a company is the subject of an auction process, there will typically be at least two rounds of bidding before a single appointed acquirer is invited to finalize contract terms. The professional adviser community is small. If an acquirer gains a reputation for bidding high in first rounds, but making sudden unjustified changes to their price in second or subsequent rounds, their initial offers and indeed the solidity of any offer comes into doubt. The better PE funds are careful to build a reputation as reliable bidders.

When a PE firm is selling, EV calculations will be used by the PE fund to establish minimum price expectations. PE will however seek to maximize price further through establishing a competitive auction and by exploring other exit routes such as an IPO. In both regards, most buyer/investor interest is likely to be attracted to a company in which the PE firm has actively invested and grown market position during its ownership period.

MORE ON VALUATION MULTIPLES

A valuation multiple is an expression of the market value of a company relative to a key statistic driving that value. Multiples provide a market-based, "apples to apples" method for determining the value of a target using data drawn from a comparable set of companies. Ideally, the multiple ultimately used to value a target takes into account long-term historical prices and cycles in the industry. Given the amount of information contained in a multiple and its importance in determining company valuations in PE investments, the selection of appropriate multiples receives significant attention in the valuation process. Let's have a closer look at how to derive suitable multiples.

IDENTIFYING COMPARABLES: PE investors typically draw on publicly listed companies and recent mergers and acquisitions transactions when identifying a target's comparable set of companies. They will consider the underlying drivers of the target company's value and look for companies with similar business and product lines, asset size, number of employees, revenue growth, margins, return on invested capital and cash flow. In the process, PE firms will focus on key metrics such as growth rate, margins and leverage to explore whether a firm's value is driven by its operating performance rather than market dynamics.

For companies with a unique business model and few listed competitors, even identifying an appropriate comparable set can be a challenge. When pure-play comparables—based on peer companies matching the target's business model—cannot be found, PE firms may resort to comparable units of larger conglomerates or use regression analysis to isolate a portion of a more complex business for comparison. Building a robust set of comparables can be particularly challenging in emerging markets, where many companies are privately held and data on company performance can be difficult to come by or may not be presented in line with international accounting standards.

IDENTIFYING MULTIPLES

Once a group of comparable peer firms has been identified, PE investors will choose valuation multiples that best reflect the individual dynamics and value drivers of the target. A range of multiples is often used for a given transaction, which offers different valuations and price points. Exhibit 7.5 shows various multiples for the telecommunications industry from 2000 to 2015.

- *EV/EBITDA:* EV to EBITDA is the most commonly used multiple, as EBITDA is largely insulated from the impact of different global accounting standards, simple to calculate, and a proxy for operating cash flow. EV/EBIT is also commonly used.

- *EV/OpFCF:* EV to operating free cash flow (OpFCF) is often used in capital-intensive industries. OpFCF adjusts EBITDA by subtracting estimated maintenance capital expenditure and the estimated change in working capital. OpFCF thus provides a business's earnings after deducting the spending required to maintain the profitability and competitive position of the company.

Exhibit 7.5 Historical Valuation Multiples of the Telecommunications Industry

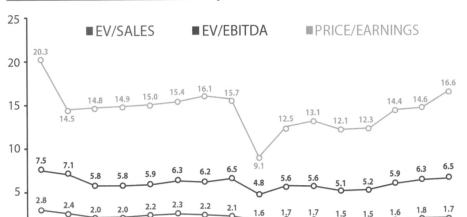

- *EV/Sales:* Sales multiples are typically employed for companies with strong growth but high cyclicality and low or negative profitability. However, sales multiples are an incomplete comparison as they do not consider profitability or cash flow.

- *EV/Book Value:* EV to book value, or net asset value, is used for asset-heavy companies. Book value provides an intuitive, simple figure for comparison as it represents the residual value to the company's owners after subtracting the value of liabilities from the value of assets.

Multiples are typically considered on both a historical (last 12 months, or LTM) and forward-looking basis to reflect a company's current and forecast performance. Depending on the relevance of capital markets, equity valuation multiples (such as price/earnings, or price/earnings to growth multiples) are also employed to complete the picture. More specific multiples based on company-specific site due diligence (such as EV/container vessels) can provide additional insight into the target's value.

CLOSING

Arriving at a company's valuation is a critical (and at times contentious) part of PE investing, as it translates the business plan and investment thesis into an estimate of the business's value. It establishes the basis for the price that a PE fund is willing to pay for a target company (or an equity stake therein). Yet valuation does not equal the bid or purchase price, as we discuss in the next chapter. Valuation continues to play a part during the holding period; Chapter 19 goes into greater detail and covers performance reporting to limited partners. Lastly, valuation resurfaces in the exit process (Chapter 15) when the PE fund switches to the role of a seller.

KEY LEARNING POINTS

• At the core of any valuation process stands a detailed business plan that translates a target's forward-looking risks and opportunities into a multiyear financial forecast.

• For VC investments in early-stage companies, valuation is typically used as a tool to determine the equity stake a VC firm requires for a given dollar amount invested, taking into account the VC's target return.

• For growth equity and buyout investments in mature companies, valuation is typically based on a target's profit and cash flow and corresponding multiples of comparable businesses.

• An important part of the valuation process is to develop a consistent way to compare potential investments. Specifically, investors will use a valuation multiple—which provides a market-based, "apples to apples" method—to determine the value of a target using data drawn from a comparable set of companies.

RELEVANT CASE STUDIES

from *Private Equity in Action—Case Studies from Developed and Emerging Markets*

Case #5: Sula Vineyards: Indian Wine?—Ce n'est pas possible!

Case #10: Investor Growth Capital: The Bredbandsbolaget Investment

Cases #11 and 12: Chips on the Side (A and B): The Buyout of Avago Technologies

REFERENCES AND ADDITIONAL READING

Goedhart, M., Koller, T. and Wessels, D. (2005) *The Right Roles for Valuations*, McKinsey on Finance, Spring, http://www.mckinsey.com/business-functions/strategy-and-corporate-finance/our-insights/the-right-role-for-multiples-in-valuation.

International Private Equity and Venture Capital Valuation Guidelines (2015) Developed by the IPEV board with endorsement from over 20 PE and VC associations globally, December, http://www.privateequityvaluation.com/valuation-guidelines/4588034291.

Salman, William A. (2009) Basic Venture Capital Formula, HBS class note, May.

Vild, J. and Zeisberger, C. (2014) Strategic Buyers vs Private Equity Buyers in an Investment Process, INSEAD Working Paper No. 2014/39/DSC/EFE (SSRN), May 21, http://centres.insead.edu/global-private-equity-initiative/research-publications/documents/PE-strategic-buyer-workingdoc.pdf.

The valuation of a target company as discussed in the previous chapter represents only the first step of determining the ultimate bid or purchase price in a private equity (PE) transaction. Indeed, the initial valuation is based on an incomplete set of information and assumptions around business plan drivers such as revenue growth, margins and the likelihood of various operating scenarios to play out, as well as a number of assumptions around imperfect pricing inputs such as multiples or discount rates. Given these uncertainties, a target's initial valuation will likely be adjusted as further due diligence uncovers additional risk factors or challenges to the planned improvement or growth of the company's business.

Although price is often the main consideration in a transaction, particularly for existing owners selling a 100% stake in a business, it is not the only driver that seals a deal, and the highest price will not guarantee a winning bid. Sellers will consider other factors when selecting a suitable PE buyer or partner in a live transaction setting, such as the form of purchase consideration (e.g., cash versus non-cash financing), the likelihood of a buyer achieving a successful closing (closing certainty), the operating and strategic know-how a buyer brings to the table and the professionalism and speed with which a buyer progresses through the sales process.

This chapter covers three major steps in deal pricing: (1) bidding for a deal (i.e., what you have to pay to "win"), (2) buyout pricing adjustments to the bid and closing mechanisms, and (3) post-closing price adjustments. We focus on PE investments in mature companies, specifically leveraged buyouts (LBOs) and deals in a competitive process, given that they are the most complex.[1]

BIDDING FOR A DEAL
SETTING THE PRICE AND WINNING THE DEAL

In an LBO, PE firms often pursue targets in a competitive sales process. It is in a PE firm's interest to bid as low as possible both to account for the assumptions and execution risk of a target's business plan and to boost returns (buy low–sell high). However, buyers need to meet the seller's acceptable reservation price—or a price that is perceived to be "fair"—and outbid (not necessarily only monetarily) the competition. Aside from explicit pricing terms and implicit value-add, in most processes the buyer needs to build trust and avoid triggering a defiant response by the seller.

Bids for target companies are often made with varying degrees of access to the target's financials, strategy and management, i.e., based on imperfect information.

---

1. The dynamics in venture investments is different and is addressed in detail in Chapter 2 Venture Capital and Chapter 7 Target Valuation.

The amount of data available to the PE firm will change over the course of the due diligence process and bidders revise their bid as new facts emerge and competitive tension comes into play.

For example, two key reference points for valuation in buyout investments are the last 12 months (LTM) or, alternatively, the forward looking next 12 months (NTM) earnings before interest, taxes, depreciation and amortization (EBITDA) and the respective EBITDA multiple.[2] Throughout the process, EBITDA adjustments may be required as more information becomes available. Adjustments to EBITDA may be driven by a number of factors: revenue and cost recognition policies, pro forma adjustments for acquisitions and disposals, and management compensation and expenses. Such modifications may also affect the overall funding structure of the deal, given EBITDA's role in determining the amount of debt financing available in a buyout. In addition, new information can drive adjustments to the EBITDA multiple, as performance and market-adjusted risk at comparable companies change and new comparable transactions are executed. All these changes filter through and drive adjustments in the enterprise valuation on which a PE fund's bid hinges.

Another key input factor for the bid price is the planned amount and structure of debt in the transaction. While EBITDA and debt multiples[3] serve as a guide to the amount of debt available, buyout firms ultimately determine the exact debt package in cooperation with their lead financing banks. Buyout firms typically consider multiple debt offers from a range of competing banks when pursuing a buyout; these packages can have a distinct impact on the bid pricing. For instance, a higher dollar amount of debt allows a buyout firm to increase its bidding price while maintaining a steady target internal rate of return (IRR). As shown in Exhibit 8.1, higher debt levels allow for a more competitive bid while maintaining the same target IRR (in this case 24%). Total equity capital actually decreases in this example, while the financial risk of the target company increases. After selecting the most appropriate debt package, buyout firms will also model an investment's expected return for different bid prices based on a fixed amount of debt and a variable amount of equity capital.

Exhibit 8.1 Leverage, LBO Pricing and Return

FIXED IRR				FIXED DEBT			
TARGET IRR	DEBT	EQUITY	BID	TARGET IRR	DEBT	EQUITY	BID
24%	630	578	1208	30%	720	440	1160
24%	720	540	1260	24%	720	540	1260
24%	810	502	1312	19%	720	640	1360

When settling on the final debt structure, the predictability of the target company's cash flows and the overall risk–return profile of the transaction will be key determinants.

---

2. EBITDA is often used as a proxy for cash flow. However, in many cases, the characteristics of the business may require the buyer to cross-reference the resultant price with other metrics like EBITDA-maintenance capex or EBITDA less net cost of providing vendor financing to customers.

3. Debt multiple is a measure of a company's ability to manage and pay off its debt. It is a ratio of debt/EBITDA.

TWO-STAGE AUCTION

Frequently, and almost always in deals concerning large and mega buyouts, multiple parties compete for the right to acquire a target company. This competition is typically organized by an investment bank (the sell-side advisor) to maximize the price and certainty realized by the seller. In such a sales process, bidders enter into a structured auction process designed to produce a winner from a progressively narrowing field of interested bidders. While there are many formats and types of auctions, we explore the competitive dynamic in a typical two-stage auction process, shown in Exhibit 8.2.

Exhibit 8.2 Two-stage Auction Process

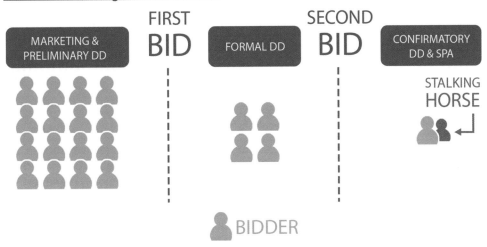

An auction is typically launched after the seller and its advisors have marketed the opportunity to a number of potential buyers. After conducting preliminary due diligence based on a restricted amount of information provided by the target, interested parties are invited to submit an initial, non-binding bid within a certain time period to show commitment to the process. This process helps to narrow the field of potential buyers to identify the most committed bidders. This bid can be a number or a target range based on the bidder's initial assessment of the target's value. Based on bids collected in the first round, the seller invites a select group of bidders to conduct formal due diligence on the company by providing, for example, expanded access to management, access to a physical or virtual data room, and the opportunity to conduct site visits.

Unless the target company is a public company, the bidding parties and the bid values from the initial round are sealed. Nevertheless, as sellers and their advisors are incentivized to realize the highest price for a sale, bluffing and gamesmanship are to be expected in the auction process. The seller and its advisors may communicate an indicative range from the initial round of bidding to anchor bidders or try to entice the most promising bidders to increase their bids to win the auction. Any actual references to competing bids would typically be a breach of non-disclosure agreements with the bidders, yet sell-side advisors at times do push the legal boundaries.

After reviewing the bids from the first round, the seller invites a limited number of bidders to submit a second, binding bid, which will determine the winner of the auction. To draw out key terms in addition to price, second-round bidders receive sample sale and purchase agreements (SPAs), which they mark up and return to the seller on the final bid date. The winning party will typically request and be granted exclusivity—or enforcement of standstill provisions—to conduct confirmatory due diligence and negotiate the final transaction documentation. These measures restrict the seller from engaging with other potential buyers over a specified period of time and protect the interests of the winning bidder, as finalizing an SPA and other transaction documentation incurs heavy legal and accounting expenses. A bidder may also request cost cover or a break-up fee to dissuade the seller from using its bid as a tool to attract more favorable bids from other interested buyers; a provision which allows it to match any higher or topping bid may also be added. Additionally, a runner-up bidder could consent to act as a stalking horse, in the hope that the winning bid might fall apart or drop. Yet, given the small chance of this happening this bidder might expect a generous break-up fee or at least cost cover in return for staying engaged.

Box 8.1

BIDDING STRATEGIES IN AN AUCTION

Determining an appropriate bidding strategy in an auction is a subjective process. Bidders must develop valuation and bid values under the time pressure imposed by the auction process and based on an information set that is typically managed closely by the target company. In the first round, parties invited to the auction typically "bid on the book" (meaning the information memorandum provided); their conviction of the target's attractiveness will be the key consideration when deciding how aggressive a bid to submit and how to marshal resources to proceed to the second round. Compounding the pressure and uncertainty leading up to the second round of bidding is the lack of information on other competing bidders, competitors' activity and, in some instances, uncertainty on the number of contenders involved in the auction. So, all bidding parties rely to varying degrees on rumors and information about the process in the market.

Changes from first-round bids must be carefully considered based on additional information on the target provided by the seller, any feedback on the auction process garnered from the seller and its advisors and a bidder's target return. A bidder may consider employing a jump bid in the second round, representing a substantial increase above perceived bids in the first round in an attempt to lock up the deal. At the same time, bidders are wary of the "winner's curse" where they end up paying substantially more than other bidders often more than the fair value of the company as it turns out later. The price implied by a fund's minimum target return theoretically represents the bidder's maximum bid. A PE fund interested in a target may also choose not to participate in an auction, and rather extend a pre-emptive bid in an attempt to clearly surpass rivals taking part in the auction, or may wait for a failed auction and step in on short notice.

Deal Pricing Dynamics Outside the Financial Model

By Veronica Eng, Retired Founder Partner, Permira

Imagine the following situation:

Due diligence suggests that you have a plausible business plan. Benchmarking of most of the parameters of the business plan against competitors' indicates that the assumptions are ambitious but not overstretched. The price range derived from applying the average/median industry LTM and NTM EBITDA and cycle multiples to your business plan appears supported by other valuation methodologies. At this price, using the proposed funding structure, the returns are at the lower end of your acceptable risk adjusted returns.

You have submitted your preliminary bid. The vendors' advisers have indicated that you have just got into the next round of the auction but your bid is still not compelling enough—they always say that!

What other factors, outside of the traditional valuation methodologies, could encourage you to improve your bid or what implicit risks are there in the existing valuation which would strengthen your resolve that you have already put your best foot forward?

- Don't assume EBITDA is a proxy to Cash Flows

  Should a company which is already well invested and does not require significant ongoing capex be valued at the same EBITDA multiple as one with a much lower cash conversion? Whilst cash generation is implicit in the overall LBO model, insufficient attention tends to be given to the sustainable cash conversion (free cash flow as a percentage of EBITDA) characteristics of the target. Could you pay more because the business is more cash generative?

- Management Capability

  The veracity of the business plan is dependent inter alia on the quality of the management team. An experienced and well-rounded management team will give you higher confidence in their ability to achieve or exceed the business plan. A serial PE CEO/CFO in the team will give you a better and more experienced platform for the transition from a subsidiary of a conglomerate to a lean, fast paced leveraged stand-alone company. Could your bid be improved as a result of this confidence?

- Uniqueness of the Final Exiting Asset

  The value of the final exiting asset ultimately depends on what others will be willing to pay at that point of time. This can depend on its strategic value as much as its profitability. Will the final exiting business have any comparative uniqueness? Will the business become an interesting "must-have" asset for some? Will they be prepared to pay a premium then but not now? Why? Is your management team capable of delivering such a business? In such a situation, would you be prepared to pay up?

- Foreign Exchange Risk

  Most PE funds are denominated in US dollars or Euros. The funds invest in businesses in countries whose base currencies are different from those of the funds. In addition, most companies today are affected by foreign exchange movements whether it be selling outside the home territory, sourcing from abroad or competitive advantage from where it operates. Whilst PE transactions are often structured to mitigate some of the forex risk suffered at the investee company level, there is little consensus on how to deal with it at the fund level. Do you synthetically price future currency movements of the investment into the returns calculation? If so, do you use the forward rates or the cost of options or…since you are unlikely to know the exit quantum or timing? What aspects of this risk are implicit in your returns calculation for this target? Do you have a fund currency advantage in this investment vs competitive bids from funds denominated in a different currency?

- Fund Portfolio Construction

  Is the investing PE fund already a well performing fund? If this is the case, the envisaged lower returns from this investment at a marginally higher price are not likely to have any material effect on the overall acceptable range of outcome for the fund. As such, would the fund accept a lower risk adjusted return investment to complete its investment program?

  Some food for thought, after all there is no prize for coming second in an auction.

BUYOUT PRICING ADJUSTMENTS AND CLOSING MECHANISMS

Once a winning bid has established a headline purchase price—i.e., an in-principle agreed upon price—the buyer and seller negotiate the final purchase price. Although the broad principles are set out in a bid letter or a marked-up SPA, the exact amount and composition of transaction proceeds are subject to a series of pricing adjustments. These adjustments require clear definitions of two balance sheet entries—net debt and target working capital—as well as a closing mechanism defining how and when they are measured. The starting point for defining net debt and target working capital is typically a company's historical financial statements. Both these definitions and closing mechanisms are ultimately formalized at signing in the SPA. See Exhibit 8.3, for a starting definition.

NET DEBT: A company's net debt is subtracted from the headline purchase price to determine the portion of transaction proceeds that flow to selling equity shareholders. The main components of net debt are interest-bearing bank borrowings and cash, two components that can be clearly derived from the balance sheet and are typically not negotiated. Which elements of the remaining components, debt-like liabilities and

Exhibit 8.3 Net Debt and Target Working Capital Definitions

$$\text{NET DEBT} = \left(\begin{array}{c} \text{INTEREST-BEARING LIABILITIES} \\ + \\ \text{DEBT-LIKE LIABILITIES} \end{array} \right) - \left(\begin{array}{c} \text{CASH} \\ + \\ \text{CASH EQUIVALENTS} \end{array} \right)$$

$$\text{TARGET WORKING CAPITAL} = \left(\begin{array}{c} \text{ACCOUNTS RECEIVABLE} \\ + \\ \text{INVENTORY} \\ + \\ \text{PREPAID EXPENSES} \end{array} \right) - \left(\begin{array}{c} \text{ACCOUNTS PAYABLE} \\ + \\ \text{ACCRUED LIABILITIES} \end{array} \right)$$

cash equivalents, will be included in net debt is often the subject of intense negotiation. Debt-like liabilities include capital and financial leases, pension liabilities, deferred tax, taxes payable, deposits and balances between the target and its affiliates. Cash-like items include outstanding checks, restricted cash, foreign cash and credit card payments in transit.

WORKING CAPITAL: Typically, buyers and sellers determine a normalized working capital or base case working capital required to operate the target at a "steady state." Defining this base case can be a contentious point, particularly in the context of a fast-growing business, where revenue may expand substantially between signing and closing. For deals priced on a debt-free/cash-free[4] basis, the definition of working capital includes accounts receivable (net of reserves), inventory, prepaid expenses, accounts payable and accrued liabilities. In such deals, key negotiated items include how to value the largest components of working capital—accounts receivable, inventory and accounts payable—and which items to include in the prepaid expenses and accrued liabilities. Yet, given that businesses often need to carry a cash balance to continue operations, a buyer may require a seller to leave an amount of petty cash on the balance sheet that will be added to the purchase price in the working capital adjustment.

CLOSING MECHANISMS

The closing mechanism set out in a transaction's SPA defines the manner in which net debt and target working capital will be measured. The two main mechanisms used in a buyout are the locked-box mechanism and the completion accounts mechanism.

LOCKED-BOX MECHANISM: A locked-box mechanism is a fixed-price mechanism that sets the value of net debt and working capital at a specific date (known as the locked-box date) before the signing of the SPA. This date is usually a relatively recent

---

4. Most M&A deals are priced on a debt-free/cash-free basis, which means that the seller receives all cash and pays off all debt from the target at the time of sale.

one, between the last annual balance sheet date and the date of SPA signing. When this mechanism is employed, the economic risk of the target is transferred to the buyer as of the locked-box date, and the buyer receives all cash profits generated by the target from that date onward. As both net debt and target working capital values are clearly defined in the SPA, the exact proceeds flowing to existing equity shareholders are known as of deal closing. As the seller will continue to run the target between the locked-box and closing dates, the buyer often pays an interest charge or daily profit rate to compensate the seller for running the target.

COMPLETION ACCOUNTS MECHANISM: A completion accounts mechanism adjusts the preliminary purchase price based on the difference between a company's net debt and target working capital at signing and the actual balance sheet values at closing. This mechanism thus protects both the buyer and seller from deviation in these balance sheet items pre-closing. Adjustments may also be made for items including target and realized capital expenditure. Completion accounts are typically prepared within an agreed period after transaction closing. The adjustment of the purchase price can either result in the seller receiving a lower adjusted purchase price or the buyer increasing its payment to the seller. When completion accounts are employed, both the economic and legal risks of the business pass to the buyer only at closing.

The primary difference between the locked-box mechanism and the completion accounts mechanism is the date when the economic risk of the target company is transferred. With the locked-box mechanism, the economic risk of the target passes to the buyer at the locked-box date; given that the buyer does not yet control the business between signing and closing, there is a mismatch of the transfer of financial risk and the transfer of legal risk and control over management between buyer and seller. This mismatch is mitigated by provisions included in the SPA that grant the buyer some control over the target company and provisions that protect the buyer from leakage[5] between the locked-box date and closing. Completion accounts, on the other hand, pass both economic and legal risk to the buyer at transaction closing.

POST-CLOSING PRICE ADJUSTMENTS AND REMEDIES

The final purchase price determined by the closing mechanism is delivered at closing. However, in some instances, the conclusive purchase price is subject to change and proceeds may change hands after the closing date. Two of these instances include a contingent payment making up part of the purchase price or a breach of contract.

---

5. Leakage comprises any transfer of value from the acquired business to the seller between the locked-box and closing dates, often in the form of dividends, bonuses or other cash transfers. Transfers that do not constitute leakage are typically made explicit in transaction documentation.

CONTINGENT PAYMENT: A contingent payment defers settlement of a portion of the purchase price to a later date. This final payment is subject to the performance of the target company, typically tied to a metric such as EBITDA, over a specified time period following transaction closing. When the target company is performing well (poorly), the contingent payment will result in a higher (lower) total purchase price via the contingent payment mechanism.

BREACH OF CONTRACT: Post-closing monetary remedies due to a breach of contract are typically paid from the seller to the buyer and result from, among other things, breaches of seller representation and warranties and post-closing covenants.[6] An SPA often includes indemnification provisions that set out monetary remedies for specific contractual breaches and a mechanism to calculate the exact remedies due. Indemnification mechanisms typically specify the maximum dollar amount rewardable under a specific breach (the cap), the minimum amount at which a claim can be made given a specific breach (the "de minimis" amount), and a cumulative dollar threshold for all remedies subject to indemnification, which, once crossed, triggers payment (the basket). The basket can be structured in two ways: if the threshold is reached, the indemnitor has to pay either the total amount of losses accrued or only the amount of losses in excess of the threshold. Funds released under an indemnification claim are subject to adjustments based on other indemnification obligations or claims between the parties.

Box 8.2

PUBLIC-TO-PRIVATE

In a public-to-private (P2P) transaction, a buyout fund acquires and delists a publicly traded company. Motivations for taking a company private include reducing agency risk by focusing ownership, implementing a governance structure that increases accountability of management teams, using a more aggressive financing structure and embarking on a strategic or operational repositioning of the company. The public nature of the target and regulation designed to protect the interest of retail investors introduce unique elements to the sales process. P2Ps were particularly prevalent during—and a major driver of—the 2006/07 peak in buyout activity, accounting for 43% and 50% of the total capital invested in buyouts in each year, respectively (see Exhibit 8.4).

P2P transactions are heavily regulated by both financial regulators and the national stock exchanges on which targets are listed. Therefore, relevant regulation can differ significantly from country to country. In general, buyout investors can initiate a P2P transaction in one of three ways: by executing

---

6. Please refer to Chapter 10 Transaction Documentation for additional information on representations and warranties and post-closing covenants.

Exhibit 8.4 Public-to-Privates as a Share of Total Buyouts

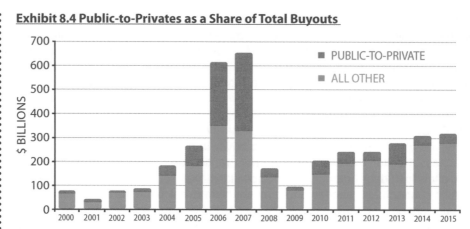

Source: Preqin

a merger agreement, proposing a scheme of arrangement, or making a tender offer for the company's shares. Merger agreements and schemes of arrangement require buyers to engage with the company and its board and are thus considered friendly takeovers; a tender offer represents an unsolicited bid for a company and is considered a hostile takeover. Regardless of which process is employed, a public company's board of directors must negotiate with a prospective investor and decide whether or not to recommend the offer to shareholders based on its fiduciary duty to the same; shareholders ultimately vote to approve or reject the proposal.

A board of director's fiduciary duty adds an additional layer of complexity to a P2P buyout. Public boards' core duty is to maximize shareholder value in the event of an acquisition. If the buyer is a controlling shareholder or includes members of a company's management team represented on the board (as in a management buyout), an independent committee of directors will assume the board's responsibility; existing shareholders participating in the buying group will not be included in the shareholder vote to accept or reject the deal. In the context of a sale with multiple competing bids, the board is obligated to seek the transaction offering the best value; in addition to price, the certainty of a bidder's funds is a crucial consideration, and a lower priced bid with "certain funds" may be selected over a higher bid with less certain financing. To satisfy the board's duty to search for the best possible offer, merger agreements can include a "go shop" provision in which the board may solicit competing offers over a set period and terminate the merger agreement with the original bidder if a superior offer is found.

PE firms typically end up paying a premium to a company's market capitalization in a P2P. A common misconception is that pricing is based on a need to explicitly pay a control premium. In reality, the premium results from the gap between the valuation calculated by the PE firm and that derived from the current market value (market capitalization + unlisted minority interest − net debt) and is meant to entice existing shareholders to tender/sell. In a final check of the transaction, an investment bank or accounting firm will render a fairness opinion that states whether or not a transaction is fair, with a focus on price.

CLOSING

This chapter offered insights into some of the tangible and intangible elements in the PE deal process, bidding strategies, pricing adjustments and closing mechanisms, respectively. While a thorough understanding of the deal pricing mechanics in LBOs is crucial, this is a rather ambiguous part of the investment process that is heavily influenced by experience. It requires the ability to relate to and negotiate with various parties, to recognize and adjust to changing circumstances and in particular lever one's network of professional relationships. We will return to more solid ground in the following chapters as we focus on deal structuring and deal documentation.

KEY LEARNING POINTS

• **The bidding price, based on an initial valuation of the business, is only the starting point in an M&A process. Sellers will consider additional factors when selecting a suitable PE buyer such as the form of purchase consideration, closing certainty, the operating and strategic know-how of a buyer and the professionalism and speed with which a buyer progresses through the sales process.**

• **In many situations, multiple parties compete for the right to acquire a target company. In such cases, bidders enter into a structured auction process—the most common of which is the two-stage auction process—designed to produce a winner from a progressively narrowing field of interested bidders.**

• **In the context of LBO transactions, it is important to understand the different bidding strategies, deal closing mechanisms and post-closing adjustments customarily employed by PE buyers.**

RELEVANT CASE STUDIES

from *Private Equity in Action—Case Studies from Developed and Emerging Markets*

Case #13: Going Places: The Buyout of Amadeus Global Travel Distribution

REFERENCES AND ADDITIONAL READING

Benson, M. and Shippy, J., The M&A Buy Side Process: An Overview for Acquiring Companies, Stout Risius Ross, http://www.srr.com/assets/pdf/mabuysideprocess.pdf.

Brams, Steven J. and Mitts, Joshua (2014) Mechanism Design in M&A Auctions, *Delaware Journal of Corporate Law (DJCL)*, 38(3), https://ssrn.com/abstract=2422577.

Davis Polk and Wardwell LLP, Going Private Transactions: Overview, https://www.davispolk.com/files/uploads/davis.polk.going.private.pdf.

Fidrmuc, Jana P., Roosenboom, Peter, Paap, Richard and Teunissen, Tim (2012) One Size Does Not Fit All: Selling Firms to Private Equity versus Strategic Acquirers, *Journal of Corporate Finance*, 18(4): 828–848.

Hege, Ulrich, Lovo, Stefano, Slovin, Myron B. and Sushka, Marie E. (2013) Asset Sales and the Role of Buyers: Strategic Buyers versus Private Equity, February 25, available at SSRN https://ssrn.com/abstract=1787465 or http://dx.doi.org/10.2139/ssrn.1787465.

Moore, R. and Jenkins, A. Issues in Negotiating Cash-Free Debt-Free Deals, RSM US, http://rsmus.com/pdf/wp_tas_cash_free_debt-free_transactions.pdf.

Sautter, Christina M. (2013) Auction Theory and Standstills: Dealing with Friends and Foes in a Sale of Corporate Control, *Case Western Reserve Law Review*, 64(2), https://ssrn.com/abstract=2207693 or http://dx.doi.org/10.2139/ssrn.2207693.

Tattersall, C., Roth, P. and Pütz, V. (2012) *Share Purchase Agreements: Purchase Price Mechanisms and Current Trends in Practice*, Ernst & Young, http://www.ey.com/Publication/vwLUAssets/EY_TAS_-_Share_Purchase_Agreements_spring_2012/$FILE/EY-SPA%20brochure-spring-2012_eng.pdf.

DEAL STRUCTURING 9

Deal structuring is a process during which private equity (PE) firms secure various forms of capital to fund a buyout transaction and set up a framework of investment vehicles through which the capital will flow. From the PE fund manager's perspective, the process focuses on optimizing a portfolio company's capital structure in terms of timing, cost and contractual obligations, and developing a legal structure of investment vehicles that solidifies the rights and interests of capital providers while minimizing tax and regulatory bottlenecks. These two processes develop in tandem, as the sources of capital influence the optimal legal structure and vice versa.

PE investors use the full array of corporate finance instruments to fund their investment in a target company. The instruments employed establish a clear priority of investors' claims on the target company's cash flow and assets. PE funds typically structure their investments by using a series of special purpose vehicles (SPVs) to ensure the ranking of all stakeholders is clearly defined.

While the instruments and structures used to fund a venture capital (VC) or growth equity investment are relatively straightforward—given these strategies rarely employ debt—deal structuring in a leveraged buyout (LBO) setting is significantly more complex.

In this chapter, we focus our discussion on the funding instruments and SPVs employed in LBO investments; these are the principal considerations underpinning deal structuring. The equity considerations discussed will broadly apply to VC and growth equity investments as well.

BUYOUT FUNDING INSTRUMENTS
DEBT AND EQUITY

Buyout investors fund the acquisition of a target through a mix of debt and equity instruments. The debt portion is typically sourced from a wide range of lenders (mainly banks), while the equity portion in a buyout is contributed by the buyout fund and the management team involved. Buyout investors often employ multiple tranches of debt and equity to optimally align the interests, cost and economic risk of capital providers in the transaction.

Exhibit 9.1 provides an overview of the commonly used financing instruments for PE transactions and their specific characteristics. While it and this section broadly represents the "market standard," the terms governing debt or equity agreements are subject to the specific attributes of a deal and are therefore freely negotiated.

Exhibit 9.1 Characteristics of PE Financing Instruments

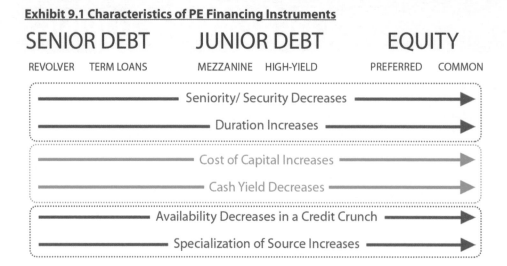

DEBT INSTRUMENTS

In an LBO, buyout firms use significant amounts of debt provided by a range of parties to fund a transaction. The amount of debt available to finance a buyout transaction is driven by the target's ability to generate cash flow for debt servicing and the broad debt market environment.[1] Buyout firms engage with lenders during due diligence and negotiation with the seller to gauge interest in the transaction in the market and develop a suitable funding structure for the acquisition. The characteristics of the main types of debt instruments are described in detail below.

SENIOR DEBT: Senior debt provided by investment banks makes up the majority of leverage in a typical LBO and has a senior claim on the target company's cash flow and assets ahead of all other forms of transaction funding. Moreover, senior debt is often secured by specific assets (collateral) at the target company, strengthening senior debtholders' claims on the company in the event of bankruptcy. Senior debt agreements typically incorporate maintenance covenants tested on a regular basis— for example, an interest coverage ratio (EBITDA/interest expense)—that allow senior lenders to monitor company performance.[2] Seniority, security and covenants reduce the risk for senior debtholders and allow them to lend to the target at the lowest interest rate in the capital structure.

Buyout firms typically run a competitive process among senior lenders, who have access to transaction information under non-disclosure agreements, to secure the most attractive funding terms for the deal. In large buyouts, bank debt is typically provided by a consortium—a group of banks—when the required loans exceed a single lender's capacity. A lead arranger heads due diligence, structures and negotiates the

---

1. Please refer to Chapter 4 Buyouts for additional details on sizing the debt portion.
2. Please refer to Chapter 10 Transaction Documentation for additional information on debt covenants.

commercial terms of the debt agreement, and represents the consortium throughout the investment and holding period; other banks are invited to participate in the offering on the same terms as co-arrangers. The arrangers might later decide to sell some of their exposure in a syndication process to other banks. Senior bank debt may also be securitized and sold on as individual leveraged loans or via collateralized loan obligations.

Senior debt typically consists of the following tranches, in order of seniority:

- *Revolving credit facility (RCF):* An RCF (or revolver) is a line of bank credit predominantly used to fund a target's working capital needs. At the time of the acquisition, revolvers are used to repay the target's existing RCF and to fund working capital adjustments to the target's purchase price. Post-closing, the borrower may draw and repay loans from an RCF up to an agreed limit throughout the term of the facility. These facilities typically have mandatory repayments once or twice a year and may require that any excess cash be used to repay the facility before dividend payments are made to shareholders (a so-called "cash sweep").

- *First lien term loan:* First lien term loans make up a large portion of an LBO's acquisition financing. These loans are typically senior secured, providing a robust claim on company assets in the instance of bankruptcy. LBOs are typically financed through multiple tranches of first lien term loans (e.g., term loans A, B and C). Term loan A typically has the lowest interest rate and the shortest maturity (between five and seven years) and is amortized—or repaid—on an annual basis over the life of the loan. Term loans B and C typically have a slightly higher interest rate, slightly longer maturity (between five and eight years) and are repaid via a single, "bullet" payment at loan maturity (although they might also require some nominal amortization).

- *Second lien term loans:* Second lien loans are used as a bridge between core, first lien term loans and junior debt. Providers of second lien term loans often range from syndicate banks to other institutional debt investors. These loans have higher interest rates and longer maturities (9 to 10 years) than first lien term loans and are typically repaid via a single, bullet payment. Second lien loans are secured against the same collateral as first lien loans but are only entitled to claims on secured collateral after the first lien debtholders are paid in full. In contrast, second lien debtholders typically have an equal claim on unsecured assets as first lien debtholders.

JUNIOR DEBT: Junior debt consists of a range of unsecured, subordinated debt instruments and ranks second to senior debtholder claims in the event of bankruptcy. Maturities for junior debt typically extend a few years beyond senior debt maturities with bullet repayments due at maturity. Junior debt often features both cash interest and interest paid-in-kind (PIK), which defers a portion of interest payments until the repayment of the loan itself. Junior debt covenants are both fewer in number and are mostly structured as incurrence covenants, which are only tested (incurred) in specific situations, for example when the company plans to pay a shareholder dividend. As a result, junior debtholders typically let senior debtholders take the lead in monitoring the operating performance of the company. To compensate for the higher risk taken, junior debt instruments are typically priced at a significant premium to senior debt.

Common forms of junior debt are mezzanine loans and high yield bonds.

- *Mezzanine loans:* This form of junior debt is raised in the private institutional market from a single lender or a small group of lenders; mezzanine providers include specialist mezzanine funds, PE funds, hedge funds, and institutional investors. In addition to the terms listed above, mezzanine loans may offer additional upside to lenders by employing an "equity kicker" through a convertible debt feature or attached warrants.[3] These "kickers" are typically included to increase the return profile of an issue and in turn attract investor participation in the offering.

- *High yield bonds:* High yield bonds are marketed and sold in the public debt market. Unlike senior and mezzanine financing, high yield bond issuance is tightly regulated and typically requires a rating, listing on a stock exchange and reporting throughout the life of the bond.[4] Due to the rules and regulations governing the marketing and sale of securities to public investors, issuing high yield bonds can be a lengthy process relative to private debt placements; as a result, these bonds are often used to replace bridge loans or other short-term debt after a buyout transaction has closed.[5] As the listing process and ongoing obligations associated with this debt can be timely and expensive, PE firms expect to pay lower interest rates than for mezzanine and other forms of junior debt.

BRIDGE LOANS: Bridge loans are typically short-term, secured credit facilities that provide temporary debt capital at transaction closing while a PE fund secures longer-term financing. Bridge loan commitments are typically secured from investment banks but may in some instances be provided directly by the PE fund or other capital providers. Oftentimes a bridge loan commitment is never drawn, as long-term financing is frequently secured between deal signing and closing. If a bridge loan is drawn, the company will try to refinance it with permanent, long-term debt quickly as the interest rates of these facilities are normally higher than those of other LBO loan tranches and increase—often to an agreed-upon cap—the longer the bridge loan is in place. If a borrower does not repay a bridge loan at the end of its term, the bridge will automatically convert into a long-term loan with an interest rate at a significant premium to market rates. These escalating interest rates are designed to encourage the prompt refinancing of the bridge.

VENDOR FINANCING: Vendor financing reduces the cash required to execute a transaction by rolling over or delaying full payment of transaction proceeds. This type of financing typically comes in two forms: vendor debt and earn-outs. As the name implies, vendor debt is provided by the target's existing owners and essentially rolls a portion of seller proceeds back into the target company. Vendor debt is typically unsecured and subordinated to junior and senior debt, but senior to shareholder loans and equity; interest payments are typically moderate to high and PIK. An earn-out, on the other hand, represents an agreement to pay a portion

---

3. Warrants are options to purchase the target's shares at a predetermined price when certain trigger events occur (for example, a change of control, a sale or an internal public offering).
4. Rating agencies monitor the debt throughout its life, and a bond's rating affects its price and marketability.
5. As high yield debt issues can take longer to place than bridge facilities, high yield debt issues may be under way, but not yet closed, prior to an LBO deal closing.

of seller proceeds at a later date. The magnitude of an earn-out is typically subject to a company's operating performance post-closing, and only strong performance will result in additional payments to the seller. Earn-outs are commonly employed when a vendor continues to manage the business post-closing—for example, in a management buyout—and demonstrates the seller's willingness to keep some "skin in the game."

SHAREHOLDER LOANS: Shareholder loans are the most junior form of debt and are provided by equity shareholders; these loans are principally provided by buyout funds and, to a lesser extent, management teams. Shareholder loans typically provide interest PIK, with the cumulative interest and loan principal repaid at exit or refinancing. Shareholder loans are often employed to establish the seniority of equity investors and to structure management compensation plans. Given their quasi-equity status, cash interest payments serving shareholder loans are not tax deductible in many jurisdictions.

EQUITY INSTRUMENTS

The equity portion of an LBO is typically underwritten by a single PE fund or a group of PE funds and company management. PE funds usually provide the majority of the equity capital, with management teams co-investing to align economic interests with the PE firm. Management often rolls existing equity stakes in the target into the LBO funding structure. The characteristics of the most common forms of equity are detailed below.

PREFERRED SHARES: Preferred shares are a senior form of equity that provides shareholders with certain preferential rights relative to common equity shareholders. PE funds typically hold the majority of preferred shares in an LBO, although a portion of management's co-investment may also be made through preferred shares. Economic rights typically include a liquidation preference, which provides a senior claim on residual cash flow in the event of exit or bankruptcy, and a dividend preference, which provides a cash or accumulated annual dividend payment. Control rights include special voting rights and the ability to force the 100% sale of company equity.

COMMON EQUITY: Common equity is the most junior instrument in a company's capital structure and provides a residual claim on cash flow and company assets after claims of all other capital providers are satisfied. Common equity ownership in a PE transaction is the primary tool used to align the interests of PE sponsors and management teams via a management incentive plan. Management team members typically own a larger proportion of common equity—or fully diluted common equity when options are employed in the plan—relative to their proportion of total equity capital invested. Thus, this "sweet equity" can provide a high return on investment if the company does well; however, if an investment performs poorly, management's stake is at risk of being wiped out.[6]

---

6. Please refer to Chapter 12 Securing Management Teams for further information on management incentive structures.

The Art of Deal Structuring

By Guy Hands, Chairman and Chief Investment Officer, Terra Firma

Private equity has two main advantages over public markets. The first is that shares are not marked day-to-day; the second is that investors stay with you for longer. Whereas the average holding period for US stocks in 2015 was around 17 weeks, private equity firms held on to buyout investments for five-and-a-half years or longer.

Operationally oriented PE firms can take advantage of this longer time horizon to create significant value by fundamentally transforming businesses. This can mean changing their strategy, strengthening management teams, investing in capital expenditure, growing through M&A and, importantly, improving their capital structure. With a robust capital structure in place, regardless of where the market goes, a business should succeed if it has the right strategy.

Many private equity investors implement capital structures designed to maximize returns, assuming their original business plan will work out. In reality, business plans rarely match expectations; businesses invariably either over-perform or under-perform.

What I have learned over three decades of investing is that it is essential to outline a realistic downside scenario for every business. You then must be confident that the capital structure you put in place is sufficiently robust to withstand this downside scenario, or indeed a broader downturn in financial markets. If your capital structure is sufficiently prudent, then the business can survive difficult circumstances. If not, then regardless of the operational strength of the business, there is a significant possibility that you can lose control and not benefit from the business's future recovery.

Terra Firma experienced both of these scenarios following the global financial crisis in 2007–2008. The first was with Tank & Rast, the leading operator of service stations on Germany's Autobahn, which was acquired in 2004. The second was with EMI, which was one of the world's largest music companies.

Both businesses were refinanced in 2007 on terms that were realistic at the time. However, once the financial crisis hit a few months later, the terms in both cases were no longer considered appropriate by their lenders.

Tank & Rast had four lenders, and while none of them were happy with the loan, no single lender felt the need to take action. Terra Firma was left to implement its strategic transformation of Tank & Rast, and as a result EBITDA grew from €179 million in 2007 to €208 million in 2011 generating further value for investors, contributing to an ultimate return of 7.5x invested capital upon the final sale of the business in 2015.

In contrast, EMI had a single lender, whose loan to EMI was one of its largest single-lender loans. Terra Firma also implemented a transformational strategy at EMI, which by 2011 had borne fruit. EMI's EBITDA grew from £68 million in 2007 to £334 million in 2010, an outstanding increase in profitability, especially considering revenues fell slightly over the same period.

Despite this success, and despite the fact that EMI was meeting its interest payments, the lender seized the company in 2011, relying on the balance sheet insolvency covenant in the loan documentation. As it happened, markets and multiples recovered from 2012 onwards; with the transformation of EMI's EBITDA over this period and the recovery of multiples, EMI's value would have likely materially exceeded the debt and the equity would have had real value.

From these experiences, we learnt two valuable lessons. First, it is essential to keep control of a business throughout the economic cycle. Second, syndicating debt as widely as possible reduces the risk that a single lender will feel the need to seize a company mid-transformation.

This is important, as history shows that sizeable shocks occur in financial markets every five to 15 years; or, in private equity terms, once in approximately every three funds. Putting in place robust capital structures therefore allows businesses with a solid strategy to succeed over the long term, without having to depend on markets to create upside on their behalf.

INVESTMENT STRUCTURES AND SPVs

A typical LBO structure consists of a series of newly established SPVs each funded by an individual debt or equity instrument. Capital from each SPV flows through the investment structure to a "BidCo," the legal entity that executes the acquisition of the target company from its vendor. Channeling capital through this type of investment structure reinforces the contractual rights of different capital providers.

To clarify the rationale and mechanics underpinning an LBO investment structure, we will explore two hypothetical structures, beginning with a simple structure (Exhibit 9.2) and progressing to one that is more complex.

Our simple LBO is financed by—in order of seniority—senior debt, a shareholder loan and common equity. Senior debt is secured directly by BidCo, while funding from the shareholder loan provided by the PE fund and common equity injected by the PE fund plus management flow into a separate vehicle, which we have labeled EquityCo. All capital invested into EquityCo then flows into BidCo, typically through an intercompany loan, and BidCo is fully financed to execute the acquisition of the target. Given the nature of the funding instruments employed at each layer of the structure, EquityCo—and in turn the PE fund and management—control the target.

Why do PE funds employ this type of holding structure? For one, SPVs can be set up in different jurisdictions to help maximize access to collateral for lenders and optimize regulatory and tax treatment of the LBO. Employing individual entities reduces the

Exhibit 9.2 Simple PE Investment Structure

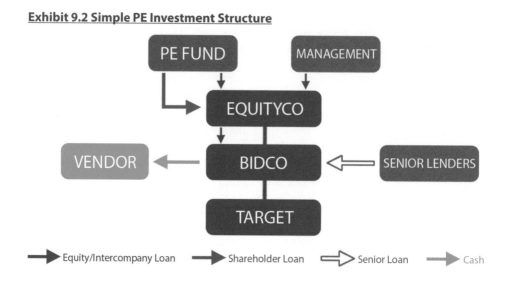

risk that debt capital will be treated as equity and interest payments will be treated as dividends, which would eliminate the tax deductibility of interest payments to debtholders. While BidCo is typically situated in the same jurisdiction as the target, other SPVs in the investment structure may be set up in various onshore and offshore jurisdictions to optimize the tax treatments of dividends, capital gains and interests. Establishing holding companies in different jurisdictions can also address the needs of individual capital providers and prepare the business for future strategic activities including the exit of the PE investor.

DEBT CONSIDERATIONS—STRUCTURAL AND CONTRACTUAL SUBORDINATION

A buyout needs to accommodate various stakeholders, in particular multiple debt providers; it is therefore vital to ensure that the subordination of claims on the target business is clearly defined and documented. Contractual relationships are supported by structural subordination, which we explain by referencing the complex investment structure in Exhibit 9.3. In this example, separate vehicles are established for each funding instrument: a senior loan, a mezzanine loan, a shareholder loan and common equity (listed in order of seniority). As in our simplified structure, funding flows through the structure via intercompany loans to fund the acquisition of the target by BidCo.

Structural subordination is achieved as follows: claims on cash flow and assets for the loan provider to each SPV must be satisfied before cash is available to pay the intercompany loan to more junior SPVs. For example, the claims of senior lenders on BidCo must be satisfied before cash is released to MezzCo (the SPV funded by the mezzanine loan); the claims of mezzanine lenders must be paid before cash is released to PrefCo (the SPV funded by the shareholder loan), and so on. As a result, the seniority established in loan documentation—referred to as contractual subordination—is reinforced by employing acquisition SPVs in this manner. This type of investment structure is required by debt providers in an LBO.

Exhibit 9.3 Complex PE Investment Structure

After an LBO is executed, senior lenders often require a debt pushdown that shifts their claim from BidCo to the operating company.[7] A debt pushdown can be achieved by merging BidCo and the target, transferring income-generating assets from the target company to the acquisition vehicle (BidCo), repaying acquisition debt through a new debt issue of the target company with the same senior lenders, or through novation.[8] By executing a debt pushdown, senior lenders have a direct claim on operating company assets and eliminate the structural subordination of senior lenders to trade creditors. Debt pushdowns are also beneficial from a tax standpoint as they eliminate uncertainty with regards to the deductibility of interest payments from taxable income generated by the operating company.

EQUITY CONSIDERATIONS

Equity capital providers in a PE investment often employ multiple SPVs to segregate their funding in a buyout. To highlight the process, we add a co-investor to our simple PE investment structure (Exhibit 9.2) and focus on the capital flowing into EquityCo in Exhibit 9.4. In this transaction, capital flows from the PE fund and co-investor into an intermediate SPV that owns a predetermined mix—often referred to as the

---

7. The obligation to execute a debt pushdown is often included in senior debt loan agreements.
8. Novation involves replacing one party with another in a contract; in this case, for example, the operating company would replace BidCo in the debt agreement between senior debt providers and BidCo.

Exhibit 9.4 Equity Vehicles in PE Investment Structure

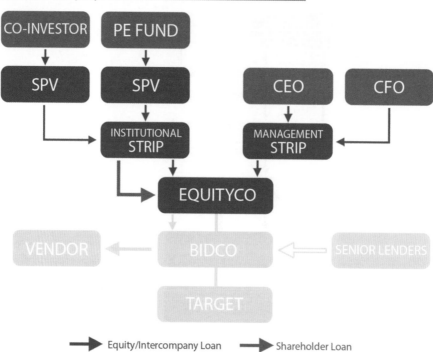

institutional strip—of shares in EquityCo. Management capital flows into a separate vehicle that owns a different mix—which we call the management strip—of shares in EquityCo. The aggregated capital in EquityCo is again transferred to BidCo through an intercompany loan.

Typically, each capital provider sets up its own SPV to clearly separate streams of equity capital with different rights. Arranging an investment in this manner also insulates a PE fund from liabilities associated with a specific portfolio company and allows for more flexibility if an individual shareholder wishes (and is permitted) to exit. In addition, it can provide a beneficial tax treatment (depending on the chosen jurisdiction of the SPV). In a buyout context, various entities are often set up to isolate the different co-investors or to separate the PE fund from management, while in a growth capital or venture capital investment, different SPVs may be used to separate the investments in a syndicated round.

CLOSING

Structuring a (buyout) transaction is a complex undertaking. A variety of considerations (tax, seniority, cost) go into selecting the preferred instruments and investment structure. While professional advisors can help at every step along the way, experience in structuring can be a competitive advantage and not only speed up execution but also increase the certainty of closing.

KEY LEARNING POINTS

• **Buyout investors use a variety of debt and equity instruments with specific characteristics to fund an LBO; VC and growth equity investors typically only use equity.**

• **When structuring a debt package, investors can chose from a wide range of debt instruments with different price points, cash cost and levels of flexibility, in a market that continues to innovate and expand rapidly.**

• **Debt and equity capital provided to fund an LBO typically flows through a series of SPVs that reinforce the seniority of the capital providers' economic claims on a target's cash flow and assets via structural subordination.**

RELEVANT CASE STUDIES

from *Private Equity in Action—Case Studies from Developed and Emerging Markets*

Cases #11 and 12: Chips on the Side (A and B): The Buyout of Avago Technologies

Case #13: Going Places: The Buyout of Amadeus Global Travel Distribution

REFERENCES AND ADDITIONAL READING

Axelson, Ulf, Jenkinson, Tim, Weisbach, Michael S. and Strömberg, Per (2007) Leverage and Pricing in Buyouts: An Empirical Analysis, Swedish Institute for Financial Research Conference on the Economics of the Private Equity Market, August, available at SSRN: https://ssrn.com/abstract=1027127 or http://dx.doi.org/10.2139/ssrn.1027127.

Darley, Mark (2009) Debt, in *A Practitioner's Guide to Private Equity*, Soundy, Mark, Spangler, Timothy and Hampton, Alison (eds), Sweet and Maxwell, https://www.skadden.com/sites/default/files/publications/Publications1877_0.pdf.

Demiroglu, Cem and James, Christopher M. (March 5, 2010) The Role of Private Equity Group Reputation in LBO Financing, *Journal of Financial Economics (JFE)*, 96(2 May): 306–330, available at SSRN: https://ssrn.com/abstract=1032781.

Gompers, Paul, Ivashina, Victoria and van Gool, Joris (2013) Note on LBO Capital Structure, Harvard Business School Module Note 214–039, October.

Ivashina, Victoria (2013) Note on the Leveraged Loan Market, Harvard Business School Module Note 9-214-047.

Yates, G. and Hinchliffe, M. (2010) *A Practical Guide to Private Equity Transactions*, Cambridge University Press.

All venture, growth equity and buyout deals are complex and require clear and detailed documentation to ensure that the parties involved understand the risks as well as their rights and responsibilities in the respective transaction. The number of stakeholders involved will vary from deal to deal and may include one or several private equity (PE) firms and funds, the target company, equity owners of the target, debt providers, and any number of consultants, advisors and other service providers. Legal documentation clarifies the key terms and conditions governing a transaction, establishes rights, protects the interests of all parties during the holding period, and provides guidance for a future exit process.

This chapter begins by discussing the key negotiation points and the essential documentation in a PE transaction. It is a highly technical chapter—reader beware—designed to draw out important commercial considerations of the various deal documents. We round up the chapter with a review of the documentation for debt and equity investment.

PE TRANSACTION DOCUMENTATION

A PE fund enters into a range of contractual agreements with the target company and its owners that define everyone's rights and obligations at specific points in an investment process. While the documents employed vary from jurisdiction to jurisdiction and deal to deal, we identify the primary transaction documents governing the deal sourcing, due diligence, and negotiation processes. We focus predominantly on documentation for the buyout of a mature company, as shown in Exhibit 10.1.

Exhibit 10.1 Key Transaction Documentation in a Buyout

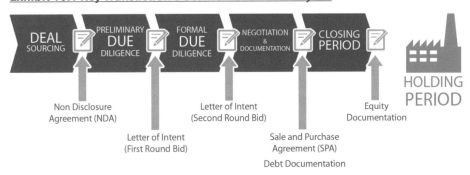

NON-DISCLOSURE AGREEMENT (NDA): At the beginning of any due diligence process, a PE fund and the target company execute a non-disclosure agreement (NDA) to exchange confidential information. An NDA places an obligation on both parties to refrain from sharing privileged information with external parties post-signing; this obligation does not apply to information that becomes publicly available, through no fault of the parties, while the NDA is in force. The NDA covers confidential information shared throughout the due diligence, negotiation, and closing processes and parts may continue to apply even when the business is not acquired. NDAs can be structured to protect a one-way or a mutual flow of information. For PE transactions, these agreements are usually one way, as the target does not generally need to access privileged information about the PE fund. Key points of negotiation for an NDA include its term, coverage and the inclusion of indemnities to define monetary remedies in the event of a breach. Obligations established by an NDA may be replaced or amplified by other confidentiality agreements entered into throughout the investment process.

THE LETTER OF INTENT (LOI): Letters of intent (LOIs) function as bidding documents and set out key economic and procedural terms that form the basis for further negotiations in a buyout process. General economic terms include the dollar amount of a PE fund's bid, sources of funding and the envisioned transaction structure. These economic provisions are non-binding and seen as a "good faith" representation of a fund's intent and an initial indication of the terms to be included in a sale and purchase agreement. PE firms and sellers use LOIs to ensure that there is general alignment on key terms before incurring the expense of in-depth due diligence and before negotiating a definitive sale and purchase agreement. An exclusivity provision, which grants the PE fund the sole right to purchase the business for a specific time period is often included in the final bid's LOI. A signed LOI can allow parties to initiate regulatory and government approval processes for the transaction and, specifically, a PE fund to credibly approach banks and other capital providers for transaction financing.

SALE AND PURCHASE AGREEMENT: A sale and purchase agreement (SPA) is the main contract entered into by a PE fund and the existing owners of a target company; it governs the terms and conditions of the envisioned transaction and the acquisition process. The SPA reflects key findings from due diligence, target valuation, deal pricing, deal structuring and other commercial, accounting and legal considerations negotiated between the PE firm and the seller. The two pivotal stages of an SPA are "signing" or execution, when parties enter into an SPA and agree to satisfy certain pre-closing obligations, and "closing" or completion, when all terms and conditions of an SPA come into force, funding for the transaction is released and the PE fund formally acquires the target company. Signing and closing may occur on the same date, but there is typically a period of time in between.

While each transaction is unique, most SPAs include a set of common provisions describing the responsibilities of the buyer and seller. These agreements typically detail a sale and purchase of either a target's assets (asset purchase agreement) or its existing equity shares (share purchase agreement). The section that follows outlines provisions common to these agreements.

- *Purchase and sale:* In this clause of the SPA, a fund agrees to purchase and existing owners agree to sell either the assets—such as the rights, titles and interests of the target company—or the equity interest in the target. The purchase price for the transaction and the specific instruments used to fund the transaction are also detailed here.[1] The counterparties to the SPA may agree to a purchase price fixed at signing via a "locked-box" mechanism or a preliminary purchase price to be

---

1. Please refer to Chapter 9 Deal Structuring for a description of the common instruments used to fund a PE transaction.

adjusted at closing via a completion accounts mechanism.[2] The purchase and sale clause also sets out the time and location for transaction closing and a long-stop date, by which time the transaction must close or parties to the SPA can effectively terminate the agreement.

- *Representations and warranties:* Representations and warranties ("reps and warranties") are statements of fact and promises that underpin specific elements of the transaction set out in the SPA. A representation is a statement of fact that was influential in inducing a buyer or seller to enter into the SPA; a warranty is a promise that a statement of fact is true. Reps and warranties are principally used to offer protection to a buyer in case a vendor's statements of fact regarding the target business prove to be false, to allocate a portion of performance risk at the target company to the seller and to provide an opportunity for a buyer to gain additional information on the target. The effects of a breach of reps and warranties and the remedies available to an aggrieved party vary across jurisdictions but can range from a party being entitled to terminate the SPA to damages.

- *Covenants:* Covenants are contractual promises that require the parties in an SPA to take or refrain from specific actions before or after transaction closing, and are typically made by the seller in favor of the buyer. Covenants may describe actions that a party is required to take (affirmative covenants) or actions a party must avoid (negative covenants). The primary purpose of pre-closing covenants is to ensure that at closing the buyer finds the target in substantially the same state as at signing of the SPA. The primary purpose of post-closing covenants is to restrict the seller from taking actions over a defined period of time that would harm the competitiveness or destroy value at the target company. Failure to comply with a pre-closing covenant results in a breach of contract, with remedies available to the aggrieved party ranging from termination of the SPA to seeking damages. A failure to comply with a post-closing covenant also represents a breach of contract, with remedies available to the aggrieved party limited to seeking damages.

- *Indemnification:* Indemnification provisions set out monetary remedies that protect a party to an SPA from losses associated with identified risks of a business. These provisions provide both the buyer and seller with certainty as to their legal rights and responsibilities in the instance of a specific breach, removing the uncertainty of pursuing a legal claim in court or arbitration. Indemnification provisions typically apply to breaches of seller reps and warranties or post-closing covenants related to the performance of the target company and provide monetary remedy limited to a maximum dollar amount to the buyer. These clauses are thus key drivers for allocating risk post-closing, as the seller's liability for losses sustained by the business post-closing are typically limited. To ensure that the seller has sufficient funds to satisfy any indemnity if needed, the buyer typically pays part of the purchase price into an indemnity escrow account at closing.

---

2. Please refer to Chapter 8 Deal Pricing Dynamics for a description of "locked-box" and "completion accounts" mechanisms.

- *Conditions precedent (CPs):* CPs are specific events or states of affairs that must be satisfied or waived for the transaction to proceed. The SPA assigns responsibility to either the buyer or the seller to satisfy a CP on a best efforts basis. If a CP is not met, the other party can choose to walk away from the transaction or waive that right. The main consideration regarding CPs for the buyer and seller is to ensure that the other party does not have too much flexibility to walk away from a transaction. Pre-closing covenants form the basis of CPs in an SPA. A standard CP for mid-sized and larger transactions are antitrust and other regulatory approvals from relevant governmental agencies.

- *Material adverse change (MAC):* A MAC clause provides a buyer with the right to terminate the SPA in case of a material event that impairs the value of the target company. The specific definition of what constitutes a MAC at the target company varies from transaction to transaction and is formalized in the definitions of an SPA. Buyers seek to define a MAC in broad terms to maximize optionality while the seller seeks narrow terms to limit the buyer's ability to terminate the SPA.

- *Termination rights/Break-up fee:* Termination provisions describe the circumstances that allow a party to terminate the acquisition agreement prior to closing. Some of the most common circumstances are: mutual written consent of both parties, a material breach of the reps and warranties, failure to perform a covenant, a legal impediment or the failure to have met all the closing conditions by the long-stop date. The SPA sometimes includes provisions that impose financial penalties on the party terminating the agreement, referred to as break-up or break fees in the case of termination by the seller or reverse break-up fees in the case of termination by the buyer. These fees are intended to cover the transaction costs of the party not terminating the transaction.

DEBT COMMITMENT LETTERS: Debt commitment letters are typically addressed to a buyout fund's acquisition vehicle by the lead arranger[3] of a leveraged buyout (LBO)'s debt financing. Securing a debt commitment letter is often required before a seller will sign an SPA to provide funding certainty for the seller. These letters are often subject to specific closing conditions—principally negotiation of loan documents—for the envisioned loan to come into force. A market flex provision allows for certain terms to be changed in the event of a significant change of conditions in the lending market.

EQUITY COMMITMENT LETTERS: Equity commitment letters, addressed by a PE fund to its acquisition vehicle, provide a limited guarantee for the equity financing detailed in an SPA. Securing these letters is often required for the PE fund to enter into an SPA and to satisfy buyer financing reps and warranties. These letters typically set out specific terms and conditions that must be satisfied for the enforcement of the fund's commitment. In some instances, the PE fund may directly provide a limited guarantee for the equity component of the transaction.

---

3. Please refer to Chapter 9 Deal Structuring for a description of the lead arranger and other bank roles in an LBO.

Deal Documentation—"Clean Exit" vs. Purchaser Protection

By Heiner Braun, Partner, Freshfields Bruckhaus Deringer LLP

These days, M&A transactions are often won or lost in competitive auctions, and deal documentation is a key factor in winning those auctions. When selecting its preferred bidder, a seller will not only look at the valuation and purchase price offered by the bidder, but also consider its approach to documentation. The Sales and Purchase Agreement (SPA) is typically the place where parties' interests must be reconciled.

Usually, a bidder will seek a certain level of protection and, therefore, ask for warranties regarding its investment. In contrast, private equity sellers in particular strive towards a "clean exit." This can be achieved by excluding potential post-closing liabilities as far as possible. In an ideal seller's world, the warranties under the SPA are limited to capacity (authority to bind signatory party) and title to shares.

Private equity buyers are typically more flexible in terms of entertaining the concept of a "clean exit" than strategic buyers, who need to show a certain set of protections for their shareholders and internal compliance purposes. This holds true in particular for listed companies and state-owned enterprises, such as from China. Rather than asking for protection under the deal documentation, private equity buyers may improve their position by taking a commercial approach. Based on a comprehensive legal, financial and tax due diligence review, potential risks associated with the target may be evaluated and deducted from the purchase price.

When selling a company, private equity firms will consider their approach to deal documentation very early in the process. The appropriate set up should be determined from a tactical point of view, taking into account which bidders the asset will attract and how competitive the process can be run. An attractive asset to be sold to other private equity firms may allow the seller to kick off the process with only a few or no warranties at all. As a fall-back position, the seller may always offer broader protections subject, however, to its liability being capped.

Depending on the timing of the process, the seller may involve a warranty & indemnity insurer right from the beginning. This could, at a premium, cap the seller's liability at even one dollar, with the insurance covering the real exposure. These insurance policies have become extremely prevalent in mature M&A markets in recent years, but are less common in emerging markets where assets are generally perceived as involving higher risk.

The auction process can be kicked off not only with a more buyer-friendly SPA but also with a "stapled" warranty & indemnity insurance policy ready to be signed by the purchaser. Alternatively, the seller may simply offer a very small liability cap and ask the bidders to take out insurance on their own. Having a "shadow set of warranties" on the shelf might help the seller to quickly react to achieve a compromise on this point.

Where the seller knows that warranties will be required, in less mature markets or for a less attractive assets, or an asset where strategic buyers will have an edge over financial sponsors (because of synergies or otherwise) it may be useful to prepare, in close cooperation with the target company's management, a set of operational warranties that can be offered. This allows the seller to make an informed proposal on the warranty and liability concept.

BUYOUT DEBT DOCUMENTATION

In an LBO, a PE fund negotiates two main agreements with debt providers, that govern the borrowers' and lenders' rights during the transaction and the period the loans remain outstanding: loan agreements and intercreditor agreements. The section that follows presents the main provisions included in these contracts.

LOAN AGREEMENTS

Loan (or credit) agreements are entered into between a PE fund's acquisition SPV and a debt provider for an LBO. These documents set out the terms and conditions governing the debt issuance process, economic rights of the lender and the performance requirements of the target company following loan disbursal. The commercial intent of the main provisions of a loan agreement is set out below.

AMOUNT AND TERMS OF LOAN: This section of the agreement describes specific characteristics of the loan, including but not limited to:

- The amount of capital provided by the loan
- The loan's interest rate, usually a market rate (e.g., LIBOR) plus a spread[4]
- The fees associated with the loan (frequently spelled out in a separate fee letter)
- The loan's term and repayment schedule
- Any collateral provided as security for loan repayment (typically specified in great detail in separate security documentation)

REPRESENTATIONS AND WARRANTIES: The key function of reps and warranties in a loan agreement is to provide the lender with a mechanism to terminate the loan agreement in the event of a breach post-signing. Specific reps and warranties included in the loan agreement are typically aligned with those found in the SPA that allow the buyer to terminate the transaction; these provisions focus on the state of the target company and the accuracy of information provided describing the target. Borrower reps and

---

4. Please refer to Chapter 9 Deal Structuring for a description of the costs and other characteristics of different types of debt.

warranties are often reasserted at specific dates during the loan's term to reconfirm the state of the operating company and the accuracy of information shared.

CONDITIONS PRECEDENT (CPs): As mentioned earlier, CPs are specific events or states of affairs that must be satisfied or waived for the transaction to proceed. In loan agreements, CPs fall into two categories: documentary CPs and event CPs. Once again, CPs in loan agreements typically align closely with CPs included in the SPA to reduce uncertainty (they are "back to back"). Documentary CPs may include delivery of due diligence reports, legal opinions, latest financial reports, the agreed-upon base case financial model and—ultimately—an executed SPA. Event CPs include the accuracy of reps and warranties and the absence of a default.

CONDITIONS SUBSEQUENT: A condition subsequent clause sets out details of outstanding conditions at closing and the date by which the borrower must satisfy them (often 90 days). In some instances, where a borrower does not satisfy a condition precedent in time for drawdown, the lender may still disburse the loan if the borrower agrees to satisfy the condition by a future date. Failure to fulfill a condition within the set time period will usually trigger an event of default.

COVENANTS: Covenants are the key monitoring mechanism following a loan's disbursement and are divided into financial and non-financial covenants. Financial covenants define certain thresholds of operating performance within which the target company must perform; the failure of doing so results in a breach of contract. Common financial covenants include interest coverage and debt-to-equity ratios; Exhibit 10.2 details how a company's financial performance feeds into a covenant calculation—in this, a cash flow to total debt service covenant—and the available margin for error (headroom) the company has. Financial covenants are either maintenance or incurrence covenants.[5] Non-financial covenants can be divided into general information and business covenants, which ensure that lenders are provided

Exhibit 10.2 Cash Flow Cover—Cash Flow to Debt Service

COVENANT TIMING		2015			
		Q1	Q2	Q3	Q4
FINANCIAL PERFORMANCE	**CASH FLOW**	**251.4**	**274.5**	**283.6**	**291.1**
	TOTAL NET INTEREST COSTS	(109.6)	(108.6)	(107.4)	(105.5)
	DEBT REPAYMENT	(44.5)	(63.5)	(63.5)	(86.7)
	TOTAL DEBT SERVICE (LTM)	**(154.1)**	**(172.1)**	**(170.8)**	**(192.2)**
COVENANT TEST	ACTUAL RATIO (x)	1.63	1.60	1.66	1.51
	COVENANT (x)	1.00	1.00	1.00	1.00
	HEADROOM (TOTAL)	97.3	102.4	112.8	98.9
	HEADROOM (% OF CASH FLOW)	38.7%	37.3%	39.8%	34.0%

---

5. Please refer to Chapter 9 Deal Structuring for information on the various covenants that apply to different types of debt.

the information required to monitor the target and that the target company is operated according to applicable law and commercial regulation. The number and stringency of these covenants range from minimal (known as covenant-lite) to major. Breach of these covenants results in an event of default.

EVENTS OF DEFAULT: Events of default in a loan include a long list of occurrences or circumstances that provide a lender with the right but not the obligation to, for example, accelerate loan repayment or require immediate repayment of the loan. Common default events include failure of the borrower to meet interest or principal payments, breach of a financial covenant, or breach of a representation or warranty. Default can also be triggered due to an event of default in another loan agreement, which is referred to as a cross-default.

INTERCREDITOR AGREEMENT

Intercreditor agreements govern the various rankings and rights among debt providers in an LBO. This agreement principally serves to protect the rights of senior lenders by clearly defining the rights of each debt provider in the event of default. In addition to debt providers, all counterparties to the loan agreements of an LBO—including acquisition SPVs and the target company as well as equity providers—may be party to the intercreditor agreement. Intercreditor agreements only come into effect upon completion of the SPA. The key provisions of an intercreditor agreement are described below.

PAYMENT SUBORDINATION: Payment subordination determines the order of claims on unsecured assets for all of a company's creditors in the event of default. This type of subordination ensures that the claims of senior debtholders are paid in full before junior debtholders receive compensation.

LIEN SUBORDINATION: Also referred to as security subordination, lien subordination determines the order of claims on collateral for a company's secured creditors in the event of default and security enforcement. Secured lenders can be divided into first lien lenders and second lien lenders; in the event of default, the total amount of debt provided by first lien debtholders must be repaid before second lien lenders have a claim on residual value. The intercreditor agreement may set a cap on claims of first lien creditors before second lien lenders become eligible for security claims.

STANDSTILL PERIODS: Standstill periods prevent junior debtholders from taking any action to enforce their claim in the event of a default—including declaring a default in the first place, accelerating debt payment, or taking legal action—over a predetermined time. Standstill periods are designed to allow senior debtholders ample opportunity to determine an optimal course of action without interference from junior debtholders.

PAYMENT BLOCKAGE: Payment blockage provisions restrict the borrower from making payments to junior lenders in the event of default before claims of senior debtholders are satisfied. Where there is only breach of a financial covenant in the senior loan agreements, the payment blockage period is potentially infinite. Some junior lenders insist on a limit on the aggregate term of payment blockage periods in a given year, and request that catch-up payments be permitted once the senior default is cured or solved.

TURNOVER PROVISION: If junior debtholders do receive compensation in the event of default before senior claims are satisfied, a turnover provision requires that these proceeds be turned over to senior creditors to satisfy their claims.

SENIOR DEBT LIMIT: These provisions limit the amount of additional senior debt that can be issued by a borrower without the consent of junior debtholders. These limits protect junior debtholders and increase the likelihood that they will receive compensation in the event of default.

EQUITY DOCUMENTATION
FOR MAJORITY AND MINORITY INVESTMENTS

Given that venture capital (VC), growth equity and buyout funds all acquire an equity stake in a target business, the equity documentation and provisions detailed below apply to all three types of PE investments. Some terms and conditions are more relevant to one particular strategy than others.[6]

The articles of association (AOA)—also referred to as the Articles of Incorporation, Certificate of Incorporation, and other names depending on the jurisdiction—and the shareholder agreement (SHA) are the key documents governing the rights and obligations of shareholders in PE investments. An AOA is a mandatory agreement entered into between the portfolio company and its shareholders and is filed with a government institution post-closing; an AOA typically includes a limited amount of information that the company and its shareholders are required to disclose. Additional shareholder rights and obligations not included in the AOA are then included in an SHA, a private agreement that defines the relationship among all shareholders and between shareholders and the portfolio company. An SHA is more flexible than an AOA and can include nearly any provision; as a private document, it often includes more sensitive agreements among shareholders.

Broadly speaking, AOAs define the economic rights of different equity shareholders while SHAs define each shareholder's control and additional economic rights, as shown in Exhibit 10.3 and detailed in the section that follows.

Exhibit 10.3 Key Provisions in Equity Documentation

ECONOMIC PROVISIONS	CONTROL PROVISIONS
Shareholding Structure	Board of Directors
Liquidation Preference	Board Deadlock
Dividend Preference	Share Transfer Restrictions
Good Leaver/Bad Leaver	Drag-along/Tag-along Provisions

6. Readers interested in specific terms governing VC investments should refer to Chapter 2 Venture Capital for a discussion on term sheets, and those more interested in minority shareholding rights in a growth equity deal should refer to Chapter 3 Growth Equity.

ECONOMICS

The economic provisions of equity documentation in a PE-backed company deal mainly with the types of shares issued by the company and their return characteristics.

SHAREHOLDING STRUCTURE: Most PE-backed companies issue at least two types of shares, preferred shares and common shares. In a buyout, PE funds typically invest the vast majority of their capital into preferred shares, with a small portion allocated to common equity. For management teams it is the opposite, with the majority if not all of their capital invested into common equity. This shareholding structure allows for the implementation of management incentive schemes to ensure that the interests of both parties are aligned.[7] In a VC round or growth equity investment, the incoming PE fund typically invests in a newly issued preferred shareholding class.

LIQUIDATION PREFERENCE: Preferred shareholders typically hold a priority claim on the proceeds realized from a liquidity event—including outright sale of the company, change of control or bankruptcy—relative to common shareholders. This liquidation preference is typically equal to the dollar amount invested in the preferred shareholding class. Once the liquidation and any dividend preference are satisfied, the residual proceeds from an exit flow to common shareholders.

DIVIDEND PREFERENCE: Preferred shareholders are often entitled to a preferred return in the form of a dividend preference. Frequently, dividends awarded under this clause are not paid out but rather accumulate during the holding period and are settled at exit. The cash dividends due to preferred shareholders must be paid before common shareholders receive any dividend or proceeds from exit.

GOOD LEAVER/BAD LEAVER: The good leaver/bad leaver provision determines what value is assigned to the shares of a management team member if he or she leaves the company before an exit event. The provision differentiates between a management team member who resigns for acceptable reasons—a "good leaver"—and one who resigns for unacceptable reasons—a "bad leaver." The value received for such shareholdings ranges from the share's fair market value for a good leaver in the best case to merely the reimbursement of a manager's investment in a buyout for a bad leaver in the worst case. This provision sets out the mechanism for determining the appropriate compensation for the resigning manager.

CONTROL

Equity documents in both minority and majority transactions lay out details of the board of directors and define additional control rights for shareholders and those related to managing liquidity events.

BOARD OF DIRECTORS: This provision describes the structure of the board of directors and defines the voting rights of shareholders. A PE board typically consists of representatives of the PE fund, existing owners, management team members like the

---

7. Please refer to Chapter 12 Securing Management Teams for further details and examples of management incentive schemes.

CEO or CFO, and independent directors.[8] When a co-investor—typically a PE fund's limited partner or another PE fund—participates in a buyout it may receive rights to appoint a board representative or observer.

BOARD DEADLOCK: A deadlock occurs when a board resolution fails to achieve majority support. Board deadlock provisions set out a mechanism to prevent such a situation from occurring.

SHARE TRANSFER RESTRICTIONS: Share transfer restrictions give existing shareholders the right to purchase the shares of another shareholder if he or she decides to sell. These rights enable existing shareholders to block sales of shares to investors not acceptable to the existing owners.

DRAG-ALONG/TAG-ALONG PROVISIONS: A drag-along provision provides the majority shareholder with the right to force other shareholders to sell their shares in a third-party transaction. This provision enables the majority shareholder to sell all the shares in a company to achieve a clean break at exit, and is often a prerequisite for sale to a strategic investor. Conversely, a tag-along provision provides minority shareholders with the right to sell their shares in conjunction with the majority shareholder, allowing minority shareholders to participate in a liquidity event pro rata with an exiting majority shareholder.

CLOSING

Transaction documentation—as technical a topic as it may be—is indeed crucial in the context of the complex investments made by PE funds and concludes our section on PE deal-making. With the deal successfully executed and the investment made, it is now time to start managing the acquired portfolio companies and executing on the investment thesis to work towards a successful exit in a few years' time.

KEY LEARNING POINTS

• **Transaction documentation—principally the NDA, LOI and SPA—represents the key contracts entered into between a PE fund and a target company's owners during the investment process.**

• **Debt documentation—principally credit agreements and intercreditor agreements—governs the rights and obligations of lenders and the target during the PE holding period and at exit.**

• **Equity documentation—in particular a company's AOA and its SHA—governs the economic and control rights of shareholders during the investment period and at exit.**

---

8. Please refer to Chapter 11 Corporate Governance for additional details on the composition and role of boards in a buyout and minority setting.

REFERENCES AND ADDITIONAL READING

Cunningham, R.L. and Galil, Y.Y. (2009) Lien Subordination and Intercreditor Agreements, *The Review of Banking & Financial Services*, May, http://www .gibsondunn.com/publications/Documents/Cunningham-Galil-LienSubordinationInter creditorAgreements.pdf.

Darley, Mark (2009) Debt, in *A Practitioner's Guide to Private Equity*. Soundy, Mark, Spangler, Timothy and Hampton, Alison (eds). Sweet and Maxwell, https://www .skadden.com/sites/default/files/publications/Publications1877_0.pdf.

Marrocco, A.J. (2016) Negotiating Critical Representations and Warranties in Franchise Mergers and Acquisitions—Part I, *Franchise Law Journal*, 36(1), Summer, http://www .americanbar.org/content/dam/aba/publications/franchise_lawyer/summer2016/flj-v36-1-marrocco.authcheckdam.pdf.

SECTION III
Managing PE Investments

The third section of our book covers the post-investment period during which value is created and ultimately realized upon exit. This may be the most crucial phase of the investment process, when the ability to execute well-laid plans will ensure a positive return on investment and when a private equity (PE) firm will need to contend with risks and opportunities not identified during the due diligence. As PE professionals say: "any fool can make an investment; it is what you do afterwards that counts."

The foundation of the post-investment phase is a solid corporate governance model implemented by the PE investor, which begins with clear monitoring mechanisms to keep all stakeholders informed and to fulfill the firm's fiduciary duty towards its limited partners (LPs).

However, PE investors are known to be hands-on owners and it is through active and, in the case of buyouts, tightly controlled boards that they supervise, guide and ultimately improve a company's prospects and value. Of course, senior management and their executive teams are the key to a successful transformation of the company as they translate strategic plans into actionable agenda items and steer execution. Senior executives will enjoy the opportunity to effect real change when working with a dedicated and engaged PE owner and will participate handsomely in the financial upside. But then PE owners are also demanding task masters and their relentless push for improvements creates a high-pressure environment not all managers will appreciate.

With an appropriate governance structure and an aligned management team in place, operational value creation becomes the central value driver in the PE model and the true source of "alpha" (excess return); in fact, it may well be the sole factor to differentiate PE firms from their peers in the long run. Operational value creation requires identifying the key initiatives that will deliver the highest potential impact, resourcing them adequately and monitoring them closely until completion. These initiatives may target to improve a company's profitability or to de-risk the investment, both ultimately leading to an improvement in value.

De-risking investments was also the main impetus behind the PE industry's early efforts to incorporate sustainability and responsible investment criteria into their portfolio management frameworks. By now, PE firms have widely adopted environmental, social, and governance (ESG) practices to improve operations and clean up companies for the eventual exit thereby enhancing returns.

PE raises closed-end funds and their finite lifespan requires that PE firms exit their investments in due time; cash-on-cash return is what matters to LPs. High-profile public market offerings obscure the fact that the vast majority of PE exits are made through a sale to either strategic buyers or, increasingly, other financial buyers. Yet no matter what exit route is chosen, only a successful sale validates the investment thesis, enables the fund to show strong returns and allows the PE firm to restart the cycle of fundraising.

Section Overview

The chapters in this section will walk the reader through the post-investment period all the way to the point of exit.

Chapter 11. Corporate Governance: The key features of PE corporate governance—a sense of urgency, active ownership and an alignment of interests with portfolio company management—are vital ingredients on the way to a successful exit. We discuss the role of portfolio company boards in both minority and majority investments.

Chapter 12. Securing Management Teams: PE firms work closely with the management teams in their portfolio companies. It is therefore critical to ensure that their interests are aligned with that of the PE investor, a target that is achieved through shared equity ownership. We explore the dynamics between management teams and PE owners and the structure of PE management compensation plans.

Chapter 13. Operational Value Creation: An active ownership model and hands-on governance allow PE firms to drive operational value creation during the holding period. This chapter describes the key levers for operational value creation, and touches on the need for measuring the impact those initiatives have on the portfolio companies.

Chapter 14. Responsible Investment: Attention towards considerations beyond financial returns has increased alongside LPs' growing appreciation that non-financial factors can have a strong positive impact on sustainable company performance. We explore the role that ESG plays in today's investment environment, explaining why it has become an integral part of modern private equity investing.

Chapter 15. Exit: A PE firm's ability to achieve timely and profitable exits is its key measure of success. It allows PE firms to return capital to its investors and raise follow-on funds successfully. This chapter details the key considerations that drive the exit process and explains the main exit strategies employed by PE funds, stepping through the process and discussing motivations of the various parties involved.

Corporate governance in private equity (PE) refers to the practices, processes and rules put in place to align the interests of owners, investors and management. A sound corporate governance framework is crucial to oversee and coordinate activities at a funds' investee companies. Governance effectively decentralizes decision-making, identifies appropriate performance measures and reward systems, and implements effective tools to monitor performance; it is a fundamental part of PE's formula for success.

Talk to PE practitioners or managers in PE investee companies and three core principles of PE governance stand out: a sense of urgency, active ownership and alignment of interest between the PE fund and its management teams; these elements provide a structure through which portfolio companies are transformed (Exhibit 11.1).

After defining corporate governance in the PE context, we take a closer look at the main institution through which PE firms exert control or influence over their portfolio companies, namely, the board of directors, differentiating between boards in control (buyout) and minority investments [venture capital (VC), growth equity].

Exhibit 11.1 Core Governance Principles in a Buyout

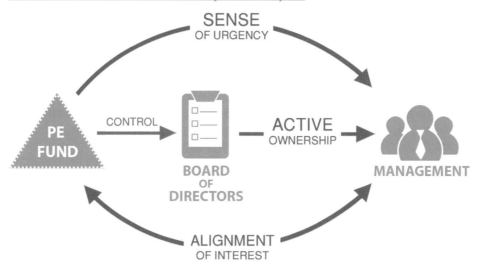

SENSE OF URGENCY

In PE, the formal governance, monitoring and decision-making processes—from the board down to the management team ultimately responsible for implementation of the business plan—are unambiguous and relentlessly focused. The sense of urgency in PE investments results from the ambitious return expectations that need to be realized over a defined investment horizon. PE firms can achieve their desired returns only if they act as transformation agents during their relatively short period of ownership.

The standard return measure in PE, the internal rate of return (IRR), contributes to this urgency by including both the time value of money and the length of the holding period in its calculation.

While there is no single ingredient or "secret sauce" that enables the success of PE investors, it is the focus and urgency across a number of dimensions that make its ownership culture different in aggregate, leading to a high-pressure environment but also a shared sense of direction.

STRATEGIC ALIGNMENT: PE investors, management teams and independent advisors work to reposition the business, reformulate strategy and closely monitor its progress post-investment. A portfolio company's initial strategy predominantly draws on the incumbent management team's vision for the business and other areas identified by the PE investor during due diligence. The company's strategy is discussed with management throughout the pre-deal process not only to receive their input but also to ensure their buy-in for its subsequent implementation. However, the strategy is not set in stone as PE's active ownership model allows ongoing reviews and revisions of strategy and business plan.[1]

LEVERAGE: In leveraged buyouts (LBOs) the presence of (large amounts of) debt creates not only discipline but also focus. Given the uncertainty inherent in the business plan—also referred to as operational risk—PE firms and management focus on reducing financial risk through debt repayment, ideally ahead of schedule. By generating financial headroom as early as possible, a business becomes resilient if operational adversity surfaces or its equity becomes more valuable at an earlier stage in the case of strong business performance. The secret to achieving early deleveraging is of course the generation of excess free cash flow, a clearly defined performance indicator (one single number).

DRIVING OPERATIONAL CHANGE: PE investors, particularly those with a controlling stake, often create special task forces or working groups consisting of board members, the second layer of senior management and outside specialists (as needed) to address high-priority initiatives. These working groups flatten the decision-making hierarchy to increase accountability, concentrate resources and drive execution. The board will rarely introduce more than two or three working groups at any one time to maintain focus on the highest value-add opportunities. Experts from the PE firm may also engage in these groups; however, PE owners will ensure that those groups are well separated from decision-making at the board level to avoid potential liabilities and negative perceptions about the PE firm "running" the company.

MANAGEMENT CHANGE: Backing the right management team is an essential component of success in PE investment, as the chief executive officer (CEO) and the executive team will be the ones to translate the business plan into actionable initiatives and business processes. For PE investors with a controlling stake or considerable influence over a portfolio company's board, changing the management team is always an option; in fact, some sources cite a replacement rate of top management for buyouts in excess of 50%.[2] For existing management teams, this

---

1. Please refer to Chapter 13 Operational Value Creation for details on how PE firms develop strategy and execute value creation plans.
2. Cornelli and Karakas (2012); Gilligan and Wright (2012); Schneider and Lang (2013).

well-understood dynamic and the interest of self-preservation provides additional motivation to execute on the company's strategic plan.[3]

MONITORING: Boards of PE-backed companies continuously monitor key performance indicators and business performance to intervene when necessary. PE partners and independent directors will engage regularly with the firm—be it through frequent meetings of the entire board, ad hoc conversations concerning financial performance, or meetings with junior executives, middle management and line employees—to form a robust view of the value creation levers and risks associated with the business. Timely information sharing and a clear understanding of current performance enabled by robust monitoring practices are critical to making optimal decisions. In the context of LBOs, boards will carefully monitor free cash flow within the organization to ensure compliance with debt covenants and debt servicing agreed with the lenders.

PRIVATE EQUITY AS ACTIVE OWNERS

As highlighted by Michael Jensen in his 1989 article "Eclipse of the Public Corporation" in the *Harvard Business Review*, "active ownership" has been the bedrock of PE investing from the start.[4] Active owners engage closely with their investee companies to shape strategy and management style, monitor performance and drive change. This level of engagement and deep familiarity with the business allows PE investors to leverage their own experience and provide the executive team with timely observations, immediate feedback and coaching when appropriate.

Private Equity's active ownership model is shown in Exhibit 11.2. The board of directors is the main channel through which PE investors execute their rights as owners and influence the performance of their portfolio companies. In addition, PE firms typically

Exhibit 11.2 Active Ownership in PE

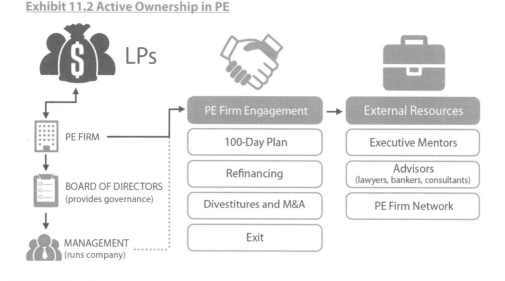

---

3. Please refer to Chapter 12 Securing Management Teams for further thoughts on finding the best management team and management replacement.
4. Jensen (1989).

engage beyond the board, specifically when their expertise can add value, for instance during mergers and acquisitions and refinancing situations. As a repeat player in the acquisition markets and regular buyer of associated services, PE firms can bring domain expertise to their portfolio companies. In high-impact situations, a PE firm will leverage its network of portfolio companies, managers, and external advisors.

THE BOARD IN BUYOUTS AND MAJORITY DEALS

In control situations, PE investors use the board of directors as their main mechanism to monitor and influence the company and management. While they also engage with management directly through informal working relationships or operational teams on the ground, major strategic reviews and planning activities happen at the board level.

Accordingly, PE-backed boards meet much more frequently than publicly listed boards and have a significantly lower percentage of independent directors than do public companies. Due to the limited number of shareholders in most buyouts, boards are typically small and efficient; directors consist of partners of the controlling PE firm, management team members, and a few select independent directors. Each director owes the portfolio company a duty of care, loyalty and confidentiality requiring them to apply best effort to act on behalf of the portfolio company. Partners and employees of the PE firm—or multiple PE firms in the event of a club deal[5]—typically occupy at least half of the seats on a board, and hold the right to effect a decision in the event of a board deadlock.[6]

We look in closer detail at the responsibilities of each type of board member.

PE INVESTORS: The PE firm's board representatives are responsible for setting the strategic direction of the business and provide the key interface between the PE fund and the portfolio company. PE firms typically nominate senior deal team members and/or operating partners as board members. The deal team's lead partner usually occupies a seat on the board to supervise the execution of the investment thesis and take overall responsibility for the investment. Operating partners, often former senior executives with an extensive network and expertise in a given sector, bring operational knowledge and industry expertise to a board setting. PE's financial partners will have repeat experience in managing, restructuring and directing companies in their respective industries, making their advice valuable and often complementary to the company's senior managers.[7]

INDEPENDENT DIRECTORS: Independent directors bring strong networks and overall pedigrees that augment and complement a specific operational, industry or strategic expertise, missing at the PE fund. The expertise of independent directors is becoming more and more relevant with the increased focus on operational value creation post-global financial crisis. Sometimes a senior director, experienced in corporate governance, will be asked to take the role as chairman of the board; this may be

---

5. "Club deals" are buyout investments involving two or more PE funds that pool their capital to execute the deal.
6. Please refer to Chapter 10 Transaction Documentation for more information on board deadlock provisions.
7. PE partners must be cognizant of their multiple fiduciary duties when serving on a portfolio company's board of directors. In addition to their obligations towards the respective company, they must also act in the best interest of their limited partners, i.e., the investors in their fund. Adding further complexity, PE partners may sit on multiple portfolio company boards. In such cases, they have an added obligation to consider the needs of each portfolio company independently, and to ensure that information received when acting on behalf of one is not shared inappropriately with another. .

particularly useful if multiple (prior) owners are involved and a steady hand is needed to balance the various interests. Independents usually receive equity incentives combined with a small board fee to cover expenses.

MANAGEMENT TEAM MEMBERS: Following the closing of a buyout, board representation from management may consist of one or two directors, typically the CEO and the chief financial officer (CFO). These board members are the key interface between owners and secondary layers of management at the operating business. A clearly articulated strategic plan is the tool that helps build and maintain alignment between the management team and its PE investors. CEOs typically work proactively with their teams and board members to translate the strategic areas of focus for the business into day-to-day implementation plans.

Box 11.1

GOVERNANCE IN MINORITY SETTINGS
VENTURE CAPITAL AND GROWTH EQUITY

The corporate governance dynamics on a board with PE as a minority investor are quite different from those found in buyouts. While many of the governance activities highlighted earlier—namely, strategic alignment and rigorous monitoring—apply in a minority context as well, a key differentiating factor is VC and growth equity funds' lack of (equity) control (Exhibit 11.3). As a result, minority investors are not able to initiate activities by leveraging their board majority. Rather, VC and growth equity investors must work alongside the majority shareholder (e.g., an entrepreneur or owner/manager) to complement their skillset and jointly drive value creation. While minority shareholding rights may provide investors with the power to block decisions of the majority shareholder under certain circumstances, such veto rights must be used sparingly and when the stakes are high, given the risk of a backlash from the controlling shareholder.[8]

Exhibit 11.3 Corporate Governance Principles in Minority Settings

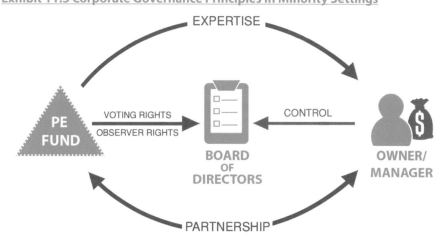

---

8. Please refer to Chapters 3 Growth Equity and Chapter 10 Transaction Documentation for additional information on minority shareholding rights.

Incoming VC or growth equity investors typically secure a board seat or at a minimum board observation rights to participate in formal company decision-making.[9] Minority investor's engagement beyond formal board functions follows no set pattern, with some assuming a highly active, hands-on role and others remaining passive investors. Regardless of an investor's level of formal or informal engagement, minority investors secure information rights that provide regular access to business and financial information on the portfolio company, such as monthly profit and loss statements, the right to visit a company's premises and engage with management and the right to inspect a portfolio company's books.

Specific board dynamics at a VC and growth equity-backed company are described below.

VENTURE CAPITAL: Early-stage VC funds are often the first institutional investor in a start-up, and VC fund representatives may find themselves on a board with an entrepreneur and angel investor who, as first-time board members, are quite inexperienced. Given the often technical rather than business expertise of founding teams, an important role of VC board members is that of a mentor. As a start-up continues to raise money, more VC funds might join the board, adding expertise but also increasing the number of chefs in the kitchen and the potential for conflict; a syndicate of investors in a funding round presents a controlling entrepreneur with an additional layer of complexity when making a decision. In contrast, in a late-stage VC-backed company, control of the board may shift from the entrepreneur to a bloc of VC and growth equity investors, often with one lead investor, as the entrepreneur gives up incrementally more control in exchange for capital.[10]

GROWTH EQUITY: Growth equity investment in small and medium-sized enterprises (SMEs) is often the first external equity raised by the portfolio company, especially in the case of a family business. Business owners are therefore accustomed to running their business independently, often leaving growth equity investors to influence majority owner/managers indirectly. Even so, some elements crucial to PE firms are negotiated upfront, chief among which is an exit provision that allows the minority investor to control the timing—and in some instances the price—of its exit. These provisions may include a "put" right to sell the PE stake back to the company or the right to force the sale of the entire business to an interested strategic buyer, a so-called "drag-along" right. To ensure the overall success of the investment, minority investors will try to influence the "institutionalization" of portfolio firm governance by adding processes and systems to bring the firm up to international standards.

---

9. Observation rights allow a fund's representative to attend all formal board meetings but do not provide voting rights; minority investors often prefer observation rights relative to a board seat to avoid the fiduciary duties associated with the latter.
10. Please refer to Chapter 2 Venture Capital for additional information on the risk and return profile of VC investment.

"Govern a family as you would cook a small fish—very gently"[11]: About growth capital investments in family-owned SMEs in emerging markets

By Idsert Boersma and Martin Steindl, FMO (the Dutch Development Bank)

Many minority investments are made in owner-manager type of small and medium enterprises (SMEs) in which the governance structure is substantially different than what we see in companies with widely dispersed ownership. It implies that a single owner, or a few owners, is deeply involved in the day-to-day management of the company. While this does effectively mitigate agency risk, it—as the flip-side of the coin—also reduces proper checks and balances, because effectively the owner is monitoring his or her own work and wearing (too) many "hats."

In the case of a family-owned SME, family members may be owners, board members, managers or all of the above at the same time. As a matter of fact, the family is another dimension in the triangle of owners—board members—managers that frequently follow different incentives and motivations than those functions that are fully integrated into the company. ***This family dimension is a key complicating factor in the standard PE model according to which interests are mainly aligned by financial incentive-based models (Exhibit 11.4).***

This may come across slightly critical, yet the special family glue is what often made the business successful in the first place. That is something one needs to appreciate and work with as a minority investor.

Exhibit 11.4 The Classic Triangle of Governance vs. Governance in a Family-owned Business

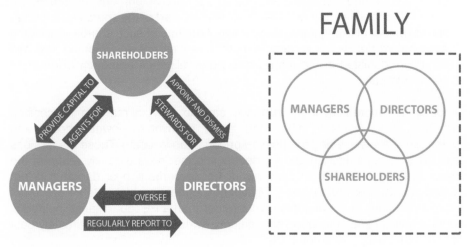

When investing in a family business some of the family members not involved in the company may still have a strong say in how the family should further shape the business. In particular, they might hold a different view on the extent to which outside managers will be involved in the running of the company, compared to the family members one is regularly in contact with as an investor. In other words, when one deals with a family business one must work on the assumption that decisions are not always made where one thinks they are. For example, in one of our investments in India the important issues were discussed during family dinners in the multi-generational family house, frustrating and reducing the influence of our nominated board member.

As a consequence, growth capital investors taking a minority equity stake will have to align with the majority of the original promoter/sponsor family. While entitled to nominate board members, such entitlement, however, will only be in line with the overall minority position. The governance and its potential amendments when entering as a new minority owner therefore become a key due diligence item from a risk point of view but also a paramount value driver for the future exit.

In some cases, a governance-related risk identified during due diligence can effectively be mitigated by nominating a director with a special expertise to the board of the investee company.

- One of our investments, a truck assembler in Asia, was also providing credit/loans to its customers. The credit decision, however, was made by commercial staff, who were incentivized by selling a truck and not by reducing a non-performing loan (NPL). By inviting a former CFO of a truck company to join the board of our investee, who had dealt with the same issue in the past, we were able to strengthen the credit function, reduce NPLs and design a proper incentive mechanism for commercial staff.
- In another deal in East Africa by reaching out to family members exclusively on a one-on-one conversational basis as part of our due diligence, we understood that the "founder" held a substantial part of the shares as a trustee for his mother allowing her to decide about the fate of such shares—including exit—before her death. A "special right" that was not documented and had not been identified in the more classic due diligence approach of our lead co-investor fund.

Another key ingredient in governance can be how to manage succession planning at all levels in which the family is involved—owner, board and managerial levels—during the holding period of an investee. These discussions can become quite intense and go deeply into the "private" family realm of the *pater familias*, especially in case his or her favourite son or daughter is not suited to take over the company. Multiple dialogues in which one needs to act more as a coach to the majority owner rather than a PE "deal maker" helped in various investments to support the majority owner to do what is ultimately best for his "other baby"—the company.

PE GOVERNANCE IN SPECIFIC SETTINGS

The degree and form of engagement with a PE fund's portfolio company varies over its ownership term. PE firms are particularly active immediately following investment and again at exit, with additional engagement depending on the performance of and select activity at the company. We elaborate on these specific contexts below.

THE FIRST 100 DAYS: PE investors engage heavily with their portfolio companies immediately following investment, when the so-called "First-100-Day" plan is launched based on findings from due diligence and initial engagement with the business. The PE firm's board representatives and independent directors will work closely with management to develop an understanding of the intricacies of the business and build a good working relationship. Boards will define immediate business priorities, reach consensus on company strategy, assign roles and responsibilities, and review decision-making and monitoring processes.

STEADY STATE: The degree of interaction during the holding period varies by firm, and changes with the complexity of the deal, the company's strategy and of course its performance. When the business is performing well, PE firms will deploy minimal resources and passively monitor company activity. In the case of a struggling investment, a PE firm may tap partners or independent directors with industry experience to support the company. In particular, changes in the composition of the management team require a high degree of involvement to ensure a smooth transition and keep the risk of losing institutional knowledge to a minimum. In some instances, PE firm representatives may step into an executive role on an interim basis.

ROLL-UPS, ACQUISITIONS AND DEBT: The engagement of the PE firm's partners increases when a portfolio company pursues a roll-up strategy and acquires several competitors to reach economies of scale and improve its market position. As roll-ups are a frequently employed strategy by PE owners, experienced partners can be an invaluable asset to ensure smooth execution. PE investors' familiarity with the full range of financial instruments adds value beyond structuring a fund's initial investment: these investors frequently engage with portfolio companies to assist with new debt issuance, debt refinancing, and monitoring of debt covenants and the cash flow needed to comply with mandatory repayments.

MANAGING THE EXIT: The PE partners' engagement at a portfolio company also ramps up as exit approaches and the business is prepared for sale, potential buyers are identified, and the sale process is launched. Communication and coordination between the PE firm and the management team is crucial to ensure full value is realized for the fund's equity stake and to mitigate conflicts. While incentive schemes will have aligned parties up until exit, the diverging path ahead may introduce conflicting interests between management teams (who are likely to remain with the business following exit) and the PE fund (which will end its relationship with the company at exit). Typical areas for conflict include the preferred exit path,[12] company valuation and management equity roll-over.

---

12. Please refer to Chapter 15 Exit for a detailed discussion on the exit process and the interests of different parties.

ALIGNMENT OF INTEREST
MANAGEMENT INCENTIVES

The last of our three PE governance elements is arguably the best known. Incentivizing management teams and external board members appropriately and in line with the PE owner's goals is a crucial ingredient of the PE model. Aligning interests is typically achieved by requiring managers to co-invest alongside the PE fund in order for them to have real skin in the game. Yet in addition an upside option is typically structured into the package to provide managers with outsized returns in the event of a positive investment outcome for the PE fund. By inviting managers to become co-owners and sharing both the risk and (extra) upside, PE firms reduce the principal–agent conflict prevalent in the today's modern corporations. We will discuss this important corporate governance element further in Chapter 12 Securing Management Teams, including a worked-out example of a management compensation plan.

CLOSING

PE funds are active investors approaching their investments with, as often described, "relentless focus" and a sense of urgency. A clear purpose and short lines of communications combined with PE's ownership philosophy allow PE investors to effectively control their investments in line with a fund's mandate and their fiduciary duty to LPs as well as to influence the value creation process in their portfolio companies.

KEY LEARNING POINTS

• **Three core principles of corporate governance within PE firms stand out: a strong sense of urgency, active ownership and alignment of interest between owners and managers.**

• **The sense of urgency results from a fund's short ownership period and the preferred return measure in PE context (i.e., IRR).**

• **The main forum for setting strategy and monitoring performance is a portfolio company's board of directors, for both minority and majority PE investors.**

• **Engagement with the portfolio company changes throughout the holding period and depends very much on the business's performance.**

RELEVANT CASE STUDIES

from *Private Equity in Action—Case Studies from Developed and Emerging Markets*

Case#10: Investor Growth Capital: The Bredbandsbolaget Investment

Cases #11 and 12: Chips on the Side (A and B): The Buyout of Avago Technologies

Case #13: Going Places: The Buyout of Amadeus Global Travel Distribution

REFERENCES AND ADDITIONAL READING

Acharya, V., Kehoe, C. and Reyner, M. (2008) The Voice of Experience: Public versus Private Equity, McKinsey, http://www.mckinsey.com/business-functions/strategy-and-corporate-finance/our-insights/the-voice-of-experience-public-versus-private-equity.

Beroutsos, A., Freeman, A. and Kehoe, C.F. (2007) What Public Companies Can Learn from Private Equity, McKinsey, http://www.mckinsey.com/business-functions/strategy-and-corporate-finance/our-insights/what-public-companies-can-learn-from-private-equity.

Cornelli, F. and Karakaş, O. (2012) Corporate Governance of LBOs: The Role of Boards, May, available at SSRN https://ssrn.com/abstract=1875649 or http://dx.doi.org/10.2139/ssrn.1875649.

Cumming, Douglas J., Siegel, Donald S. and Wright, Mike (2007) Private Equity, Leveraged Buyouts and Governance, *Journal of Corporate Finance*, 13(4): 439–460, SSRN: https://ssrn.com/abstract=983802.

Davis, E.H. (2009) Minority Investments by Private Equity Funds, Kirkland & Ellis LLP, November 5, https://www.kirkland.com/siteFiles/Publications/8E62BE0BF5EC88C8FCDEF4065D6180E3.pdf.

EVCA Corporate Governance Guidelines (2010), https://dato-images.imgix.net/45/1459783870-F_EVCA_CorporateGovernanceGuidelines_2010.pdf?ixlib=rb-1.1.0.

Gilligan, J. and Wright, M. (2012) Private Equity Demystified: 2012 Update, ICAEW.

Jensen, Michael C. (1989) Eclipse of the Public Corporation, *Harvard Business Review*, retrieved from https://hbr.org/1989/09/eclipse-of-the-public-corporation

McDonald, John J. (2008) Actions That Private Equity Fund Representatives on Corporate Boards Can Take to Help Avoid Liability, *Journal of Private Equity*, 11(4 Fall): 6–11.

Schneider, A. and Lang, N. (2013) Private Equity and the CEO, The Boston Consulting Group, November.

Van Den Berghe, Lutgart A.A. and Levrau, Abigail P.D. (2001) The Role of the Venture Capitalist as Monitor of the Company: A Corporate Governance Perspective, SSRN https://ssrn.com/abstract=294280 or http://dx.doi.org/10.2139/ssrn.294280.

One of private equity (PE)'s secrets to success is the manner in which the firms work with management teams at their portfolio companies. Regular, intense interaction between managers and PE professionals is a given as are open lines of communication. But true alignment is achieved through shared equity ownership of the investee company. While board dynamics and the form of equity ownership vary across different strategies, a PE investor's goal vis-à-vis its engagement is consistent: optimize decision-making and provide clear economic incentives to drive above-average investment returns.

For the executive, managing a PE-controlled portfolio company brings a unique set of opportunities and challenges: on the one hand, PE owners provide management teams with a degree of freedom and generous compensation packages unmatched by most publicly held corporations or family-owned businesses; on the other hand, PE investors expect results in the short term and those with control will not hesitate to replace individual managers or executive teams at struggling companies. Senior executives working for the first time with a PE firm may need to get used to a different pace of activity and highly engaged owners.

This chapter explores the relationship between PE professionals and management teams in a buyout from both the investor's and management's perspective, and explores the characteristics and practical application of management compensation plans in PE. The final section discusses the alignment of interest between founders and investors in venture capital (VC)-backed companies.

WORKING WITH MANAGEMENT
PE'S PERSPECTIVE

The board of a PE-controlled company sets the tone and the high-level strategy at the portfolio firm; ultimately, however, the management team is responsible for its execution translating it into a clear day-to-day plan. Given the management's focal role, PE firms spend a significant amount of time and resources assessing managers, incentivizing them and, when necessary, bringing in new managers to complement or replace an existing team. Exhibit 12.1 provides an overview of a PE firm's engagement with management.

ASSESSMENT AND APPRAISAL: Management teams and PE deal teams get to know each other during the intense months of due diligence leading up to the signing and closing of an investment. PE partners observe management in action and form an opinion about their ability to implement and execute a company's strategic plan. In doing so, the potential new owners consider several questions: is this the right team going forward? Do they have the professional skillset and experience to drive performance during the holding period and will their personality align with that of the investor? Oftentimes the "type" of senior management needed post-investment differs from that pre-investment, as best illustrated by the case of a "take-private" in which a

Exhibit 12.1 Assessing and Incentivizing Management Teams in Buyouts

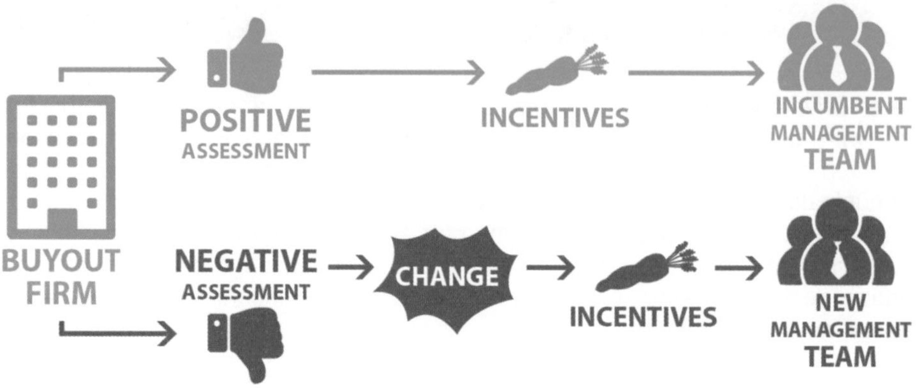

PE fund acquires a publicly listed company: the chief executive officer (CEO)'s role changes from that of a shareholder-facing "chairman-type" in a public company to that of a "chief operating officer-type" in a cost- and change-focused buyout.

MONITORING: Once the investment is made, PE owners work with management to put in place appropriate governance and monitoring processes. Management teams— especially those with little or no experience working in a PE-controlled company— must quickly adapt to direct lines of communication and a performance-driven environment. Ideally, the management team will develop a strong relationship with the experienced, hands-on and financially astute owners, which PE can be at its best, and communicate regularly and transparently with the company's board, especially when things do not go to plan.

In addition to formal channels, management team members and PE owners regularly engage on an informal basis to test ideas and maintain open lines of communication. This informal interaction fosters a positive relationship, provides a sounding board for management, and limits the amount of formal preparation required for each interaction.

At times, PE firms will engage with their portfolio companies on a more granular, operational level. Operating partners, affiliated with the PE firm or engaged as advisors for their specific expertise, and operating teams will then work hand in hand with management to identify and implement value-accretive projects.[1] As much as operating partners provide dedicated, on-site expertise, they constitute yet another communication channel the management team must astutely manage.

INCENTIVES: PE owners implement management compensation plans to align their economic interests with that of the senior managers. Through stock options or "sweetened" equity, management teams have the opportunity to achieve a return several multiples of that realized by the PE fund in a successful investment; however, in the case of a poorly performing portfolio firm, management team members are at risk of losing their investment. See later sections of this chapter for a detailed discussion of these compensation plans.

---

1. Please refer to Chapter 13 Operational Value Creation for more information on operating partners.

CHANGING MANAGEMENT TEAMS: PE owners carefully select and monitor the management teams in their portfolio companies and will make changes early on if and when needed. Studies of leveraged buyouts have shown that management change is particularly prevalent during the acquisition process and the initial ownership period; turnover during the holding period has been found to be in line with, or slightly lower, than that experienced at comparable publicly listed companies.[2] Indeed, studies on the topic cite a replacement rate of top management for buyouts in excess of 50%.[3]

However, contrary to popular belief, working with existing management teams is clearly the preferred route, even for majority PE owners; after all, replacing C-suite executives is not only difficult and costly, but may delay the implementation of the business plans and introduce unnecessary distractions. Nevertheless, should the existing team be unable to execute the planned operational improvements, a change will be made.

PE firms regularly draw on experienced managers from prior portfolio firms to replace departing senior executives; in fact, it is not unusual for senior managers to follow PE owners from one investee company to the next. At times, operational partners from the PE firm may also step into leadership roles, but this can only be a temporary measure until a new manager is found.

WORKING WITH PE OWNERS
MANAGEMENT'S PERSPECTIVE

Working with a PE-controlled board means aggressively driving, growing and expanding a business, and managing teams to meet short-term goals while not losing sight of a company's overall expansion strategy. It is a role that will not fit every executive's style. Senior executives transitioning to a PE-backed portfolio company will see drastic changes in expectations: while a conservative 3% annual growth target may have been sufficient for a steady-state publicly listed company, they may now be driving international expansion with a target to double the profit of the business within the investment period of three to four years.

These transformational growth expectations require a management team with the ability to thrive in a fast-paced, resource-constrained and key performance indicator (KPI)-driven environment, while keeping a close eye on the balance sheet: given the high debt level and financial covenants associated with leveraged buyouts (LBOs), a team's ability to generate consistent cash flow, tightly control costs, and achieve financial targets is particularly important. At the same time, senior managers must implement strategic change, grow the top line and prepare the business for exit over a holding period of three to seven years. For new management teams the challenge is magnified, as they must achieve all this while learning the intricacies of an organization on the fly.

---

2. Acharya, Kehoe, C. and Reyner (2009); Cornelli and Karakaş (2015); Gong and Wu (2011); Why some private equity firms do better than others (2010).
3. Cornelli and Karakas (2012); Gilligan and Wright (2012); Schneider and Lang (2013).

For the right executive, this can be an exciting ride: the PE-backed operating environment provides a platform unique in the corporate world. PE investors' experience in mergers and acquisitions and their broad, often sector-specific networks provide portfolio company management with access to deep expertise and willing support. PE ownership frees managers from certain reporting requirements (especially compared to publicly listed firms), allowing them to focus KPIs that drive performance throughout the holding period. The smaller companies, leaner management teams and the limited bureaucracy at a PE-backed company allow managers to implement change faster and affect a wider range of company activities relative to management at a publicly owned corporation. However, the lean approach cuts both ways, as PE owners will often allocate limited resources to certain corporate functions, set strict budgets and reduce non-core activities, providing managers with limited room to delegate responsibility.

Certain personality traits and types of experiences prepare executives well to succeed in a PE-backed environment. Prior experience with portfolio firms is of course an advantage, and PE firms therefore often back the same managers over several investments. Larger PE organizations are known to create portfolio company advisory boards—consisting of senior executives from their investee companies—who meet regularly to discuss shared concerns and value creation opportunities and focus on portfolio firms in critical condition.

Experience leading across all key functions of a company is also highly valued in senior executives, as well as the willingness to roll up one's sleeves and tackle problems across the organization; being able to juggle multiple tasks and prioritize between potentially conflicting KPIs is a must. PE firms also look for managers with situational experience—for example, executing turnaround, carve-out or roll-up strategies—that aligns with a company's specific needs or stage of development.

Executives with the right mix of commendable ethics, confidence and humility, who make decisions independently, have the flexibility to revisit and adjust strategy and tactics frequently, and the ability to make difficult decisions are likely to do well in a PE-backed environment.

Box 12.1

CONFLICTS BETWEEN MANAGEMENT AND PE OWNERS

Over time, differing opinions regarding roles and responsibilities in a PE-backed company can lead to tension between management teams and PE owners. According to a Boston Consulting Group survey (Schneider and Lang, 2013), there is a significant divergence of views regarding the importance of a PE firm's role in relation to operational and revenue-related topics between portfolio company CEOs and PE investors (Exhibit 12.2). This relates specifically to the planning period of the first 100 days post-investment and the definition of KPIs, two activities on which PE owners often focus their attention. Other sources of tension cited include a lack of transparency and accountability, and of course poor business performance.

Exhibit 12.2 The PE Owner's Role: Two Views

Source: The Boston Consulting Group

Despite the demanding nature of the work, lower job security and potential for disagreement due to the hands-on involvement of PE professionals, an overwhelming majority of portfolio company CEOs from the same survey— more than 90%—credited PE ownership as having a positive effect on company performance and enabling them to succeed in their role. Senior managers, reflecting on their experience with PE firms, often highlight that the industry's commitment to performance and decisiveness makes them preferable employers to publicly listed companies.

MANAGEMENT COMPENSATION PLANS
IN BUYOUTS

The critical role of management teams in a PE-backed company is underscored by the incentive schemes employed in a buyout. Implemented at the time of the PE fund's acquisition, these schemes provide management with substantial equity ownership of the portfolio company and align the economic interests of PE investors and the teams in charge of execution in a powerful way. These compensation plans are typically made available to senior executives only—meaning the top two layers in the management team—and up to 20% of a company's common equity is often set aside for them. The opportunity to participate in these schemes comes at a price, as senior managers must personally co-invest alongside the PE fund to secure their equity interests and show their commitment to the company (i.e., demonstrate they have skin in the game).

To determine the size of management's co-investment, several methods are used, including salary multiples, reinvesting a portion of a manager's gain realized from a prior transaction, or a certain percentage of a manager's personal wealth. PE professionals often comment that they like to see a manager's commitment to be the second-largest commitment in his personal finances, exceeded only by his mortgage. Indeed, getting the balance right is important: the equity upside focuses managers on value maximization while the personal investment discourages excessive risk taking (a tendency common with free options).

The specific instruments used to structure management compensation plans vary by jurisdiction. In Europe, management teams typically hold shares of common equity, while the PE fund holds both preferred and common equity or common equity and a shareholder loan. This two-tiered shareholding structure allows for management's co-investment to be "sweetened"[4]—where management receives a common equity share in the order of five to seven times the value of its investment— to offer a return several times that of the PE fund if the investment performs well (see Box 12.2 for an example).[5] In the United States, on the other hand, management typically holds options on common equity, exercisable over time or upon hitting certain company performance milestones, or a profit interest in the company. Management plans in Asia vary even more widely, with different markets employing sweet equity, options and profit interests, and no real established best practices.

The expected payout of these compensation plans differs significantly from those offered by incentive schemes at publicly listed companies. For example, a study of CEO compensation packages for US LBOs found that CEOs received on average twice the amount of equity in the businesses than their peers in publicly listed companies, underscoring the prevalence of equity compensation in PE-backed transactions.[6] The PE-backed CEOs in the same study received salaries that were 10% lower than their peers' at publicly listed companies, with 13% more of their annual cash compensation structured as variable pay, again placing a premium on performance. Unlike equity compensation awarded to managers of public companies—which often takes the form of options vesting on an annual basis and is supported by a publicly traded instrument—management equity in PE-backed companies is highly illiquid and can only be sold alongside the PE investor, further strengthening the alignment of interests.

---

4. Also referred to as "sweet equity."

5. The preferred shares or shareholder loans typically provide an annual return of 8–12% PIK, with interest accruing to holders rather than cash. In the event of an exit, the cumulative compound return plus principal of these preferred securities must be repaid before any residual profits are shared with common equity owners in effect creating a liquidation preference for the preferred shareholders. Please refer to Chapter 9 Deal Structuring for additional information.

6. Leslie and Oyer (2008).

Box 12.2

MANAGEMENT COMPENSATION PLANS
AN EXAMPLE FROM EUROPE

To highlight the upside potential and downside risk in management compensation plans, we step through an example with a simplified two-tiered "sweet equity" structure based on a hypothetical LBO.

"Capital Partners" acquires a semiconductor business with an enterprise value of €1 billion, funded by 65% bank debt and 35% equity. The existing management team remains in place and co-invests €3 million in the transaction, all of which will be invested in common equity.[7] Capital Partners and management agree to a structure that awards just under 7% of common equity to management. In addition to common equity, Capital Partners will hold preferred equity with a 10% annual dividend paid-in-kind (PIK), resulting in the capital structure shown in Exhibit 12.3.

Exhibit 12.3 Two-tiered "Sweet Equity" Structure

CAPITAL STRUCTURE AT DEAL CLOSE		
SECURITY	SECURITY HOLDER	€ MILLIONS
DEBT	BANK	650
PREFERRED SHARES	CAPITAL PARTNERS	305
COMMON EQUITY	CAPITAL PARTNERS	42
COMMON EQUITY	MANAGEMENT	3
TOTAL EQUITY		350

MANAGEMENT EQUITY "SWEETENER"		
	CAPITAL INVESTMENT	COMMON EQUITY SHAREHOLDING
CAPITAL PARTNERS	99.1%	93.3%
MANAGEMENT	0.9%	6.7%

Management contributes 1% of shareholder funds but holds nearly 7% of common equity.

The implications of this incentive structure are best illustrated through various business scenarios and possible outcomes at exit—a downside case, a base case, and an upside case. We assume a holding period of five years, with a varying amount of bank debt remaining on exit. After five years, the balance due to preferred shareholders amounts to €491.2 million, consisting of principal (€305.0) and annual dividend proceeds (€186.2). The cash flows and returns generated in the three scenarios are shown in Exhibit 12.4.

As shown, a well-structured management compensation plan can deliver significant upside to management teams if and when they deliver on a PE firm's base case return (in our example roughly 2.5 times invested capital) or outperform the set target. Conversely, the downside case underscores the risk that management's equity stake will be wiped out in an underperforming investment, particularly in a structure that employs a shareholder loan and preferred shares held solely by the PE investor.

However, in the instance of poor performance outside of management's control (or when a new management team is brought in to take over), PE firms frequently restructure compensation plans to ensure that incentives remain aligned and some payout is achieved upon reaching the reset performance targets.

7. We chose a simple equity structure for our example. In practice management participation is often structured as a mix of common shares and preferred shares or shareholder loans.

Exhibit 12.4 Cash Flow and "Sweet Equity" Returns at Exit

CAPITAL STRUCTURE AT DEAL CLOSE			
€ MILLIONS	DOWNSIDE CASE	BASE CASE	UPSIDE CASE
EXIT PROCEEDS	820	1300	1600
LESS BANK DEBT	500	400	300
PROCEEDS AVAILABLE TO SHAREHOLDERS	320	900	1300
PREFERRED SHARE PRINCIPAL	305.0	305.0	305.0
PREFERRED SHARE ANNUAL RETURN	15.0	186.2	186.2
CAPITAL PARTNERS COMMON EQUITY	0.0	381.5	754.9
MANAGEMENT COMMON EQUITY	0.0	27.3	53.9
CAPITAL PARTNERS - CAPITAL INVESTED	347	347	347
MANAGEMENT - CAPITAL INVESTED	3	3	3
CAPITAL PARTNERS - TOTAL CAPITAL RETURNED	320	872.7	1246.1
MANAGEMENT - TOTAL CAPITAL RETURNED	0	27.3	53.9
CAPITAL PARTNERS MoM	0.9	2.5	3.6
CAPITAL PARTNERS IRR	-2%	20%	29%
MANAGEMENT MoM	0.0	9.1	18.0
MANAGEMENT IRR	Ø	55%	78%

What Makes a Great Private Equity CEO?

By Tony DeNunzio CBE, Chairman, Pets at Home and formerly Chairman, Maxeda BV

There is no magic in private equity's success at driving performance. In many ways, managing a company well in a private context is no different to managing a company well in the public markets. The need for clear leadership, a compelling vision, a well-defined strategy and strong execution skills apply in both cases. The need to engage employees, who will in turn satisfy customers, who will in turn drive business results, applies in both cases. However, there are subtleties in what makes a great private company CEO and having recruited a good number over the years, some of whom have been phenomenally successful and others who did not hit the mark, I would identify five characteristics of the successful PE CEO: Leadership, Team Building, Entrepreneurship, Change Management and Financial Drive.

Leadership (Walk on Water?)

The best PE CEOs demonstrate an extraordinary ability to define the value creation strategy, build a team to execute the plan and drive business results. They have to be equally people oriented and results focused. They set the bar high and expect people to deliver. They have to manage and satisfy all stakeholders from equity investors, lenders, customers, communities, colleagues and senior management. The helicopter approach is important allowing the CEO to cover a lot of ground and then to land and spend time on big issues or opportunities. Finally, the best CEOs are excellent communicators, inspire trust and motivate the whole organisation. In the words of General Foch in WW1 *"The most powerful weapon on earth is the human soul on fire!"*

Team Builders (the Smiling Assassin!)

Jack Welch stated that *"I never regretted making a people decision. I only regretted not making it sooner."* Speed is one of the competitive advantages of a PE company and that speed is applied to driving value creation strategies at the same time as building the best team. The top CEOs assess their team very quickly and decide on who to keep and who to replace. In today's highly competitive world, it's not one man or woman at the top that can drive outstanding results, it requires harnessing the talent of a highly motivated and coordinated team.

Entrepreneurship (Owner Driver Mentality)

The most exciting aspect of being a leader in a private equity company is that it is as close as one can get to owning and running one's own company. CEOs are given a significant amount of freedom (within a governance framework) to lead the company and drive results. They have *"real skin in the game"* having invested into the management equity plan which can really focus the mind. In many investment decisions, I have heard managers say *"This is my money we're talking about!"* This focus leads to a balanced risk/reward approach, bold strategic and operational programs and real innovation.

Change Management (Get Me from A to B!)

The best CEOs are brilliant at change management. They can move an underperforming business to a top performer or turnaround a failing business to one with a sustainable growth strategy. This is all about change management, getting the business from A to B by focusing the organisation on the big strategic value levers. And not chasing too many rabbits—otherwise they will all get away! Mario Andretti encapsulated this beautifully: *"If you think you are in control, you are not driving fast enough!"* Organisations have an ability to cope with significant change as long as it is planned and coordinated.

Financially Driven (Where's the Money?)

Lastly, the top CEOs are very financially driven both in terms of remuneration and performance. One could say they are hungry for success. They have invested in the management equity plan and they aspire to a life changing outcome. The easiest way of articulating this is with simple math. Let's assume a management team own 10% of the equity and a business is valued at 10× EBITDA. Every €1m of EBITDA increase is valued at €10m enterprise value and results in €1m of cashflow. The Management Equity Plan accrues 10% of the €10m and of the cashflows—so every €1m of EBITDA increase delivers €1.1m directly to the management pot. This is highly motivating to management. Consequently, they embrace the performance metrics and scrutiny of their private equity investors. They thrive on seeing the EBITDA increase and the net debt go down.

A great private equity CEO recognises that to get the best exit value for their business they have to create a business that has a sustainable growth strategy, a strong management team and a consistent track record of financial performance. If they get this formula right they will probably hit the jackpot!

ALIGNING VC FUNDS AND ENTREPRENEURS

A central element for successful VC investment is identifying and backing the right team. VC-backed founders are often serial entrepreneurs, and VC investors may back the same entrepreneur more than once, with the expectation that lessons learned along the way will be applied to future businesses. Given the volatility of early-stage companies, the right team may receive backing even without a fully formed business model, with the investors trusting their ability to adapt or pivot as the venture evolves. Conversely, a weak team with a great idea may not receive backing, as restructuring a founding team post-investment can be a challenge.

The future value of early-stage companies depends on the founding team's ability to realize the company's vision and growth opportunities. In VC, particularly at an early stage, investors have little to no leverage to change the team: equity control typically rests with the entrepreneur. Given the risk of early-stage investing, VCs heavily structure their investment (see Chapter 2) through preferred stock with distinct rights. This favorable treatment comes at the expense of the founders who typically hold common stock and are diluted in every subsequent funding round.

In effect the founders will win (big) only if and when the investor wins. Cash compensation and salaries are therefore kept to a minimum and will start to increase only following later fundraising rounds. Venture funds will be careful to observe that the founding team retains a respectable share in their company post-investment to ensure motivation and continued engagement in the firm. This applies especially to early-stage start-ups (i.e., pre-profit and pre-revenue) where major future fundraising rounds and the resulting dilution have to be anticipated. VCs may include ways for founders to increase their stake in the company if and when certain milestones are hit; such schemes are referred to as "earn-ins" and will offer the founding team additional equity from the VC's share pool.

Getting a start-up's incentive structure right starts with the conditions laid out in the respective round. They often include a preferred return (liquidation preference) for investors; yet, once that has been achieved, founder and management may participate in the upside to a larger extent, motivating the team to push for a stellar exit. The opposite order applies when a carve-out for founders is employed. Assuming founders negotiate a 10% carve-out, this stake will have a priority claim on exit proceeds (after any debt) before the various preferred shares from multiple VCs receive consideration.

As the company evolves, both parties—founders and investors alike—will strive to reach milestones in line with their business plan. After all, subsequent rounds of funding are usually raised within 12 to 18 months, and reaching the next stage in a company's development—a so-called "fundable" milestone—will help support a higher valuation, which is crucial: the same dollar amount raised at higher valuations will not only benefit founders (who will need to give up less equity), it will also prevent a down-round for the earlier venture investors.[8]

---

8. For further details on VC down-rounds and dilution, please refer to Chapter 2 Venture Capital.

CLOSING

Given the critical role management plays in executing a portfolio company's business plan, it is little wonder that PE firms spend a significant amount of time selecting, monitoring and devising incentive schemes for senior management. While the financial rewards for a successful management team can be spectacular in well-performing cases, it should be noted that managers in a PE-invested company typically face a high-pressure environment, tight targets, limited resources and a high risk of getting replaced when failing to perform. However, for the right individual it can be an opportunity to enact real change with a dedicated owner and the support of a professional board and ultimately reap the rewards of a successfully executed strategy.

KEY LEARNING POINTS

• Working closely with a motivated management team is one of the drivers of success in PE investing.

• Managers working with PE-controlled boards must adjust their expectations and adapt to a fast-paced environment and a sophisticated new owner.

• Management compensation plans are key in creating the right incentive structures in PE-backed companies.

RELEVANT CASE STUDIES

from *Private Equity in Action—Case Studies from Developed and Emerging Markets*

Case #8: Private Equity in Emerging Markets: Can Operating Advantage Boost Value in Exits?

Case #15: Vendex KBB: First Hundred Days in Crisis

REFERENCES AND ADDITIONAL READING

Acharya, V.R., Kehoe, C. and Reyner, M. (2009) Private Equity vs. PLC Boards in the U.K.: A Comparison of Practices and Effectiveness, *Journal of Applied Corporate Finance*, 21 (1 Winter): 45–56.

Cornelli, F. and Karakaş, O. (2012) Corporate Governance of LBOs: The Role of Boards. http://ssrn.com/abstract=1875649.

Cornelli, F. and Karakaş, O. (2015) CEO Turnover in LBOs: The Role of Boards, December, available at SSRN https://ssrn.com/abstract=2269124 or http://dx.doi .org/10.2139/ssrn.2269124.

Gilligan, J. and Wright, M. *Private Equity Demystified*: 2012 *Update*. London: Institute of Chartered Accountants in England and Wales.

Gong, J. and Wu, S. (2011) CEO Turnover in Private Equity Sponsored Leveraged Buyouts, *Corporate Governance: An International Review*, 19 (3): 195–209, http://ssrn.com/abstract=1851603.

Jensen, Michael C. (1989) https://hbr.org/1989/09/eclipse-of-the-public-corporation

Leslie, P. and Oyer, P. (2008) Managerial Incentives and Value Creation: Evidence from Private Equity. Working Paper. http://www.nber.org/papers/w14331.

Management Compensation: Eu vs US vs Asia. http://peblog.wpengine.com/wp-content/uploads/2016/02/95615261_1.pdf

Schneider, A. and Lang, N. (2013) *Private Equity and the CEO*. The Boston Consulting Group.

Stenholm, G. (2006) *Positioning the Private Equity Portfolio Company CEO for Success*. Spencer Stuart.

This PWC 2016 survey shows the trend in management compensation: http://www.pwc.com/us/en/hr-management/publications/assets/pwc_private_equity_stock_compensation_survey_2016_pwc.pdf

In the past decade and a half, we have witnessed a nearly fivefold increase in private equity (PE) assets under management on the back of strong performance and growing investor interest.[1] In the wake of the steady rise in dry powder and as a result of the lessons learned from the global financial crisis, the PE industry has increasingly focused its attention on the fundamental drivers of PE performance.

As the industry has matured, the ability to access debt and structure deals is no longer considered a unique, differentiating skill for PE firms (except maybe for very large deals and special situations). Instead, operational value creation has become the key topic on today's PE agenda. Limited partners (LPs) consider it a core differentiator when committing to PE funds and companies enquire about operational support before deciding on a suitable investor.

Operational value creation focuses on driving performance improvements in a company's existing operations to build a more efficient, better-run business. Leveraging PE's active ownership model and hands-on governance, PE investors are well positioned to focus company resources and support the necessary improvements. As repeat buyers-improvers-sellers of companies, the best PE firms bring industry expertise, pattern recognition and finely tuned processes to the table that assist in the identification and planning of the most appropriate value creation initiatives.

This chapter describes the levers used by management to execute in line with a portfolio company's business plan and implement operational improvements successfully. With the increased focus on value creation capabilities in PE investments, LPs have started to ask for ways to measure the impact of PE ownership on company performance; we discuss a model developed by INSEAD's PE center to isolate and measure unique operational value generated over time.

THE VALUE CREATION ROADMAP

The execution of operational improvements during the PE holding period requires careful selection, prioritization and management of company resources. While most operational improvement initiatives have the potential to add value, they should not be considered a shopping list applied in every situation. In fact, PE is typically very selective, choosing to concentrate on three or four areas in any given business at any one time; attempting to tackle more may overburden management and produce poor outcomes. Once initial core areas have been covered, further improvements can be delivered in subsequent phases.

Due diligence conducted by the PE firm pre-investment will have identified low-hanging fruit—i.e., areas with obvious potential for operational improvement—for value creation, which are likely to be at the core of the initial "100-day plan."[2] A careful

---

1. Source: Preqin.
2. A 100-day plan outlines clearly the changes to be achieved during the first months post-investment.

examination of the previous owner's operating model will not only aim to build on the company's established strengths but also look for new ways to release cash or increase profit margins. Typical initiatives include working capital controls and the adoption of more sophisticated pricing strategies.

Where an improvement is expected to be self-funding, PE will assess the opportunity using conventional measures such as payback period, return on investment and return on capital employed. In contrast, in cases where injection of additional (equity) capital is required, the PE firm will evaluate whether the project will increase company value and achieve the required hurdle return on this "fresh" equity. Once a value creation plan has been initiated, explicit operating and financial metrics are defined to track the progress of the operating initiative.

Box 13.1
LEVERS FOR OPERATIONAL VALUE CREATION

The tools used to drive operational value creation at a PE-backed company are no different from those available to public corporations or family firms; yet PE firms have a reputation for excelling at execution. Exhibit 13.1 lays out the generic tools used to improve operating performance and the section below places them into the context of PE investing.

SALES GROWTH: Driving revenue growth through increased sales volume is the preferred lever for value creation in PE, based both on a survey of PE investors' rank of value creation levers and on an analysis of PE-backed companies' past performance.[3] New market entry, new product introduction and improving sales force effectiveness are the main initiatives employed to drive sales growth. Given the amount of time needed to realize these strategic changes, sales growth initiatives are introduced very early in the holding period.

Exhibit 13.1 Operational Value Creation Levers

3. Gompers, Kaplan and Mukharlyamov (2015) Capital Dynamics and the Technische Universität München (2014).

GROSS MARGIN IMPROVEMENT: PE-backed companies drive margin improvement through a mix of improved sales and cost savings. Price increases, supply chain and distribution optimization, reduced procurement costs and improved capacity utilization are among the primary initiatives employed to improve margins. While not unique, a PE firm's focus might drive management to reduce SKUs, bringing down complexity and associated manufacturing cost. As mentioned, the strong emphasis on and associated investment in sales, including the occasional new customer from a PE firm's network, might result not only in better volumes but also higher average sales prices, further improving the gross margin.

OVERHEAD REDUCTION: Reducing overhead is one of the most common value levers used immediately following a PE fund's investment in a portfolio company. Typically assessed carefully during due diligence, reduced overhead provides a quick win for the bottom line and short payback periods. PE-backed companies focus on reducing general and administrative expenses, and tend to outsource non-core functions, while focusing research and product development efforts on products with the highest (near-term) commercial potential. In the context of a roll-up strategy, effective acquisition integration provides an opportunity to eliminate redundancy and indirect costs among merged entities. Conversely, one area in which buyout firms often add cost is in finance and reporting (e.g., IT systems), linked to the tighter control and oversight model, and the use of extensive debt financing.

CAPITAL EFFICIENCY: PE investors work closely with their portfolio companies to optimize the use of short- and long-term capital, helping them to release cash from operations. Managing the use of capital is particularly relevant in leveraged buyouts (LBOs), as excess cash can be used to repay debt or pay early distributions to the PE fund and improve an investment's internal rate of return. Short-term capital management focuses on the optimization and permanent release of cash from working capital through inventory reduction and improved payment terms with customers and suppliers. Fixed asset optimization revolves around ensuring that capital expenditure delivers value within the PE holding period and identifying assets to be shut down or sold to release cash.

SHARED SERVICES: PE firms can drive profitability improvements across fund portfolios by introducing shared services and by leveraging the combined negotiating power of their portfolio companies. The benefits of shared services are usually realized through joint procurement of insurance and outsourcing of common back-office and business services. Joint procurement can pay additional dividends for PE firms with industry-focused funds as cross-portfolio purchasing can extend into inventory and consumable goods. The most common spend items targeted for joint procurement include the selling, general and administrative account, where scale can be leveraged to achieve cost savings (see more on value creation levers below). PE firms also leverage the breadth of their portfolios by hiring subject matter experts—for instance, in environment, social and governance or IT—and applying their expertise across different portfolio companies.

More than Private Equity-Skilled Industrialists
By William L. Cornog, Member and Head of KKR Capstone

At its core, private equity is an industrialist endeavor. With company ownership comes great responsibility, including significant influence over the welfare of employees, customers, suppliers and the communities in which a company operates.

Increasingly and understandably, private equity firms are judged not only by their returns, but also by how returns are generated. Decisions regarding compensation and benefits, onshore versus offshore job creation, supplier selection, employee health and safety practices and facility engineering are scrutinized by multiple stakeholders. These decisions impact not only a company's competitiveness, but also its reputation and in some cases even its license to operate. Consequently, private equity firms, through their ownership and governance of companies must look beyond the numbers into the operations of their companies.

Private equity firms must also focus on operational value creation because it is fundamental to generating superior returns. As the industry has matured, attracting thousands of PE firms and billions of dollars of capital, the source of returns has shifted dramatically from deleveraging and multiple expansion to EBITDA growth. Today, generating top-quartile returns involves buying well and applying responsible leverage, but most of all it requires building better businesses. The best firms infuse an operational perspective across every stage of the deal lifecycle as they identify, purchase and improve businesses.

Operational value-added begins in diligence as firms make their most important decision: whether to buy a business. PE firms can't weave straw into gold, turning a bad company into a good company. Success requires "good clay." Operational diligence must examine the strength of a company's end markets, business model, and barriers to entry while identifying the profit improvement opportunities that underpin the required stretch of a winning bid.

Once a company is purchased, the first order of business is strengthened governance since at the heart of private equity is a "governance arbitrage" advantage. An operational perspective is required to increase transparency with upgraded metrics and reporting, to more closely align pay and performance, and to focus the board room agenda on the highest priority opportunities. While many public company boards approach governance from a defensive posture, focusing on managing risk and reputation, private equity boards play to win, focusing on driving performance and generating top-quartile returns given the tight coupling of ownership and governance.

A "100 Day Plan" has become the industry's instrument for achieving alignment between ownership and management on the value creation priorities for the business. Ambiguity undermines execution, so ruthless prioritization ensures that management and the overall organization remain focused, which results in better execution.

Since the best team usually wins, PE firms also quickly assess and, where necessary, upgrade management talent. As a former consultant, I initially approached my portfolio operations role as helping our companies determine what to do and how best to do it. Today, I focus more on the *who* than the *what* and *how*, moving swiftly to upgrade management rather than support executives that are not fit for purpose. There is significant opportunity cost for PE firms that fail to do this. There is no bigger value creation lever than building a human capital advantage.

Finally, with a foundation of strong governance, management and strategic focus success boils down to execution. Academic studies consistently confirm that PE owned firms grow faster, drive more productivity and even out innovate (producing more patents) than publicly owned companies in the same industry. This execution advantage is the product of strong governance, a focused strategy, management top grading and direct value-added support from the PE firm.

Private equity firms should not meddle in the day-to-day operations of their businesses. Management is accountable for and must be given latitude to run the business. However, private equity firms must actively govern and support the value creation programs that drive success in the marketplace and returns for investors, which is why today's best private equity firms are not only good investors, but also skilled industrialists.

RESOURCES FOR OPERATIONAL VALUE CREATION

While the PE firm and the board of directors play an integral role in overseeing and driving operational value creation initiatives, management teams are ultimately responsible for all aspects of execution and the delivery of the desired results. Given the high demands on PE-backed management teams, they may at times lack the bandwidth or change management expertise to develop and optimally execute these plans on their own. As a result, PE-backed companies draw on four primary resources—two provided directly by the PE firm and two external resources—to offer support throughout the planning and execution of value creation initiatives: executive mentors, operating partners, consultants, and operating teams. While shown in Exhibit 13.2 as individual options, several of these resources can be used at the same time.

Exhibit 13.2 Operational Value Creation Support

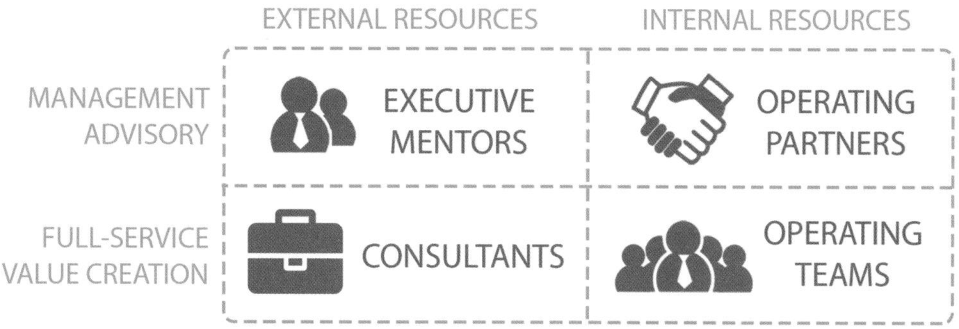

	EXTERNAL RESOURCES	INTERNAL RESOURCES
MANAGEMENT ADVISORY	EXECUTIVE MENTORS	OPERATING PARTNERS
FULL-SERVICE VALUE CREATION	CONSULTANTS	OPERATING TEAMS

MANAGEMENT ADVISORY

PE-backed companies engage seasoned corporate executives to advise their management teams. These corporate executives come with many years of experience and credibility as senior executives in a corporate setting and their networks can open doors, accelerate decisions and assist with regulatory approvals if and when needed. In particular, these executives can help assess opportunities for operational improvement and assist in developing value creation plans. They provide a critical link between PE owners and senior management teams and may assume a formal seat on a company's board of directors. This type of coaching is particularly relevant for management teams working with a PE investor for the first time, as they may need guidance to adjust to their new responsibilities (e.g., focus on cash over net income or dealing with lending banks) and the high-pressure environment.

EXECUTIVE MENTORS: PE firms often draw executive mentors from their established network of senior executives for engagement with a specific portfolio company. Mentors typically work with one portfolio company at a time, often on a part-time basis. Executive mentors bring industry-specific or change management experience and may have worked for a PE-backed company before. These executives are usually incentivized through equity stakes in the business in an arrangement similar to management compensation plans.[4]

OPERATING PARTNERS: Some PE firms have full-time operating partners who work next to the deal team and are on hand to advise management on value creation. Operating partners may have a broad general management background coupled with specific sector experience or functional expertise in a given element of operations (e.g., procurement or IT). Operating partners often engage with a number of management teams at the same time and provide a direct link to the PE firm. These professionals are salaried employees of the PE firm and are typically compensated through carry in a fund or equity in the businesses they work with. Operating partners may also serve as interim chief executive officers (CEOs) during leadership transitions.

FULL SERVICE VALUE CREATION

PE-backed companies regularly involve teams of professionals to engage in various aspects of the planning and execution of operational value creation. Working hand-in-hand with management, these advisors provide both high-level guidance and on-the-ground execution capability.

CONSULTANTS: Management teams draw on consultants with deep industry, technical or functional expertise to assist in the execution of value creation plans. A team of consultants may complement a PE firm's operational team or other in-house resources. Consultants are typically hired on a project or contract basis, either pre- or post-investment, and may engage at reduced rates during due diligence in hopes of securing more sizable work post-investment.

---

4. Please refer to Chapter 12 Securing Management Teams for additional information on management incentives.

OPERATING TEAMS: Operating teams are employed directly by PE firms to engage in operational value creation and to manage the funds' portfolio company investments. Operating partners—as described above—lead these teams and are complemented by a supporting cast often with consulting backgrounds. These teams are typically built to provide generalist support to a portfolio firm but may focus on a specific technical or functional area. In addition to engaging post-investment, operating team members may participate in a deal to provide perspective on a company's operations as early as deal sourcing and often are formal members of the deal team during due diligence. Yet, most operating teams only start engaging when the probability of closing the deal is high to avoid diverting resources to uncertain investment opportunities.

Given the related overheads, operating teams can usually be found at larger PE firms with the financial resources, and a large number of portfolio companies to benefit from and fully utilize internal teams. Smaller funds are less likely to employ clearly specialized financial and operating specialists; rather, partners tend to have a more diverse skillset to cover both the investment and portfolio management processes.

Box 13.2

IN-HOUSE OR OUTSOURCED?

PE firms must decide whether to build in-house teams or rely on outsourced capabilities to drive operational value creation during the holding period. Aside from the obvious evaluation of fully loaded cost for maintaining in-house resources versus employing external resources on an as-needed basis, consideration must be paid to the question of which entity (PE firm, fund, portfolio company) will bear the cost of an in-house team.

Historically, the expense of services rendered by an operating team was charged to the portfolio company, yet recently the model has been rethought and certain practices corrected. Most *limited partnership agreements* now stipulate that management fees are to be used to pay for internal teams. When portfolio companies reimburse the general partner (GP) for these services, LPs will argue that they are charged twice. Some GPs have therefore scaled back on internal teams, have tried to make them more independent of the GP, or have improved their disclosure to LPs; a number of GPs have also given rebates to their LPs for some of the fees paid previously. In any case, whether services rendered by an operating team will ultimately be borne by the portfolio company or the GP, the initial investment required to start the program needs to be made by the PE firm itself.

Also, while in-house resources provide a direct line of communication between operating partners on the ground and other decision-makers, it introduces the potential for conflict between operating teams and deal teams as well as operating teams and management teams.

PE firms that employ in-house resources must carefully manage their engagement in a company's operations for two primary reasons: first, the risk of liability and second, potential conflict with management. While close monitoring and active support is a principle of active ownership, becoming overly engaged raises the PE firm's risk of liability related to activity at the portfolio company. Taking too much control of an operating initiative also risks demotivating management, breeding dependency on the PE firm's resources, or driving a wedge between the PE firm and management. In-house operating professionals thus must strike the right balance among setting the strategic direction, playing a supporting role in day-to-day operations, acting as a sounding board and resource to management and empowering management teams to effect the desired change.

A different problem arises when PE operations teams are spread too thinly over a large number of portfolio companies. CEOs can feel like victims of "seagull management"—with teams flying in when there is a problem, making a lot of noise, and then flying out. This approach often goes hand in hand with asking for vast amounts of information without explaining how it will be used. To CEOs, it can appear that the team is more interested in monitoring than helping the business. This tension is of course exacerbated in situations where the business underperforms.

MEASURING OPERATIONAL VALUE CREATION

Identifying appropriate levers, devising suitable plans and deploying resources in a timely fashion are vital steps for driving operational value creation. To develop a systematic and repeatable approach it is critical to accurately measure the operational value created and then calculate its contribution to fund-level returns. Yet, this is no small task. The ambiguity around value creation lies partly in the standard measures applied by PE firms to show the sources of investment returns at the portfolio company level. Historically, GPs have used the three drivers presented in Exhibit 13.3 to break out performance drivers.

While an industry standard, this rather simplistic model neither provides insight into the drivers of operational change realized under PE ownership, nor does it benchmark the performance of a PE-backed company against its current (pre-PE ownership) trajectory or the dynamics in its industry.

Exhibit 13.3 Standard Measures of PE Value Creation

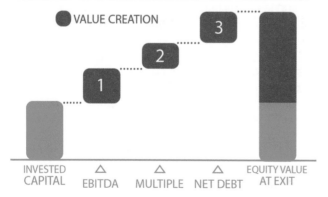

VALUE CREATION

1 Change in annual operating cash flow, typically using EBITDA as a proxy.

2 Change in valuation multiple (usually EBITDA multiple).

3 Change in net debt, a measure showing cash generation during the holding period.

INVESTED CAPITAL — △ EBITDA — △ MULTIPLE — △ NET DEBT — EQUITY VALUE AT EXIT

To address these limitations, INSEAD's Global Private Equity Initiative (GPEI) developed a framework that brings clarity to the operational value creation debate.[5] INSEAD Value Creation (IVC) 2.0 incorporates the main strengths of existing frameworks and introduces a few new concepts. Specifically, it measures value creation across various operational and financial levers and isolates company-specific value created by PE investors and management teams during the holding period. Exhibit 13.4 illustrates the output from the IVC 2.0 model applied to an anonymized US mid-market LBO investment.

Exhibit 13.4 IVC 2.0 Value Creation Drivers

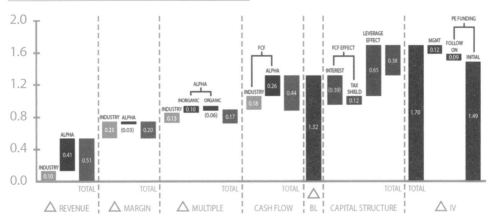

Source: INSEAD GPEI

IVC 2.0 deconstructs the investment return (as a multiple of invested capital[6]) into five categories of value creation. Value created in the first four of these categories—change in revenue, change in margin, change in multiple, and cash flow—is attributed to either industry performance or company-specific performance (which we call "alpha"). In our example, for instance, the total value created through change in revenue (0.51) was predominantly accounted for by company-specific operating improvements (0.41 or 80%) relative to industry performance (0.10 or 20%).

In addition, IVC 2.0 explicitly breaks down the impact of leverage on investment returns in a fifth value creation category called capital structure. The "leverage effect" captures the increased return on equity realized by funding a significant portion of the transaction with debt. The "free cash flow effect" captures the reduction in the cash available to shareholders resulting from additional interest expense, which is partially offset by an increase in a company's tax shield. In the final category, IVC 2.0 allocates the return generated by the investment—Δ IV in Exhibit 13.4—to different sources of funding, according to ownership group (PE and management in this case) and round of investment (initial and follow-on funding).

---

5. An in-depth review of IVC 2.0 methodology can be found at http://centres.insead.edu/global-private-equity-initiative/documents/INSEAD-ValueCreation2.0.pdf
6. Excess return (i.e., total investment return as per industry convention) is 2.7×.

With levers of value creation decomposed in this manner, IVC 2.0 output can be recombined (Exhibit 13.5) to isolate the unique value created by the PE-backed company. Here, of the 1.7× money multiple, 0.64× comes from favorable industry dynamics, 0.38× from the application of leverage and 0.68× from "alpha," the fabled outperformance that justifies the PE model.

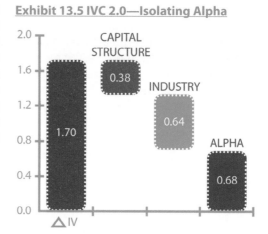

Exhibit 13.5 IVC 2.0—Isolating Alpha

Source: INSEAD GPEI

CLOSING

With operational value creation on every LP's mind (so much so that most PE firms make operational capabilities a centerpiece of their investor pitch), different philosophical approaches are being tested, ranging from hands-off to deeply engaged, from internal resources to hiring the best specialists on an as-needed basis. There are no special (secret) levers in a PE fund's toolkit; all instruments are familiar to the experienced executive or management consultant. The difference lies in the PE owners' willingness to execute decisively and provide management with resources and incentives to accomplish the set goals.

KEY LEARNING POINTS

• Achieving operational improvements in portfolio companies has become a major differentiator in PE.

• Tools to drive those improvements are no different from those used in any other company; but PE-owned firms go beyond the mere identification of the right levers; they excel at execution through rigorous focus.

• PE firms support their portfolio companies and management through operating partners, mentors, consultants and specific operating teams.

• Models are emerging to measure the value createds by PE during the holding period.

RELEVANT CASE STUDIES

from *Private Equity in Action—Case Studies from Developed and Emerging Markets*

Case #8: Private Equity in Emerging Markets: Can Operating Advantage Boost Value in Exits?

Cases #11 and 12: Chips on the Side (A and B): The Buyout of Avago Technologies

REFERENCES AND ADDITIONAL READING

Borom, M.P. (2012) Assessing Operating Teams and Capabilities across Different Private Equity Models, Strategic Resource Group, www.thl.com/media/17856/cie_srg_whitepaper.pdf.

Capital Dynamics and the Technische Universität München (2014) Value Creation in Private Equity.

Davis, S.J., Haltiwanger, J., Handley, K., Jarmin, R., Lerner, J. and Miranda, J. (2014) Private Equity, Jobs, and Productivity, *American Economic Review 2014*, 104(12 December): 3956–90.

Ernst & Young (2014) *Taking Stock: How do Private Equity Investors Create Value? A Study of 2013 European Exits.*

Gompers, P., Kaplan, S.N. and Mukharlyamov, V. (2015) What Do Private Equity Firms Say They Do? Harvard Business School Finance Working Paper No. 15-081, available at SSRN http://ssrn.com/abstract=2600524.

INSEAD/Duff & Phelps (2014) Value Creation 2.0, INSEAD GPEI, http://centres.insead.edu/global-private-equity-initiative/documents/INSEAD-ValueCreation2.0.pdf.

Lieber, D. (2004) Proactive Portfolio Management: Manage Now to Realize Returns Later, *Journal of Private Equity*, 7(2 Spring): 72–82.

RESPONSIBLE INVESTMENT 14

Private equity (PE) firms affect stakeholders involved in their portfolio companies well beyond the improvements targeted in the business plans. Examples of this impact in the ordinary course of business are the creation of employment, the improvement of working conditions in their portfolio companies and higher tax revenues due to the growth experienced at PE-backed companies.

Going beyond these added benefits, PE firms are increasingly called upon to approach their investments more systematically and proactively with the broader stakeholder community in mind, a trend referred to as responsible investment. This focus on considerations beyond financial returns has evolved alongside limited partners' (LPs) growing appreciation that non-financial factors can have a positive impact on value creation, sustainable company performance, and the health of civil society.

Adding a chapter on responsible investment to a book on PE shows how much the authors believe that PE can serve as a force for good. PE firms are well positioned to implement responsible investment strategies and promote sustainable business practices due to their active ownership and corporate governance model. The PE industry has in the past decades created considerable wealth and employment in the advanced economies; as it expands its reach into emerging markets, its ability to impact the economic, social and ecological environment of communities might be even larger.

This chapter first puts the various approaches and definitions of responsible investment into perspective before focusing on the role of environmental, social, and governance (ESG) factors within the PE industry. We explore the role ESG plays in today's investment environment, explaining why it has become an integral part of modern PE investing.

RESPONSIBLE INVESTMENT DEFINED

Although there is no commonly accepted definition of responsible investment, we consider it to be a mandate to go beyond a narrow target of financial returns and incorporate a commitment to do good or, at a minimum, be a responsible guardian of the portfolio company and its environs.

Indeed, the ways in which PE funds can implement responsible investment strategies range widely: from negative screening, to proactive ESG management strategies, to impact investment funds. The framework below (see also Exhibit 14.1) distinguishes five main approaches to investment based on the importance assigned to social returns.[1] Along a sliding scale, they range from pure financial focus to pure philanthropy.

---

1. From a talk on Impact Investing & Marketing to the Bottom of the Pyramid, INSEAD (2016).

Exhibit 14.1 Responsible Investment Continuum

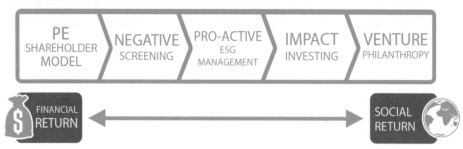

SHAREHOLDER MODEL: Traditionally, PE funds focused purely on financial return, in a clear implementation of the "shareholder model," separating investment decisions and management of a portfolio company from wider stakeholder considerations. This should in theory lead to the most efficient allocation of resources. In this model, it is up to the shareholders to dedicate part of their profits to wider social causes if they choose to follow a specific agenda.[2]

NEGATIVE SCREENING: "Do no harm" is the mandate for PE funds in the second group of our framework. This investment mandate may require a PE fund to abstain from investment in controversial sectors, such as tobacco, gambling, fossil fuel production or arms manufacturing. Such an approach may be instigated by the investment firm's partners' ethical beliefs, the wish to minimize reputational risk or requirements of fund LPs. Negative screening fits easily into a standard due diligence process and simply narrows the universe of available investment opportunities.

PROACTIVE ESG MANAGEMENT: In contrast to the previous group, PE firms employing this strategy define their responsible investment mandate in a prescriptive and proactive manner (i.e., "do some good"). LPs and PE firms have started to actively and systematically manage environmental, social and governance factors by establishing structured programs that integrate ESG policies and procedures into pre- and post-investment decision-making processes. PE firms will often require their investee companies to have adopted such polices pre-investment or include raising ESG standards as part of their improvement plans. While the focus remains on financial returns, there is an explicit and implicit belief that following an active ESG investment approach is good not only for company stakeholders, but also for investment performance by building better, more robust business.

IMPACT INVESTING: Impact investment funds stand out from conventional PE funds as their mandate adds from the start a social return component to their financial return target, with an upfront intention to generate change on both dimensions. The levers and key performance indicators (KPIs) used to derive and monitor a social return are manifold and depend on the funds' focus and industry. At a minimum, however, they will include ESG standards with specific themes pursued such as financing opportunities for the bottom of the pyramid (microfinance), improvement of employment and education opportunities, access to affordable healthcare and

2. A recent INSEAD Knowledge article argued the point of a social mandate in any public equity environment (Vermaelen, 2016).

housing, and sustainable agriculture and clean technologies. Competitive financial returns and a positive social impact are not mutually exclusive: evidence shows that adding a social return target does not mean that financial returns are compromised, with multiple impact investment firms raising follow-on offerings after achieving their target internal rates of return.[3]

VENTURE PHILANTHROPY: At the far end of the scale—and opposite to investors seeking a pure financial return—are approaches with a pure social mandate, represented by venture philanthropy. Compared to pure philanthropy, venture philanthropy introduces additional levels of rigor, coordination and monitoring to increase the efficiency and impact of the grant-making process. Venture philanthropists often engage on broader themes and draw on an array of funding to initiate change. While venture philanthropy always has a social impact target, it rarely has a profit target beyond prolonging the use of the capital base, thereby differentiating itself from impact investing. It therefore concerns mainly the actions of foundations, rather than general partners (GPs) or PE firms.

ESG IN TODAY'S PE INDUSTRY

Historically, the PE industry had emphasized avoiding negative headlines and other reputational risks resulting from ESG issues at minimal cost, often focusing on legal compliance with local regulation. A change in attitude became visible in 2005 when the United Nations Environment Programme Finance Initiative published a report that linked the managing of ESG factors to investors' fiduciary duty. In doing so it attracted the attention of PE players and propelled ESG into the mainstream investment industry.

Since then, ESG management has evolved into an essential activity for GPs looking to go beyond basic regulatory demands. While GPs' interest in ESG was initially driven by LP expectations, over time many GPs started seeing commercial benefits from incorporating ESG practices into their investment program. Thought leaders have adopted comprehensive and structured processes to leverage risk management and value creation opportunities. Progressive thinking on ESG has been formalized in industry guidelines that have become widely adopted. Exhibit 14.2 charts the evolution of ESG in PE.

LP EXPECTATIONS: The growing demand for public accountability and transparency around environmental and social issues from the investor community and their constituents has led LPs to push for increased ESG awareness. Many LPs' requirements related to ESG have been formalized in their internal guidelines and form part of their duties to their beneficiaries. For US public pension plans—the largest allocators to PE—and other government-affiliated LPs, direct oversight from government institutions and regulatory requirements leads to additional emphasis on

---

3. Despite this success, impact investment may struggle to achieve scale as the investable universe is constrained by the dual financial and social mandate. A linked challenge to institutionalizing impact investing arises from the perceived fiduciary risks and agency costs of considering non-financial returns. However, legislation has been enacted in some jurisdictions that allows authorized investors to explicitly consider non-financial terms while still fulfilling their fiduciary duty.

Exhibit 14.2 ESG Evolution: From Risk to Opportunity

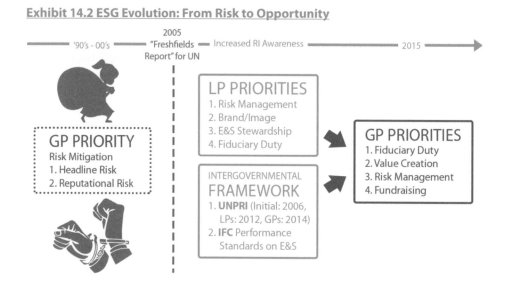

ESG. As LP beneficiaries are often large groups of citizens, there is strong motivation for institutional investors to improve sustainable practices and increase accountability on their behalf.

GP MOTIVATION: LPs were the initial instigators for GPs to take a closer look at ESG. Given today's competitive fundraising environment, established PE firms are expected to have a well-developed approach to ESG, with a credible framework and evidence of ESG-related projects and initiatives executed during the holding period. However, many firms are well aware that an active ESG program can also be a lever for value creation and value protection during the holding period. Viewing a company through an ESG lens expands the opportunity set for value creation, be it through eco-efficiency, reduced employee turnover, or improved corporate governance processes. Value at a portfolio company can be protected by proactively mitigating ESG risks—such as pollution, work stoppages, corruption and money laundering—through timely initiatives and execution of targeted programs. So the impact of thoughtful ESG policies on both fundraising and value creation are powerful reasons to implement a robust program.

INDUSTRY GUIDELINES: Various institutions and industry bodies have contributed to the conversation on ESG by developing frameworks and guidelines for best practice. The United Nations-supported Principles of Responsible Investment (UNPRI), drafted by an international network of investors, provide guidelines for both LPs and GPs. For LPs, UNPRI developed a due diligence questionnaire and made a set of guidelines based on best practices available to incorporate into their allocation process. For GPs, the UNPRI provides a framework for incorporating sustainability and ESG considerations into investment decisions and ownership practices. In emerging markets, standards have often been set and adoption driven by development finance institutions. The International Finance Corporation (IFC) Performance Standards on Environmental and Social Sustainability, for example, provide guidelines for developing a framework focused on the priorities of global growth markets.

Industry guidelines combined with internal responsible investment policies often provide the foundation for a PE firm's ESG framework.

THE CHALLENGE OF MEASURING IMPACT

Not surprisingly, measuring the impact of ESG initiatives is a serious challenge.

Typically, PE boards and ESG subcommittees will identify specific ESG-related KPIs against which to compare a company's progress performance. While tracking most ESG KPIs—for instance, greenhouse gas emission—is relatively straightforward, measuring the impact on company value is often not. Many KPIs may be hard to express in dollar terms as they often lack a financial element or a readily available translation into one.

The best proxy for direct financial measurement—provided a link to value can be established—might be tracking performance improvement over time. Key to this effort is collecting solid data and using targeted analytics. The board will work with management to identify meaningful metrics relevant to the business that drive value without unnecessary administrative efforts.

Currently, environmental improvements are arguably the most commonly valued, ranging from improved eco-efficiency to green product development. Indirect value such as that from enhanced reputational risk management, improved governance, or better labor standards is recognized but typically not explicitly measured. However, the impact of less-quantifiable improvements related to ESG may be a way to increase exit valuations, or at a minimum to reduce a company's cost of capital, given the reduced business risk.

Several research efforts are under way to develop tools to measure economic and social impact in PE investments holistically and to develop—over time—a widely accepted standard. One recent paper explores the measurement of an external rate of return and proposes a platform where companies, investors and third parties can transparently report their activities across various social parameters, thereby allowing themselves to be measured against their peers.[4] Further work will be needed to arrive at a globally accepted standard.

Box 14.1

WHERE DOES YOUR FIRM STAND?
Esg, eSg or esG

The ESG considerations most relevant to investment decision-making vary from GP to GP. For some, environmental factors are at the fore; for others, social or governance issues are more important. Ultimately, which aspect of ESG takes priority will be largely driven by a fund's individual investments, its geographic focus and its investment mandate. Exhibit 14.3 provides insights into the three categories of ESG and highlights some of the most commonly executed initiatives in each.

4. Florman, Klingler-Vidra, and Jacinto Facada (2016).

Exhibit 14.3 Three Categories of ESG

PE firms predominantly focus on value creation by improving eco-efficiency to reduce cost or by developing environmentally sustainable products and services to expand the product offering and capture consumers' willingness to accept a higher price point for such products. KKR's Green Portfolio Program and Carlyle's EcoValuScreen are two initiatives that help portfolio companies identify opportunities to reduce both costs and their environmental footprint.

PE firms carefully manage developmental impact on a portfolio company's stakeholders, starting with labor and health and safety standards, but also including employee training and development programmes. Managing social considerations and the impact on a portfolio company's community may be particularly relevant in emerging markets, where core business models—such as affordable housing and health care delivery—have been developed to address challenges faced by the bottom of the pyramid.

PE firms ensure that portfolio companies have a robust governance structure that enables effective business review and control. Effective governance has long been an integral facet of PE ownership; additional attention is paid to anti-bribery and anti-corruption policies in the context of ESG. From establishing board subcommittees with appropriate charters to creating protocol for reporting environmental and social matters to management, corporate governance improvements are a key PE value driver.

EMERGING ESG FRAMEWORKS

A PE firm's ESG framework ensures that relevant considerations are consistently incorporated across all portfolio companies. Frameworks range from broad flexible guidelines that govern a PE firm's activity on a high level, to targeted due diligence checklists and processes. PE funds may employ in-house staff dedicated exclusively to championing ESG considerations, or rely exclusively on external consultants to conduct this work. As discussed, the reasons to implement an ESG framework vary and are often a combination of several aspects, including industry best practices, LP expectations, and guidelines tailored to a specific GP's investment strategy.

Although managing environmental, social and governance factors in isolation is not a new concept in PE investment, developing and applying a broad framework to manage ESG investment considerations holistically very much is. Given the relatively early stage of development, the industry is still in search of definitive best practices. However, by examining the experiences of various PE firms in a recent

Exhibit 14.4 Emerging ESG Frameworks

RISK FOCUS

ESG risk factors are assessed mainly during the pre-investment process and primarily evaluate a target company's compliance with local laws and regulations. The primary goal of a risk-focused ESG program is to mitigate reputational and headline risk for the portfolio company and PE firm. Significant ESG risk will often lead an investment committee to reject a proposed investment, unless major risks can be mitigated.

PROGRAM DRIVEN

PE firms actively manage ESG investment considerations through targeted initiatives. Steps taken are pro-active and tailored to the needs of a specific company, an industry sector, or the portfolio as a whole. Firms implementing this framework typically hire an experienced ESG specialist to understand their portfolio companies' needs, identify value creation opportunities, execute initiatives, and validate performance.

INTEGRATED APPROACH

A broad framework defines ESG activity across all relevant functions at the PE firm, including investment, portfolio operations, investor relations, and legal. Policies and procedures are typically integrated into existing systems and reviewed by an ESG governing body. Such frameworks provide investment professionals and ESG-dedicated staff with clear guidelines to manage ESG considerations over the life of a fund.

study undertaken by INSEAD's Global Private Equity Initiative (GPEI),[5] we have identified three structures currently employed to manage ESG considerations. These frameworks are not necessarily mutually exclusive, and a single PE firm may fall into more than one category. As global ESG themes and the ability to manage them continue to evolve, we expect the techniques and methods to converge towards a best practice (Exhibit 14.4).

As PE firms begin to develop their own parameters, specific decisions related to structure, capabilities, and resources must be made. The ESG framework will then be applied across the entire investment process:

• Prior to investment, GPs focus on identifying ESG risks that may render a negative investment decision and on value creation opportunities during the holding period. Investment professionals identify material ESG risks and opportunities at the target, oftentimes with the help of a detailed ESG due diligence questionnaire. In addition to the identification of the risk or opportunity, its magnitude is also considered; for

5. INSEAD GPEI (2014).

example, the risk of pollution, while real, may only affect a small business subsidiary and is therefore easily mitigated or ring-fenced from the main business. This initial assessment is used to identify more in-depth due diligence requirements on specific topics, often conducted by external subject matter experts.

- Material ESG considerations are typically included in the final investment memorandum to a PE fund's investment committee and enter negotiations (e.g., indemnities) with the seller. They also become high-priority considerations in the first 100-day plans.

- During the holding period, ESG levers are one of the many value creation drivers available to a portfolio company.[6] Responsibility to execute specific ESG programs and initiatives falls to the management team with the support of PE partners and external consultants. Some PE firms have cross-portfolio programs in place to leverage their knowledge and provide ESG solutions to common challenges across all portfolio companies. Improved ESG policies can enable a company to access capital at a lower cost due to a lower risk rating. At a minimum these measures enhance a company's reputation and in turn mitigate headline risk.

- Consideration of ESG factors extends to the exit review process, during which a broad assessment of ESG performance is undertaken and the operational capabilities and reputation of potential purchasers are screened.

ESG IN EMERGING MARKETS

ESG considerations play a particularly important role in emerging markets as investments often affect local communities on a larger scale than in developed economies. In developed markets, explicit sets of rules of engagement with different stakeholders are in place, such as social contracts, regulations and government fiat. In emerging markets, however, this socioeconomic framework typically does not exist to the same degree, leaving a company to decide on a responsible path ahead.

ENVIRONMENTAL IMPACT: Environmental considerations are no less important in emerging markets than in developed ones; in fact, they can be more critical given the fragility of local communities and the lack of government resources to combat environmental problems. Implementing standardized operational best practices can have a major impact on resource efficiency, driving down waste, improving energy efficiency, and increasing yields in the context of agriculture and fisheries.

SOCIAL IMPACT: While the focus in developed markets is often on environmental and governance factors, PE firms active in emerging markets have a distinct opportunity to deliver value by managing social factors in their investments. To do so, they draw heavily on a range of sustainability and governance frameworks developed specifically for investment in emerging economies, notably the IFC Performance Standards on Environmental and Social Sustainability.

In particular, targeted investment plus improved management and operational techniques lead to better, safer products and services at lower prices. This in turn

---

6. See Chapter 13 for more information on operational value creation.

combats one of the paradoxes of global development, namely, that the poorest pay the highest prices for everyday necessities. In addition, increased commercial activity by portfolio companies improves the standard of living for employees and their families through higher wages as well as investments by the company in better access to training, healthcare and schooling. Communities also stand to benefit from higher tax returns and improved infrastructure.

GOVERNANCE IMPACT: As in developed markets, PE firms active in emerging markets tend to focus on governance as the core of their business model. Yet better governance serves a purpose beyond the specific company by signaling that firms embracing transparency as well as checks and balances can succeed (often contrary to the prevailing modus operandi in emerging markets). The implementation often occurs through training of existing management and expanding a management team's expertise through external hires, and through enhancing the transparency of boards by appointing external and truly independent directors. Measuring and sharing financial and non-financial KPIs provides additional governance levers to drive improved business performance and control.

Responsible Investing: In Growth Markets, It's Common Sense

By Tom Speechley, Partner at The Abraaj Group

To judge from recent surveys, private equity funds and limited partners increasingly agree that environmental, social and governance considerations are a crucial component of their investment process and practices. To borrow from the title of a recent study,[7] however, fund managers and investors have yet to "bridge the gap" in understanding how to achieve their responsible investment objectives. Amid a confusion of acronyms and divergent definitions, it found that expectations and approaches have yet to align.

In the growth markets we operate in, seeing eye-to-eye on defining "impact" matters a lot less than the simple truth that responsible investing boils down to common sense. For limited partners and general partners alike, applying the policies and procedures that companies and investors in their home markets take for granted not only protects against reputational and financial risk, but also creates value. And, in the absence of codified governance, labor and environmental standards in many of these markets, private equity becomes an important driver of positive change in businesses that are as a result both profitable and sustainable. Success with a social purpose.

We have learned over the last 15 years that to deliver robust returns, ESG must be an integral element of the investment process, from screening and

---

7. https://www.pwc.com/gx/en/sustainability/publications/assets/bridging-the-gap.pdf

due diligence, to operational management and oversight, through to exit. Our experience has taken us from regarding ESG as a tool to reduce risk and liabilities to embracing it as an opportunity to increase business performance and strengthen valuations.

Take Southey Holdings, one of the largest privately owned groups in South Africa where upon investment "service with safety" was put at the core of the company's ship and oil rig repair business. Through enhanced staff training, equipment upgrades and rigorous monitoring, Southey was able to further improve its ESG record and win significant assignments from oil majors that had shied away from local contractors because of safety concerns. Health and safety or good business practice?

At Condor Travel, Peru's leading inbound tourism operator, the business provides market opportunities for a large number of local micro-enterprises that would not otherwise be able to reach customers and promote their services. It also now offers U.S. and European eco-tourists travel packages that come with carbon credits to mitigate deforestation in the Tambopata National Reserve in the Amazon Basin. Saving the planet or smart marketing?

And at Crossland Logistics, a leading cross-border trucking operator in Thailand, the executive team adjusted driver compensation levels to match industry standards and hired alternate drivers directly on its payroll. This is uncommon in an industry where companies only pay their main drivers who in turn pay second drivers, usually at a significant discount and without the security of employment benefits. Having two drivers is critical on long-haul journeys as it improves driver safety and security and enables higher utilization of trucks. As a result, attrition rates have fallen by 30% and there has been a reduction in accident rates by 14%. Worker protections or superior and focused client service? Taken from this perspective, responsible investing is not a trade-off, as in "the cost of doing business." It is a long-term investment imperative that time and again creates healthier businesses and healthier societies.

ESG factors are crucial to business now more than at any time in the history of private enterprise—and all indications point to a move towards a common understanding of the reasons why ESG protects and enhances value. Until that time comes, let's agree on two things. Responsible investing is not just the right thing to do, it's the sensible business choice.

CLOSING

The institutionalization of responsible investment best practices is increasingly aligning the fiduciary duty of GPs with the ESG interests of the LP community. With this expansion of the PE mandate beyond financial returns, regulation and improved benchmarking tools continue to emerge that will drive development and enforcement, allowing the PE community to continue to home in on the practices that deliver social impact and those that don't.

KEY LEARNING POINTS

• Responsible investing is an increasingly important item on today's PE agenda. Investment strategies can range from those with pure financial to those with pure social mandates; we define a range of drivers behind the strategies with blended returns.

• Different stakeholders (e.g., GPs, LPs, and industry organizations) have their own motivations to expand their investment mandate beyond financial targets.

• Tracking and measuring the impact of responsible mandates is a challenge. Currently, there is no globally accepted standard; therefore, PE boards and ESG subcommittees need to identify specific ESG-related KPIs to effectively track their companies' progress.

RELEVANT CASE STUDIES

from *Private Equity in Action—Case Studies from Developed and Emerging Markets*

Case #17: Rice from Africa for Africa: Rice Farming in Tanzania and Investing in Agriculture

REFERENCES AND ADDITIONAL READING

Florman, Mark, Klingler-Vidra, Robyn and Jacinto Facada, Martim (2016) A Critical Evaluation of Social Impact Assessment Methodologies and a Call to Measure Economic and Social Impact Holistically through the External Rate of Return Platform. LSE Enterprise Working paper #1602, February.

Freshfields Bruckhaus Deringer (2005) A Legal Framework for the Integration of Environmental, Social and Governance Issues into Institutional Investment, Asset Management Working Group of the United Nations Environment Programme Finance Initiative, October, accessed here http://www.unepfi.org/fileadmin/documents/freshfields_legal_resp_20051123.pdf.

INSEAD (2016) Impact Investing in the Spectrum of Responsible Investment Approaches, INSEAD, January.

INSEAD/GPEI (2014) ESG in Private Equity: A Fast-Evolving Standard, http://centres.insead.edu/global-private-equity-initiative/research-publications/documents/ESG-in-private-equity.pdf.

InvestEurope (2013) Environmental, Social, and Corporate Governance (ESG) Disclosure Framework for Private Equity, http://www.investeurope.eu/media/21433/ESG_disclosure_framework.pdf.

Malk Sustainability Partners (2015) ESG in Private Equity – 2015, June, accessed here http://malkpartners.com/wp-content/uploads/2015/06/ESG-in-Private-Equity-%E2%80%93-2015.pdf.

Principles for Responsible Investment (PRI) report, an investor initiative in partnership with UNEP Finance Initiative and UN Global Compact (2014/15). https://www.unpri.org/about/pri-teams/investment-practices

WWF/Doughty Hanson & Co., Private Equity and Responsible Investment: An Opportunity for Value Creation, http://www.doughtyhanson.com/~/media/Files/D/Doughty-Hanson-Co/Attachments/WWF%20report%20Final.pdf.

Vermaelen, T. (2016), Doing Good by Investing in Sin, INSEAD Knowledge, http://knowledge.insead.edu/blog/insead-blog/doing-good-by-investing-in-sin-4774.

In private equity (PE), the proof is in the exit (rather than the pudding), meaning that only after cash-on-cash returns have been realized and distributed will limited partners (LPs) know if the fund has lived up to their expectations. Interim valuations represent at best an attempt at assessing fair value, but do not paint a complete picture nor guarantee a successful outcome.[1] PE investments are made for a limited time and with a clear goal of selling the equity stake at a profit and to return money to the LPs invested in the fund. As we highlighted in our first chapter, PE is, after all, a simple business: one buys, improves and then sells a portfolio company, the exit being the final stage of the PE investment process.

A PE firm's ability to achieve timely and profitable exits reliably across multiple funds is a key measure of success applied by financial market players; it allows the PE firm not only to return capital and excess profits to investors in line with a fund's mandate, but also to approach those institutional investors again for future fundraising. Thus, "exit shaping"—the process of positioning a portfolio company for sale and choosing the best exit strategy—is a top priority for a PE firm's partners from the start. Indeed, when considering an investment, committees will favor potential investee companies with multiple and clear future exit avenues.

This chapter covers the key considerations that drive the exit process and how exit shaping impacts various stages of the investment process. We explain the main exit strategies employed by PE funds, highlighting not only the processes but also the motivations of the various parties involved. To put our discussion into perspective, Exhibit 15.1 shows the amount of unrealized value in PE portfolios since 2000—investments made, but not exited.[2] Of particular interest is the $1.6 trillion in unrealized value as of 2015 (broken down by fund vintages) awaiting exit in the near future.

Exhibit 15.1 Unrealized Value in PE Funds

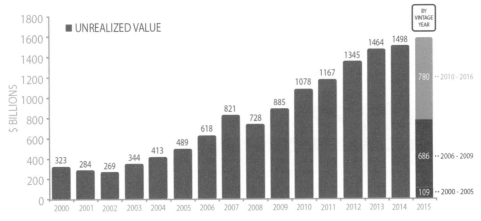

Source: Preqin

---

1. Refer to Chapter 19 Performance Reporting for further information on interim valuation.
2. Unrealized Value in Exhibit 15.1 is for venture, growth, buyout investment strategies. Source: Preqin.

EXIT CONSIDERATIONS

To understand the dynamics surrounding the exit from an investee company, it is useful to remind the reader of the PE fund management model: raise closed-end funds from external institutional investors with the mandate to invest in private companies, hold for a limited time period and, upon successful sale, return capital to investors, all within the finite lifespan of a fund. The returns generated (in aggregate) will determine fund-level profits and have a direct impact on the PE firm's ability to raise a follow-on fund.

First to note is that not all LPs have a uniform view on returns or how to measure them. Target returns vary by each individual investor's perceived riskiness of a fund's investment strategy and investment destination, as well as the role of a given fund in its overall PE portfolio. Also, some LPs might prioritize high internal rates of return (IRRs) over high money multiple returns, typically if they have plenty of attractive reinvestment opportunities, while others prefer money multiples ("you can't eat IRR"[3]) to maximize actual dollar returns.

The timing of those exits impacts the returns in PE, particularly at the beginning and end of a fund's term.

EXIT CONSIDERATIONS EARLY IN THE FUND'S LIFE: Successful exits early in a fund's life are essential when raising follow-on funds; returning cash earlier than expected to the LPs helps them justify the decision to re-up in the next-generation fund. Exiting investments quickly will also have a positive impact on the IRR for the fund (known as "locking in" the IRR) due to the assumptions implicit in the IRR model. On the other hand, by leaving money on the table, early exits may adversely affect the total cash return (or multiple of money) realized from an investment.

EXIT CONSIDERATIONS LATER IN THE FUND'S LIFE: The dynamic shifts during the second half of a fund's term, when the PE model produces an incentive for fund managers to delay exits to maximize money multiples and thereby carry (assuming the fund is performing above its hurdle rate), potentially at the expense of the fund's LPs who are looking for earlier returns. These conflicting views on exit timing are exacerbated in the context of "zombie" funds, funds managed by PE partnerships that have failed to raise a follow-on fund and hold on to the remaining investments for fee income stream.[4]

PREPARATION FOR SALE—EXIT SHAPING

For a PE fund to realize the value created over the course of a holding period, its equity stake must be sold to a suitable acquirer. Planning for a successful sale starts months or even years earlier. Some firms refer to it as the 500-day plan, during which

---

3. A saying in PE and also the title of a memo by Howard Marks, founder of Oaktree Capital, to Oaktree Clients (12-07-2006).
4. See Chapter 20 Winding Down a Fund for more on tail-end funds.

a detailed top-down review is undertaken and a value creation plan is developed for the potential buyer. Exit considerations prior to investment and during the holding period are highlighted below.

DEAL SOURCING, DUE DILIGENCE AND EXECUTION: The path to exit (and its likelihood) is an important factor during the investment committee's initial deliberations of a potential target company. As often in PE, optionality is key, meaning that portfolio companies should ideally come with a range of possible exit avenues, with the final one to be determined at a later stage. As the investment is being assessed and structured, PE firms will seek specific contractual terms maximizing their influence or control over the future exit process. This is particularly important for growth equity and venture funds, which are minority investors. Such terms may include registration rights, drag-along and tag-along rights, and redemption rights.[5] Furthermore, to facilitate an attractive exit, management incentive packages will be structured to reward the team (i.e., vesting of their options or shares) only after management has stayed with the company for a specific time post-exit. This provides a new buyer with a period of stability after ownership is transferred. These contractual terms are typically documented in shareholding agreements, corporate charters and registration rights agreements.

MANAGING PORTFOLIO COMPANIES: PE investors regularly fine-tune their exit plans throughout the holding period. While monitoring company performance versus its business plan, special consideration is paid to the potential impact of value accretive projects on a company's value at exit (i.e., how much recurring profit will the project deliver around exit time, what multiple can be assumed for this profit stream and how does this compare to the cost of the project and any alternative usage of capital?). Additional emphasis may be put on enhancing processes and governance, not only to improve and de-risk the company's performance but also to boost exit prospects; this is especially relevant when planning to exit to large international strategic buyers or through a public listing. Lastly, the exit environment is monitored, from overall market conditions such as liquidity, debt multiples and initial public offering (IPO) activity to industry-specific dynamics such as capital expenditure cycles, mergers and acquisitions (M&A) activity and purchase prices and multiples paid, all to optimize exit timing.

EXIT PREPARATION: Once the timing of an exit is selected, PE firms must prepare their funds' portfolio companies for sale (see Exhibit 15.2). The sales process is by no means standardized and the path chosen and the parties driving the sale will depend on a number of variables, including the internal capabilities of the portfolio company, the resources the PE firm can commit, and the complexity of the operating business.

At a minimum the seller will prepare up-to-date historical and forward-looking accounting statements and collect key operating, financial and legal information. All will typically be summarized in an information memorandum that is used to approach more than one buying party, and made accessible in full to potential buyers in electronic form, at times in a staged process.

---

5. For further details on protective provisions for minority investors, please refer to Chapter 2 Venture Capital and Chapter 10 Transaction Documentation or the Glossary.

Exhibit 15.2 PE Exit Preparation

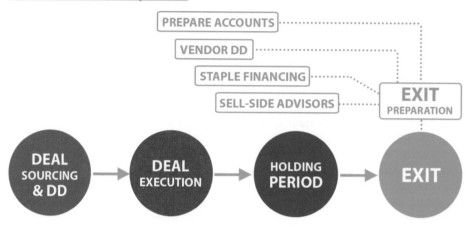

To facilitate a sales process, a portfolio company may commission vendor due diligence (VDD) on the financial, legal and—less frequently—the commercial standing of the company. The use of a VDD allows for a wider sales process and more intense bidding given that the cost associated with due diligence is reduced for each participating bidder. While the portfolio company hires and pays for the service providers that execute VDD, they will eventually assign their work with all legal obligations to the winning bidder and its financing banks.

A related concept for speeding up the sales process and to enhance price and closing certainty is the use of staple financing. In a staple financing, a bank prearranges financing for the acquisition and makes it available to any of the bidders involved in the sales process. The staple financing is negotiated by the seller on the basis of a VDD report and will need to be fully credit approved by the bank, subject to final transaction documentation. The use of staple financing minimizes execution risk for the buyers and, with a committed debt package and reasonable assumption for the equity portion in the capital structure, installs a floor for the purchase price. It also provides buyers with a starting point to explore more attractive debt packages with their own banks.

Lastly, PE firms might hire a sell-side advisor (usually an investment bank) to manage the sales process. This tends to be the standard for larger and more complex processes with multiple parties. It also frees up resources at the PE firm and portfolio company, where oftentimes only the senior management is informed of and involved in the sales process, placing a huge burden on them in addition to their regular responsibilities of managing the company.

EXIT PATHS

Achieving successful exits lies at the core of PE investing and affects decision-making throughout the investment process. PE investors carefully consider the pros and cons of different exit scenarios and market conditions to maximize financial returns. Exhibit 15.3 shows the share of the three most prevalent exit paths for buyouts—sale to a strategic, sale to a PE fund and IPO—over the last decade.

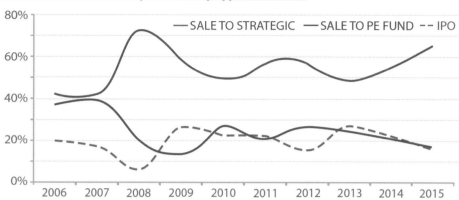

Clearly, the most common avenue is a sale to a third party—be it a strategic buyer or another PE fund—followed by an IPO, and finally, as a partial realization only, a dividend recapitalization. PE investors may pursue more than one exit strategy in a dual-track or triple-track process to create optionality, potentially to generate a price premium, and limit the risk of a failed exit. However, such an approach brings with it additional financial costs and increased demand on management bandwidth.

Each exit strategy—sale to a third party (strategic or financial buyer), IPO, and dividend recapitalization—has its strengths and weaknesses that will affect the speed, complexity and certainty of an exit.

SALE TO A THIRD PARTY

The most common exit path from a majority investment is the sale to a third-party investor.[6] These transactions typically ensure a full exit with a full cash payment. They offer the PE fund significantly more transaction flexibility and control over the exit process than an IPO—where the terms are often determined by security laws, exchange rules and underwriters—and are usually completed faster and at lower cost than an IPO.

Third-party buyers may include strategic investors—domestic and international corporations—or financial investors—in particular PE funds but also hedge funds and family offices. The advantages and disadvantages of an exit involving a strategic buyer may differ significantly from one involving a PE buyer, as highlighted below.

STRATEGIC BUYERS: Strategic investors' operations and expertise in an industry will inform their approach in a sales process. The perceived synergies between their existing operations and the business to be acquired often entice "strategics" to propose a higher valuation than financial investors. Familiarity with a given industry often reduces the due diligence required on a target, and hence the time and resources spent on it by portfolio company management. However, additional time during the process will be spent on evaluating potential synergies. More time post-signing might be required to file for cartel approval and comply with antitrust regulation. These points together with the lack of M&A resources, as few strategics engage frequently in M&A activity, might limit their ability to execute a transaction quickly.

---

6. La Lande (2011).

Strategic investors typically seek a controlling stake (or path to control) when investing in a business, which complicates the sale of minority PE investments. In addition, engaging industry peers in the sales process introduces the risk that competitors gain access to sensitive company information during due diligence. Moreover, management may not support the sale to a strategic investor, given the risk of redundancies post-acquisition.

PRIVATE EQUITY BUYERS: PE funds regularly acquire stakes via secondary and tertiary transactions from other PE investors. As experienced buyers with capital to deploy for a predefined investment period, they offer a higher degree of certainty of closing, as well as the ability to execute faster than strategic investors. Only minimal governance and strategic alignment with the target tend to be required given that their needs are broadly similar to those of the exiting PE investor. Financial buyers might also provide a partial exit bridging unfavorable market conditions for a full exit via IPO or strategic sale later. However, unlike strategic buyers, financial buyers typically require extensive due diligence to become familiar with a company and its sector, are hard negotiators and are often more price sensitive.

Box 15.1
CONCERNS ABOUT SECONDARY BUYOUTS

Large LPs often have exposure to PE funds investing in similar industries or geographies—a fact that becomes problematic in the context of a PE-to-PE or secondary buyout, a particularly popular exit strategy especially during times of high levels of dry powder. LPs invested in both the purchasing and selling fund do not realize liquidity on a portfolio level and find themselves paying management fees, transaction fees and carried interest for exposure to the same asset at a higher price. Moreover, assets sold in secondary or tertiary transactions may offer less upside after multiple PE owners have tried their hands at optimizing and improving the firm.

In rare cases, two funds managed by the same sponsor may execute a secondary transaction, referred to as an affiliate transaction. For LPs invested in both sponsor's funds—as is common because they often participate in a successful sponsor's follow-on fund—such transactions raise the issues outlined above. Yet, for LPs invested in only one fund, the lack of external valuation implies a potential conflict since an under- or overvaluation will jeopardize performance for one of the funds. To mitigate the risk of conflict, an independent valuation is often sought from an external party or an independent PE fund is asked to co-invest. Fund documentation typically requires the approval of LPs in both funds before this type of affiliated transaction can be completed. For these reasons, PE firms try to avoid such transactions.

DESIGNING AN AUCTION PROCESS: PE investors pursuing a third-party sale must consider the trade-off between creating positive competitive tension and speed, certainty and cost when devising the sales process. The third parties approached can range from a single investor or small group of investors in a targeted solicitation, to an investment bank-led auction where a large number of investors go through a multistage bidding process.[7] Both strategic and financial investors are often included in the sales process as this offers both upside valuation potential and increases the certainty of closing the deal. While approaching a small number of investors limits the complexity, the time committed by management and the confidentiality risk, approaching a large number of investors can increase the number of competing bids and lead to a more favorable winning bid. Yet, an excessively competitive process may reduce investors' willingness to commit time and resources to the process given the number of competing bids.

In the event of a successful exit via a third-party sale, PE investors will try to negotiate a clean break from the portfolio company by limiting the extent and duration of liabilities related to the sale. All sellers are typically required to provide contractual representations and warranties reflecting the state of specific aspects of the portfolio company in the transaction documentation. Should these prove to be untrue, acquirers have the right to seek redress. Indemnification clauses set out the remedies (typically cash or liquid assets) available to the buyer in the case of a breach and define the compensation period. PE investors will seek not only to limit the duration of the indemnity clause but also restrict compensation to a percentage of the purchase price (up to 100%) to shield the fund from recourse. Escrow accounts, deal insurance and deferred payment of the purchase price are used to guarantee the buyer that assets are available for recourse.

INITIAL PUBLIC OFFERING

An IPO allows a PE investor to exit from its ownership stake in a portfolio company via the registration and sale of its shares on a stock exchange. A public offering will rarely allow the PE fund to divest fully from the portfolio firm; rather, proceeds from the initial share offering typically allow only for a partial exit, as a portion of IPO proceeds is often used to fund the business itself or repay debt from the LBO. In most cases, PE investors achieve full exit through follow-on offerings of shares after the expiry of a lock-up period commonly lasting 3 to 12 months.

ADVANTAGES: IPOs have historically provided the highest returns relative to other exit strategies for PE-backed companies.[8] In addition to the value realized via the listing, the retained ownership allows PE investors to benefit from future appreciation of the business and the liquidity and daily price discovery of a listed company allows them to optimize the timing of follow-on offerings. Beyond the financial returns, the publicity and reputational benefits of a high-profile IPO have been found to help especially up-and-coming PE firms in their next round of fundraising.[9] IPOs tend to receive strong support from management as the dispersed nature of public ownership provides a platform to maintain a company's independence and avoid reductions in headcount often required after the sale to a strategic investor. And lastly, an IPO announcement alone can prompt bids from strategic and financial investors, which—if accepted—may produce a superior outcome for the investment.

---

7. Though expensive, employing a sell-side advisor—or even two—frees management from the procedural side of the transaction, allowing them to focus on managing the business. Such advisors can be valuable during the initial screening and identification of interested buyers; however, management teams will still need to be heavily involved in individual investor meetings and addressing questions raised during due diligence.
8. Chinchwadkar and Seth (2012).
9. Ibid.

DISADVANTAGES: Pursuing an IPO has several drawbacks. Failure at any stage in the listing process can adversely affect the credibility of both the company and the PE firm, tainting subsequent exit attempts. The IPO market is notoriously cyclical and market and macroeconomic shocks can result in a rapid withdrawal of investor demand for new issues. Selecting the right geography for a listing adds further complexity as market liquidity, competitive listings, and local investors' familiarity with the business vary from market to market. Moreover, not all companies are suitable candidates for IPO, particularly those that do not wish to disclose sensitive information through a publicly available prospectus.

IPOs are expensive relative to other exit strategies. Companies are typically priced at a discount to encourage investor uptake, requiring PE investors to "take a haircut" at least for the initial listing. Associated fixed costs include underwriters, legal and accounting fees, printing fees and listing costs, altogether ranging from 5 to 15% of capital raised, with a larger fee burden for smaller offerings.[10] In addition, management teams must commit significant time to manage the listing process, including attending investor roadshows.

Liquidating a fund's remaining stake following an IPO and the expiry of the lock-up period also presents challenges. Achieving a full exit through follow-on offerings can take years, and large block sales can place downward price pressure on a stock with insufficient liquidity. While an IPO provides an opportunity to capture additional upside via the remaining stake, a partial exit also exposes the fund to downside pricing risk. As the fund's position is liquidated, all the directors associated with the PE fund typically resign from the listed company's board to avoid insider trading issues. This limits the fund's ability to influence a company in which it may still hold a sizable stake.

In some cases, PE funds distribute the remaining shares directly to the fund's LPs (a so-called "distribution-in-kind"). While this can help institutional investors optimize tax exposure, the complexity of managing the publicly listed stake—which often falls to a different team within an institutional investors' organization—can outweigh the benefits and may have negative feedback on the PE fund.

DIVIDEND RECAPITALIZATION

A dividend recapitalization allows a PE investor to extract cash from a company and reduce its capital at risk without affecting the company's ownership structure. Recapitalizations are typically funded either from cash on hand in the portfolio company ("non-leveraged dividend recapitalizations") or by releveraging the balance sheet through issuing new debt securities ("leveraged dividend recapitalizations"). Non-leveraged recapitalizations may be funded through excess operating cash flow or the divestment of a business line and are typically smaller than those funded through new debt issuance. A leveraged recapitalization is often employed when a company's debt-servicing capacity has improved thanks to strong operational performance, or when credit market conditions are more favorable than at the time of the initial buyout transaction. The latter can of course quickly revert, changing the amount of cash available through the debt-raising exercise.

ADVANTAGES: There are several benefits to employing a dividend recapitalization. First, it reduces or even eliminates a fund's downside risk in a portfolio investment

10. PwC (2012).

through the repayment of a portion or all of a fund's invested capital, providing a free upside "option" from its remaining equity stake. With no dilution or new shareholders, buyout investors maintain control of their investment—the board remains unchanged. Second, a recap relieves some of the pressure of achieving a sale to return money to fund LPs and can provide a backup solution if other exit strategies fail. Both forms of dividend recapitalization can be quickly completed with limited involvement of senior management.

DISADVANTAGES: First, a dividend recapitalization only provides a partial exit for investors. So, there is no high-profile exit. Second, there is no independent company valuation by an external investor providing impartial input for mark-to-market pricing. Leveraged recapitalizations increase a portfolio company's debt-servicing requirements, and introduce a fresh set of tighter covenants, both factors limiting the operational flexibility of the company and increasing the risk of default.

Exhibit 15.4 offers a brief summary over the advantages and disadvantages of the various exit options.

Exhibit 15.4 Exit Alternatives and Considerations

PATH	ADVANTAGES	DISADVANTAGES
SALE TO STRATEGIC	i. Full exit ii. Often pay a premium (synergies) iii. Pay in cash	i. Less sophisticated buyers prolonging process ii. Strategics require a majority stake
SALE TO PE FUND	i. Ample dry powder in market ii. Can 'warehouse' company until eventual IPO	i. Sophisticated & demanding buyers ii. Minority stake may reduce pool of potential investors
IPO	i. Potential for high returns ii. Access to future liquidity iii. Often preferred by management iv. High profile exit	i. Lock-up ii. Risks of going to market iii. Uncertainty of returns iv. Strain on management time
DIVIDEND RECAP	i. Returns cash to LPs ii. No new shareholders iii. Does not dilute equity stake	i. Partial exit ii. Value of investment unknown iii. Not a high profile exit

The Proof is in the Exit
By Marco De Benedetti, Managing Director and Co-Head of European Buyouts, The Carlyle Group

Optimizing an exit from a portfolio company is one of the most challenging parts of the private equity business model. As a General Partner, you are faced with a multitude of variables—valuation multiples of comparable companies, the availability of financing and the favorability of terms, M&A activity amongst strategics, strength of capital and foreign exchange markets—all of which factor into the decision to move forward with a sales process, and ultimately, the exit method that will maximize value for the fund and its investors or so-called Limited Partners (LPs) on a risk-adjusted basis.

When investment opportunities are underwritten, a great deal of time is spent evaluating the most likely exit route—and what it will take to get there. More often than not, investments that are not *"take-privates"* lack certain governance, financial reporting, legal and compliance, and/or management capabilities that public companies are required to have. As a result, even in instances where a business is underwritten *knowing* that it is not fit for an IPO, by professionalizing a business towards the standards of a publicly traded company, not only is transparency increased—allowing the deal team to identify and address issues more quickly from reliable and expedited financial reporting—but a narrative of professionalization is shaped which should ultimately help drive a higher sales price.

Maintaining an active dialogue with advisors, industry experts, and management, in conjunction with completing regular internal-valuation analyses, will help to make cyclical valuation trends more transparent and to guide exit timing. However, the cyclical nature of valuations may not always align with exit timelines given the constraints of the fund life. Regardless of these constraints, businesses that generate strong, consistent cash flows enable the General Partner to return capital to shareholders through dividend recapitalizations despite broader industry or sector headwinds.

Portfolio management also plays a critical role when evaluating exit opportunities for a fund. A fund's fixed life cycle generally provides some structure over the expected cadence of realizations to LPs. As a result, situations may arise where holding an investment to realize incremental upside is attractive on a stand-alone basis; however, from a portfolio management perspective, the General Partner may ultimately decide to pursue an exit to manage risk across the broader portfolio. Another aspect to consider is where any given investment is relative to the life of the fund. In the event of funds that have generated a successful return for the Limited Partners, the General Partner might want to expedite the liquidation of the fund and focus on the successor fund. One needs to remember that the Limited Partners are interested in the performance of the overall fund in addition to each individual investment.

Running an exit process is never a speedy endeavor, given it requires countless hours of preparing materials for prospective buyers, traveling for road-shows and/ or management meetings, completing complex regulatory filings, and ultimately negotiating the terms of the sale agreement. Management at the portfolio company serves a critical role throughout this process, while also ensuring that the business continues to operate at its full capacity. Given the significant efforts often demanded from management, it is imperative that when structuring an investment, both economic and timing incentives are aligned between the fund and management team, thereby ensuring all parties are mutually incentivized to achieve a value-maximizing exit outcome.

There are no easy exit paths. Whether it's an IPO, sale to strategic, or dual-tracked process, all exit opportunities require careful ongoing evaluation of the broader market. However, in certain instances, some options may be completely unviable or inopportune. For example, public new issue markets can be closed for extended periods of time; however, this does not necessarily imply a slowdown in M&A activity or unfavorable pricing. Therefore, maintaining flexibility with regards to both timeline and exit-route is critical to maximizing value.

CLOSING

Exit activity in the PE industry is closely monitored by all financial market players as a way to keeping the finger on the pulse of PE. Strong exit years bode well for future fundraising activities, as LPs are more inclined to reinvest in successor funds if and when funds are returned after successful exits.

Exiting from investments in portfolio companies can be a tricky process, fraught with uncertainty; volatile market conditions and unexpected macroeconomic shocks can easily derail the sale of well-managed portfolio firms. This is particularly true in emerging markets, where liquidity is difficult to assess. In addition, minority investors will need to manage majority owners to ensure that their desire to exit aligns with their own timeline and needs.

KEY LEARNING POINTS

• Exits in PE are crucial; they validate the GP's investment strategy and prove its value add during the holding period.

• Exit shaping—the process to prepare the portfolio company for a sale or IPO—is a focal point for PE investors, starting at due diligence and extending throughout the holding period.

• PE firms look for optionality in exits: they consider multiple avenues to sell their stake in the future.

• The three main exit avenues from a control investment are sale to a strategic or PE investor, an IPO, or a dividend recapitalization.

RELEVANT CASE STUDIES

from *Private Equity in Action—Case Studies from Developed and Emerging Markets*

Case #8: Private Equity in Emerging Markets: Can Operating Advantage Boost Value in Exits?

Case #9: Slalom to the Finish: Carlyle's Exit from Moncler

REFERENCES AND ADDITIONAL READING

Aggarwal, V.A. and Hsu, D.H. (2014) Entrepreneurial Exits and Innovation, *Management Science*, 60(4): 867–87.

Bayar, O. and Chemmanur, T.J. (2011) IPOs versus Acquisitions and the Valuation Premium Puzzle: A Theory of Exit Choice by Entrepreneurs and Venture Capitalists, *Journal of Financial and Quantitative Analysis*, 46(6): 1755–93.

Chinchwadkar, R. and Seth, R. (2012) Private Equity Exits: Effect of Syndicate Size, Foreign Certification and Buyout Entry on Type of Exit. SSRN Electronic Journal, 08/2012.

Ferreira, D., Manso, G. and Silva, A.C. (2014) Incentives to Innovate and the Decision to Go Public or Private, *Review of Financial Studies*, 27(1): 256–300.

La Lande, Rashida K. (2011) Private Equity Strategies for Exiting a Leveraged Buyout, Gibson, Dunn & Crutcher LLP via Practical Law Company.

PwC (2012) Considering an IPO? The Costs of Going and Being Public May Surprise You.

Fund Management and the GP–LP Relationship

We have so far focused on the investment side of private equity (PE): how to identify, execute, manage and exit a single investment. We now turn to a central relationship in PE: that between general partners (GPs) and limited partners (LPs), the PE firms that raise and manage funds and the investors that back them. The GP–LP model allows for specialized roles, separating the investment function from the capital allocation function and thereby limiting the liability of LPs. With this blueprint, the industry was able to scale and grow significantly over the past four decades.

Yet the separation of roles adds substantial legal and fundraising cost to the PE model. To reduce the legal complexity, standards for documents and processes have evolved, most notably the limited partnership agreement.

The separation of activities can also lead to resource and information asymmetries between a fund's GP and its LPs. From the LP's perspective, selecting a manager and managing a portfolio of PE funds are the main tasks requiring significant (and not always available) resources.

One feature embedded into the model to minimize the principal/agent conflict is the finite lifetime of funds. This instills discipline in the GP, focuses their attention on exits to return proceeds to investors and gives LPs the ability to reconsider the relationship at regular intervals.

Section Overview

The chapters in this section cover the main elements of the institutional GP–LP fund model, from raising to winding down a fund (for GPs) to allocation decisions when developing a PE program (for LPs).

Chapter 16. Fund Formation: The PE fund model determines the rules of engagement for GPs and LPs over the life of a PE fund. We touch on the structural and contractual foundations of a PE limited partnership, examine key considerations for GPs and LPs and discuss the limited partnership agreement.

Chapter 17. Fundraising: Fundraising is the first step in a PE fund's lifecycle. The capital raised from investors will not only be used to invest in portfolio companies but will also finance the fund manager's business as a going concern. We describe the standard steps, key considerations and documents involved in this process.

Chapter 18. LP Portfolio Management: An LP's allocation to PE must be considered within the context of its broad investment mandate and its overall portfolio construction. Key elements discussed in this chapter include the benefits and challenges presented by the PE asset class, defining parameters of a PE program, fund manager selection and managing an existing portfolio of PE funds.

Chapter 19. Performance Reporting: The challenge of evaluating PE performance comes from its very nature as an illiquid asset class with long investment horizons. This chapter explains the steps taken to derive a fund's gross and net performance and highlights potential issues to be considered in the process. We conclude with a closer look at methods to compare PE performance to public equity performance.

Chapter 20. Winding Down a Fund: This chapter closes the loop by discussing how to wind down a PE fund and bring the parties' legal obligations to an end. We describe the standard process of dissolving, liquidating and terminating a fund and investigate specific end-of-fund-life solutions in the case of unrealized assets at the end of a regular—and irregular (zombie)—fund life.

Private equity (PE) funds today—be they venture capital, growth equity or buyout funds—operate in a global market and invite investors with distinct mandates to deploy their assets via a single fund vehicle. As the PE industry has grown over the past 40 years, investors have increasingly demanded more transparency and flexibility to accommodate their specific needs. With greater visibility of and interest in the PE asset class than ever, the demands on fund formation have expanded.

The fund formation process determines the rules of engagement for general partners (GPs) and limited partners (LPs) over the life of a PE fund. While many of the provisions found in fund formation documentation are standardized or revolve closely around a market standard, an effective and expertly executed fund formation process can optimize a fund's structure and its key terms for LPs and GPs alike. Due to a fund's longevity—often 10 years or more—setting clear and transparent rules is essential for the GP's ability to attract investors, mitigate potential risks and navigate a complex and changing regulatory, tax and investment landscape in the process.

In this chapter, we touch on the structural and contractual foundations of a PE fund—the PE limited partnership—elaborating on the broad terms laid out in Chapter 1. We begin by examining the key considerations for GPs and LPs during the fund formation process; we then present the various vehicles typically employed to channel capital to a fund and its investments. We conclude with a discussion of the key legal document in the fund formation process: the limited partnership agreement (LPA). Please note that this chapter is highly technical, making it more of a source of reference for the general reader.

SETTING UP A PE FUND

The primary goal in fund formation is simple: structure a collection of vehicles that allows for an optimal flow of capital from LPs to the fund—and ultimately to its portfolio companies and back to the LPs upon exit—preferably with minimal tax impact at the fund level.[1] The most common and effective structures allow for the flexible management of the fund's capital throughout the PE investment cycle (i.e., investment phase/divestment phase) and avoid double taxation on distributions of income and capital for LPs in the fund.

PE funds are usually set up as limited partnership closed-end funds; we will focus the discussion in this chapter on this legal structure. Less commonly employed fund structures include search funds, deal-by-deal structures, opt-in/opt-out funds and open-ended (evergreen) vehicles.[2]

---

1. A note on taxation: Limited partnerships have in general no entity-level tax. Each GP, manager and LP will respectively manage its own tax situation. Nevertheless, much attention is paid to withholding taxes for proceeds coming to the fund upon exit of deals. Also, the much-discussed topic of tax treatment for carry—should it be treated as capital gain or ordinary income—is no longer a US issue only, but incurs greater scrutiny in many jurisdictions.

2. Please refer to our Glossary for a brief definition of these vehicles.

Frequently employed onshore limited partnership structures include Delaware Limited Partnerships for funds primarily investing in the United States, English Limited Partnerships for funds primarily investing in the United Kingdom and various limited partnership structures employed in European and Asian jurisdictions. PE funds may also employ offshore limited partnership structures—including Cayman Islands, Jersey and Guernsey Limited Partnerships—to optimize a fund offering. When offshore vehicles are employed, tax treaties and other bilateral/multilateral agreements can help mitigate unfavorable tax treatment of the offshore fund.

On the one hand, PE firms aim to establish a simple funding structure with entities in as few jurisdictions as possible to minimize cost and the complexity of fund operation, administration, reporting and regulatory compliance; on the other hand, demands from LPs and the desire to operate in multiple countries may make this a futile effort. From the GP's perspective, PE funds are ideally structured as onshore vehicles within the jurisdiction and location of its target portfolio companies. This eliminates any red tape or restrictions imposed on foreign investment vehicles and can cast a favorable light on the fund's activity in the public eye. However, more often than not, circumstances may lead the fund to a more flexible offshore vehicle—for instance, in the Cayman Islands, Luxembourg or Jersey. In such cases, a primary fund is established offshore, with capital invested through wholly-owned subfunds or acquisition vehicles domiciled in the onshore jurisdiction.

LPs look for a familiar structure in a recognized onshore or offshore jurisdiction when considering capital allocations to a PE fund. Investors will ensure that the structure limits their own liability to the capital committed to the fund and that the laws supporting their limited liability are familiar and robust. For US domiciled LPs, a fund structure that optimizes outcomes under the US tax and regulatory system (for example, UBTI, ERISA, CFC, PFIC) is a paramount requirement.

FUND VEHICLES

GPs have a variety of fund structures and supporting vehicles to choose from when establishing a closed-end PE fund. To optimize specific tax, regulatory and other structuring needs of one or more LPs, multiple fund vehicles are often established to channel investments alongside a single primary fund. These include parallel funds, feeder funds, and co-investment vehicles. Exhibit 16.1 provides an example of a fund structure with a variety of supporting vehicles; their primary functions are described in the section that follows.

PRIMARY FUND: The primary fund is the main vehicle to which the GP and the majority of LPs commit. The provisions of a primary fund's LPA govern substantially all investment, divestment, and fund management activities made through any vehicle associated with it.

PARALLEL FUND: Parallel funds are usually set up to accommodate the special legal, tax, regulatory, accounting or other needs of an individual LP or group of LPs participating in a fund offering. These vehicles invest and divest side by side with the primary fund in fixed proportions typically based on each vehicle's capital commitments; both funds will usually maintain the same percentage of invested-to-committed capital over the

Exhibit 16.1 PE Primary Fund and Complementary Vehicles

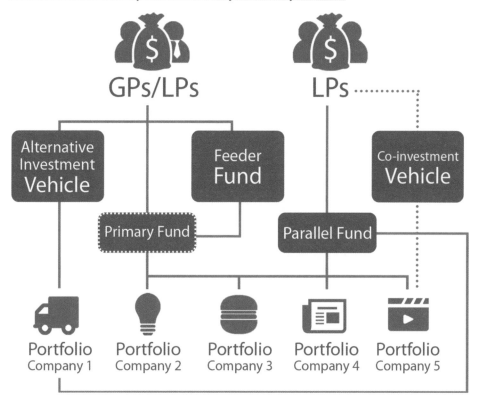

life of the fund. LPs in the parallel fund share in all expenses related to managing the funds and fund investments on a pro-rata basis. The terms of the parallel fund are substantially the same as the primary fund, except as is reasonably necessary to address the needs of LPs in the parallel fund. Parallel funds are often established to accommodate, for example, foreign investors subject to taxes from an onshore vehicle, the need for opt-out from LPs (for example, Sharia compliance), or when the terms of a single investor are difficult to disclose in full to other fund investors.

FEEDER FUND: Feeder funds aggregate commitments from one or more investors and invest directly into the primary fund as an LP. Feeder funds are primarily formed for tax purposes; as such, they may, for instance, file and pay taxes in a specific jurisdiction (rather than each investor paying individual taxes) or may have special tax attributes. A feeder may allow foreign investors to avoid onshore taxes. Feeder funds may also be established by banks and other institutions that pool capital from multiple clients to meet the minimum check size required for investment in a PE fund; in this case, they are at times referred to as "platforms." Investors in a feeder fund are responsible for meeting capital calls and paying expenses and fees on the same terms as LPs in the primary fund.

ALTERNATIVE INVESTMENT VEHICLE: Alternative investment vehicles (AIVs) are structured to accommodate one or more special investments made outside of the primary fund (and/or a parallel fund). These vehicles are employed when the main fund is not the optimal vehicle for a particular investment, whether for tax, regulatory or other legal reasons. GPs have broad discretion to establish an AIV but they are typically deal-specific or established for a group of related deals. AIVs may invest in parallel to or in lieu of a primary fund and have full rights to draw on LP capital commitments on substantially the same terms as the primary fund.

CO-INVESTMENT VEHICLE: These vehicles are set up by the GP to invest alongside the master and parallel funds in a portion of a single investment. The co-investment is typically provided by one or more of a fund's LPs at lower (or no) fee and carried interest terms than the primary fund; at times, capital may be drawn from an external party. Co-investors may be granted more flexibility than fund LPs around exit timing, allowing them to stay on post-exit of the primary fund. LP co-investment rights are subject to negotiation and may provide preferential access to co-investment opportunities for a cornerstone LP or may be granted on a case-by-case basis at the full discretion of the GP. The primary fund typically needs to receive its full allocation of an investment opportunity before co-investment can be sought, with the co-investment amount typically being smaller than the investment from the primary fund.

LIMITED PARTNERSHIP AGREEMENT

A fund's LPA sets out the general terms and conditions applicable to all participants in a PE fund. This document establishes the rights and responsibilities of a fund's general partner and limited partners related to fundraising, capital calls and distributions, expenses and profit sharing, fund governance and reporting, and fund termination. The section that follows outlines the key provisions found in an LPA.

ORGANIZATION

This section of the LPA sets out basic information on the fund, including but not limited to:

- The laws and regulations governing formation of the partnership
- The name, place of business and registered agent of the partnership
- The purpose of the partnership and the types of investment it will make
- The term of the partnership, typically 10 years with two, one-year extensions
- The investment period and the minimum capital a fund must deploy before its GP can raise a follow-on fund
- The additional fund vehicles associated with the fund

PARTNERS AND CAPITAL

In this section of the LPA, key stakeholders and the ways in which they contribute capital to the fund are defined. An entity affiliated with the sponsoring PE firm will serve as a fund's GP and will typically commit from 1 to 5% of a fund's total capital, with the GP commitment rarely exceeding 10% of a fund's capital. A GP admits an initial group of LPs to the fund and the GP then commences investing.

CAPITAL CALLS: As soon as a fund has had its first closing, the GP may issue capital calls to LPs to make investments and cover deal expenses, pay fund fees and expenses related to establishing the fund up to a cap, and settle the general obligations and liabilities of the partnership. The capital called by a fund is referred to as contributed capital. LPs must meet capital calls within a limited period (e.g., 10–20 days) of receipt; an LP that fails to meet capital calls suffers severe penalties such as the loss of the right to make future capital contributions, the loss or reduction of its stake in existing investments, or the forced sale of its stake in the fund. An LP may be excused from meeting a capital call for investment if its participation would result in violation of a law or regulation. The GP may request that the other LPs meet the shortfall from an excused or defaulting LP.

SUBSEQUENT CLOSINGS: GPs may at their discretion admit additional LPs into a fund via subsequent closings within a specific time period—typically 9 to 18 months—following the first closing. LPs that are admitted post-first closing will typically participate in fund investments made prior to their admittance and are required to pay all fund fees and expenses as if they had committed on the first closing date. At the time of their subscription, these LPs must contribute capital to the fund equal to their proportionate share of total contributed capital plus interest. This contribution is distributed to a fund's existing LPs to align the ratio of capital called to capital committed for all LPs while the interest payment compensates existing LPs for effectively "covering" a new LP's capital commitments.

LP LIMITED LIABILITY: LPs' liability in a fund is limited to their capital commitment; an LP is under no obligation to commit any additional capital to the fund beyond its unused capital commitments at any point during the fund's term. GPs may be permitted to recycle committed capital during the investment period if an investment is exited within a certain period, often one to two years (so-called "quick-flips"), or to the extent distributions represent a return of capital drawn for fees or expenses. An LP may also be required to return distributed capital to a fund to meet indemnity or partnership obligations.

DISTRIBUTIONS POST-EXIT AND CARRIED INTEREST

Distributions to LPs and GPs from a limited partnership consist of current income generated by fund investments and proceeds realized from the sale of fund investments, net of outstanding and reserved partnership expenses and obligations. Distributions may be made in the form of cash or marketable securities; marketable securities typically represent "in-kind" distributions of listed equity resulting from an initial or secondary public offering. LPAs set out the period within which current income and sale proceeds must be distributed to fund investors, for instance 60 days following the close of the fiscal quarter for current income and 45 days after proceeds are received from a sale of fund assets. In addition, distributions may be made to cover the proportionate tax expense incurred by fund investors for investments held in the portfolio.

DISTRIBUTION WATERFALL: The order of priority and timing of distributions made to a fund's LPs and its GP are set out in an LPA. Priority is typically defined by a waterfall consisting of four steps: the first two steps allocate distributions to fund LPs, the third allocates proceeds to the GP, and the fourth allocates distributions to both fund LPs and the GP. Proceeds shared with the GP in the third and fourth step are referred to as a GP's carried interest (or profit share)—the key incentive for PE professionals—and is most frequently set at a 20% share of a fund's net profits. An example of the generic language defining the steps in a distribution waterfall is set out in Exhibit 16.2.[3] It should be noted that venture funds typically do not have a hurdle rate.

---

3. In recent years, some of the most sought-after funds started to lower or even omit the hurdle rate (traditionally 8%).

Exhibit 16.2 Distribution Waterfall and Carried Interest

STEP 1: Return of LP Contributed Capital

Distribution of capital until each LP has received 100% of its aggregate contributed capital for investment, fees and fund expenses.

STEP 2: Hurdle Rate

Distribution of capital to each LP until a hurdle rate – a preferred return typically in the range of 8% to 10% per annum – on contributed capital has been achieved.

STEP 3: GP Catch-up

Distribution of capital until the GP has received carried interest equal to 20% of the distributions made to fund LPs in Step 2 and to the GP in Step 3.

STEP 4: 80/20 Split

Distribution of remaining capital in the ratio of 80% to fund LPs and 20% to the GP.

CARRIED INTEREST: PE funds employ two common methodologies that determine when a GP is entitled to carried interest: all capital first carry and deal-by-deal carry with loss carry-forward. When an all capital first carry (also known as a European-style waterfall) is employed, a GP is entitled to carried interest only after all LP capital contributions made to the fund have been returned and a hurdle rate on all contributed capital has been achieved.

In the case of deal-by-deal carry with loss carry-forward (also known as an American-style waterfall), a GP is entitled to carried interest following the sale of each investment in a fund, after LPs' capital contributions have been returned and the hurdle rate for that investment and all previously exited investments has been achieved. See Box 16.1 for worked-out examples of both carried interest methodologies.

CLAWBACK: If, at the end of a fund's term, a GP has received carried interest in excess of the agreed share of fund-level profits (usually 20% of net profits) or has received carry without the LPs realizing their hurdle rate, a clawback provision is triggered that allows LPs to reclaim any overdistribution and align the share of fund profits with the terms set out in the LPA.[4] Clawback provisions are most commonly activated in an American-style waterfall, and rarely in the context of a European-style waterfall. The clawback covers the whole life of a fund and essentially looks at the economic position once all the dust settles (and all investments have been made, exited and proceeds distributed). At times, LPAs may define an interim clawback. If in place, return distributions will be measured half-way through a fund's term and (if necessary) overdistributions may be "clawed back" or future distributions diverted to the LPs until alignment has been restored. The obligation to meet clawback payments sits with all carry recipients at a PE firm, unless extremely junior, and a portion of the GP's carried interest may be held in an escrow account (especially if there is no guarantee in place).[5] Nevertheless, it should be added that experienced PE partners will avoid a clawback situation and forego carry if and when the risk of overdistribution arises.

---

4. GPs typically provide clawback payments that are "net of taxes."

5. Where the GP is a special purpose vehicle, the "owners" of the GP often guarantee the GP's clawback obligation. In some cases, the sponsor itself may guarantee the clawback, or much less frequently the "key" principals may jointly guarantee the clawback obligations of all carry recipients.

Box 16.1

CARRIED INTEREST IN PRACTICE
ALL CAPITAL FIRST VS. DEAL-BY-DEAL

The example below shows the impact of the two carried interest models on the timing of cash flows to both the GP and LPs as exit proceeds are distributed.

Our sample fund makes only two investments—$100 million in PortCo 1 in year one and $140 million in PortCo 2 in year two—and exits each after five years. PortCo 1 is sold for $300 million, generating an excess return of $200 million (MoM of 3×), and PortCo 2 is sold for $280 million, generating an excess return of $140 million (MoM of 2×); see Exhibit 16.3. We further assume for simplicity a hurdle rate of 8% per annum, carried interest of 20% and no management or portfolio fees.

Exhibit 16.3 Fund Investments

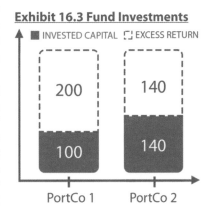

An all capital first waterfall follows the sequence of steps shown in Exhibit 16.4 and detailed below.

Exhibit 16.4 All Capital First Waterfall

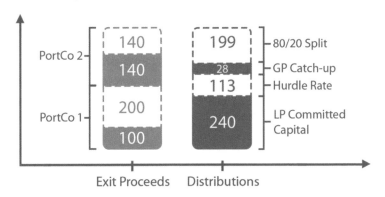

Exit PortCo 1: ($300 million) → funds are used to:
- Step 1: return all of the LP capital drawn by the fund ($240 million).
- Step 2: part one of the $113 million[6] hurdle rate paid to LPs ($60 million).
- No carry for the GP—all proceeds from the exit have been distributed to LPs.

6. The hurdle rate calculation = ($240 million * 1.08^5) – $240 million.

Exit PortCo 2: ($280 million) → funds are used to:
- Complete step 2: part two of the $113 million hurdle rate paid to LPs ($53 million).
- Step 3: GP entitled to carried interest "catch-up" ($28 million).
- Step 4: remaining proceeds from exit are divided between LPs and the GP on an 80/20 basis (total: $199 million; LPs: $159 million; GP: $40 million).

A deal-by-deal waterfall follows the sequence of steps shown in Exhibit 16.5 and detailed below.

Exhibit 16.5 Deal-by-deal Waterfall

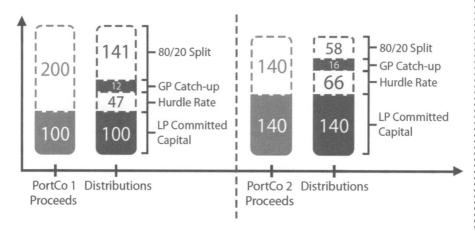

Exit PortCo 1 ($300 million) → funds are used to:
- Step 1: return all of the LPs' capital invested in PortCo 1 ($100 million).
- Step 2: hurdle rate for PortCo 1 is paid to LPs ($47 million[7]).
- Step 3: GP entitled to carried interest "catch-up" ($12 million).
- Step 4: remaining proceeds from exit are divided between LPs and the GP on an 80/20 basis (total: $141 million; LPs: $113 million; GP: $28 million).

Exit PortCo 2 ($280 million) → funds are used to:
- Step 1: return all of the LPs' capital invested in PortCo 2 ($140 million).
- Step 2: hurdle rate for PortCo 2 is paid to LPs ($66 million[8]).
- Step 3: GP entitled to carried interest "catch-up" ($16 million).
- Step 4: remaining proceeds from the exit are divided between LPs and the GP on an 80/20 basis (total: $58 million; LPs: $46 million; GP: $12 million).

Within the setting of our straightforward example, the fund's GP receives the same amount of carried interest independent of the model applied; yet, the timing under the deal-by-deal waterfall is more favorable to the GP (carry is received earlier).

---

7. The hurdle rate calculation = ($100 million * 1.08^5) – $100 million.
8. The hurdle rate calculation = ($140 million * 1.08^5) – $140 million.

RIGHTS AND DUTIES OF THE GP

A PE fund's GP is solely responsible for operating, managing, administering and controlling the affairs of a PE limited partnership, notably including all decision-making related to investing and divesting the fund's capital. GPs are required to maintain a fund's status with properly authorized regulatory authorities so that it may carry out its duties within the jurisdictions in which it operates, or appoint an authorized investment manager to carry out those functions on its behalf. While fund LPs have no input on investment decision-making, the LPA sets out certain limits and obligations that govern GP investment and portfolio management activity to protect LP interests and align with the fund strategy presented during fundraising. These may include but are not limited to:

- Limits on the amount of capital the GP may invest in a single investment, in a single year or before certain fund milestones
- Limits on the sectors, geographies, strategies and types of instruments within which the fund can invest
- An obligation to value fund portfolio companies and report those values to fund LPs on a regular basis
- An obligation for the GP to prepare and pay taxes on behalf of the partnership, and use certain efforts to secure relevant tax exemptions or refunds on behalf of fund LPs
- The right to offer co-investment rights to certain LPs in case the fund does not take up the entire investment amount
- Rights to secure fund-level debt, incur expense, and hedge portfolio exposure on behalf of the fund
- The right to hire consultants and advisors to execute investment and portfolio management activity

KEY PERSON CLAUSE: The LPA will clearly define the key personnel or "key persons"—typically senior partners—responsible for the fund's activities. In general, key persons are required to devote substantially all of their time to managing the fund. In the case of one (rarely) or several key persons leaving, the following remedies may apply: termination of the investment period (most commonly), removal of the GP or dissolution of the fund.

AFFILIATED FUNDS: LPAs will clearly lay out any restrictions of investment activities for the fund's GP and its affiliates. Provisions typically limit the GP or its affiliates from raising a follow-on fund during the fund's investment period or until a certain portion of fund commitments have been invested. Specifically, the provisions will detail the "devotion of time" of the key persons in the fund and the "allocation of deal flow" in the case of a family of funds. Any violation of these provisions/duties can lead to the suspension of a fund's investment period. Investment activity of the GP and its affiliates outside of the fund is typically limited to investments previously earmarked from an existing fund, follow-on investment in portfolio companies of existing funds, investments that fall outside of the fund's mandate and an affiliate's co-investment in the fund's investment. GPs may also be required to disclose any opportunity that falls within the fund's mandate but is pursued by an affiliated fund to the fund's LP Advisory Committee (LPAC), which may need to provide consent before the investment is executed by the affiliate.

MANAGEMENT, PORTFOLIO AND OTHER FEES: A fund's LPA typically includes a provision that requires the fund to enter into an investment advisory agreement with a third-party investment advisor, typically an affiliate of the GP. The investment advisor manages the day-to-day activity of the PE fund—including but not limited to evaluating investment opportunities, providing advisory services to portfolio companies, and managing the fund audit and reporting function—in exchange for a management fee. The management fee usually ranges between 1.3% and 2.5% during the investment period and often steps down to a lower percentage and/or a lower capital base—for instance, invested capital rather than committed capital—at the expiration of the investment period. The investment advisor, the GP and its affiliates often generate fee income—including but not limited to transaction fees, monitoring fees, break-up fees, directors' fees and acquisition and disposal fees—for services rendered to the fund or its portfolio companies. A large proportion of this additional fee income—historically between 50% and 100%, now trending towards 100%—is shared with a fund's LPs via a management fee offset.

FUND-LEVEL FEES: A fund's GP and investment advisor incur significant expenses in the set-up and throughout the term of a PE fund. LPAs set out a mechanism for a GP to recoup the organizational expenses incurred in establishing a fund from its LPs through an initial capital call immediately following an LP's subscription to the fund. Additional expenses incurred in the management of a PE fund include broken-deal expenses, taxes imposed on the partnership, the cost of fund-level borrowing, and fees and expenses for attorneys, accountants, advisors and consultants. To the extent that fund-level expenses incurred are not reimbursed by a prospective or actual portfolio company, the fund will pay directly or reimburse the GP or the investment advisor for the payment of these expenses.

INDEMNIFICATION: This clause protects or limits the liability of individuals involved in the fund. LPAs include clauses that remove the liability for a fund's GP and its investment advisor—as well as their directors, officers, partners, members, employees, agents and other affiliates—for any action or inaction made in good faith that results in a liability, claim, cost or expense against the fund. The indemnification typically does not extend to liabilities resulting from fraud, willful misconduct, violation of a law or breach of contract. These clauses typically include give-back provisions that allow the GP to claw back a portion of distributions made to fund LPs to satisfy indemnification obligations.

OTHER PROVISIONS

LP ADVISORY COMMITTEE: An LPAC is formed to advise the GP on select issues over the course of a PE fund's term. LPAC members are nominated by the GP and consist primarily of the largest LPs in the fund. A fund's LPAC generally does not owe a fiduciary duty to the fund or its LPs, and the activities of an LPAC should be limited strictly to review of fund matters—as opposed to active management—to preserve the limited liability of the LP with which an LPAC member is associated. Key functions of the LPAC include:

• Reviewing valuation methodologies, portfolio company valuations and proposed write-ups/write-downs of fund assets

- Reviewing and providing or withholding consent for any potential conflict of interest in any potential transaction, particularly those concerning related party transactions
- Reviewing and providing or withholding consent for issues related to changes in the fund's governing documents, including but not restricted to extension of the investment period, removal of investment restrictions and approval of changes to key personnel within a fund

TRANSFERABILITY OF FUND INTERESTS: The LPA sets out specific guidelines and circumstances under which a GP's or LP's interests in a fund may be transferred to a different party.

- *GP interests:* The voluntary withdrawal or forced removal of a GP from a fund is typically subject to a supermajority of votes from fund LPs. In the event of a transfer, the outgoing GP remains responsible for all activity related to managing the fund until its departure, and maintains all indemnities granted by the fund. The treatment of economics in the context of a transfer of GP interest is subject to negotiation; for example, the outgoing GP may retain its rights to carried interest on a portion of the portfolio. In addition to a for-cause termination right, many LPAs provide LPs with the right to remove and replace the GP on a no-fault basis. The "cause" triggers for GP removal and the voting thresholds required to remove a GP are often heavily negotiated.

- *LP interests:* LPs are typically not permitted to transfer their interest in a fund without the express consent of its GP. Other LPs in a fund may have a right-of-first-offer, which requires the LP transferring the interest to first field offers from existing LPs before seeking an external buyer with a superior offer.

DISSOLUTION, LIQUIDATION AND TERMINATION OF THE FUND: LPAs typically lay out a specific process for winding down a fund. An LPA will typically define specific events that will cause a PE fund to dissolve, including, for example, the sale of all fund investments, a supermajority vote by fund LPs, or the bankruptcy of the GP. Following the dissolution of the fund, remaining fund investments will be liquidated in a prudent manner over a stated time period. If a fund's GP or its assigned liquidating trustee determines that the sale of investments within that time period would result in undue losses to the fund, liquidation for such investments may be delayed. Termination results in the partnership coming to an end.[9]

REPORTING: LPAs typically set out specific guidelines under which a GP must report a fund's activity to each of its LPs. GPs issue formal reports on a quarterly basis and an annual report at financial year-end that include a fund's net asset value (NAV), descriptions of new investments and follow-on investments, the sale of fund assets, cash or in-kind distributions, and the amount of management fees due. Key among the information reported is the NAV, which is prepared on a quarterly basis and represents the sum of each portfolio company's fair market value.[10] Fund NAVs are a particular focus as they determine the number of shares for distributions-in-kind or set the headline price in the context of a sale of an LP's interest in the fund.

---

9. Please refer to Chapter 20 Winding Down a Fund for a full discussion of this topic.

10. Please refer to Chapter 19 Performance Reporting for an overview on valuation methodology.

SIDE LETTERS

Side letters are contractual agreements that alter the terms of individual investors' participation in a PE fund without impacting the LPA and other governing documents. These agreements are widely used during the fundraising process to provide preferential rights for large or cornerstone investors in a fund or to cater to the specific needs of an LP without renegotiating a fund's LPA. Typical provisions addressed in a side letter include:

- Preferential fees (management fees or terms on management fee offsets)
- Preferential information or disclosure rights
- Co-investment rights
- Provisions related to the tax, legal or regulatory status of an investor
- "Most favored nation" (MFN) provisions

Not on the Side
By Andrew M. Ostrognai, Partner, Debevoise & Plimpton LLP

One of the biggest trends in the negotiation of private equity funds has a name that ironically suggests it is a small detail to be wrapped up right before closing: *the side letter*. The side letter is simply a side agreement between an investor and a fund's general partner or manager, and the right of the general partner or manager to enter into side letters is well-accepted in the market and is typically spelled out in the fund's limited partnership agreement (LPA) and private placement memorandum. But this simple explanation belies the growing role and importance of the side letter.

The practice of entering into side letters has grown over the last decade or so from something rather small and truly on the side—confirmation of a bespoke tax issue, or granting an investor the right to see draft financial accounts earlier—to lengthy and complex agreements central to many fundraisings. They can and do cover every topic imaginable, from favorable economics, to reporting, to compliance with laws (even those which the general partner would not otherwise need to comply with), to opt-outs, and the list goes on.

For the most sophisticated investors in the largest funds, side letters are far from being on the side of anything; they may well be the main attraction, and the subject of the most negotiation during a fundraise. Indeed, for a well-established fund that has been through multiple fundraises, the LPA or other constitutive document may change little, but the side letters may vary greatly from fund to fund in terms of number and nature of issues they address.

Sophisticated sponsors will spend considerable time thinking about the interplay of the LPA and side letters. For example, if a sponsor moves terms from side letters to the LPA, it may obviate the need for some negotiation, but the sponsor may also lose the ability to generate some goodwill in negotiations by giving investors some of the terms they have sought. At the same time, if a sponsor saves everything for the side letter—even terms it is otherwise quite willing to give to all investors—the grinding process of negotiating scores of provisions with dozens of investors may finally outweigh any joy investors would otherwise have received in getting the terms they seek.

On top of that, a sponsor may at times wish to stash a particular provision in a side letter—for privacy's sake, or because they don't want to clutter the negotiating history of the LPA—but find the provision simply won't work unless it is in the LPA. Such provisions include those that put burdens or obligations on the other investors if they are exercised, such as withdrawal rights.

As if all of this was not already complex enough, these side letter negotiations are conducted against a backdrop of most favored nations (MFN) provisions. MFN provisions at their most basic simply mean the sponsor needs to treat investors equally in what it gives them in side letters. But the process is never that simple.

It is common in the market today to group investors by the amount committed, a practice often referred to as *economic tiering*. In this way, investors get the benefit only of provisions given to investors committing the same amount or less to a fund. The benefit of MFN to an investor may be further limited by carving certain rights found in side letters from the MFN provisions, such as rights to seats on the fund's advisory committee. Additionally, it is not uncommon for MFN for a particular investor to apply only to those rights of benefit to that investor; for example, a non-US taxpayer would not be offered a special right that benefits only US tax-exempt investors.

These are only the most common modifications and adjustments to the MFN concept, but there are many others. So MFN is equality of a sort, but heavily caveated and footnoted.

The rise of the side letter should not be surprising. This business is, after all, called *private* equity. With a name like that, it should be expected that, for the most sophisticated investors and funds, private side deals have become business as usual.

CLOSING

Getting the legal structure and rules of engagement right while ensuring that all parties involved understand their rights and responsibilities is key in fund formation; after all, GPs face many obligations, chief among them fiduciary duty towards their investors. Given the long duration of the typical closed-end PE fund, any structure must be sufficiently robust to ensure investor's rights yet flexible enough to adapt to changing circumstances.

KEY LEARNING POINTS

• PE funds are usually set up as closed-end limited partnerships to facilitate the investment and divestment of capital in the fund's mandated jurisdiction.

• When setting up the legal foundations of a PE fund, GPs will carefully consider the requirements of their LPs with regards to tax issues. Feeder funds, parallel funds, and co-investment vehicles may be set up to accommodate different classes of investors.

• The LPA sets out the terms and conditions applicable to all parties involved in a fund and defines their rights and responsibilities.

• In particular, the LPA clearly defines the rules related to distributions, carried interest, fee structure, the rights and duties of the GP and the process to terminate and dissolve the fund.

RELEVANT CASE STUDIES

from *Private Equity in Action—Case Studies from Developed and Emerging Markets*

Case #1: Beroni Group: Managing GP–LP Relationships

Case #6: Adara Venture Partners: Building a Venture Capital Firm

Case #18: Private Equity in Frontier Markets: Creating a Fund in Georgia

REFERENCES AND ADDITIONAL READING

Debevoise & Plimpton (2015) Private Equity Funds: Key Business, Legal and Tax Issues, Debevoise & Plimpton LLP.

Naidech, S. (2011) Private Equity Fund Formation. Chadbourne & Parke LLP, with Practical Law Corporate & Securities.

The speed at which private equity (PE) firms raise funds is a clear indicator of the industry's well-being, reflecting investors' level of satisfaction with historical performance and their expectations for the future. In the years prior to 2008, funds were raised within a record 8 to 12 months, at times faster. That rate increased to well over 24 months immediately after the global financial crisis—a sign that limited partners (LPs) had become rather cautious amid the turmoil. In recent years, however, the time has returned to pre-2008 numbers, a fact that may say as much about the (out-) performance of PE as it does about the relative (under-) performance of many other asset classes.

Fundraising is the first stage of the PE fund lifecycle: no money, no deals. The capital raised from investors will be used not only to invest in portfolio companies but to finance the fund manager's business as a going concern. While proactively maintaining a good relationship with fund LPs throughout a fund's term is important, general partners (GPs) test the real value of these relations during the fundraising process.

Before approaching potential investors, PE firms must develop a clear message of how their strategy, systems, and people fit together to implement the investment strategy and ultimately deliver the required strong performance.

This chapter describes the standard processes involved in fundraising and explains the main documents used throughout.

THE GP FUNDRAISING PROCESS

Fundraising begins long before the first meeting with potential investors. The fundraising approach depends on the longevity and track record of the PE firm. In the case of a first-time fund, the PE firm must develop a clear and differentiated investment strategy and assemble a team with the expertise to execute its stated strategy before approaching their first investors. In the case of a well-established PE franchise with an existing family of funds, fundraising will start with those LPs who have participated in prior funds; they will typically be invited to "re-up" and invest in the new fund to be raised.

There is no secret to a successful fundraising campaign: it very much depends on the attractiveness of the strategy and the track record of the team relative to competing funds in the market. Credibly matching these strategic considerations to a well-defined plan to deliver exceptional returns is key to securing LP capital commitments. All aspects of the fund lifecycle must be appropriately (and convincingly) addressed, from efficiently deploying capital to adding value through partners' engagement during the holding period to achieving successful exits, and clearly reflected in the fundraising documents.

With an appropriate strategy, team and target fund size in place, it falls to a PE firm's partners and, where relevant, the investor relations team to manage the fundraising

Exhibit 17.1 PE Fundraising Process

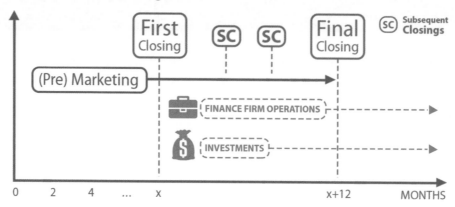

process. No two firms will raise a fund in the exact same manner; nevertheless, the process for raising a closed-end fund can be divided into phases shown in Exhibit 17.1 and detailed in the section that follows.

PRE-MARKETING: Seasoned PE professionals often comment, "Fundraising is an ongoing process" or "We are always fundraising." After all, it takes time to build relationships and trust with LPs to ensure they are open to considering a commitment to one of the firm's future funds. Investors won't write a check to anybody without having reached a level of familiarity with and confidence in a PE firm and its team.

During this so-called pre-marketing stage—when activities ramp up in preparation for the next fundraising round—PE firms engage with investors via one-on-one meetings and road shows to determine their overall interest in the strategy and establish the kind of trust one needs to build a solid relationship. At this stage, PE partners will share general information on the prospective fund while trying to assess how the formal offering can be tailored to align with investor demand. Pre-marketing can significantly reduce the time period that a PE fund is formally in the market by securing in-principle indications of interest or assessing pent-up demand before a formal process is launched. For seasoned PE firms with a large family of funds and diverse investment activities, maintaining contact with and determining the needs of the LP community is a continuous process.

Box 17.1

MARKETING REGULATIONS

In recent years, a variety of new national regulations have added complexity (and pain) to the marketing of PE funds and other investment vehicles. These regulations address to whom PE funds can market and how they can make their funds known in the investor community. For the former, while rules vary from country to country, in nearly all instances the PE fund must raise capital via private placements to qualified investors only (often defined by having a minimum of investable assets or being registered as qualified individuals). Marketing to high-net worth and sophisticated investors is permitted in some jurisdictions, while any general public offering of the fund or marketing to retail investors is usually prohibited. GPs must therefore personally approach the appropriate investors and may not employ mass-communication methods to market a fund.

In addition, national regulators may impose a varied—and at times opaque—set of rules. For instance, national regulation may prescribe contrasting guidelines for marketing onshore versus offshore funds; they may also require—or not—a PE firm to register before marketing any fund offering. PE firms failing to comply with these regulations may be subject to regulatory, criminal and civil action.

Most jurisdictions provide some exemptions to these regulations, be it for offerings made to a small number of investors in their region or for a fundraising below a certain dollar amount. In addition, PE firms may freely market a new fund offering to existing LPs in their funds or gain access to other potential investors through reverse solicitation—where potential investors enquire about a fund offering of their own accord. However, reverse solicitation is risky and closely scrutinized by the authorities, as it can be difficult to establish who initiated the conversation.

MARKETING: After testing the waters during pre-marketing, a PE firm will finalize its fund offering and formally launch the marketing process. At this stage, it will present investors with a clear picture of all material aspects of the fund, including its target size,[1] its investment strategy, key personnel associated with the fund, minimum LP and GP commitment sizes, and fund economics. This information is typically set out in short form in a fund's term sheet and in more detail in a fund's private placement memorandum. PE firms supplement information on the fund offering with supporting documentation on the team, its track record and previous investments in a detailed data pack or virtual data room for investor due diligence.

The reasoning behind the sizing of a new fund is best explained with an example: assume a firm is raising a mid-market European buyout fund and has established that there will be ample opportunity to deploy capital in the years to come. Each of the six partners has bandwidth for on average two deals over the four-year investment period and the subsequent portfolio work. The "sweet spot" for the fund, i.e., the target equity check size per investment matching the PE team's expertise, will be around €200 million. With 10 to 12 investments in the fund the target amount for this round of fundraising will therefore be €2 billion, with a hard cap at €2.5 billion.

PE firms are likely to follow a specific hierarchy when approaching potential investors in a fund. It is natural to start with investors from prior funds with an existing relationship with the GP, co-investment partners or LPs known to anchor new funds. PE firms raising successor funds will try to secure initial commitments from a core group of returning LPs to send a strong "user-approved" signal to the investor community. Approaching existing LPs first can have some drawbacks: while it may increase the certainty of fundraising (and the speed of reaching a first closing), a successful GP might be able to obtain better terms from new investors. Yet, long-term investors with the PE firm will expect (or have contractual rights) to be invited and continuity

---

1. The target size is defined at the beginning of the process by a limit called a soft cap and ultimately a hard cap. In the instance of strong interest from LPs and heavy oversubscription of the fund, a hard cap may be breached, but only with the consent of existing fund LPs. However, GPs need to remain cognizant of their capacity to execute additional or larger deals within their stated mandate when allowing the fund to grow significantly beyond its target size.

with its investor base might pay off for the GP in case of a one-time weaker fund. GPs therefore need to carefully balance their desire to diversify and strengthen their investor base by accommodating their existing LPs.

Educating potential investors on a new fund offering is a lengthy process and requires patience. Several meetings are typically needed to reassure interested investors and familiarize them with all aspects of the investment offering, even with existing LPs. A tailored pitch book is developed for each individual meeting, incorporating additional information and answers to the various questions arising throughout the process. In addition to face-to-face meetings, interested investors will submit detailed due diligence questionnaires, requiring the GP to commit time and resources to provide feedback.

Investors satisfied with their due diligence will request the proposed fund's governing documents, most commonly a limited partnership agreement (LPA). Most investors in a PE fund will ask for changes or additions to the proposed LPA and subscription agreements[2] before committing capital. Negotiating terms simultaneously with several potential investors can be a delicate and time-consuming process, and PE firms will typically try to limit the number of changes granted. If the PE firm and an investor agree to a change, that change will either be incorporated into the fund's LPA, and applicable to all investors in the fund, or granted to an individual LP via a side letter.[3]

FUND CLOSINGS: A PE fund's GP secures capital commitments from investors through a series of closings held over a period of 6 to 18 months. At each closing, a fund's LPs will sign subscription agreements and LPAs, and the GP may begin drawing down capital for investment and fund-level fees. A fund's first closing typically represents a significant percentage of the PE firm's fundraising target; reaching it quickly sends an important signal to the LP community. A GP will only hold a first closing when sufficient capital commitments have been secured to execute its investment strategy. Capital commitments secured during fund closings are immediately available for investment.[4]

Following the first closing, a fund's LPA sets out a fixed period of time—usually 6 to 12 months—during which the GP may secure additional capital commitments through subsequent closings. Few significant changes are made to a fund's LPA after the first closing, aside from those requested by significant investors, as any change must be approved by existing LPs. Once a GP secures commitments matching a fund's target size, a final closing will be held and no new investors can enter the fund (a defining criterion of a closed-end fund). Exhibit 17.2 shows the average number of months taken to reach final closing and the percentage of a fund's original target size reached for fund vintages 2006–2015. It can be easily seen that funds prior to the financial crisis closed quickly and regularly above their hard caps, which changed during the financial crisis when fundraising goals were rarely achieved.

---

2. Subscription agreements governing the terms of investment in the first closing set out the dollar amount committed by each investor and conditions that must be met before the first closing can be completed.
3. Please refer to Chapter 16 Fund Formation for more on side letters.
4. PE firms work continuously on generating deal flow to ensure a solid deal pipeline and to be ready to draw down and invest capital as soon as a new fund is raised or a closing has been achieved.

Exhibit 17.2 PE Fundraising Timing and Success

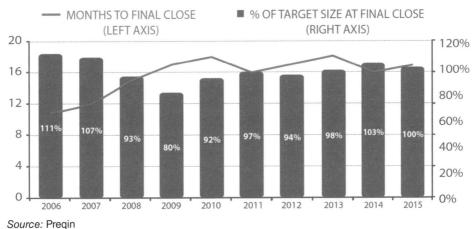

Source: Preqin

FUNDRAISING DOCUMENTATION

PE firms use various documents throughout the fundraising process.

PITCH BOOK: PE firms prepare a pitch book to present a fund offering to potential investors and generate discussions. Pitch books provide investors with an overview of the fund's strategy, its target return, the risks involved, the fund's historic performance, its investment process, the investment team supporting the fund and their individual track record, as well as the key commercial aspects of the fund. GPs will often customize the pitch book on an investor-by-investor basis to highlight specific aspects of the strategy and the team.

TERM SHEET: Term sheets provide detailed information on the key commercial and legal aspects of a fund offering. These documents offer an approachable, short-form summary of terms contained in a fund's LPA. These may include, but are not limited to, the terms shown in Exhibit 17.3.

Exhibit 17.3 PE Fund Term Sheet

Fund Structure	Limited partnership
Fund Size	Targeted dollar amount
Minimum LP Contribution	Typically 5% of a fund's targeted size
GP Contribution	1-10% of the aggregate capital commitments
Fund Term	10-year, with two, one-year extensions
Distribution Waterfall	All Capital First or Deal-by-Deal
Management Fee	2% per annum on committed capital during the investment period and—typically—a reduced rate on invested capital thereafter
Carried Interest	Typically 20% of a fund's net profits, subject to an 8% hurdle rate
Portfolio Construction	8-12 investments during the investment period
Investment Limits	Single investment limit: 20% of total fund commitments

PRIVATE PLACEMENT MEMORANDUM (PPM): A PPM expands upon the elements highlighted in a pitch book and term sheet to provide a robust overview of the fund offering and the PE firm sponsoring the fund. This document is typically sent to investors after an initial meeting. It provides investors with information on the offering and protects fund managers from the liability associated with selling unregistered securities.

One of the most critical sections of the PPM is the team's track record. Given the historically strong linkage between past performance and future performance ("stickiness") in PE, investors are particularly interested in the track record of the investment team and that of its individual members.[5] Best practice is to include all funds previously managed and all investments made to avoid selective disclosure.

Raising a First-time Fund

By Javad Movsoumov, Managing Director, Head of APAC Private Funds Group, UBS

Here is an ideal set of circumstances for a first-time fund:

A team of professionals (the "Spin Out Team") that has worked closely together for a considerable number of years is leaving their current employer to set up a new fund. The Spin Out Team consists of several senior individuals who have led the entire investment process for a number of portfolio companies. The Spin Out Team's track record is in the top quartile vis-à-vis benchmark returns across a number of investment cycles. The Spin Out Team has a formal letter of attribution from the prior employer stating that the team has been responsible for leading a number of investments, confirming the returns generated and permitting the team to use this track record. Post-departure, the Spin Out Team retains the ability to source deals, add value or exit investments, while continuing to operate effectively outside of the former institutional eco-system. The investment strategy of the team is supported by the team's track record, the current macroeconomic environment and also by the team's pipeline of investment opportunities.

Few new funds are fortunate to have all or most of these ingredients; however, the absolute minimum required to stand a chance of raising institutional capital is (i) strong and repeatable track record; and (ii) ability to prove that you have generated the track record.

LPs "buy into" a GP's investment thesis, an integral part of which is confidence derived from past investment experience. However, if either investment thesis or the circumstances under which past returns were achieved drastically change, the value of that past investment experience to LPs diminishes.

This is a critical obstacle for all first-time funds as there is clearly a significant change in circumstances.

---

5. While this correlation of past returns to future performance seems to be less reliable in the most recent decade, LPs continue to focus on track record as a starting point. It helps to understand the GP's investment style and assess whether the partners' experience will fit with the new fund's proposed investment mandate.

Will the new firm be able to find the same investment opportunities as it did in the past? Will it be able to replicate and deliver the same returns? Ironically, the best way to convince LPs to invest in a first-time fund is to allay their concerns by presenting the new team as a well-experienced, institutional platform, i.e., not a first-time fund.

As a guide, a first-time fund may consider the following sequence of steps:

1. Prepare marketing documentation and due diligence documentation detailing track record, track record attribution and other basic materials to enable anchor investors to conduct their analysis;
2. Secure anchor investors and hold a first closing;
3. Finalize full set of due diligence documentation;
4. Make the first investment(s); and
5. Approach the broader LP community to finalize the fundraise.

Raising a first-time fund (even with a fully-attributable strong track record) is by no means a walk in the park. The first point to consider is that a majority of institutional investors do not invest in first-time funds. Hence, the addressable universe of LPs shrinks significantly. To complicate the process, many LPs often meet new managers and conduct significant due diligence before declining the opportunity.

Even if an LP can participate in first-time funds, getting this LP into the first closing is difficult. By participating in the first close of a new fund, an LP risks getting "stuck" in a small fund if further closings do not materialize. Such a smaller fund may have to change its investment strategy to target smaller deals or have an overly-concentrated portfolio. This is where anchor investors come into play.

Anchor investors are relatively large LPs that commit a sizable amount of capital for the fundraise (e.g. 20–30% of the fund size), but do so on special terms. These may include preferential economics (reduced management fee and carried interest), special co-investment rights and even a stake in the management company. Most importantly, there will be a strong feeling of mutual trust between the anchor investors and the manager. Typically, anchor investors would know the new fund manager from his/her past career. In some cases, they may even encourage the fund manager to leave their current firm and set up a new firm with the promise of support. Sealing an anchor LP commitment may help with: (i) validating the first-time fund story (particularly if the anchor is an established and respected LP); (ii) providing capital to start making investments; and (iii) providing a management fee stream to run the new GP.

While raising a first-time fund is not easy, one should remember that every fund manager at some point raised a first-time fund. New private equity teams keep the industry exciting and competitive.

THE FUNDRAISING ROADMAP

The time and complexity involved in raising a PE fund varies; established PE firms may raise multibillion dollar funds in a matter of months, while fundraising for first-time funds may take years and not succeed. The maturity of the PE firm, competitor funds in the market and investors' appetite for PE investments all influence duration and success of the fundraising process.

A critical step for all PE firms is securing credible LPs, at times large anchor investors, for a fund's first closing. Credible, established investors help validate a fund's value proposition in the LP community and greatly facilitate the remaining fundraising process. To entice investors to participate in a first closing, preferential fund terms are often granted, including but not limited to reduced management fees and superior co-investment rights. At times, anchor investors might even take a stake in a fund's GP.

To reduce risk from the origin of a fund's capital commitments, established GPs aim to build an LP base diversified by type and geography. They also conduct in-depth background checks to assess the quality, reliability and investment constraints of potential investors before allowing them to commit.

The process and degree of difficulty of raising a PE fund is markedly different between fund managers raising a first-time fund and those raising successor funds. Not all investors with an allocation to PE invest in first-time funds, narrowing the pool of available investors. It is therefore crucial for the first-time fund manager to target investors with the appropriate risk appetite and a history of supporting first-time managers. Common investors in first-time funds include endowments, family offices, specialist fund-of-funds and development finance institutions.

For first-time PE teams raising capital, the common closed-end fund structure may not be the easiest model. Funding investments on a deal-by-deal basis allows a newly established PE firm to show its access to proprietary deal flow, deploy capital and establish relationships with the investor community without requiring LPs to commit to a closed-end fund and lock up their capital for the long term. With fees paid on a deal-by-deal basis typically lower than those paid for a fund, "carry" or profit sharing arrangements tend to be similar; as a result, such structures are attractive for LPs. For the GP, though, this approach comes with a high degree of execution risk, as securing funding for deals it works on will take extra time and there is no guarantee of it coming together as expected.

Raising capital for a PE firm's second fund is still a significant challenge, as most investments in fund one will still be awaiting exit, with the majority of returns not yet realized. However, investments in fund one offer important information about the GP and its ability to execute in line with its proposed investment strategy. By the time the third fund is raised, prospective LPs will have multiple data points to evaluate the GP—especially with fund one showing cash-on-cash returns to substantiate the fund's investment thesis (or not).

PE firms may also raise smaller funds with sizable co-investment[6] programs to fund large transactions. In addition, a significant and above average commitment from the GP can help enhance the attractiveness of the offering. All new funds should consider the use of placement agents to help them shape their message and reach a wider and better-targeted audience of LPs.

---

6. Please refer to Chapter 21 LP Direct Investment for more information on co-investment strategies.

Box 17.2

PLACEMENT AGENTS

A placement agent acts on behalf of a PE fund during the fundraising process, introducing the fund manager to potential investors and providing services related to all aspects of fundraising. These can include developing the fund's pitch, providing information on market trends, and assisting in the due diligence process. A placement agent can rationalize and accelerate the fundraising process, allowing the GP to spend more time on managing investments. Similar to the relationship between an LP and a PE fund, relationships between GPs and placement agents are often long term, with the same agent involved in multiple fundraisings.

The main service provided by placement agents is access to their LP network. Given their constant engagement with the LP community, placement agents have a clear understanding of the needs of different LPs. Their detailed knowledge of the GP landscape at large may also improve the efficiency of the LP's investment process; nevertheless, it is usually the GP who engages the agent. For GPs, broad access to the LP community can be particularly beneficial for first-time funds, fund managers looking to raise progressively larger funds, and those looking to diversify their LP base.

Placement agents are typically either a boutique outfit or part of an investment bank. Boutiques typically take on a limited number of mandates per year and provide a more tailored, targeted solution. Investment banks offer a GP a global distribution network and a range of follow-on services. While the choice may be an obvious one for some GPs—venture capital funds tend to employ boutique placement agents, while buyout funds have a symbiotic relationship with investment banks—the ability of some boutiques to also raise larger funds often muddies the water.

Placement agents are typically engaged on a retainer-based advisory fee plus a success fee paid by the fund manager. The latter makes up the bulk of a placement agent's compensation and can range from 1 to 5% depending on the target size of the fund. In addition to the fees directly related to fundraising, investment banks also often bundle additional follow-on services into a single fee proposal.

CLOSING

Raising capital for a PE fund is a requisite first step to finance both investments and the business activity of a fund manager. A professional fundraising process includes multiple steps, adherence to a certain protocol including standard documentation and, most of all, a convincing investment thesis backed up by track record and a firm's resources. A successful fundraising is the first step in establishing a long-term relationship between fund managers and their investors.

KEY LEARNING POINTS

• **Fundraising and the speed at which it can be executed is very much a measure of a PE firm's success. It is also seen as a gauge for the overall industry's well-being and performance.**

• **Once the team (GP) and the overall strategy have been defined, raising a new fund starts with establishing its target size, a clear marketing plan and a consideration of the LPs to be approached.**

• **Fundraising documentation includes pitch books, term sheets and PPMs; at times placement agents are engaged to assist.**

• **The process of raising a fund differs for first-time fund managers and their more established peers.**

RELEVANT CASE STUDIES

from *Private Equity in Action—Case Studies from Developed and Emerging Markets*

Case #3: Pro-invest Group: How to Launch a Private Equity Real Estate Fund

Case #6: Adara Venture Partners: Building a Venture Capital Firm

Case #17: Rice from Africa for Africa: Rice Farming in Tanzania and Investing in Agriculture

REFERENCES AND ADDITIONAL READING

Debevoise & Plimpton (2015) Private Equity Funds: Key Business, Legal and Tax Issues, Debevoise & Plimpton LLP.

InvestEurope (2015) AIFMD Implementation & Fund Marketing: A Closer Look at Marketing Under National Placement Rules across Europe, edition 3, March, http://www.investeurope.eu/media/453360/AIFMD-Fund-Marketing-Guide_March-2015.pdf.

InvestEurope (2016) European Private Equity Activity—Statistics on Fundraising, Investments and Divestments, May, http://www.investeurope.eu/media/476271/2015-european-private-equity-activity.pdf.

Sorrentino, T., Wainwright, F. and Blaydon, C. (2003) Note on Private Placement Memorandum. Dartmouth College Center for Private Equity and Entrepreneurship, https://www.tuck.dartmouth.edu/uploads/centers/files/Private_placement_memo.pdf.

Stone, Heather M. (2009) Raising Capital for Private Equity Funds, Aspatore, https://www.amazon.com/Raising-Capital-Private-Equity-Funds/dp/0314209905.

For further information:

- On policy related to PE in Europe (in particular post-Brexit) you may refer to InvestEurope's repository (http://www.investeurope.eu/policy/key-topics/)

- For PE in the United States refer to the NVCA (http://nvca.org/research/stats-studies/) or the American Investment Council (http://www.investmentcouncil.org/news-and-policy/)

- For emerging market issues please refer to EMPEA (http://empea.org/research/legal-regulatory-issues/).

As investors in the private equity (PE) asset class, limited partners (LPs) build and maintain portfolios of investments in a range of PE funds. As an LP's allocation to PE typically makes up only a fraction of its total assets under management (AUM), PE must be considered within the broader context of its investment mandate and overall portfolio construction.

LPs will determine how much capital (typically as a percentage of AUM) to allocate to the PE asset class based on a host of factors including their annual cash flow needs, their risk appetites, the target return of their overall portfolios and the internal resources available to manage a PE allocation. Certain characteristics of PE—such as its private and illiquid nature, the opaque process of fund manager selection, capacity constraints at some of the best-performing fund managers, and the uncertain timing of cash flows from a PE portfolio—make investments in the asset class difficult even for astute and experienced public market investors. Despite these concerns, PE has moved from its humble origins in the 1970s to become an integral part of most institutional investors' portfolio.[1]

This chapter opens with a discussion of the pros and cons an LP must understand when considering an allocation to PE. If the LP decides to move forward, the next steps are to construct, maintain and manage a PE portfolio. To execute these successfully, an investor needs to develop a clear mandate and performance target for its PE program and set up an internal process for manager selection and portfolio management, all of which we discuss in this chapter.

DECIDING ON AN ALLOCATION TO PE

Let's start with a hypothetical LP, a large institutional investor such as a pension plan or endowment, which has been investing in global markets for decades—but only through public equity and fixed income. While it has used external fund managers and been willing to explore innovative tools, including derivatives, to date it has not added PE to its portfolio. Its investment committee (IC) has decided to give this fast-growing and, at first glance, attractive asset class serious consideration and is lining up the arguments in favor of and against such a move; needless to say, the IC must consider the risk of not allocating to PE and thereby depriving its beneficiaries of attractive future returns.

Investors new to the asset class and accustomed to the world of clear-cut and liquid public market investing will need to adjust their expectations not only with regard to the liquidity and transparency of their positions, but also with regard to their ability to calibrate and easily adjust the riskiness of their allocations to PE.

---

1. For the purpose of this chapter, we will define institutional investors broadly, including not only pension plans, endowments and sovereign wealth funds, but also family offices.

BENEFITS OF INVESTING IN THE PE ASSET CLASS

RETURNS AND ALPHA: By foregoing exposure to PE, investors may miss out on alpha or excess returns over a market portfolio. Top-quartile PE funds in particular have produced robust and consistently superior performance relative to other asset classes in the past and have done so over different market cycles. Exhibit 18.1 compares the 5-, 10- and 15-year returns generated by the broad PE asset class with those of public equity and global bond markets.[2]

Exhibit 18.1 PE in an Institutional Investor's Portfolio

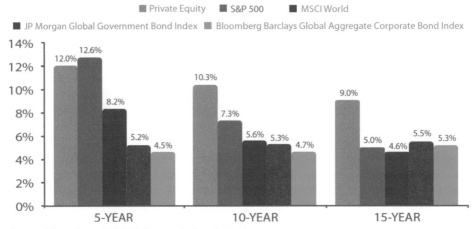

Source: Bloomberg, INSEAD-Pevara, Author Analysis

CORRELATION AND DIVERSIFICATION: In theory, adding a PE allocation—and therefore exposure to the private, unlisted companies in PE funds—to a broad portfolio will diversify an LP's source of returns and, in turn, reduce portfolio volatility and the overall risk of a large negative performance move. This argument needs to be carefully tested against an investor's existing portfolio with the result naturally depending on the correlation between its existing investments and the PE funds it targets. The goal will be to add an uncorrelated source of returns to the portfolio.

ACCESS TO EMERGING ECONOMIES: Given its liquidity and overall ease of execution, public market investing may appear to be an easier choice to gain diversified equity exposure compared to PE investing. While this may be the case for developed markets, the argument fails when building exposure to the world's global growth or emerging markets. Public exchanges in emerging markets only capture a portion of the overall economy and are often underweight with respect to a large number of interesting growth sectors. A PE fund's investments in private companies provide a way to gain exposure to these sectors.

---

2. PE returns were calculated based on the INSEAD-Pevara dataset of 3,000 funds using quarterly modified internal rates of return. Source for the MSCI World and JP Morgan Global Government Bond Index: Bloomberg.

CHALLENGES OF INVESTING IN THE PE ASSET CLASS

Introducing PE into a traditional portfolio of public equity and fixed income investments presents LPs with a novel set of challenges. These primarily relate to implementation, due to the specific characteristics of PE investing, including illiquidity, cash flow management, and organizational challenges. We look at each below.

ILLIQUIDITY: PE demands a long-term commitment from its investors and a high comfort level with illiquidity; the required 10-year commitment of capital to a PE fund is necessary to execute its investment strategy, be it venture, growth or buyout. An LP's capital commitment is drawn down gradually over a four- to five-year investment period; once called, the capital typically remains invested for three to seven years, and in many instances significantly longer, until exit.

CASH FLOW MANAGEMENT: The limited liability provided to LPs through the blind pool structure of PE funds requires that investment decisions sit firmly with the GP only.[3] LPs have limited visibility on size and timing of cash inflows and outflows, aside from the regular reporting and informal dialogue with the GP. Therefore, LPs must have a ready source of capital at hand to fund capital calls made by their GPs and fulfill their obligations.

Large institutional investors often have investments in over 100 PE funds; while the exposure to multiple funds may smooth out the erratic cash flows from single funds, in times of market dislocation, PE funds often exhibit synchronized behavior (at times even with other, usually mildly correlated asset classes). Examples of synchronized behavior include the near complete breakdown of distributions during the two years following the global financial crisis of 2008 and the high distributions in the subsequent bull market, both of which created allocation challenges (the second example of course being the more benign problem).

ORGANIZATIONAL CHALLENGES: The relative novelty of PE compared to traditional asset classes such as public equity or fixed income, and the challenge of building and maintaining an allocation to PE, requires an LP's IC to provide resources to effectively execute and supervise such a strategy. Not only must a team be built, typically with new talent from outside the organization given the specific experience required, but the team must also be given sufficient budget and (especially) time to establish a comprehensive program.

It will take many years to see meaningful returns and even longer to be able to form an opinion on the success of the program. Judging and tracking performance requires custom benchmarks to reflect the characteristics of the actual portfolio, as generic industry returns published can only be a starting point; this in turn requires investment in systems and people to build up a sufficient knowledge base. The long time horizon and consistency required for a successful PE investment program often clashes with the short stay of talent in investor organizations (especially public pension funds and other government-linked institutions) given the incentive to move to another role in the industry with a better financial package and a higher degree of autonomy.

---

3. Please refer to Chapter 1 Private Equity Essentials for a clear explanation of the mechanics of PE funds.

PORTFOLIO CONSTRUCTION CONSIDERATIONS

Once a positive decision on starting a PE program has been reached, processes and guidelines need to be put in place to govern the program's portfolio construction, manager selection and the overall decision-making process. The following points must be considered.

TARGET ALLOCATION: An investor's risk appetite will determine its target allocation to PE. The distinct mandates of different types of institutional investors have a direct impact on their appetite for PE. Public and private sector pension funds, while the largest allocators of capital to PE in absolute dollar terms, on average have an allocation of 6–8% of AUM due to their regular cash flow needs and the investment restrictions associated with these plans. Family offices and endowment funds have lower liquidity needs and on average make substantial, double-digit allocations to the asset class. Exhibit 18.2 shows PE target allocations as a percentage of AUM for different types of institutional investors over the years.

Exhibit 18.2 PE Target Allocation by Investor Type

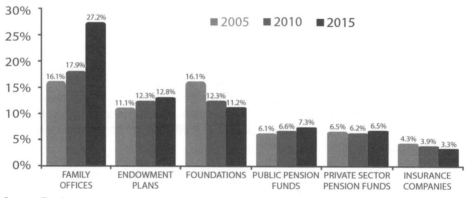

Source: Preqin

DIVERSIFICATION: The degree of diversification within a PE portfolio and specific allocation decisions depend on an LP's risk appetite, its target return for the asset class and the resources available to build and manage a PE portfolio. LPs diversify their PE allocation across a range of factors including manager, investment strategy (venture, growth, buyouts), geography, industry and vintage year. Aside from the "risk smoothing" common to all diversification efforts, allocation across vintage years in particular helps create a steadier investment program, especially in light of the J-curve effect from individual fund allocations. Oftentimes, an LP's diversification strategy and allocation decisions are shaped by views on the macroeconomic environment, preferences for or against specific countries or investment strategies and the overall experience of the investment team. These dynamics mirror in some way the discussion on active and passive investment in public equities.

TARGET RETURN: An LP's target return for its PE allocation will have a direct impact on manager selection, portfolio construction and regional allocation. Return expectations for developed markets tend to be lower than those for emerging markets; similar for later stage investment strategies versus early stage investment strategies. The level

Box 18.1

LP COMMITMENT STRATEGIES

Achieving and maintaining a desired allocation to PE is an ongoing process, as an LP's exposure to the asset class is subject to the unpredictability of capital calls and distributions and the evolution of fund net asset values (NAVs). When building a PE program through primary fund commitments, an LP's exposure to the asset class grows gradually as managers in its portfolio draw down and invest capital; achieving an LP's target allocation to PE takes time. Even once fully invested, the challenge remains to maintain a steady exposure to PE: GPs may already begin returning capital during a fund's investment period—due to early exits—and unexpectedly reduce an LP's invested capital in PE.

Given that GPs typically do not call 100% of a fund's committed capital, LPs expect a gap between capital invested and capital committed to the fund. To reach their desired exposure, LPs will typically overcommit to the asset class, allocating—say—120% or 130% of their target AUM to PE. Secondary, direct and co-investments provide tools for an LP to proactively manage an existing portfolio and build up its exposure to PE more quickly, but these programs are normally much smaller in scale than the primary investments.

Exhibits 18.3 and 18.4 show the evolution of a hypothetical LP's PE portfolio with a $1 billion target allocation. As shown in Exhibit 18.3, an LP's PE portfolio is simply an overlay of multiple J-curves,[4] each representing the cash flow profile of a distinct fund.

Exhibit 18.3 LP PE Portfolio J-curves

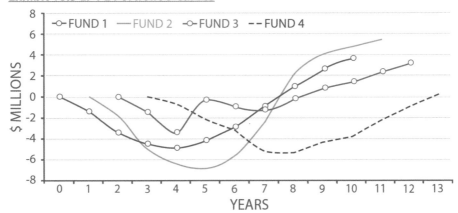

---

4. J-curves were introduced in Chapter 1 Private Equity Essentials; the J-curves in Exhibit 18.3 plot the LP's cash flows from four separate $10 million commitments to the funds shown in the exhibit.

Exhibit 18.4 shows the evolution of the LP's PE portfolio in aggregate.[5] To hit its $1 billion target allocation to PE, our hypothetical LP decided to commit $1.2 billion to the asset class over each five-year period (i.e., an overcommitment of 20%). The PE portfolio shows annual net cash outflows for the first seven years before beginning to generate a net cash inflow from year eight onwards. The cash flows and NAV modeled in Exhibit 18.4 must be taken with a grain of salt, as the actual capital calls, distributions and NAVs of underlying funds will evolve in a less predictable manner.

Exhibit 18.4 LP PE Portfolio Evolution

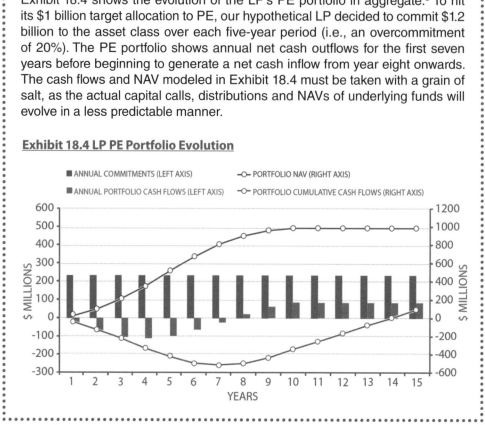

of diversification in a portfolio also has an impact on its expected return: broadly, diversified portfolios reduce the volatility of returns by smoothing out the impact of individual funds' outperformance or underperformance, while concentrated portfolios provide a wider range of expected returns (for better or worse) as the impact of an individual fund's performance will be more pronounced.

IN-HOUSE OR OUTSOURCED TEAMS: LPs must decide whether to execute a PE program in-house or outsource the investment function. This build or buy decision with regards to investment decision-making defines how much internal resources and know-how are required. In-house programs require a team with investment expertise, skills to construct a well-diversified portfolio, experience in manager selection and a large network to access attractive fund offerings. LPs often start with an allocation to PE through a fund of funds[6] or engage advisors to craft custom mandates to PE, then gradually build expertise to allocate directly to PE funds. Even seasoned LPs will at times rely on the selection skills of external managers to access markets outside their expertise (especially emerging markets) or, in the case of large investors, allocate to smaller funds that are unable to accommodate their minimum check size. Secondary

---

5. All funds in the hypothetical LP's portfolio have the cash flow characteristics of the J-curve detailed in Chapter 1 and a steady evolution of fund NAV. Commitments are made to the portfolio on January 1 of each year and the hypothetical LP can allocate the exact amount it desires to the hypothetical fund.
6. Fund of funds aggregate capital from multiple investors and invest in a diversified portfolio of PE funds. They act as a single LP in a fund and may be able to negotiate fee discounts on behalf of their clients.

fund investments, co-investments and minority direct investments are often a natural progression.[7]

INVESTMENT RESTRICTIONS: Institutional investors usually have strict guidelines on where and, more often, where not to invest (negative screens). These restrictions can be industry, geography or governance specific, and may reflect local laws or norms (e.g., Sharia law) or specific environment, social and governance requirements.[8] Side letters will address an individual investor's concerns and formalize the agreement.

PE FUND MANAGER SELECTION

The success of a PE investment strategy hinges on the selection of the right managers and their funds. Returns vary widely between top-quartile and bottom-quartile funds (see Exhibit 18.5) and the stickiness of top-quartile fund managers and their ability to consistently outperform their peers—while proven for earlier periods—has been called into question in recent years.[9]

Exhibit 18.5 PE Fund Performance Quartiles by Vintage Year

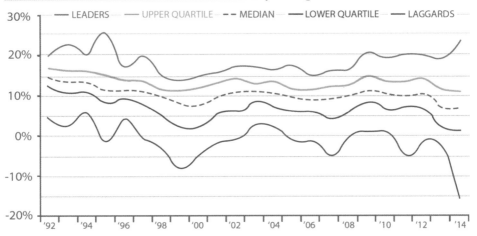

Source: INSEAD-Pevara

In addition, gaining access to funds from reputed managers introduces an additional challenge—the funds are often oversubscribed and priority is given to established and known LPs, making it difficult for those launching a new PE program.

With a clear and diversified commitment strategy in hand, the LP's investment team begins the process of assessing the various PE funds in the market, starting due diligence on a select few and ultimately committing capital to even fewer. With over 8,000 PE firms globally,[10] LPs have on the face of it no shortage of investment opportunities; however, the more specific the investment strategy, the more constrained an LP's selection may become. We will take a closer look at the four main phases of the fund manager selection process as shown in Exhibit 18.6.

---

7. Please refer to Chapter 21 LP Direct Investment for more on LP co-investment and direct strategies.
8. See Chapter 14 Responsible Investment for more on environmental, social and governance considerations.
9. Harris, Jenkinson, Kaplan, and Stucker (2014).
10. The number refers to professional fund management firms; but estimates vary widely on the number of active fund managers (source: Prequin 2016).

Exhibit 18.6 LP Fund Manager Selection Process

TOP-DOWN REVIEW: The investment process begins with a top-down review of the existing PE portfolio vis-à-vis its target PE allocations (unless the investor is new to PE and has no existing positions, in which case screening is step one). Over- or underweighted exposure to a specific strategy, sector or geography within the portfolio may require rebalancing and dictate the priority for new commitments. In conjunction with a portfolio review, LPs typically assess the attractiveness of their overall strategy within the prevailing macroeconomic environment, current capital market dynamics and the competitive landscape in PE.

SCREENING: LPs begin the manager selection process by assessing the following criteria: the respective track record of the fund's GP, the GP's investment team, the fund's strategy and its fit with the LP's existing portfolio. The depth of this initial screening varies from fund to fund; first-time GPs will be subject to closer scrutiny than GPs who have received allocations from the LP in the past. During this initial engagement, the LP will decide whether to conduct formal due diligence on the fund offering.

DUE DILIGENCE: This step consists of a deep dive into all aspects related to a fund's investment strategy, team and structure. The fund must present a sustainable strategy that is well positioned in the current market environment. The strategy has to be consistent with the skills of the team, its experience, cohesiveness, and history of working together. All past investments made by the GP related to the fund's strategy are reviewed and interactions with the GP help in assessing the manager's impact on value creation. In addition to investment activity, LPs typically review the structure of the investment team, the GP's investment in the fund (referred to as its "skin in the game"), the GP's governance structure, responsible investment policies and overall key risk factors. The fund's legal and tax structures and its incentive system need to ensure that the interests of the GP and LPs are aligned.

RECOMMENDATION AND SUBSCRIPTION: At the conclusion of the due diligence process, an investment paper is submitted to the LP's IC outlining the risks and opportunities associated with a fund manager's offering. Deliberations at the IC level will likely result in additional questions, requiring a further round of due diligence for funds passing the first cut. Funds that get the go-ahead from the IC enter the subscription process, where terms related to the LPA, side letters and other documentation are agreed.

Of course, every LP intends to commit capital (only) to future top-quartile funds. However, predictability of the returns down the road remains an elusive goal. Therefore many investors flock towards funds raised by PE firms with historically strong performance. These funds therefore often become heavily oversubscribed and in turn hard to access. This bias (or herd-like behavior), combined with a desire by some of the larger investors to reduce the number of their GP relationships has led to a bifurcation among the GPs, splitting PE firms into those able to raise funds in record time and those not able to achieve a first closing.

Relative Value Approach to Enhance Portfolio Returns

By Christoph Rubeli, Partner and Co-CEO, Partners Group

Private equity investing has undergone a massive transformation over the past five to ten years, as the asset class has become more and more institutionalized. The drivers of this transition are multifold: first, target companies are increasingly international and buyout transactions have become more complex. Secondly, it has been acknowledged that private market return drivers are similar to their public market peers, capturing market volatility and reflecting global transitional trends, while at the same time offering upside from value creation opportunities.

Private markets portfolio management is no longer about simply picking the best managers: managers may be closed for an extended time between funds or not accessible to new investors at all. If capital is allocated at an unfavorable time in the cycle, even the best manager may underperform its peers, as was the case for select 2001 US venture vintages and select 2006/2007 European vintages. At the same time, LPs no longer desire operating through fund-of-funds structures due to the deep J-curve effect and high costs. As a result, private markets have progressed from a bottom up, boutique-style, opportunistic approach to a more mature, process-driven and systematic industry.

This trend has been exacerbated by the fact that LPs have become more sophisticated. LPs' expectations of private markets portfolio management have evolved accordingly and their requirements have widened significantly. Demand for country- or sector-focused GPs is often limited to the best-in-class managers or for diversification purposes. Instead, many LPs are consolidating their GP exposures, thereby reducing their overall private market exposure to a handful of managers. More and more institutional investors are looking for GPs offering an integrated, global investment approach across primary, direct and secondary investments in order to more effectively mitigate the J-curve effect, reduce underlying fees, provide earlier distributions and enhance liquidity. More often than not, public and private pension funds, sovereign wealth funds or other institutional investors demand a customized mandate solution which can be implemented via comingled funds or via direct lines.

Direct lines are allocations to a single investment through client-specific vehicles; they can cater for specific investment demands, such as:

- an accelerated private markets portfolio ramp-up to reach a desired target allocation,
- meeting specific responsible investment criteria,
- yield vs. capital-appreciation focused portfolios, or
- following a dynamic, and point-in-time specific relative value investment approach where the relative value may be characterized by region, type of investment, financing stage, and at a more granular level, identifying areas where assets benefit from transformative growth.

This relative value approach often reaches beyond private equity, to also include other private market offerings such as private debt, private infrastructure or private real estate. This broader approach optimizes portfolio implementation by allocating capital across the private markets spectrum to where the best relative value can be found. For instance, intense competition in the private equity secondary space may have driven up prices, while real estate secondaries are less intensely competed over and offer compelling investment opportunities.

Moreover, empirical evidence shows that adding private equity to a traditional public markets portfolio is primarily return enhancing. Broadening the private markets allocation across the wider spectrum does not only enhance returns (albeit admittedly to a lower extent than by solely adding private equity) but also offers superior diversification benefits by notably lowering the expected volatility of a portfolio.

LPs are increasingly searching for managers who can offer long-term solutions to investment needs. Many of our LPs are demanding a target allocation to private markets as a percentage of their overall portfolio, reaching beyond the initial commitments to build up the portfolio, as well as asking for proposals that outline a long-term strategy to maintain the target allocation. Finally, an offering for an LP may be rounded out by capabilities complementing proactive portfolio management such as risk management, customized reporting and structuring solutions, further broadening the traditional fund-of-funds approach towards an integrated portfolio solution.

MANAGING AN EXISTING PE PORTFOLIO

Once established, PE portfolios require constant monitoring to maintain an LP's target allocation, manage irregular cash flows and consolidate and assess the fund reports received from its various GPs. Investors in PE face a few challenges during that process, some of which we detail below.

MONITORING: Monitoring fund performance is an ongoing process and forms a crucial element of portfolio management; it is no different for private or public equity investments. Tracking the evolution of a fund—its investment and divestment activity and other activity at the fund's GP—and benchmarking performance against other asset classes and the fund's peers requires a clear modus operandi. Monitoring is the foundation of risk management and target allocation optimization. An active approach to monitoring can be resource-intensive.

LIQUIDITY MANAGEMENT: The manner in which an LP manages its uncalled capital commitments will impact the return generated by its overall investment portfolio. Unlike mutual or hedge fund managers who collect invested funds from the start, PE funds call capital from their LPs throughout the investment period—only if and when needed. This requires LPs to manage their committed capital in a way that allows them to meet impending capital calls at short notice. While it may be tempting to actively manage those idle funds to enhance net returns, such a strategy adds liquidity risk to the overall PE portfolio.[11] Over the long run, LPs can plan to meet capital calls in their PE portfolio

---

11. Please refer to Chapter 23 Risk Management for further discussions on risks and risk mitigants in PE.

out of distributions from mature, divesting funds. Proactively managing a portfolio of PE funds can help maintain an LP's target exposure to PE and align capital drawdowns with distributions.

BALLOONING PORTFOLIO: Most investors strive to maintain relatively constant gross exposure (as a percentage of AUM) to every asset class in their investment portfolio, as defined by their IC. In the PE context, this requires that a sizable proportion of funds returned after successful exits are promptly reinvested. Of course, new commitments can only be made to PE funds in the market—i.e. those that are fundraising—a fact that over time will add to a slowly but surely expanding number of GP relationships that need to be managed. The increase in relationships can be somewhat slowed down by preferentially allocating capital to follow-on funds by existing GPs. Still a "ballooning" of relationships is hard to avoid in the ordinary course of business, making it difficult for LPs, with their often moderate number of investment professionals, to effectively engage with an ever-expanding number of individual GPs. Exhibit 18.7 highlights this dynamic for our hypothetical LP presented in Box 18.1, tracking the increase in the total number of both funds and fund manager relationships in its portfolio as it maintains its annual commitment strategy to PE at a steady $240 million.[12]

Exhibit 18.7 LP Ballooning PE Portfolio

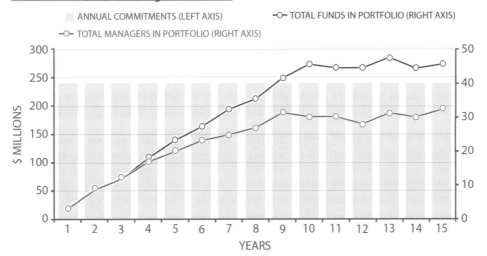

SECONDARIES, CO-INVESTMENTS AND DIRECTS: Aside from primary allocations to funds, LPs have other options to grow their exposure to the PE asset class. They may, for example, acquire secondary stakes in mature funds to backfill vintage year exposure, provide access to promising GPs and help diversify their PE portfolio.[13] Secondary transactions may also be used to manage a ballooning portfolio by selling off LP interests. Increasing exposure to PE funds already in the portfolio via secondaries transactions is another attractive option to prevent an inflating portfolio (i.e., doubling down on known entities). Seasoned LPs may over time develop an appetite for co-investments—investing directly into portfolio company equity side by side with a GP—and direct investments to improve economics and fine-tune their investment allocation.[14]

---

12. We assume a fund life of 10 years for all funds in the portfolio, which causes the number of funds and fund manager relationships to flatten from year 10 onwards as new funds replace those funds at the end of their terms.
13. Please refer to Chapter 24 Private Equity Secondaries for additional information.
14. Please refer to Chapter 21 LP Direct Investment for further reading.

DENOMINATOR EFFECT: The denominator effect refers to an asset allocation problem caused by a sudden drop in the value of an LP's public equity portfolio in times of market turmoil. During market shocks, valuations of illiquid assets—and PE in particular—adjust more slowly, if at all. As a result, the value of an LP's overall portfolio (the denominator) drops more quickly than the value of its PE allocation, causing an increase in an LP's exposure to PE as a percentage of total AUM, often significantly beyond its target allocation. As many LPs have a mandate to maintain exposure to an asset class within a target range, this scenario may lead to a forced reduction of PE exposure—for instance, through secondary transactions—or a temporary halt in new investment allocations during times of stress.

CLOSING

The decision to shift a significant portion of their portfolios to PE has been top of mind for many large institutional investors in recent years; with interest rates near historical lows, achieving respectable long-term target returns with a traditional portfolio has become a challenge. However, to execute a PE investment strategy well requires a good understanding of the specifics of the industry, a long term strategy and the build-up of dedicated resources.

KEY LEARNING POINTS

• Institutional investors must take the time to understand and assess a range of characteristics (both pros and cons) of PE before allocating to the asset class.

• An LP's risk appetite, target returns, internal capabilities and investment restrictions must be considered when constructing a diversified PE portfolio.

• Choosing the right PE funds and managing an existing portfolio within its mandate are the final (and ongoing) steps in the LP investment process.

RELEVANT CASE STUDIES

from *Private Equity in Action—Case Studies from Developed and Emerging Markets*

Case #2: Going Direct: The Case of Teachers' Private Capital

Case #4: Hitting the Target: Optimizing a Private Equity Portfolio with the Partners Group

REFERENCES AND ADDITIONAL READING

Harris, Robert S., Jenkinson, Tim, Kaplan, Steven N. and Stucke, Rüdiger (2014) Has Persistence Persisted in Private Equity? Evidence from Buyout and Venture Capital Funds, Darden Business School Working Paper No. 2304808; Fama-Miller Working Paper, February 28, https://ssrn.com/abstract=2304808 or http://dx.doi.org/10.2139/ssrn.2304808.

Jenkinson, T., Harris, R. and Kaplan, S. (2016) How do Private Equity Investments Perform Compared to Public Equity? *Journal of Investment Management*, 14(3): 1–24.

Lichtner, K. (2009) How to Build a Successful Private Equity Portfolio, *Thunderbird International Business Review*, 51(6), Version of record online: October 19, http://onlinelibrary.wiley.com/doi/10.1002/tie.20296/pdf.

Private Equity Navigator (PEN). Model portfolio published twice annually by INSEAD's Private Equity Center (GPEI). http://centres.insead.edu/global-private-equity-initiative/research-publications/private-equity-navigator.cfm.

Performance reporting is the formal process through which general partners (GPs) communicate a fund's activity and interim returns to limited partners (LPs) throughout the holding period. While the cash-on-cash return of an investment (or a fund) is not determined until a full exit (or realization) has been achieved, interim fund performance provides crucial information for both the GP and the LPs in a fund. For a GP, a fund's interim performance plays a key role in its ability to raise a successor fund; for LPs, it provides important information for allocation decisions within its private equity (PE) portfolio.

Given the central role of interim performance reports, the methodologies and metrics used and their application are closely scrutinized by a fund's LPs. Although the steps to determine interim fund performance are relatively straightforward, different valuation techniques at each step in the process can produce results that are not always directly comparable. This, combined with the subjective assumptions underlying unrealized investment valuations, makes interim fund valuation one of the most contentious aspects in the GP–LP relationship.

This chapter explains the steps taken to arrive at a fund's interim performance report—individual company valuation as well as gross and net performance at the fund level—and highlights potential issues to be considered in the process. The chapter concludes with a closer look at methods used to compare PE performance with public market performance.

INTERIM FUND PERFORMANCE

The performance of a PE fund is reported to its LPs on a quarterly basis. These quarterly reports offer insight into the value of a fund's portfolio companies and the overall performance of the fund to date. Exhibit 19.1 shows the basic steps taken to translate the value of a fund's portfolio companies to its gross and net performance metrics.

Most limited partnership agreements require that a GP reports the fair market value of a fund's investments, a fund's net asset value (NAV) plus its gross multiple of money

Exhibit 19.1 Evaluating PE Fund Performance

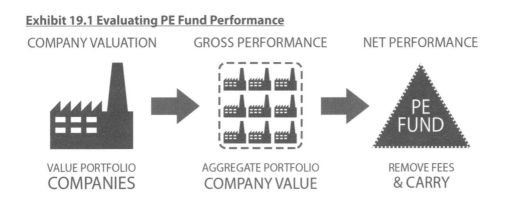

COMPANY VALUATION

GROSS PERFORMANCE

NET PERFORMANCE

VALUE PORTFOLIO **COMPANIES**

AGGREGATE PORTFOLIO **COMPANY VALUE**

REMOVE FEES **& CARRY**

PE FUND

invested (MoM) and its internal rate of return (IRR) as of the reporting date. (See the section on gross performance below for additional details on how to make these calculations.) Starting with the gross performance data, further adjustments need to be made to appropriately recognize the fees and carried interest associated with the fund and to estimate the net, cash-on-cash returns to be received by the LPs. In fact, it is now common practice for GPs (or their external fund administrators) to calculate both gross and net returns. LPs just need to be able to replicate the report and if necessary make it comparable to that of other funds.

We take a closer look at the three steps in interim performance reporting in the sections that follow.

COMPANY VALUATION

The valuation process begins by establishing the realized and/or unrealized value in each portfolio company. Determining an investment's realized value is straightforward, as it equals the proceeds generated from a successful partial or full exit from the fund's position in a company. Determining a company's unrealized value is a more involved and subjective process. Historically, GPs reported the unrealized value in a portfolio company at cost to their LPs and held that value constant throughout the holding period until exit only accounting for impairments but rarely writing the value up (with the exception of a market-based transaction such as a new investment round or sale of a substantial asset). However, following the 2009 global financial crisis, the concept of "fair value" became the market standard.[1]

"Fair value" is defined as the price that a fund would realistically receive for the sale of an asset (or would pay for a liability) in a transaction between market participants on the reporting date. A GP sets a portfolio company's unrealized fair value the same way it determines a company's initial valuation: via multiples from recent industry transactions, comparable public companies, and investments in the portfolio company itself. After establishing an investment's unrealized, illiquid enterprise value, adjustments must be made for any excess assets or liabilities. All instruments senior to a PE fund's equity in terms of their creditor ranking need to be deducted to arrive at the fair equity value of a fund's stake.

While GPs exercise a degree of judgment in determining the unrealized value in their unlisted investments, preference is given to methodologies that draw on market-based measures of risk and return that are minimally influenced by accounting techniques. In addition to metrics from comparable businesses and recent transactions, fair value also takes current market conditions into account, yet rules out abnormally high or low valuations resulting from temporary market imbalances or distressed sales. Techniques used to determine fundamental value, including discounted cash flow or real option valuation, may also inform fair value and can balance market-based assessments.

---

1. The concept of "fair value" is clearly explained in the International Private Equity and Venture Capital Valuation Guidelines published originally by the IPEV board in 2009 and supported by over 20 PE and venture capital associations globally. (The latest edition can be found here: http://www.privateequityvaluation.com/valuation-guidelines/4588034291).

Various academic studies have highlighted the controversy and potential conflicts of interest between GPs and LPs when determining unrealized value in unlisted portfolio company investments. For example, a recent study[2] suggested that at times the valuation of unrealized investments had been used to smooth out interim fund performance, particularly by overstating portfolio company valuations during bear markets. The same study showed that the unrealized portfolio value early in a fund's term was not strongly correlated to a fund's ultimate cash-on-cash performance.

Box 19.1

UNREALIZED VALUE IN PUBLIC EQUITY

PE investments in publicly listed companies—for example holdings resulting from a direct private investment in public equity, a residual equity stake following an initial public offering, or the acquisition of a portfolio firm by a listed entity—are valued in a different manner. Even though a market price for the equity holding is available, adjustments may be required to reflect the fair value of the stake. For example, a PE fund may hold a high percentage of the company's free float or listed shares; while owning a large portion of listed equity might offer a "control premium" (especially when secured by additional rights such as preferred dividends or board control), it may also justify an (il-) liquidity discount, since its sale, or the expectation of an eventual sale, may depress the share price.

In addition, GPs and LPs may take different views on the market risk of such unrealized investments in public equity. Some may prefer to hold investments longer—be it to maximize money multiples or to take advantage of scarce investment opportunities in a specific sector—while others may prefer to exit earlier as a way of maximizing an investment's IRR and avoid paying PE fees on a position in a public security. A GP may therefore decide to distribute the shares of publicly held companies in the fund "in-kind," allowing each LP to act according to its preference.[3]

GROSS PERFORMANCE

With realized and unrealized valuations of its portfolio companies in hand, a GP will calculate a range of fund-level performance metrics, including the fund's MoM, NAV and IRR. Calculating the MoM of each investment—and ultimately of the fund—is fairly straightforward; it is simply realized plus unrealized equity value divided by the capital invested in the company. Similarly, calculating the NAV is simply the sum of the unrealized equity value in a fund's portfolio companies. Calculating a fund's IRR, on the other hand, is far from straightforward and can prove contentious, as different IRR methodologies will produce different fund performance results.

---

2. Phalippou and Gottschalg (2009).
3. However, the cost, logistics and accounting issues connected with this approach make it a rarely used option.

Exhibit 19.2 Gross Performance Statistics

| | FUND EXAMPLE | | | | | | | BACKGROUND | | |

Great Returns Growth Fund III
Investment Schedule, September 30, 2015
$ Millions

COMPANY	INDUSTRY	DATE OF INITIAL INVESTMENT	TOTAL $ INVESTED	REALIZED VALUE	UNREALIZED VALUE	TOTAL VALUE	TOTAL MoM	GROSS IRR	VALUE BASE	EXIT YEAR	EXIT TYPE
Company A	Services	Mar-12	18.5	18.5	0.0	18.5	1.0	0%	Realized	2013	Buyback
Company B	Technology	Apr-12	15.0	60.0	24.0	84.0	5.6	64%	Realized/Contract	2015	Trade sale
Company C	Consumer Staples	Sep-13	22.1	0.5	0.0	0.5	0.0	-100%	Realized	2014	Write off
Company D	Cleantech	Jan-14	9.1	0.0	40.9	40.9	4.5	136%	Quoted	2015	IPO
Company E	Industrial	Jun-14	61.5	0.7	82.1	82.8	1.3	25%	Multiple	not exited	
Company F	Financial Services	Sep-14	32.2	0.0	45.0	45.0	1.4	36%	3rd party transaction	not exited	
Company G	Financial Services	Nov-14	65.9	0.0	65.9	65.9	1.0	0%	Cost	not exited	
TOTAL			224.3	79.7	257.9	337.6	1.5				

Average	23%
Value weighted Average	12%
Aggregated CFs IRR	33%

Exhibit 19.2 shows a report from a fictitious fund detailing the gross performance statistics usually sent to LPs on a quarterly basis. We highlight especially the varying results for fund-level IRRs, depending on the method chosen. In the case of our fund, gross performance ranges from an IRR of 12% to 33% for the same portfolio—a significant variance purely driven by the choice of methodology. (For more on the challenges associated with IRR reporting, see "The IRR Conundrum" below.)

NET PERFORMANCE

To arrive at a fund's net performance, LPs must adjust the reported gross performance—both in terms of MoM and IRR—to account for any fees or profit sharing paid to the GP, namely (but not restricted to), annual management fees and carried interest.[4] These payments have a considerable impact on the net performance or actual take-home profits realized by fund investors. A model by Towers Watson estimates that a fund's gross annual return of 20% will lead to a net return of 13.7% after consideration of all fees.[5] Exhibit 19.3 provides an example and shows how to arrive at net fund performance.

An LP's committed but uninvested capital must be managed while waiting for future capital calls from a GP. An LP's choice on how to invest such undrawn commitments will have a further impact on performance and ultimately contributes to the "real" net return achieved from its PE portfolio. LPs may be tempted to actively manage such funds; while the decision may increase returns, it will add to the risk of not being able to fulfill capital calls when required.

---

4. Please refer to Chapter 1 Private Equity Essentials and Chapter 16 Fund Formation for a description of the fees and costs associated with PE funds.
5. This assumes an even distribution of investments over the investment period and regular investment realizations. Source: Towers Watson (June 2010) PE Emerging from the Crisis.

Exhibit 19.3 Net Performance Statistics

IMPACT OF COST ON NET RETURNS	COMMENTS

Fund Size ($m):   200
Term (years):   10
Management fee: 2% on commitment during 4y investment period, 1.5% on invested capital thereafter.
Carry: 20% of European style "All Capital First" structure
                  (hurdle rates and catch-up not relevant as fund in example comfortably exceeds hurdle)
Deals: 2 per year a $20m with 4y until exit

YEAR	1	2	3	4	5	6	7	8	9		
INVESTED	-40	-40	-40	-40	-40						
REALIZED					80	80	80	80	80	❶	
MANAGEMENT FEE	-4	-4	-4	-4	-2.4	-1.8	-1.2	-0.6	0	SUM: ❷	-22
CARRIED INTEREST					0	0	-8	-16	-16	SUM: ❸	-40
GROSS RETURN	-40	-40	-40	-40	40	80	80	80	80	SUM (GAIN):	200
										MoM:	2
										IRR:	18.9%
NET CF TO INVESTOR	-44	-44	-44	-44	37.6	78.2	70.8	63.4	64	SUM (GAIN): ❹	138
										MoM:	1.69
										IRR:	13.4%

STRONGLY SIMPLIFIED EXAMPLE!

❶ Equal time distribution of investment & distributions.
Early win would impact IRR and timing for carried interest.

❷ Management fee drops substantially after year 5, building a successful GP franchise requires new fund raised by this time.

❸ First "carry" flows in year 7!

❹ Cost to investor about 5.5% p.a. or 0.31x MoM.

Performance Reporting 2.0
By Peter Freire, CEO, Institutional Limited Partners Association (ILPA)

When Limited Partners ("LPs") evaluate private equity managers ("GPs"), there are a multitude of considerations that must be weighed before making an investment decision. The most fundamental of those considerations is a robust understanding of the GP's net performance (i.e., performance after taking into consideration all fees and expenses). In today's evolving PE market, where LPs are seeking to decrease the number of GP relationships in their PE portfolio, accurate comparisons across the spectrum of GPs is of growing importance. Here, we examine three areas where LPs should ensure they're using a consistent measuring-stick when evaluating net investment performance.

First, regardless of size and organization type, nearly all LPs have increased their focus on monitoring the costs which drive the gross-to-net fee drag within their private equity fund program. By identifying the drivers that differentiate gross returns from LP net returns (an investor's "bottom line"), LPs can assess manager-efficiency, understand the opportunity cost of their fund program, and ensure that LP/GP alignment is maintained. Thanks to recent guidance by the Institutional Limited Partners Association (the ILPA Reporting Template), LPs can now point to an industry standard for the disclosure of management fees, expenses, carried interest, and portfolio company fees. As a result, LPs will benefit from the increased efficiency and accuracy of its cost and performance monitoring efforts.

Secondly, beyond fee and expense monitoring, LPs focus closely on Net IRR performance data to evaluate the historical success (and potential future success) of a GP's investment strategy. One current market trend that will impact the comparability across Net IRRs is the increasing usage of credit facilities. GPs are beginning to utilize these facilities as a means to more efficiently manage capital calls and reduce the gross-to-net fee drag early in the life of a fund. While utilization is growing, market norms for this practice have not yet been established, and usage is expected to be variable across the industry. As a result of the variability, the LP community will want to measure the portion of net returns attributable to these credit facilities in order to: i) isolate the component of performance generated from credit facilities, which will allow LPs to accurately compare net returns across a peer set of GPs, and ii) understand the portion of net returns that come from good (or bad) fund management versus fundamental investment acumen.

Finally, net multiples (e.g., Total-Value-to-Paid-In, or "TVPI"), can also vary amongst GPs for reasons other than fundamental investment performance. This may occur when there's variation in the use of recycling, which is amplified when there are inconsistencies in the treatment of recallable distributions in the TVPI calculation. To ensure a more consistent comparison across peers, the industry should use the GIPS standards approach, where recallable capital is treated like all other distributions, and not netted against cumulative contributions (i.e., TVPI calculations should add recallable distributions to the numerator, rather than netting them from the denominator).

The PE industry will continually evolve, but a thorough understanding of net returns will always be core to the LP mindset. Utilization of the ILPA Reporting Template, as well as applying consistent return comparisons, will enhance an LP's evaluation of the GP peer universe.

THE IRR CONUNDRUM

IRR is the performance metric of choice in the PE industry, and represents the discount rate that renders the net present value of a series of cash flows of an investment zero. Despite its widespread use and acceptance, the assumptions underlying any IRR calculation and the use of IRR in practice opens a Pandora's Box of controversy.

One of IRR's main weaknesses is the built-in "reinvestment assumption" that capital distributed to LPs will be reinvested over the fund's term at the same IRR generated at exit. Therefore, a high IRR (>25%) generated by a successful exit early in a PE fund's life is likely to overstate the real economic performance of the fund as the probability of finding an investment with a comparably high IRR over the remaining fund term is low—especially as the closed-end nature of PE funds prohibits investors from reinvesting capital in other funds already in the divestment stage (which would be the closest in terms of risk–return proposition to the exited investment).[6] The mechanics of the IRR calculation thus provide an incentive for a GP to aggressively exit portfolio

---

6. Huss (2005).

companies early in a fund's lifecycle to lock in a high (fund-level) IRR.[7] A related problem, although smaller in magnitude, is that the IRR fails to take into account the LPs' cost of holding capital until it is called for investment.

Beyond this main weakness, there are additional problems with IRRs. First there is the variability in how the metric is applied by GPs; in the absence of a clear industry standard, various methods are used to aggregate the IRRs of individual portfolio investments to arrive at a fund-level return (as shown in Exhibit 19.2). This makes comparisons between fund IRRs difficult for LPs. Second, the IRR is an absolute measure and does not calculate performance relative to a benchmark or market return.[8]

To date, the PE industry has not arrived at an agreed-upon and widely accepted market standard.

MODIFIED IRR (MIRR)

Modified IRR (MIRR) overcomes the reinvestment assumption problem of the standard IRR model by assuming that positive cash flows to LPs are reinvested at the cost of capital or a broad public market benchmark; it also accounts for the cost of uncalled capital, unlike the standard IRR model. By basing the IRR on more realistic assumptions for both reinvestment and cost of capital, the MIRR provides a more accurate measure of PE performance. The effects of switching from IRR to MIRR for a given portfolio are as follows: astronomic 100% + IRRs for "star" funds resulting from early exits are brought into more reasonable territory, while funds suffering from early fallouts in their portfolio are no longer penalized with the unreasonable assumption that all investments (and even uninvested capital) will lose money. The MIRR method generally results in a less extreme performance in both strong and weak funds, as shown in Exhibit 19.4.

Exhibit 19.4 Performance Comparison: IRR versus MIRR

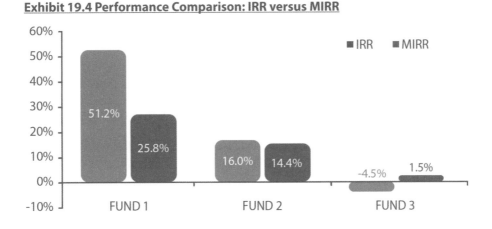

7. For more on MIRR, refer to the joint GPEI-Pevara report on performance in the PE industry at http://centres .insead.edu/global-private-equity-initiative/.
8. Ang and Sorensen (2012).

Box 19.2

COMPARING PE WITH PUBLIC EQUITY PORTFOLIOS

LP investment committees often ask to compare the performance of PE funds with that of the more traditional asset classes; however, the process is far from straightforward. Unlike listed or traded instruments, much of PE's performance reporting relies on interim valuation of unlisted and illiquid investments making the final result opaque at best and a reliable "mark-to-market" impossible. Furthermore, the PE asset class is dominated by outliers, which are difficult to "index," and shows risk–return patterns quite distinct from more traditional asset classes. It is indeed challenging to gain broad (index-like) exposure to PE, contrary to public markets where one can build a diversified portfolio in a straightforward manner.

Moreover, the standard performance measures in PE—IRR and MoM—are not directly comparable to liquid asset classes where valuations and returns are easily determined through a daily mark-to-market. IRR takes into account the timing and size of cash flows while public equity benchmarks use time-weighted return measures. Despite the issue of comparing apples to oranges, attempts have been made to arrive at a (somewhat) realistic comparison.

Public Market Equivalent

A frequently cited method is the public market equivalent (PME) approach, an index–return measure that takes the irregular timing of cash flows in PE into account. The PME compares an investment in a PE fund to an equivalent investment in a public market benchmark (e.g., the S&P 500). The method assumes that all cash flows resulting from capital calls or distributions from the PE fund are replicated in the public market index; it then compares those returns to the cash-on-cash returns (net of fees) of the PE fund. To be clear: every capital call from the PE fund will trigger an equivalent purchase in the public market index and every distribution will trigger a sale of the respective index stake; the dollar-weighted return from the index investments is then plotted as the PME for the PE fund. The choice of the benchmark index is clearly very important and only total return indices make for a meaningful comparison.

The PME approach is a useful and straightforward method, but has its flaws. PME depends on the NAV being benchmarked at the end of the time interval. This can be misleading as it depends on the NAVs reported by the fund managers and assumes that the remaining positions in the portfolio can be readily sold in the market at the quoted NAV. Therefore, the PME approach is typically only used for mature funds where the remaining NAV is minimal.

Time-weighted Returns

Enabled by modern portfolio management tools and systems, LPs today have the ability to calculate the time-weighted returns of their PE portfolios, providing output that is directly comparable to securities priced in public markets. When true time-weighted returns are not available, an approximation can be made by geometrically linking a PE portfolio's periodic MIRR returns.

To further the discussion on this topic, INSEAD's Global Private Equity Initiative applied this methodology to quarterly MIRRs produced by nearly 3,000 institutional funds in the INSEAD-Pevara dataset to produce a broad industry performance index for PE. By setting the cost of capital and the reinvestment rate equal to the long-term return generated by a comparable public index, any out- or underperformance can be attributed to PE "alpha." Based on fund-level cash flows reported by these institutional PE funds, the research finds that PE persistently outperforms comparable public market indices across time and geographies.

Using this PE index, Exhibit 19.5 shows the annualized return generated by PE and that of a comparable public market index for an investment made at any point in time and held until year-end 2015. For example, investments made at the end of 2005 generated a 10-year annualized return of 10.3% in PE and 6.3% in the MSCI, respectively.

Exhibit 19.5 Global PE versus Public Market Returns

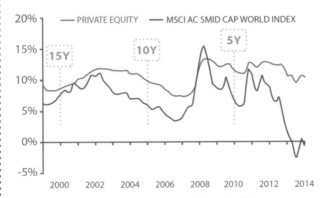

RETURN	PRIVATE EQUITY	MSCI INDEX
5-YEAR	12.0%	6.7%
10-YEAR	10.3%	6.3%
15-YEAR	9.0%	7.9%

Source: Bloomberg, INSEAD-Pevara, Author Analysis

But for one brief period immediately following the global financial crisis, a consistent allocation made to PE (on any date over said period) outperformed a comparable investment in public markets.

It should be noted that comparing performance in this manner has its weaknesses. The construction of a PE index measuring broad industry performance oversimplifies the challenges of investing in PE; for example, an assumption of a 100% exposure to the index over time masks the challenge of building and maintaining consistent exposure to PE. In addition, tracking industry-wide performance in PE is a contentious task in the absence of reliable datasets. Nevertheless, the outperformance of this PE index provides food for thought for institutional investors considering an allocation to the asset class.

CLOSING

Valuing portfolio investments during the holding period and aggregating them to evaluate interim gross and net fund performance provides vital information for GPs and LPs alike. For a GP, a fund's interim performance plays a key role in its ability to raise a successor fund; for LPs, it provides important information for allocation decisions within its PE portfolio. However, LPs must be aware of the related caveats and flaws in the interim fund performance valuation process.

KEY LEARNING POINTS

• Given the private nature of PE investments, arriving at a fair valuation of a fund's investments during the holding period can be a complex and controversial exercise.

• The standard performance measures in PE—MoM and IRR—need to be well understood to allow for a meaningful comparison of PE funds.

• Comparing the performance of PE portfolios to that of more liquid assets is not trivial; the PME and time-weighted returns are suitable methods for investors.

RELEVANT CASE STUDIES

from *Private Equity in Action—Case Studies from Developed and Emerging Markets*

Case #4: Hitting the Target: Optimizing a Private Equity Portfolio with the Partners Group

Case #8: Private Equity in Emerging Markets: Can Operating Advantage Boost Value in Exits?

REFERENCES AND ADDITIONAL READING

Ang, A. and Sorensen, M. (2012) Risks, Returns, and Optimal Holdings of Private Equity: A Survey of Existing Approaches, accessed from: http://ssrn.com/abstract=2119849.

Brown, Gregory W., Gredil, Oleg and Kaplan, Steven N. (2016) Do Private Equity Funds Manipulate Reported Returns?, Fama-Miller Working Paper, August 1, available at SSRN: https://ssrn.com/abstract=2271690 or http://dx.doi.org/10.2139/ssrn.2271690.

Huss, M. (2005) Performance Characteristics of Private Equity: An Empirical Comparison of Listed and Unlisted Private Equity Vehicles, accessed from:

http://ict-industry-reports.com/wp-content/uploads/sites/4/2013/10/2005-Performance-Characteristics-of-Listed-and-Unlisted-Private-Equity-Vehicles-Huss-Uni-Basel-Oct-2005.pdf.

International Private Equity and Venture Capital Valuation Guidelines (2015) Developed by the IPEV board with endorsement from over 20 PE and VC associations globally, December. http://www.privateequityvaluation.com/valuation-guidelines/4588034291.

Jenkinson, T., Harris, R. and Kaplan, S. (2016) How do Private Equity Investments Perform Compared to Public Equity?, *Journal of Investment Management*, 14 (3): 1–24.

Kaplan, Steven N. and Schoar, Antoinette (2003) Private Equity Performance: Returns, Persistence and Capital Flows, MIT Sloan Working Paper No. 4446-03; AFA 2004 San Diego Meetings, November, available at SSRN: https://ssrn.com/abstract=473341 or http://dx.doi.org/10.2139/ssrn.473341.

Mulcahy, Diane, Weeks, Bill and Bradley, Harold S. (2012) We have Met the Enemy… and He is Us, Kauffman Foundation, May, http://www.kauffman.org/~/media/kauffman_org/research%20reports%20and%20covers/2012/05/we_have_met_the_enemy_and_he_is_us.pdf.

Phalippou, L. and Gottschalg. O. (2009) The Performance of Private Equity Funds. Oxford University Press: *Review of Financial Studies*, 22(4): 1747–1776, SSRN: https://ssrn.com/abstract=473221 or http://dx.doi.org/10.2139/ssrn.473221.

Private Equity Navigator (PEN). Model portfolio published twice annually by INSEAD's Private Equity Center (GPEI), http://centres.insead.edu/global-private-equity-initiative/research-publications/private-equity-navigator.cfm.

After spending much of the book's fourth section on raising and managing private equity (PE) funds and limited partner (LP) portfolios, this chapter closes the loop by discussing how to wind down a fund.

In principle, a PE fund should be terminated 10 to 12 (in the case of standard extension) years after the final closing of the vehicle. Once that happens, its GP and LPs have no further legal obligations towards the fund.

In reality, however, there are many instances where a fund is not terminated after its defined term. In fact, the average (!) time it takes PE funds to exit all investments as of this writing is estimated to be 15 years, well beyond the standard 10+2 model. Extending a fund's term often allows for the prudent exit of remaining assets in a fund portfolio and can be in the best interest of both a fund's GP and its LPs. Yet in the case of a struggling GP, an extension may introduce serious principal–agent conflicts. In cases where a GP's current and prospective income consists entirely of management or monitoring fees, a "zombie fund" may result and require coordinated action by a fund's LPs to resolve.

The chapter opens with a description of the standard process of dissolving, liquidating and terminating a fund. It then continues with an explanation of specific end-of-fund-life solutions in the case of unrealized assets. The last part of the chapter focuses on zombie funds and potential actions that LPs and GPs might consider to deal with them.

LIQUIDATING A PE FUND

The legal process for winding down a PE fund structured as a limited partnership takes place in three main steps: dissolution, liquidation and termination (Exhibit 20.1).

Exhibit 20.1 Winding Down a PE Fund

DISSOLUTION: A dissolution event triggers a process that ultimately results in the end of a partnership and the GP's and LPs' obligations to a fund. Dissolution events, which are defined in a limited partnership agreement (LPA), typically include the expiration of a fund's predefined term, the disposal of all fund investments following the termination of the investment period, a supermajority vote of the LPs (no fault clause), a key person event (i.e., when a key person leaves the fund) and a GP bankruptcy. As soon as one of these events occurs, the dissolution of the fund is effective. The partnership does not end, however, until any remaining fund assets are distributed (liquidation) and the fund's limited partnership certificate is cancelled (termination).

LIQUIDATION: Once a dissolution event has occurred, the winding down and liquidation of any remaining fund assets must begin. To terminate a fund, all outstanding fund obligations must be satisfied. The GP is typically in charge of liquidating the fund's remaining assets within a short, predetermined period of time. Whatever proceeds are realized from the sale of these assets will first be used to pay expenses for the liquidation, to settle outstanding claims from fund creditors, and establish reserves to cover any future fund liabilities; any remaining exit proceeds are then distributed according to a fund's distribution waterfall.[1] Typically, a clawback is calculated upon the winding down of the fund and any excess carried interest received by the GP is redistributed to fund LPs.

TERMINATION: After liquidating any remaining assets held by a fund, the partnership can be terminated. To effect termination, a certificate of cancellation is drafted and lodged with the jurisdiction in which the fund's certificate of limited partnership was originally filed; at that point, the fund ceases to exist and has no legal persona. The LPs receive the final financial statements and tax reports of the fund.

END-OF-FUND-LIFE OPTIONS

A fund approaching the end of its life with unrealized assets that are unlikely to be liquidated in time and at acceptable terms is of serious concern to LPs. Such funds contribute to ballooning portfolios and take up LPs' time and resources for monitoring while typically contributing comparably little in terms of incremental return. In these instances, LPs' willingness to continue investing resources in a fund will play a key role in their desired path forward.

The fund's GP and its LPs have a range of options at their disposal to manage funds with unrealized assets. The option(s) chosen[2] depend on two main factors: the LPs' trust in the GP and the performance of the fund. Exhibit 20.2 organizes the end-of-fund-life options according to these criteria.

STEADY-STATE OPTIONS

If, at the end of a fund's life, the interests of LPs and the GP remain aligned and the performance of the fund is positive, a range of standard options are available to overcome the end-of-life situation. The most common will be to extend the term of the

---

1. Please refer to Chapter 16 Fund Formation for more on distribution waterfalls.
2. LPs have been known to turn their back on such funds due to the small amount of capital at risk, the limited remaining economics relating to their stake and importantly the lack of personal career benefits from dealing with a potentially contentious and time-consuming issue.

Exhibit 20.2 Options to Address Tail-end Funds

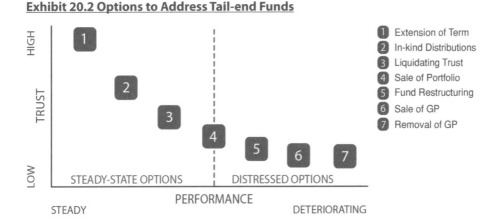

fund, providing the GP additional time to generate value within a portfolio company and exit without running the risk of being perceived as a distressed seller. Other options include in-kind distributions of portfolio company stakes to fund LPs, a transfer of the assets into a liquidating trust or the sale of the portfolio to a secondary buyer. In each of these instances, the LPs and the GP typically remain in good standing and work closely together to solve the issue at hand.

EXTENSION OF TERM AND ADJUSTMENT OF FUND TERMS: The term of a PE fund can typically be extended beyond the targeted 10 years by two one-year periods—either at the discretion of a fund's GP or by vote of its LP advisory committee. Extensions beyond two years are quite common as well; however, LPs will typically request a reduction of management fees, carried interest or a higher hurdle rate in exchange for an extension to prevent GPs from asking for a longer holding period to maximize their fee income or carried interest.

IN-KIND DISTRIBUTIONS: In this scenario, a GP will make in-kind distributions of fund assets in the form of marketable securities, typically publicly listed shares resulting from a portfolio company's initial public offering. Although in-kind distributions transfer market risk and complexity from the fund to its LPs, they still represent one of the more straightforward manners of addressing end-of-fund-life challenges.

LIQUIDATING TRUST: In this option, unrealized fund assets are transferred into a liquidating trust, a newly established entity, with the LPs of the fund as beneficiaries. This type of trust allows a GP to create a clean break from the fund and avoid playing a significant role in the liquidation process. A liquidating trust tends to have a lower fee structure than the original fund and is managed more passively on an as-needed basis.

SECONDARY SALE OF PORTFOLIO: GPs can also sell a fund's entire tail-end portfolio on the secondary market.[3] These transactions are a form of direct secondaries and involve the purchase of equity stakes in a fund's underlying portfolio companies. Often, a single secondary buyer will acquire all of the unrealized assets from a fund in this scenario. The transaction provides liquidity to LPs and allows the GP to concentrate on other funds, but may require a discount to fair value.

---

3. See Chapter 24 Private Equity Secondaries for additional information.

DISTRESSED OPTIONS

The alignment of interests of a fund's GP and LPs may break down at the end of its term. When LPs' trust in the GP erodes, more extreme measures may be needed to address the situation. Steps taken in these scenarios are typically LP-driven and include fund restructuring, the sale of the GP or—in the extreme—the removal of the GP. In these cases, at least one party is leaving the partnership: either the LPs are selling their position in the fund or the GP is being replaced.

FUND RESTRUCTURING: A fund is usually restructured with the help of secondary investors, who provide an exit option for LPs by acquiring their interests in the fund. There are several ways for a fund to execute a restructuring, starting with the straight replacement of the current LPs through a tender offer. In such a case, secondary buyers will offer to purchase the fund interests of existing investors and each LP can choose to sell out or remain in the fund. If this approach is chosen, the original fund remains in place and the buyers become the fund's new LPs.

At times, the replacement of existing investors is coupled with a new round of fundraising to recapitalize the vehicle. An alternative avenue is the rollover of the assets into a new fund where the unrealized assets of the fund are sold to or merged with a new fund set up by the secondary buyers and the GP. The LPs are given the option to either cash out or roll their interests over into the new vehicle. The terms of the new fund are drafted to give the GP more time to manage the assets and to realign the interests of the GP and the LPs.

SALE OF THE GP: LPs can (strongly) encourage the GP to reach an agreement with another established GP to merge operations and hand over control of the existing fund. This is done in the hope of stabilizing the investment team, mitigating the risk of a conflict of interest arising in the management of the existing portfolio companies, and increasing the investment team's ability to raise a new fund.

REMOVAL OF THE GP: LPs may terminate the GP's mandate to manage a fund at any time (no-fault clause), subject to the payment of a pre-agreed penalty often equal to 18 to 24 months of the management fee. However, this option is rarely pursued, since removing a fund's GP is not only expensive but adds additional risks to an already precarious situation compared to maintaining the status quo. Should LPs decide to exercise this right, they will not only incur the abovementioned penalty but will also need to engage a new GP at standard market terms. Moreover, the new GP will require time to familiarize itself with fund portfolio companies, further delaying final exits.

ZOMBIE FUNDS

Zombie funds are PE funds managed by a GP that is unable to raise a follow-on fund. Common reasons for the failure to raise a successor fund are poor performance, significant changes in the investment team combined with an unclear succession plan and, overall, the LPs' loss of faith in the GP. Exhibit 20.3 summarizes factors behind the birth of a zombie fund, key challenges raised by it and steps that a GP can take to rectify the situation and raise a new fund.

Exhibit 20.3 Lifecycle of a Zombie Fund

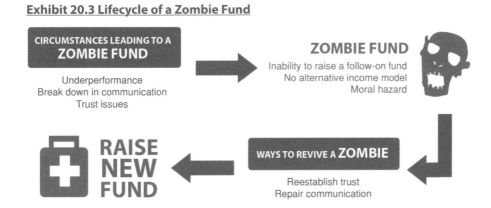

Zombie funds raise a range of issues and make life difficult for all parties involved.

First, in the case of underperformance and the failure to raise a new fund, the PE incentive structure creates a major conflict of interest between GPs and LPs. As soon as the probability of receiving carried interest from a going-concern fund is diminished—and fees from a future fund are unlikely to materialize—GPs' single remaining income stream will come from current management or monitoring fees. As a result, these GPs are incentivized to delay the sale of a fund's remaining assets to receive some fee income, as opposed to working towards a timely exit. Such behavior is, however, certain to affect a GP's reputation and chances of raising another fund.

Second, a zombie fund will lack resources to optimally execute the fund's mandate. This will primarily affect the quality of the team involved. Investment professionals in a struggling GP are likely to look for new opportunities and to show little commitment to the fund. With the quality of the investment team declining, LPs will be incentivized and feel the urgency to push for quick solutions. Moreover, portfolio company management may push for a change of shareholding structure to increase the company's prospects and opportunities. Advisors may be aware of the reduced business potential and will focus their attention elsewhere.

LP PERSPECTIVE

As described, a zombie fund presents challenging circumstances for its LPs. In the best case, the GP, even with good intentions, is unable to maximize the value of fund assets; in the worst case, the GP milks the fund and delays the sale of its assets.

While some of the end-of-fund-life options described earlier can help resolve a difficult situation at a price, LPs can proactively take steps to mitigate the risk of becoming involved in a zombie fund. Specific measures include reviewing the team composition, professional past, fund structure and the LPA during fund due diligence, and strengthening portfolio monitoring processes to identify risks at GPs early during the holding period. Another path for less resourced or more risk-averse investors is to only allocate to managers with multiple funds, given that their franchise value will discourage them from the abovementioned behavior.

REVIEW FUND STRUCTURE AND LPA: The main source of conflict between LPs and GPs is the link between a fund's invested capital and its management fees after the investment period has expired. There are several ways to mitigate this issue when drafting a fund's LPA:

- Adjust the fund's fee structure so that the management fee will be reduced by a fixed amount at the end of the investment period. This adjustment reduces the GP's incentive to postpone the sale of existing assets.
- Reduce the threshold and penalty for the GP's removal to increase the bargaining power of LPs if and when a zombie fund situation arises.
- Remove the customary one-year fund extension at the sole discretion of the GP.
- Review the key man clause. Sometimes a GP is permitted to substitute key partners in the LPA under certain circumstances. By doing so, GPs can reshuffle the initial team at their own discretion and without LP approval. Removing the ability of GPs to replace professionals ensures that funds will be managed by the same team originally backed by the LPs.

STRENGTHEN MONITORING TO IDENTIFY RISKS AT GPs EARLY: Identifying investments at risk of becoming zombie funds early may allow LPs to work on a solution proactively or sell such fund stakes in the secondary market (if necessary at a discount) and avoid the need to manage a complex situation.

BACK MANAGERS WITH MULTIPLE FUNDS: Zombie funds usually materialize only in the instance of standalone funds, i.e., when GPs manage a single fund rather than a family of funds across geographies and investment strategies. Managing multiple funds with separate revenue streams mitigates the potential conflicts of interest should one of these vehicles underperform. In addition, a GP with more than one fund will have a broader interest in maintaining its reputation and goodwill with the LP community, as it plans to continue raising follow-on funds in the future.

GP PERSPECTIVE

A GP, caught in a zombie fund situation and hampered by a lack of resources, must carefully manage an increasingly demotivated team and an increasingly acrimonious relationship with his investors. While exceedingly difficult, a GP may still be able to raise a new fund (or the team might have a professional future as part of a different set-up) by focusing on three key dimensions: trust, performance and the equity story.

TRUST: Trust is one of the most critical factors required for successful follow-on fundraising. Preserving trust can be achieved irrespective of the last fund's performance by maintaining professional conduct and transparency, and not acting against the LPs interests for short-term, opportunistic gain.

PERFORMANCE: To have any chance of raising a new fund, the team needs to deliver strong performance for the remaining portfolio companies in a zombie fund. Funds that still hold a number of portfolio companies with several years remaining until the fund's term expires have an opportunity to improve performance of these remaining assets and thereby increase the chances of raising a follow-on fund.

EQUITY STORY: While managing a zombie portfolio, a GP must shape and define its positioning and strategy in light of future fundraising. To do so, a GP must clearly identify its value proposition to LPs. This means retaining a team with skills and experience relevant to the GP's investment strategy and achieving strong exits on deals that are most similar to the strategy of potential follow-on funds.

GP-led Liquidity Solutions
By Francois Aguerre, Partner, Co-Head of Origination, Coller Capital

GP-led opportunities require selectivity, and a strong focus on portfolio quality.

Although a significant amount of today's private equity net asset value (NAV) will be realized in the normal way, another sizable portion will prove challenging for fund managers to exit within a sensible time-frame, especially because the global financial crisis has led to the extension of portfolio companies' holding periods.

According to Preqin, as of year-end 2015, approximately $676bn of unrealized value is held in 2005–8 vintage private equity funds (Exhibit 20.4). As most of these funds are reaching the end of their pre-agreed lifetimes, GP-led liquidity options are being considered to provide solutions for these aging portfolios.

Moreover, where GPs of ageing funds have little prospect of carried interest, or are unable to raise another fund, they may have little incentive to exit their investments because this would effectively put them out of business. This obviously weakens the alignment between GPs and their LPs. Because of these issues, GPs and LPs alike have increasingly been willing to see existing private equity vehicles restructured. Such

Exhibit 20.4 Unrealized Value Held in 2005–2008 Vintage Funds

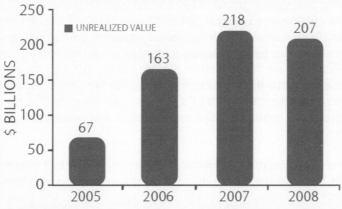

Source: Preqin

transactions tend to be initiated and led by GPs, with the active involvement of secondary buyers. Fund restructurings have a number of objectives:

- to provide a liquidity option to a fund's original investors;
- to secure additional time, and potentially more capital, for a fund's remaining assets;
- to re-align the interests of new and remaining investors with those of the GP, by re-setting some of a fund's terms and conditions.

The restructuring of a private equity fund is complex and presents many challenges—not least of which is achieving an appropriate alignment of interests between multiple parties—and restructuring solutions tend to be highly customized as a result.

On the sell side, restructurings often entail lengthy discussions with the members of a fund's advisory committee and LP base, and usually require a 75% approval threshold. On the buy side, too, there are significant challenges, especially the high level of uncertainty for bidders that a transaction will eventually take place.

Given this inherent complexity, real appetite and commitment are needed on all sides, and many mooted restructuring transactions never get off the ground. Among recent GP-led liquidity solutions that did not reach a successful conclusion, common explanatory factors include differences in pricing expectations and misalignment of interests between sellers, buyers and GPs. These factors ultimately lead to a lack of support from the LPAC, or from the LP base, to reach the minimal approval threshold.

Notwithstanding these challenges, GP-led liquidity solutions have accounted for a meaningful proportion of the overall secondary market volume in recent years, and this proportion looks likely to be maintained or surpassed in the years ahead. Restructurings have so far been predominantly a US phenomenon, since that is where the largest funds are. Larger funds tend to have more robust GP platforms and stronger assets, and therefore a greater attraction for buyers.

Successful restructurings exhibit certain features. The fund in question will have finished its initial investment phase. It will be coming to the end of its lifespan, or already have entered an extension period. There will be significant unrealized value remaining in its portfolio, which will need additional time to achieve its full potential. There must also be the potential for further value creation. For potential buyers, the key issues are the stability and quality of the GP, and strong assets. Buyers should ensure that the restructuring process is fair and transparent to all parties. At the same time, the fund's LPs should have the choice of continuing to invest on the same terms as incoming investors and receiving liquidity on attractive terms.

To make all this work, incoming secondary investors should adopt a partnership approach right from the beginning. In many cases, relationships between the parties involved in successful restructurings often pre-date the transactions themselves.

CLOSING

Although unglamorous, the professional winding down of a fund and its related obligations is part of the full lifecycle of PE. The 10-year plus duration of a typical PE fund means it is likely that the people overseeing this process, on both the LP and GP side, will be different from those that began the journey. While most funds come to an orderly end, a considerable, and by all accounts increasing, number end as "zombie" funds representing (in aggregate) a sizable amount of industry capital and requiring overproportional management attention and a negotiated solution.

KEY LEARNING POINTS

• A PE fund operates as a closed-end partnership and as such has a clearly defined term; once all portfolio holdings have been exited, a dissolution event is triggered that begins the winding down process and the end of the GP–LP relationship.

• Termination and liquidation become complex if residual holdings remain in the fund as it reaches its final year.

• Depending on fund performance and the state of the GP–LP relationship, the parties will choose from an array of solutions to bring the fund to a conclusion ranging from the extension of the fund's term to the removal of its GP.

REFERENCES AND ADDITIONAL READING

Belsley, M. and Charles, I. (2013) Phoenix Rising—Restructuring as a Solution for Zombie Funds, Kirkland & Ellis LLP, https://www.kirkland.com/siteFiles/Publications/Financier%20Worldwide%20(Zombie%20Funds_%20Belsley%20Byline)%20Sept.%202013.pdf.

SECTION V
The Evolution of PE

Private equity (PE) has become an integral component in the asset mix of every institutional investor, yet continues to innovate and grow. In the last section of our book, we consider the latest trends in the industry and take a closer look at topics concerning the evolution of the asset class. On the one hand, we see increasing innovation and differentiation; on the other, we see a trend towards institutionalization and, in certain segments, commoditization, driven at times by a changing regulatory environment.

As the industry continues to mature, the lines dividing traditional limited partners (LPs) and general partners (GPs) have become blurred. The GP–LP relationship is in flux as investors in the PE asset class not only develop direct and co-investment capabilities, but also take advantage of a liquid secondaries market to actively shape their PE exposure. This proactive stance is enabled by innovations in, and increased application of, risk management techniques that allow LPs to better monitor their exposure to the asset class. These trends represent a shift of power towards traditional fund LPs in a historically GP-dominated relationship, feeding back into a broader discussion around fees and carried interest in the traditional GP–LP model.

The maturation of the industry has also triggered innovation on the GP front. Listed PE vehicles have offered GPs a way to reduce their dependence on, and time commitment to, the fundraising process. At the same time, listed PE provides retail investors with access to an asset class traditionally open only to institutional investors and high net-worth individuals. Segregated accounts and funds with substantially longer lifespans are other ways in which GPs are addressing specific investors' needs.

We round up the book with a comment by the authors on the past, present and future challenges of the PE industry.

Section Overview

Chapter 21. LP Direct Investment: This chapter details LPs' direct investment in target companies. Ranging from passive co-investment to standalone direct investments, these investment strategies provide LPs with the means to build exposure in PE outside the GP–LP fund model.

Chapter 22. Listed Private Equity: We examine the two pure-play listed PE offerings: listed PE firms and listed PE funds. In addition to providing retail investors with access to brand names like KKR, Blackstone, and Carlyle, these vehicles give institutional investors an opportunity to "park" the funds committed to the asset class while waiting to be drawn down.

Chapter 23. Risk Management: We detail the risks faced by LPs and GPs in PE investment. A focus on risk allows both LPs and GPs to better track their activity in PE and to reduce the volatility of their returns and investment performance, respectively.

Chapter 24. Private Equity Secondaries: The PE secondaries market provides a tool for LPs to actively manage their exposure to PE through the purchase and sale of established PE investments. We detail the two core secondaries transaction types—the sale of an LP's interest in a fund and the sale of a direct stake in a portfolio company—as well as how these tools are used by LPs and GPs in practice.

Chapter 25. Evolution of Private Equity: A final word from the authors.

Generally, the modern private equity (PE) industry operates based on a model that clearly separates the role of the limited partner (LP) from the general partner (GP). This allows for specialization and ensures limits to liability for fund LPs.[1]

However, predating this institutional fund framework, influential entrepreneurs and their business empires have long been engaged in direct investing, using the financing techniques of their time. This eventually gave rise to what became known as merchant banking—providing capital to companies in return for share ownership.

Although the fund model came to dominate the investment industry over time, some players, notably family offices and some financial institutions, continued to invest directly in private, unlisted businesses. Even more relevant for the industry, over the last 10 to 15 years, institutional investors have started to embrace this trend of "going direct" as well, investing outside the conventional limited partnership structure and using direct and co-investment strategies to complement their primary fund program. This has given rise to a hybrid investment model and a new group of investors nicknamed the "GLP" (or general limited partners) by some observers.

This chapter will start with an overview of the different ways in which LPs can execute a direct investment mandate, ranging from passive co-investing to direct investing. However, the focus will be on co-investing, insofar as it maintains the traditional LP role. We will look into the reasons and attractions for co-investing, evaluate risks associated with this approach, consider (to-date inconclusive) evidence of the success of co-investment programs, and lastly discuss their implementation challenges.

GOING DIRECT
WAYS TO MARKET

LPs have two main avenues to deploy capital into PE outside the traditional closed-end fund model: direct investing, and co-investing as passive or active participants (Exhibit 21.1).

DIRECT INVESTING: When an LP spends a significant amount of its financial firepower on direct investments, it transforms itself into a quasi-GP—at least for this part of its operations. Accordingly, it requires the LP to replicate an investment structure in line with a standalone PE firm (minus the fundraising apparatus) as discussed throughout this book. Few institutional investors have attempted to do so. Many are too small to afford the required investment in people and infrastructure, while others are wary of cultural and implementation issues within their organization.

---

1. Please refer to Chapter 1 Private Equity Essentials for further information on the structure of institutional PE funds.

Exhibit 21.1 Overview—Ways to Market

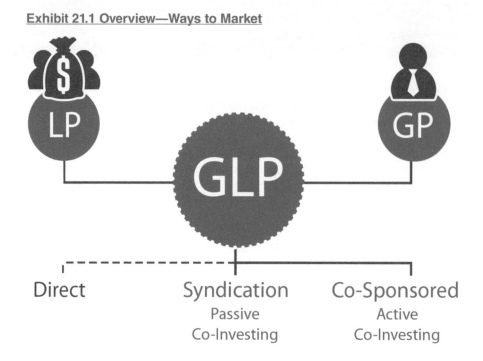

CO-INVESTING: Instead of attempting direct deals, a large number of LPs have opted to undertake co-investments on a regular basis. For a typical co-investment, a PE firm approaches one or more investors with an opportunity to invest side by side with the main fund in a single target company. Co-investment strategies of LPs range from the occasional, purely opportunistic to systematic programs. Aside from the scale and strategy employed, two forms of co-investment can be distinguished—passive co-investment (also known as syndication) and active co-investment (also called co-leading).

- *Passive co-investing:* This is by far the dominant form of co-investing. In this strategy, the GP reaches out to (mainly, but not exclusively) its investors once a deal has progressed to an advanced stage, oftentimes upon reaching exclusivity in an auction process or even post-signing of the transaction. The LP is given a deadline to decide whether to join the equity consortium and for what amount. Information on the deal is prepackaged by the GP, generally in the form of an information memorandum and due diligence reports. The LP's decision tends to be informed by its views of the general attractiveness of the opportunity (including market, company specifics and the risk profile of the transaction) and its trust in the GP's ability to execute on the investment thesis. Therefore, deep direct deal experience is not required, as the LP relies on assessment criteria analogous to the one employed in its manager selection process.

- *Active co-investment:* The active model of co-leading differs significantly from the passive model described above. Here, the LP is invited early on to join forces with a PE firm. In some (generally rare) cases, the LP may even lead or originate a transaction and invite a PE firm for its execution or operating skills. To be seen as a near equal "co-lead," the LP must possess some degree of expertise to help get the deal done or at least not slow down its progress. This requires some direct deal experience among its staff and processes that are streamlined to enable speedy decision-making and execution. An LP might provide additional value to the equity consortium through, for instance, networks of direct and indirect portfolio companies, connections to local regulators, cross-border links, local market knowledge or pattern recognition from its large investment portfolio. By engaging early on in the process the LP will also be liable for broken deal costs (i.e., the cost of an unsuccessful transaction attempt) at a time when chances of success are still lower compared to a syndicated co-investment.

ATTRACTIONS OF CO-INVESTING

The growing interest and the increasing participation of LPs in co-investments are undeniable. In a recent survey,[2] 72% of polled investors said they had asked for co-investment rights when making new fund commitments. Likewise, 50% of LPs polled are actively or opportunistically co-investing, with a further 22% considering doing so. Only 3% of LPs surveyed decided to discontinue after having co-invested in the past (Exhibit 21.2).

A range of attractions are cited by LPs engaging in co-investing.

HIGHER NET RETURNS DUE TO LOWER FEES: Historically, LPs have paid no fees on co-investments (but naturally shared transaction costs pro rata with other equity investors). Yet with the number of co-investments rapidly increasing in recent years, some sort of compensation is often used to entice GPs into sharing deal flow or to stand out from other LPs. This can take the form of one-time equity arrangement fees (analogous to a lead bank arranging debt financing), management fees and even carried interest. However, in almost all cases the fee drag[3] is lower compared to typical fund management fees and carried interest.

Exhibit 21.2 Breakdown of LPs by Current Co-investment Activiy

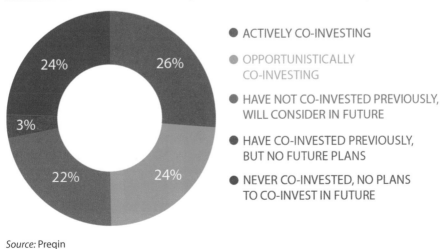

- ACTIVELY CO-INVESTING
- OPPORTUNISTICALLY CO-INVESTING
- HAVE NOT CO-INVESTED PREVIOUSLY, WILL CONSIDER IN FUTURE
- HAVE CO-INVESTED PREVIOUSLY, BUT NO FUTURE PLANS
- NEVER CO-INVESTED, NO PLANS TO CO-INVEST IN FUTURE

Source: Preqin

---

2. See Fig.15, Preqin, November 2015, https://www.preqin.com/docs/reports/Preqin-Special-Report-Private-Equity-Co-Investment-Outlook-November-2015.pdf.
3. Total fees paid for an investment.

DEAL SELECTION: Investors are looking to enhance returns or at least reduce the riskiness of their co-investment portfolio through deal selection. While this by definition requires selection skills, LPs argue that they can achieve this by avoiding certain types of investments, such as larger or riskier deals, or deals outside the fund managers' historical expertise. This helps counter the blind-pool model of PE investing, whereby once capital is committed, the LPs have limited, if any, influence on the type of investments the GP undertakes.

POTENTIAL TO FINE-TUNE PORTFOLIO DIVERSIFICATION: Given the imperfect nature of fund allocation (such as finding suitable managers for specific strategies and vintages, and the time lag of capital deployment) co-investments can round out a portfolio by adding exposure to a certain geography, market, industry sector, investment strategy or vintage year. A related perceived benefit is the LP's increased control over its investment activity throughout the PE market cycle, reducing investments and exposure during market peaks while expanding or accelerating capital deployment during down cycles.

ABILITY TO SMOOTH OUT THE J-CURVE EFFECT[4]: Co-investments enable LPs to smooth out the J-curve effect in two ways. First, they can help accelerate the pace at which capital is deployed and second, individual co-investments have a shorter holding period than a fund, leading to earlier realizations.

COMPLEMENTING AN LP'S PRIMARY FUND PROGRAM: Co-investments allow an LP to conduct due diligence on GPs where it is most meaningful, namely, in a live deal situation, especially prior to committing to a new fund. Co-investing might also be particularly useful in emerging markets where the traditional 10 + 2-year model might be too long or inflexible for the rapidly changing circumstances.

These main points, plus several idiosyncratic ones, are named by LPs in the survey cited above and summarized in Exhibit 21.3.

Exhibit 21.3 LP's Perceived Benefits of Co-investing

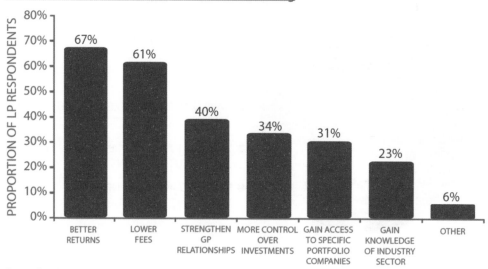

Source: Preqin

---

4. Please refer to Chapter 1 Private Equity Essentials for further details on the J-curve.

RISKS OF CO-INVESTING

Despite the attractions of co-investing, the main way in which institutional investors implement co-investment programs, namely, through a passive co-investment approach (syndication), introduces either increased risk or significant cost.

The syndication process exposes investors to the effects of adverse selection from both the GP and LP sides, may lead to poorly understood investments and offers little differentiated value to GPs. The challenges can be grouped into two main categories: selection issues (choosing the deal) and positioning (getting the deal) especially in an increasingly crowded co-investment space.

SELECTION ISSUES

When LPs choose in which deals to co-invest, they typically suffer from two distinct risks: (1) adverse selection by GPs and (2) selection problems by LPs.

GP SELECTION: We start with the hypothesis that GPs might offer LPs marginally less attractive deals for co-investment either intentionally or unintentionally through the kind of deals they select for co-investments. The rationale for doing so intentionally would be to allocate expected better performing deals fully to the fund to get full performance-linked economics (carried interest) while allocating part of the expected underperformers to the free co-investment bucket. However, even if the GPs were able to differentiate between more and less attractive investments ex-ante, in the day and age of permanent fundraising (Chapter 17) it is unlikely that GPs will knowingly offer inferior deals to their LPs, given the potential repercussions on that crucial relationship. In addition, GPs still invest fund money, which includes their own money, in every single transaction.

Although it is unlikely that GPs will knowingly offer inferior deals to their LPs, investment opportunities for co-investment do differ on average from those that are exclusively allocated to funds, along one dimension: namely, they tend to be larger, as these are the deals with the biggest need for co-investments. Anecdotal evidence suggests that larger deals are inherently riskier as their size tends to lie outside a manager's investment sweet spot of skills and experience. Also, many of the larger deals with more co-investment offerings tend to occur during market peaks, i.e., during vintage years that tend to underperform. Indeed, many of the struggling or failed megadeals from the boom era preceding the 2008 financial crisis had large co-investment allocations. While the relatively small number of these investments does not allow for meaningful statistical analysis, the negative impact on individual LPs has certainly been significant in some cases.

LP SELECTION: Even if a GP offered all potential deals to an LP for co-investment, thereby eliminating any adverse selection problems on his side, the LP would still have to make the decision where to invest. By picking investments (and therefore moving away from "buying the market" represented by all deals it has access to) LPs introduce biases into the selection process. Unsurprisingly, investors in PE are influenced by the full range of biases identified by behavioral finance research, e.g., overconfidence, confirmation bias, availability of heuristics, trend chasing, etc. These inclinations or tendencies are intensified by the lack of experience in, and rigorous processes for, direct deal execution and may lead to larger, better known assets being given a preference in the context of co-investing.

The selection process can be improved by building over time (1) internal expertise that stays within the organizations, or delegation of the selection decision to a better skilled and resourced outside party, (2) a meaningful incentive scheme linked to the long-term performance of the co-investment program, and (3) processes that ensure consistency and guard against these investment biases.

POSITIONING

Overly ambitious goals of many co-investment programs, with respect to the number of investments and dollars deployed per annum, often add pressure on the co-investment team to do deals. Without broadening the opportunity set (difficult with constrained resources in a competitive market), a higher conversion rate inevitably means less selectivity and increased risk per deal.

This links to the second challenge LPs face: positioning, or getting the deal in an increasingly crowded co-investment space with more LPs competing for the (perceived) attractive co-investment opportunities on offer. Doing so requires a two-pronged approach: first, LPs must broaden their pipeline to see more co-investment opportunities; second, after identifying its desired co-investment deals, the LP needs to receive an allocation in these opportunities.

While there are increasing attempts to create a standard operating procedure on co-investment allocation, the nature of the PE business will always afford the GP a certain degree of discretion in selecting co-investment partners. Given this gatekeeper role, LPs are well advised to consider the GP's perspective. Among the most frequently named criteria cited by GPs when selecting LPs for a co-investment are:

- Speed (making decisions quickly in a tight and often multi-geography process)
- Certainty of execution, once a decision has been made
- Enhanced fundraising prospects
- Receipt of some (reduced) economics (fees or carry)
- Value-add

The GPs' biggest concern when offering co-investment rights to LPs is, of course, speed in their decision-making process. Indeed, respondents to a 2014 survey of GPs cited "slowing and delaying the deal process" as their greatest concern about bringing in LPs.[5] As such, GPs often share deal flow with partners with whom they have co-invested before and who they trust in their execution capabilities. Therefore, it is essential for LPs to build agile internal processes commensurate with the timeliness required in co-investing. Failing to do so relegates an investor exclusively to the increasingly crowded passive co-investment space. See Exhibit 21.4 for the main benefits and disadvantages cited by GPs of offering LPs co-investment rights.

LPs can further differentiate themselves by offering an attractive fundraising prospect for the PE firm's next fund or offering (reduced) economics for participation.

---

5. Fifty-eight percent of respondents according to Preqin's February 2014 survey.

Exhibit 21.4 GPs' Perception of Offering LP Co-investment Rights

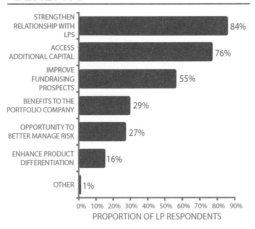

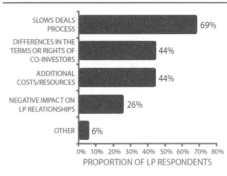

Source: Preqin

Box 21.1

ARE CO-INVESTMENT PROGRAMS SUCCESSFUL?

Based on anecdotal evidence, there is no clear answer. Most co-investment programs are too young for conclusive results. While surveys of LPs show a distinct self-reported outperformance of LPs' co-investment programs, other recent studies have found that co-investments underperform PE benchmarks (but outperform direct investment).[6] Others have focused on the outperformance of co-investments versus the funds they came from.[7]

Insofar as co-investment programs invest a high proportion of their funds on a fee-free basis, the latter studies' results are not surprising. In fact, the lack of fees would allow for some selection mistakes and still produce a better (or at least similar) outcome than the fund program on a net return basis.

However, such a passive program does require significant resources, making it hard to implement for all but the largest investors. For average size programs, the main hurdle to success seems to lie in the injection of "active" elements into the co-investment programs to better select investments and execute the process.

IMPLEMENTATION CHALLENGES

Some of the risks inherent in co-investing can be reduced by building internal co- and direct investment capabilities. Yet going direct brings with it a number of implementation challenges.

---

6. Fang, Ivashina and Lerner (2013).
7. Alpinvest (2014), Stepstone (2014) and State of Wisconsin Investment Board (2013).

RESOURCE INTENSITY: An active co-investment program requires investments in a transaction team, legal support and portfolio management. Only a sizable co-investment program can justify such a build-up of resources, ruling out many smaller investors.

ATTRACTING TALENT: Attracting good people with GP skillsets to LP organizations is difficult due to generally less generous compensation structures, the often-limited scope of the program and the risk of political interference. In particular, government-linked or publicly owned LPs (sovereign wealth funds or public pension plans) struggle to arrive at competitive compensation structures, as their rules and public scrutiny limit the potential for performance-linked compensation.

GOVERNANCE STRUCTURE: The risk of interference can be significant inside some LP organizations. Setting up an effective governance structure that clearly stipulates who the ultimate decision-makers are is a first step, followed by clarity on who manages the deal-specific risk. The latter is especially important given the more concentrated nature of co-investments versus a broad fund program, where failed investments are less visible and have less impact on overall performance. Boards and senior decision-makers will need to invest time and effort to better understand the specifics of PE co-investing.

CONFLICTS WITH ORGANIZATIONAL CULTURE: A well-designed co-investment program rarely exists independent of the larger organization. Therefore, it needs to carefully balance its specific needs with that of the overall organization in terms of compensation scheme, risk and contribution measurement and decision-making. A larger and more active co-investment and direct investment program might also lead to decisions that can negatively impact the primary fund program, for example, if allocation decisions are overly influenced by co-investment considerations (strategic partner versus best-performing funds).

Given these organizational challenges, many LPs prefer to remain passive co-investors or outsource their more active co-investment activity to external parties. In particular, fund of funds have discovered such a product offering as a way to differentiate themselves, generate (potentially) higher fees and in the process leverage their existing GP and funds relationships.

GOING DIRECT
INSTITUTIONAL INVESTORS ONLY?

In the last decade, but particularly since the 2008/09 global financial crisis, several large institutional investors have started to go direct (alone or together with like-minded LPs), investing directly into private companies without GP involvement.[8] These organizations are able to replicate the GP model in-house by leveraging their large balance sheets and global networks—all without the distractions of fundraising. In some cases, they are helped by their lower cost of capital, longer investment horizon or preferential tax treatment (pensions plans are tax exempt in many countries).

8. For an example of one of the most prominent and arguably successful proponents of this trend, consider the Ontario Teachers' Pension Plan (OTTP), which started what is now referred to as the "Canadian model." For a case study on OTTP please refer to "Case 2 Going Direct" in our related case book *Private Equity in Action—Case Studies from Developed and Emerging Markets*.

Yet, direct investing magnifies both the attractions and risks of co-investing. For example, going direct gives institutional investors more control over their investment decisions, but requires more (and different) skills. While there are no external fees, the need to build up resources internally will be costly. And although going direct may lead to potentially higher returns, it may also result in a more concentrated portfolio.

The direct approach also requires a complete redesign of the organization, increasing the potential for internal conflict with, for example, the public equities team. There is also the risk that a focus on direct investments might lead to a deterioration of the fund program's performance (paradoxically reinforcing the perception of the direct program's outperformance) by allocating resources and attention to the direct side to justify this strategy. Furthermore, the generic question for any in-house professional services function of how to stay "sharp" without the full exposure to market forces needs to be addressed.

An extensive direct investment program can also lead to channel conflicts between direct investing and fund investing, with successful GPs increasingly wary of accepting such active investors as LPs in their funds. Lastly, it exposes LPs to legal liability as well as more direct stakeholder pressure.

There is anecdotal evidence from institutional investors that direct investments work best (relative to fund investments) when they are made in well-understood mature industries, in geographic proximity to their home base, when the deal team possesses direct investment skills, during upcycles, and in mature economies. Further research is needed.

CPPIB's Partnership Centric Approach to Private Equity Investing

Julie Gray, Senior Principal—Investment Partnerships (Funds, Secondaries and Co-Investments), Canada Pension Plan Investment Board (CPPIB)

Crawl, Walk, Run

CPPIB's internal mantra when building out any new investment strategy is "crawl, walk, run" and partnerships are a critical aspect of this evolution. Accordingly, our private equity business has been rooted in a partnership model since the firm entered the market through investing in private equity funds in the early 2000s.

When in the mid-2000's, CPPIB's private equity team commenced participating in passive co-investments, it did so only with GPs where the firm had a fund relationship. This co-investment team grew both in size and capability and steadily evolved into a co-sponsorship group,[9] retaining its focus on investing alongside an existing GP partner, but focusing on relatively large transactions where CPPIB's equity commitment is greater than $300 million.

---

9. CPPIB utilizes the term co-sponsorship with respect to its active co-investment (co-leadership) program. Note: All figures are in Canadian dollars as of March 31, 2016.

This evolution left a large and growing opportunity set unaddressed until 2013 when we established a dedicated co-investment team to invest alongside our GP partners in post-close syndicated co-investments, mid- to late-stage deals, and mid-market co-underwrites. CPPIB's equity commitment ranges between $25 and $300 million in these transaction types, up to a maximum of 24.9% of total equity given our co-investment team does not seek post-close governance rights, which is in contrast to our co-sponsorship business.

Managing a Large Private Equity Program

With the private equity industry maturing, CPPIB, like many large investors, expanded its PE program to include private equity fund investing, secondaries, co-investments, co-sponsorships and direct investments on a global basis and today has more than 120 investment professionals focused on these areas. Despite the build out of a large internal team, the program continues to be highly partnership centric with the vast majority of the capital invested in or alongside our GP partners.

Making large fund commitments is core to CPPIB's private equity strategy. Over the past decade, CPPIB has invested, on average, $5 billion per year in PE funds, building a $50 billion portfolio allocated to approximately 60 core private equity managers. These relationships create opportunities not only for CPPIB's private equity business but also for other investment strategies such as private credit and relationship investments (minority investments in public or pre-IPO businesses).

Outside of the funds group, CPPIB's private equity program is predominantly focused on investing alongside its GP partners via co-sponsorships and co-investments and has invested approximately $26 billion in over 90 transactions.

As CPPIB continues to build out its internal private equity capabilities, we continue to look for complementary investment strategies that enable the firm to deploy capital at scale. Examples of which include providing partial, or more selectively, full liquidity solutions for existing portfolio companies of our GP partners.

There are also some situations where it makes sense for CPPIB to invest on our own, primarily in the natural resource and financial services sectors. Additionally, CPPIB may proceed independently in acquiring businesses where the risk profile and/or hold period is not conducive to ownership by a traditional buyout fund or where the seller has a requirement for a non-PE buyer. These direct "strategic investments" represent less than 3% of the firm's total capital invested in private equity to date.

The Only Constant is Change…and Partnership

CPPIB's partnership model was the foundation of its private equity investing discipline and remains at the core of this strategy. The development of CPPIB's private equity business has raised questions about our future intentions regarding private equity fund investing and strategic relationships, particularly since some other Canadian pension plans have evolved to a more direct private equity model. For CPPIB, our partnership based approach is even more important now given our assets are expected to reach almost $600 billion by 2030, versus approximately

$300 billion today, and keeping pace with this growth requires leveraging a number of complementary private equity strategies and relationships. Additionally, as we continue to expand our global reach, partnerships provide access to new geographies and local investment expertise. So while the PE landscape will continue to change and CPPIB's private equity business will continue to evolve, our commitment to strategic partnerships as a core component of the firm's private equity strategy can be expected to remain constant.

CLOSING

In summary, the picture that is emerging is one of a more diverse PE model: institutional investors are attempting more direct investments in larger, lower risk transactions, a trend that has been observed for some time in real estate and infrastructure investing. This may be the start of the commoditization of the PE asset class that, in line with other markets, is expected to see more disintermediation. For PE's bread and butter transactions, LPs are negotiating and receiving an increasing proportion of co-investments, thereby lowering fees and regaining some control over the allocation process.

The co- and direct investing trend is a relatively recent one, so it remains to be seen if the move into a partial GP role will achieve the desired returns for its LPs.

KEY LEARNING POINTS

• **Direct and co-investment strategies are recent trends among institutional investors.**

• **Attractions of low fees and closer involvement with investments need to be balanced with the risks of starting a co-investment program.**

• **Popular co-investors are reliable, make decisions quickly and add value to the overall investment process.**

• **Data beyond anecdotal evidence is still lacking to prove that co-investment is the way forward for all LPs.**

RELEVANT CASE STUDIES

from *Private Equity in Action—Case Studies from Developed and Emerging Markets*

Case #2: Going Direct: The Case of Teachers' Private Capital

Case #4: Hitting the Target: Optimizing a Private Equity Portfolio with the Partners Group

Case #19: Asian Private Equity: A Family Office's Quest for Return

REFERENCES AND ADDITIONAL READING

Alpinvest (2014) The Virtue of Co-Investments, White Paper 2014/2.

Coller Capital (2016–17) Global Private Equity Barometer, Winter http://www
.collercapital.com/Uploaded/Documents//Publications/2016/Coller_Capital_Winter_
Barometer_2016.pdf.

Fang, Lily, Ivashina, Victoria and Lerner, Josh (2013) The Disintermediation of
Financial Markets: Direct Investing in Private Equity, *Journal of Financial Economics*,
116(1 April): 160–178.

State of Wisconsin Investment Board (2013) Private Equity Co-Investments:
Historical Performance and Strategy Opportunities, quoted in: Privcap Reports,
The Co-investment Era Q2/2014. www.privcap.com/wp-content/uploads/2014/05/
coinvestment_final_5.14.14.pdf.

Stepstone (2014) Co-Investments: Good for Your Portfolio's Health?

Listed private equity (LPE)—an oxymoron? Publicly traded instruments may indeed appear out of place in a book on PE, but with the number of LPE vehicles on global stock exchanges growing steadily, we felt a chapter was well justified. LPE vehicles are not exactly new to financial markets: as far back as the 1970s and 1980s we saw listed firms involved in quasi-PE and venture capital activities; in recent years, though, the number has increased rapidly.

LPE vehicles fall into one of two categories: LPE firms and LPE funds.[1] While no two vehicles are alike, the capital raised through a public offering generally provides a permanent source of capital to augment a PE firm's traditional fund management business. However, once listed, LPE shares are exposed to general market gyrations and volatility linked to the overall macroeconomic cycle. A negatively trending share price may demotivate employees with equity-linked compensation and call into question investment decisions and the firm's overall strategy.

LPE vehicles promise retail investors an avenue to gain exposure to PE (see Exhibit 22.1), an asset class usually accessible only to institutional investors and high-net worth individuals due to the large minimum investments needed to subscribe to traditional closed-end funds. However, as retail investors are largely unfamiliar with the intricacies of PE investing and the PE business model overall, they must familiarize themselves with a new language and the bespoke structures of each LPE offering.

This chapter clarifies the basic mechanics and key considerations for investors in both LPE firms and LPE funds; we add a discussion of the pros and cons to be considered by the PE firms themselves before pursuing a public listing.

Exhibit 22.1 How LPE Vehicles Generate Revenue

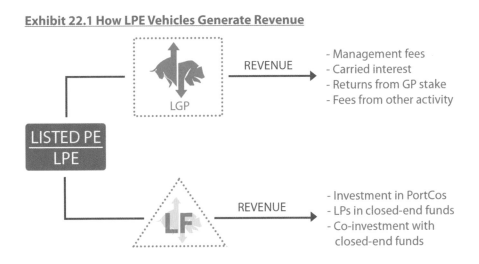

LGP → REVENUE →
- Management fees
- Carried interest
- Returns from GP stake
- Fees from other activity

LISTED PE / LPE

LF → REVENUE →
- Investment in PortCos
- LPs in closed-end funds
- Co-investment with closed-end funds

---

1. Our definition of LPE refers to "pure-play" LPE vehicles. Several sources may include a third type of LPE vehicle: listed investment companies. As these companies typically conduct a wide range of investment activities—one of which is PE—we chose to exclude them from this chapter.

LISTED PE FIRMS

LPE firms (LGPs) make up a small but influential proportion of the LPE universe. Over the past decade, the initial public offerings (IPOs) of the likes of Blackstone (2007), KKR (2010), Apollo (2011) and Carlyle (2012) not only attracted the attention of a broad retail investor base, but also raised questions about these firms' motivations. For example, observers wondered what was driving these traditionally discrete partnerships to suddenly seek the attention of the public and accept the scourge of quarterly reporting in the process.

Following an IPO, the principle business model of an LPE firm remains unchanged: it continues to raise and manage closed-end funds on behalf of an institutional and high-net worth investor base. Although a major economic interest in the PE firm may be sold via the listing, pre-IPO equity partners in the firm will remain effectively in control of the business through a combination of preferred shares or other contractual agreements. Pre-IPO equity partners also typically maintain a significant minority interest in the economics of the business. Finally, a PE firm's senior principals and other key personnel enter into long-term employment agreements with the listed vehicle. Exhibit 22.2 shows a typical, simplified holding structure for an LGP vehicle.

As for the retail investors buying into the stock, they effectively assume the same position as the partners in the PE firm. Shareholders of an LPE firm participate in all revenue generated by the PE firm; this includes not only the carried interest—a share of the profits from the investments made—but also any fees collected for its various activities and returns realized on the general partner (GP) stake. Fees (and to a lesser extent carried interest) in PE can be a very attractive, steady source of income and will provide a diversification effect for any traditional portfolio. Shareholders of an LGP vehicle gain not only (indirect) access to PE investments, they benefit as well from the fees generated by the GP through other fund management activities.

Exhibit 22.2 LPE Firm (LGP) IPO and Use of Proceeds

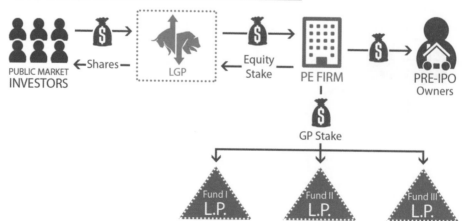

BENEFITS OF LISTING

The benefit to the founders and equity partners of these PE firms is straightforward: cash out of a successful franchise built over decades from the ground up. But some benefits of a public listing extend to the firm itself:

- *Diversified capital base:* Some IPO proceeds are retained on the balance sheet of an LGP, providing a permanent source of capital to commit to future closed-end funds and thereby reducing the pressure on future fundraising.

- *More skin in the game:* With the fresh source of capital, LGPs are able to increase their own percentage commitment in their closed-end funds, strengthening their alignment with limited partners (LPs) in the process.

- *Compensation:* A listing will make it possible to create attractive incentive structures for the next generation of partners joining the firm (e.g., shares and option pools), which will in turn provide an exit avenue for founders wishing to retire.

- *Brand building:* Listing a PE firm may increase its visibility and raise the status of its brand and in turn facilitate future fundraising for its closed-end funds, attract talent, and boost the firm's access to potential target companies.

- *Acquisition currency:* An LGP can use its shares to acquire other companies to expand its fund management activity into other asset classes.

NEW CHALLENGES FROM LISTING

COST OF LISTING: Like any listing, an IPO will require time, resources and in particular the attention of a PE firm's senior partners, thereby shifting the focus away from the business at hand. Post-IPO, time and resources must again be committed to ensure compliance with regulatory demands (e.g., Sarbanes-Oxley in the United States) and reporting requirements associated with the listing.

CONFLICTS OF INTEREST: LGPs need to carefully manage the inherent conflict between the fund's public shareholders and its LPs: a decision taken to maximize the potential return of the LPs may not necessarily benefit the vehicle's share price (at least in the near term) and vice versa. Satisfying the interests of both stakeholders can turn into a conundrum and pose a dilemma to the partners involved. Post-IPO, PE firms are usually careful to reassure their institutional investors of their continued long-term focus when making investment decisions.

DISTRACTION FROM CORE BUSINESS: Many of the LPE firms have expanded their businesses at a rapid clip in the years following their IPO; expanding not only their fund management activities to include hedge funds, real estate and infrastructure funds, but also starting to offer services ranging from mergers and acquisitions and fundraising to turnaround advisory. For example, of the US$266 billion managed by Blackstone in 2014, only US$66 billion was invested in PE, raising questions about the importance of PE next to its other business lines. In effect the IPO trend has accelerated the move of some of the largest PE firms towards becoming diversified asset managers. While there might be synergies (brand, fundraising, participation in different products in the same situation, exploring an investment thesis from different angles) there are no doubt negatives related to the increase in size and diversification of activity (additional management layers, overheads, investment in unified systems for different products, loss of focus, incentive schemes). A concern often raised is that this trend goes against the often quoted mantra of "focus" in PE.

To realize some of the benefits, especially unlocking some of the value created while avoiding the drawbacks of being listed, several larger PE firms have been selling stakes in themselves to outside investors. Initially, buyers came mostly from the sovereign wealth and large pension fund universe; however, recently new investors, including some specialized in taking stakes in management companies, have emerged.

Box 22.1

COMMUNICATING NON-GAAP EARNINGS

Starting with Blackstone's IPO in 2007, LPE firms began to communicate their quarterly earnings using economic net income (ENI) rather than net income under Generally Accepted Accounting Principles (GAAP), arguing that ENI better reflects the underlying performance of a PE firm's business. ENI captures the cash generated by the LGP business (through fund-level fees and performance fees—e.g., carried interest) and the expenses incurred to operate the business in a given period (principally salaries and performance fee-related compensation), with revenue and expense adjustments made for the effect of unrealized fund investments.

Shifting from "GAAP NI" to "ENI" caused great controversy, primarily because of the treatment of non-cash items related to compensation programs established at the time of the IPO. These programs created multibillion dollar pools of future non-cash charges that (1) translate LGP employees' pre-IPO carried interest rights into shares scheduled to vest over time and (2) provide a permanent option pool to compensate investment professionals as they progress in their career.[2] As these compensation programs are established at the time of the IPO, they are treated as one-off charges and often significantly increase the earnings results reported over an accounting period under GAAP.

While a bridge between ENI and GAAP accounting results is disclosed in earnings reports and a full explanation of the accounting methodology is included in an LGP's annual report and financial statements, the key question is: to what extent do investors rely upon a limited understanding of ENI when deciding to invest in an LGP vehicle?

In any case, resorting to an unusual (and, to some, obscure) method continues to be viewed with skepticism by some market players and remains a contentious issue. At a minimum, the use of non-GAAP measures makes these investment vehicles hard to benchmark, and as such difficult to include in large institutional portfolios.

---

2. The rationale behind creating these programs was to retain talent, align interests with LGP shareholders and ensure that the LGP could offer competitive compensation to its junior partners.

LISTED PE FUNDS

The vast majority of LPE instruments are listed funds (LFs). LFs—also referred to as evergreen funds—provide a permanent source of capital for a PE firm to conduct its investment activity. Like closed-end funds, fund managers raise LFs to execute future investments or to purchase existing PE stakes through a secondary transaction.[3] Contrary to its traditional peers, LFs recycle the funds raised and will reinvest both capital and profits in consecutive deals.

LFs engage a PE firm or its affiliates as the investment manager on an exclusive and fully discretionary basis. The right to appoint the investment manager is typically controlled by the sponsoring PE firm or its employees via, for example, service agreements established at the time of the IPO or rights associated with a preferred share class held by the PE firm. Common shareholders, who provide the vast majority of an LF's capital, typically have only an economic interest in the fund and are not involved with the selection of the GP.

An LF is typically raised and managed alongside a PE firm's closed-end vehicles. PE firms invest capital from an LF into companies on a standalone basis, alongside closed-end funds as a co-investment in private companies, or into closed-end funds as an LP. Having access to multiple pools of capital gives PE firms greater flexibility and a chance to structure their deals predominantly in-house: a traditional closed-end fund's equity stake may be complemented by mezzanine debt from the firm's LF to execute an investment in the same portfolio company. Exhibit 22.3 shows a highly simplified schematic of an LF in parallel to closed-end funds.

Investing in an LF provides retail investors with access to a return profile typically reserved for large institutional investors and high-net worth individuals. To be clear, investors in LPE funds realize value through both share price appreciation and dividends. The portion of profits an investor receives in the form of dividends depends

Exhibit 22.3 LPE Fund (LF)

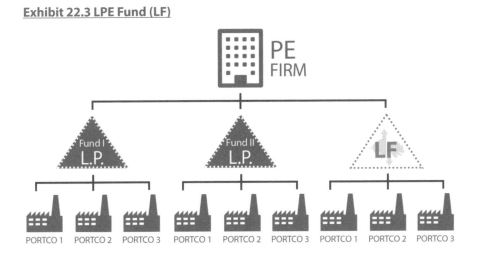

3. Please refer to Chapter 24 Private Equity Secondaries for additional detail.

on either the instrument's legal structure or the discretion of the fund manager. For example, some fund structures require that at least 90% of their taxable income be distributed to investors as dividends. Other fund structures pay out far less—if any at all—based on the manager's discretion and the opportunity cost of holding cash.

BENEFITS OF A LISTED FUND

PE firms that raise LFs are typically established managers with a history of managing closed-end limited partnerships. Raising an LF provides a host of benefits to them and their business:

- *Permanent economics:* LFs provide a permanent source of management fees and carried interest to their sponsoring PE firm.
- *Reduced fundraising requirement:* The permanent capital provided by an LF circumvents the time constraints and demands of raising a string of closed-end funds.
- *Reduced pressure to exit:* LFs have no fixed term, and proceeds from an IPO are retained on the balance sheet indefinitely, reducing the pressure to exit and return LP capital within a given period of time. Such patient capital will also open the door for discussions with family businesses looking for long-term partners rather than short-term investors.
- *Future access to capital:* A secondary offering of shares in an LF allows a PE firm to raise additional funds in the same vehicle if and when required.
- *Diversified investor base:* Raising an LF diversifies a PE firm's investor base away from the traditional LPs in closed-end funds.

LFs also offer specific benefits to its investors and shareholders:

LESS COMPLEX: LFs, a few years after the IPO, will usually no longer be exposed to the J-curve effect[4] given their established portfolio of underlying companies built over time producing regular cash in- and outflows. Retail investors therefore do not have to worry about the complex demands on liquidity management and administration associated with traditional closed-end funds.

PROXY FOR OTHER PE FUNDS: Large institutional investors may use LFs as a means to temporarily invest capital that is committed to, but to date uncalled by, traditional closed-end funds to create a proxy for their PE exposure and at the same time avoid the drag on returns caused by cash holdings.

CHALLENGES OF A LISTED FUND

The PE business model is at times hard to reconcile with the requirements of a public market listing.

ILLIQUIDITY: To achieve returns from an LF vehicle similar to that of an LP in a traditional closed-end PE fund, the public shareholders must hold their shares over

---

4. Please refer to Chapter 1 Private Equity Essentials or our Glossary for further details on the J-curve.

an equivalent long time period and ensure that their payouts are tied to the fund's performance. Therefore, LF shares are often thinly traded as investors hold their stakes as a proxy for long-term investments. This leads to illiquidity, reflected by high bid–ask spreads and in some cases little trading activity or turnover for extended periods of time; as a result, large block sales can lead to substantial depreciation in an LPE fund's share price and unexpected volatility.

PRESSURE FOR "STEADY" PERFORMANCE: While investors should ultimately be agnostic to the timing of cash flows, provided they achieve the same time weighted return, in reality there is substantial pressure on management of listed vehicles to show steady and somewhat predictable returns. This conflicts with the lumpy returns produced by PE investments, especially the occasional home runs and the not so infrequent write-offs. A natural tendency for LFs is therefore to invest in (perceived) less risky transactions, e.g., infrastructure or unlevered transactions. This in turn negatively impacts the expected return of the LF.

MINORITY SHAREHOLDER ACTIVISM: While in general most LFs are controlled by the sponsoring PE firm, in some instances, outside shareholders can gain control by acquiring a significant stake and then push to replace the GP. While this might lead to a higher realization for shareholders than the value at which the fund is trading, it typically has severe repercussions on the going concern of the PE firm.

CONFLICTS WITH TRADITIONAL VEHICLES: If a manager invests from various listed and unlisted funds, allocation and valuation problems might arise. Allocation conflicts need a robust mechanism, in particular, where the manager derives different economics from different funds or has conflicting (even implicit) mandates. As for valuation, various public market considerations, including investor sophistication or short-term market volatility, can lead to drastically different valuations of the same underlying portfolio assets between the listed and unlisted vehicle.

Box 22.2

ABOVE OR BELOW NAV?

The price of LF shares is in theory anchored by the net asset values (NAV) of its underlying portfolio investments. As compared to the NAV of a closed-end PE fund—which consists of the sum of the fair value of its portfolio companies—an LF's NAV may also include at times a significant cash balance, cash equivalents and other assets held on the balance sheet to be deployed in future investments; only a portion of the cash will be distributed to its shareholders via dividends.

In reality, the price of an LF's shares rarely aligns with its NAV; the share price will typically trade at either a premium or—more frequently—a discount to NAV per share. Reasons for such a discount are mainly anecdotal but can be explained by top-down drivers—such as the macroeconomic environment, general market sentiment, and perception of the broader PE industry—and fund-specific factors—including the amount of uninvested cash on the balance sheet, the liquidity of an LF's shares as well as the perceived strengths and weaknesses of the fund manager.

This premium or discount typically applies to the broad LF industry as a whole, as the PE industry falls into or out of favor with investors. Prior to the global financial crisis, for instance, LF funds on average traded at a premium to NAV, which swung to a broad discount post-financial crisis. Surely, as the understanding of and trust in the asset class grows, investor interest will grow and the market will deepen. As we observed with the secondaries market in PE from 2010 to 2015, more capital flowing into these instruments will help legitimize this to-date niche part of public markets, increase its liquidity and in turn reduce its price volatility and discrepancy to NAV.

Listed Private Equity Funds: Is the Market Missing an Opportunity?

By Emma Osborne, Head of Private Equity Fund Investments, Intermediate Capital Group plc, and Mark Florman, Chairman of LPEQ, the association of listed private equity investment companies

Listed private equity funds ("LFs") are an ideal way for private individuals, or small institutions, to invest in private equity ("PE"). LFs offer investors access to PE-backed companies with the added advantages of daily liquidity and greatly simplified administration.

With these benefits it is difficult to understand why LFs, at the time of writing, are trading at a discount of around 19%[5] to net asset value, while many private secondary market transactions are completing at close to par, or even a premium. Harbourvest's takeover bid for SVG in September 2016 is a clear indicator of this disconnect between public and private valuations, eventually valuing the assets at a 0.6% premium, while the market had been valuing them at a 21% discount immediately prior to the bid. Despite this public endorsement of value in the sector from a sophisticated specialist PE investor, the market appears to be missing the opportunity. But why?

Lack of liquidity is one reason. The sector is relatively small (approximately £9 bn market cap, excluding 3i) and the differences in both strategies and structures between the various entities can make it relatively complex to understand. This deters larger institutions from investing the time to understand it since it is challenging for them to deploy meaningful capital.

Another reason is a belief that PE is simply a geared play on the market. What this view misses is the fundamental value that PE creates through active ownership and the alignment of interests with portfolio company management. It also misses the fact that the types of businesses that PE firms invest in are

---

5. London listed PE investment trusts, excluding 3i.

quite different from the profile of listed companies more broadly: PE tends to have a higher proportion of more defensive businesses, selected to be able to withstand higher gearing due to their strong cash flow characteristics.

While these are undoubtedly contributory factors, we believe the main reason is the experience of the sector in the global financial crisis ("GFC"). Many investors were severely burned when NAVs were written down at the end of 2008 and, at the same time, discounts ballooned to 60–70%. The worst performance through this period tended to be in the larger, higher profile vehicles such as Candover, 3i and SVG. This tainted the perception of the sector as a whole even though many LFs performed relatively well throughout.

The current high discounts suggest investors fear another downturn, but there are a number of factors that indicate the sector could be expected to fare better in the event of another crisis:

- **Balance sheets are stronger:** In 2008, many funds had overstretched balance sheets. The extreme discounts in the GFC reflected concerns that some LFs would be unable to meet their obligations.

- **Portfolios are of higher quality, with lower leverage:** After the GFC both investors in, and lenders to, private equity backed companies became more selective. Although headline prices paid in the last few years are close to pre-crisis highs, this is on significantly lower volumes and only the best opportunities are commanding very high prices and leverage. With valuations below the last peak on a like-for-like quality adjusted basis, NAVs should therefore not have as far to fall.

- **Forced sellers magnified discounts:** Many shares across the sector were held in a small number of open-ended funds which suffered redemptions. Selling by these vehicles magnified discounts across the sector.

- **Communication with investors has improved:** LFs have invested in investor relations programmes since the crisis, which should help allay concerns during another crisis.

Most investors are keenly aware, and are reminded by legal disclaimers, that "past performance is not a guide to the future" whenever they look at investments that have performed strongly. But in looking at LFs many seem to be forgetting that the poor performance of the sector in the GFC is not a good guide to the future either. We believe the market is missing an opportunity.

CLOSING

Listing a PE vehicle provides PE firms with a fresh source of capital to conduct their fund management businesses, benefiting both the founders of PE firms and the continued operations of the franchise. Given the variety and complexity of the LPE asset class, retail investors must take the time to develop a clear understanding of a specific vehicle before investing.

KEY LEARNING POINTS

• There are two primary types of LPE vehicles: LPE firms and LPE funds.

• LPE firms sell a stake in the future revenue stream of their management companies (fees and carried interest) while LPE funds provide a permanent source of capital for a PE firm and invest directly in underlying portfolio companies themselves.

• Benefits and challenges for the PE firm, investors and traditional LPs need to be carefully evaluated and mitigation mechanisms incorporated where needed.

RELEVANT CASE STUDIES

from *Private Equity in Action—Case Studies from Developed and Emerging Markets*

Case #4: Hitting the Target: Optimizing a Private Equity Portfolio with the Partners Group

Case #9: Slalom to the Finish: Carlyle's Exit from Moncler

REFERENCES AND ADDITIONAL READING

Huss, M. (2005) Performance Characteristics of Private Equity: An Empirical Comparison of Listed and Unlisted Private Equity Vehicles, http://ict-industry-reports. com/wp-content/uploads/sites/4/2013/10/2005-Performance-Characteristics-of-Listed-and-Unlisted-Private-Equity-Vehicles-Huss-Uni-Basel-Oct-2005.pdf.

Lahr, H. and Herschke, F. (2009) Organizational Forms and Risk of Listed Private Equity. *Journal of Private Equity*, 13: 89–99, https://papers.ssrn.com/sol3/papers. cfm?abstract_id=1359091.

Preqin/LPX Special Report (2012) Listed Private Equity – Opportunities for Institutional Investors, https://www.preqin.com/docs/reports/Preqin_LPX_Listed_Private_Equity_June12.pdf.

Risk is naturally a core consideration for institutional investors managing large and globally diversified portfolios; yet the nature of private equity (PE) adds a dimension to a portfolio's risk profile that is unique from other (more liquid) asset classes. Investors, therefore, need to appreciate the inherent characteristics of PE to appropriately initiate and manage a PE program that aligns with their risk appetite.

In PE, risk management takes place long before the actual investment decision is made, rather than post-investment, as is more common in traditional portfolios of public equity and fixed income. The selection process defines the nature and location of the investment (and risk) up front; long-term lock-up periods make any adjustment exceedingly difficult, once a commitment to a fund has been made. After all, PE funds are blind-pool vehicles that reveal merely a broad mandate during fundraising,[1] while the actual portfolio investments are made over time.

The risk discussion in this chapter will add perspectives not touched on yet in this book and take both limited partner (LP) and general partner (GP) risk management considerations into account. We will explore risk management processes and the instruments used only at a high level due to the constraints of this book.

To structure our discussion, we start with investor-related risks, organized into four categories: asset class risk, portfolio risk, fund manager risk, and direct investment risk (Exhibit 23.1).

Exhibit 23.1 PE Risk for Limited Partners

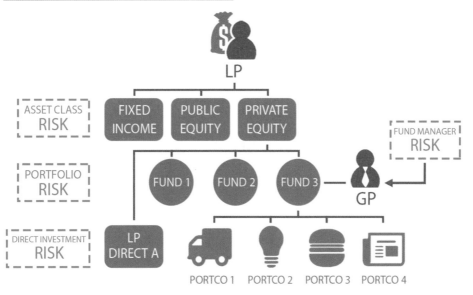

ASSET CLASS RISK

Once an investor has decided to allocate a percentage of its total assets under management to PE, the LPs' investment team will develop a detailed strategy to start the investment process and reach the desired target allocation over time. An investor's risk appetite—a measure of its willingness to put its capital at risk and accept the possibility of extensive losses in the pursuit of a target return—is a key parameter in this process. The risk appetite is closely related to the original mandate of the LP, be it liability matching for an insurer or wealth preservation for a family office.

The theoretical (risk) impact of including PE in an investor's portfolio is well understood: adding private, unlisted companies to a traditional portfolio of public equity and fixed income will help diversify the overall portfolio exposure by reducing its volatility and the risk of large drawdowns, thereby increasing its Sharpe ratio. PE's historically lower volatility of annualized returns, relative to those from a comparable public equity index, seems to fulfill the theory (see Exhibit 23.2). Of course, the argument needs to be carefully back-tested[2] since the actual diversification effect (and returns achieved) will naturally depend on the investor's existing portfolio, the choice of PE/venture capital (VC) funds it may be able to access and the correlation of those assets to its overall portfolio.

Exhibit 23.2 Global PE versus Public Market Range of Returns

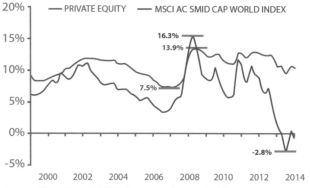

RETURN	PRIVATE EQUITY	MSCI INDEX
MIN	7.5%	-2.8%
MAX	13.9%	16.3%
RANGE	6.4%	19.1%

Sources: Bloomberg, INSEAD-Pevara, author analysis[3]

While allocating to PE may add alpha (or excess returns) to an institutional investor's portfolio, exposure to PE investment entails specific risks, mainly related to the closed-end structure of PE funds and the ensuing illiquidity of fund interests. We explore these risks in detail below.

DURATION: A typical PE fund requires a capital commitment of at least 10 years. While early realizations may occur, LPs must typically wait four to six years before receiving meaningful distributions of capital. Investors need to ensure that this time horizon matches their liabilities.

---

2. Investors typically run extensive back-tests to explore how any new asset class might have impacted the portfolio performance historically.
3. PE returns were calculated based on the INSEAD-Pevara dataset of 3,000 funds using quarterly modified internal rates of return. (http://centres.insead.edu/global-private-equity-initiative/research-publications/private-equity-navigator.cfm). Source for the MSCI World Index: Bloomberg.

LACK OF INTERIM LIQUIDITY: Once capital has been committed and invested through a PE fund, LPs must hold their stakes until the end of the fund's life. While the fast-growing secondaries market has made it possible to manage a PE portfolio and adjust portfolio holdings proactively,[4] selling an LP stake takes time and is often executed at a discount to a fund's net asset value (NAV).

LACK OF TRANSPARENCY: PE funds are blind-pool investment vehicles, with the actual investments becoming visible only over time. It gives the portfolio's risk exposure a new or opaque dimension that the LP's mandate has to allow for.

CASH FLOW AT RISK: LPs have little visibility on the timing and size of cash flows to and from a PE fund. While cash flows will theoretically broadly track a J-curve—with capital calls for investments early in a fund's life followed by capital distributions from exits as the fund matures[5]—all capital calls and distributions are made at the discretion of the GP and cannot be forecast with certainty. LPs attempt to model the timing and size of drawdowns through cash flow simulations, taking different scenarios and economic conditions into account.

COMMITTED VERSUS INVESTED CAPITAL: Less than 100% of the LP's committed capital to PE will be drawn down at any one time, as early distributions will offset subsequent investments. In addition, GPs will usually retain a portion of fund capital for follow-on investments, with the exact percentage hard to forecast. This leaves the LP at risk of an overall exposure to PE below its desired level, requiring the investor to overcommit to reach its desired target allocation.

REGULATORY AND TAX RISKS: Changes in regulation and taxation may have a dramatic impact on the attractiveness of the PE asset class; new taxation may reduce returns and stricter regulations may make allocations to PE less attractive.[6]

An allocation to PE requires custom benchmarks to measure and track its success and facilitate an arm's length assessment of the strategy's viability. Developing and maintaining suitable benchmarks is not a trivial task, as the risk–return patterns differ significantly from that of traditional asset classes, with PE returns dominated by outliers or extreme performers. However, methods exist to allow for a reasonable comparison.[7]

PORTFOLIO RISK

Assuming an LP is comfortable with the headline risks of investing in PE, it can manage its exposure by thoughtfully constructing a portfolio of PE investments. The goal is to build a diversified portfolio—diversified not only by strategy (e.g., venture, growth and buyout) and geography, but also by vintage (i.e., the year in which the fund

---

4. Please refer to Chapter 24 Private Equity Secondaries for additional detail on the mechanics of secondaries.
5. Please refer to Chapter 1 Private Equity Essentials for further details on the J-curve.
6. The introduction of Basel III, the Dodd–Frank Act and the Volcker Rule for banks and Solvency II for insurance companies (in Europe) increased the cost of owning stakes in alternative investments.
7. Please refer to Chapter 19 Performance Reporting for a detailed description of the comparison of PE performance with other asset classes.

started its investment activity)—that reduces the idiosyncratic risk linked to a single PE fund allocation. Evidence shows that vintage-year diversification is one of the most effective ways to reduce the risk of a PE portfolio as it offers consistent exposure across different market cycles.

Three distinct risks stand out in the context of PE portfolio management.

CONCENTRATION RISK: Over time, PE portfolios may lose their initial diversification; concentration may not only result from allocating to too small a number of funds, but also from exceptional performance of, or early distributions from, funds with shared characteristics.

BALLOONING PORTFOLIO: Maintaining a constant gross commitment to PE is a tricky task. It demands that capital distributed from exits be reinvested promptly; yet any new commitments can only be made to PE funds in fundraising—a requirement that over time will ensure a slowly but surely expanding number of PE funds in the portfolio. With a growing number of funds and GP relationships and a modest number of investment professionals on the LP's side, resources will be stretched.

DEFAULT RISK: Default risk may arise if an LP is unable to meet a capital call, be it due to a cash flow shortage, overcommitment, general financial market stress on the public portfolio side or simply the mismatch of capital calls and distributions from a mature PE portfolio.[8] For example, with ample liquidity available in the mid-2000s, investors were tempted to rely on bank debt to fund their PE commitments—a reliance that came back to haunt them during the 2008 global financial crisis when liquidity vanished and bank lines were cancelled. While the penalties for a "capital D" default can be drastic—in the extreme leading to an LP having to forfeit its fund interest— such situations are usually managed by the GP through a secondaries transaction.

In the past, adjusting a portfolio's riskiness to stay within a desired risk contribution from PE was an elusive target. Yet this has changed in recent years. The explosive growth of the secondaries market —from less than US$15 billion in 2009 to well over US$40 billion in 2016[9]—has opened the door for LPs to manage their PE exposure in a proactive manner quite differently from the pre-2007 days of PE. Whether driven by changes in regulations or an investment committee's desire to shift portfolio allocations from developed to emerging markets, these days LP stakes are very likely to find ready buyers, given the amount of dry powder waiting to be deployed for secondary deals.

As buyers of secondary stakes, LPs can increase exposure to specific strategies, funds or geographies and backfill a vintage year to improve portfolio diversification. The duration of secondary investments is shorter than that of primary investments commitments, which implies that returns and liquidity are seen earlier. Also, the blind-pool risk is greatly reduced so that future drawdowns and distributions can be forecast more realistically.

Of course, LPs may also choose fund of funds to achieve a balanced exposure in PE or access smaller funds unable to accommodate the LP's minimum investment. While this avenue reduces the required manpower by outsourcing the allocation decisions

---

8. Refer to Chapter 18 LP Portfolio Management for a full overview of how LPs construct a portfolio.
9. Source: Greenhill Cogent

to one of the global fund of funds managers and promises instant diversification, it comes at the cost of an additional layer of fees.

FUND MANAGER RISK

Selecting fund managers and monitoring their distinct performance over time is a key challenge for LPs. With over 8,000 professional PE fund managers globally,[10] finding those that fit their investment mandate and risk appetite requires time, experience and resources; and with large pension plans and institutional investors often managing well over 100 GP relationships, monitoring their performance is clearly a full-time job. We show some of the related risks in Exhibit 23.3 and explore them in detail below.

KEY PERSON RISK: Successful funds rely on the expertise and knowledge of a few key people: the senior partners in the organization. The so-called "key person risk"—a situation where one or two crucial partners leave a fund manager in the middle of a fund's term—is a concern for investors as it may lead to underperformance. An appropriately worded legal clause in the limited partnership agreement may allow for a withdrawal of funds or cessation of the investment period should such an event occur; nevertheless, a fund's invested capital will usually remain at risk for the remainder of its life.

STYLE DRIFT: The term defines a GP's shift away from its original investment strategy and promised mandate. For investors who have carefully selected each fund to fill a specific diversification need in their portfolios, even subtle changes may upset the balance and shift its overall risk profile. Yet, given the long duration of closed-end funds, adjustments to strategy in a changing investment environment (in particular in emerging markets) are not uncommon.

Exhibit 23.3 Idiosyncratic Risks Posed by PE Funds

STYLE DRIFT

KEY PERSON RISK

REPORTING AND TRANSPARENCY

FUND MANAGER

FOREIGN EXCHANGE RISK

REALIZATION RISK

10. The number refers to professional fund management firms; but estimates vary widely on the number of active fund managers (source: Preqin 2016).

REPORTING AND TRANSPARENCY: LPs require each individual fund to provide performance data in a consistent and timely manner, to allow for portfolio-level reporting to the LP's investment committee. Over the years, quarterly reporting has become the standard in the industry, and LP associations—in particular the Institutional Limited Partners Association—continue to develop and promote reporting requirements to develop best practices. Yet a variety of formats and systems and the discretion of the manager in valuing assets and allocating fees and expenses create risks for investors.

REALIZATION RISK: The interim valuations (i.e., NAV) of PE investments will fluctuate throughout the lifetime of the fund and may vary substantially over time from those ultimately realized. Even after the implementation of the International Private Equity and Venture Capital Valuation Guidelines in 2009 in the aftermath of the global financial crisis, calculating quarterly NAV remains an inherently subjective process.[11] For example, investments made as club deals have in the past received drastically different interim valuations by the GPs involved. Given the practice of raising successor funds every three to four years, fund managers are incentivized to report ambitious results (possibly inflating a fund's NAV) in the lead-up to the next fundraising.

FOREIGN EXCHANGE RISK: Most LPs are US-dollar based and invest and receive distributions in US dollars; nevertheless, fund managers will convert the dollars raised into local tender for investment. Respectable returns in a local currency may be significantly diminished by adverse exchange rate moves and lead to US dollar returns well below expectation.

At the time of allocation, LPs manage fund-specific risk through rigorous due diligence of a fund offering and through terms in fund documentation.[12] LPs will carefully consider a GP's track record, its investment strategy, the experience of its team and its compensation structure, as well as its reporting and monitoring processes. A GP is expected to invest in the fund to align the economic interests of the fund manager with those of its LPs.

During the investment period, monitoring and performance tracking are an ongoing process, no different from that in public equity portfolios. To benchmark the portfolio against that of its peers, data from fund of funds, advisors or data providers is used to show aggregate quartile performance of the overall industry by vintage year, geography and sector. Insights gained from this exercise will inform future asset allocation decisions.

DIRECT INVESTMENT RISK

The number of LPs with ambitions to execute direct deals—i.e., investing in private companies without going through managed funds—is increasing. We dedicate a full chapter[13] to this discussion as the risks involved and the commitment needed to

---

11. Before 2008, underlying companies were valued at cost until realization at exit, meaning that valuations of funds showed no volatility prior to the sale of the portfolio companies. This changed in 2009 with the introduction of the International Private Equity and Venture Capital Valuation Guidelines, which established a set of fair value rules. See Chapter 19 Performance Reporting for additional information.

12. Please refer to Chapter 16 Fund Formation for further details.

13. Please refer to Chapter 21 LP Direct Investment for details on LPs going direct and building co-investment programs.

make both co-investments and direct deals a successful component of an institutional portfolio are not trivial. Developing those capabilities takes time and patience and exposes the LP to all the GP risks discussed below.

RISK MANAGEMENT FOR GPs

To complete the discussion on risk management, we will now follow the money chain and explore the risks faced by a GP throughout the fund lifecycle. The earlier sections in our book covered in detail how GPs raise funds, generate deal flow, execute investments and ultimately manage their portfolio companies towards a successful exit. In this section, we move beyond the deal-related risks and explore business and market-related risks to which GPs are exposed (see Exhibit 23.4).

Exhibit 23.4 PE Risk for General Partners

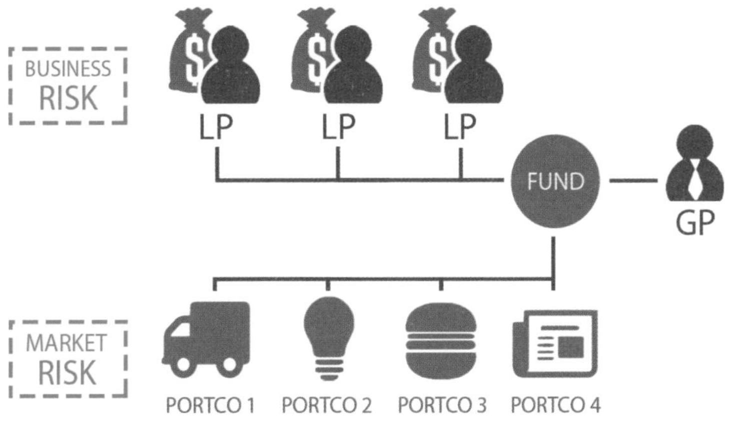

BUSINESS RISK

We define business risks as those that threaten the stability of a PE firm's continued operation, focusing on funding and human capital.

FUNDING RISK: Fundraising—even for established PE franchises—depends on external circumstances; during the so-called "risk-off" periods following crises, even successful fund franchises will find it hard to gain LPs' commitments for new investment vehicles and sustain their businesses.

DEFAULT RISK: While rare, LPs not meeting their capital commitments will present a major disruption to a GP's business. Beyond the standard KYC (know-your-client) processes, developing an LP base that is diversified in terms of geography and type helps to mitigate this risk.

REGULATORY RISK: GPs are facing increased regulatory pressure that requires greater transparency and detailed disclosure with regard to their funds' fee structures (for example, in the context of Solvency II in Europe). Equally, changes in taxation or new regulations on fundraising may negatively impact the operations of a PE firm.

HUMAN RESOURCES RISK: While successful PE firms may over time raise larger fund vehicles, growing the number of partners and the size of the deal team proportionally and in a timely fashion is not easy. This is particularly challenging if the skills needed to execute the strategy change over time (e.g., new emphasis on operational value creation or cross-border transactions).

SUCCESSION RISK: One of the major reasons PE firms dissolve or shrink can be found in the distribution of economic interests and decision-making. The ongoing tension of balancing the interests between senior and up-and-coming junior partners (and by extension intermediate-level professionals) has been the main driver for the establishment of new PE firms, resulting from spin-offs of individuals or whole teams. The topic becomes most prominent when founding partners approach retirement age, and a fair solution of how to value the firm and how to manage the transition needs to be found. The sale of a stake in the firm or its listing, increasingly popular in recent years,[14] may be one solution to this problem.

CONCENTRATION RISK: Few of the abovementioned risks threaten the survival of a PE firm. An insufficiently diversified portfolio, though, will; be it either through single-asset risk (nowadays rare) or exposure to the same sector or geography across investments, the effect on fund performance can be disastrous. Given that this is a manageable risk, LPs in general show little forgiveness for this error in subsequent fundraising.

MARKET RISK

A PE fund's performance is of course impacted by broad market trends and the macroeconomic environment.

MACROECONOMIC RISK: Similar to all financial market participants, PE funds are exposed to macroeconomic shocks and cycles. Other than a (mostly temporary) effect on investment and exit activity, the impact is mostly felt by the portfolio companies, with those with the highest operating and financial leverage the most exposed.

CREDIT RISK: All GPs are exposed to the credit cycle and its impact on a portfolio company's cost of funding. Buyout funds in particular depend on access to liquid credit markets to execute leveraged buyouts (LBOs). In times of market stress, severe disruptions in the credit market can impair the value of a portfolio company as well as the ability of buyout firms to execute LBOs.

PUBLIC EQUITY MARKET RISK: Public equity markets are a key determinant of entry and exit multiples of a fund's portfolio companies. At exit, GPs are exposed to illiquidity in the primary equity market, as initial public offering windows can open and close in short order.

FX RISK: Fluctuations in foreign exchange rates impact the net performance of a fund's investments. The risk, for example, applies when a euro-denominated fund invests in countries outside the eurozone; investments are made in the local currency and upon exit the local tender is converted back into Euros (using the respective rate at the time) and returned to the LPs. The majority of PE firms do not protect against these currency fluctuations and leave the hedging decision to their LPs.

FX: Hedge or Hope?
By Rob Ryan, Market Risk Manager, Baring Private Equity Asia

The arguments against fx hedging of Private Equity investments are well worn. Difficulties in timing fx hedges and the costs of eliminating currency risk have historically led to many fund managers adopting a strategy of hope rather than hedging. The conventional wisdom is that currencies always mean-revert in the long run, and since PE investing is a long-run activity, there's no point in hedging.

It is indeed true that currencies often exhibit mean reversion over the long term. But the problem is that such mean reversion rarely cooperates with the timing of investment entry and exit. What are the chances that the currency will be at the optimal point when the opportunity for divestment presents itself? PE investing is not exempt from Murphy's Law.

More to the point, the core competency of a PE firm is investing in Private Equity, not currency trading. And make no mistake: NOT hedging the currency risk on an investment IS currency trading, but without the usual fx market liquidity. PE firms have neither the competitive edge, nor the agility to profit from macro trading. Currency movement is an unwanted and uncontrollable risk that contributes only to volatility of returns.

A portfolio theory approach would suggest that the risk performance of an investment (as measured by the Sharpe ratio) can be improved if some of the volatility of returns can be eliminated at a suitably acceptable cost. What is deemed "acceptable" will depend upon the amount of volatility that is eliminated, but the current global trend towards ever-lower rates skews the calculation towards active currency hedging in an increasing number of cases: with interest rates in most countries at or close to zero, interest differentials have compressed, and the costs of hedging through forwards have fallen dramatically.

Indeed, the "cost" of hedging back into USD, the most common fund base currency, is now a benefit in most G10 currencies, and even in a number of Asian emerging market currencies. This means that in effect, the investment gets paid to reduce the volatility of returns. Under those conditions, it is difficult, in theory at least, to justify a decision not to hedge.

Once the decision is made to hedge currency exposure, the next step is to determine what that exposure is. Where the asset is a purely domestic business with only local currency revenues and costs, the concept is simple: the entire value of the company is exposed to a devaluation of that local currency with respect to the fund's base currency.

But what if that company does nothing but export locally made products or services, receiving USD as payment? In that case the company's value increases upon local currency devaluation, as lower costs deliver higher margins. Hedging against a devaluation of the local currency would therefore increase currency risk: on appreciation, the hedges would lose money and the company's margins would shrink.

There are further complexities to be taken into account, such as industry concentration and pricing power; currency pass-through provisions in contracts; and even second-order effects such as wage inflation as imported inflation rises. In some cases, it will be possible to come to a reasonable estimate of the impact; in others it will not be possible to get much more than a directional read. In practice, putting a number on the exposure of an asset to currency moves is often far from simple, and sometimes more art than science.

But let's assume that such a number can be arrived at: for the sake of simplicity, we determine that our $100m asset is 50% exposed to a depreciation of the local currency, i.e. for every 10% fall in the currency, the asset loses 5% of its value in base currency terms. The next question: what is an appropriate hedge size? Is it the simple $50m exposure? Or should we hedge in advance 50% of the underwritten exit multiple—or perhaps something in between?

To a large degree this will depend on the manager's level of certainty that the investment will perform as expected. A debt-type instrument that has a reasonably well-defined payout will provide more certainty than the projected payout on a riskier growth equity investment. Other factors will also come into play, including the likely timing of the exit, and indeed, the cost of hedging: hedging a 3x multiple from Day One will cost three times what it would cost to hedge just the equity cheque.

Currency hedging in Private Equity is not a simple task. But neither is it so difficult as to be something to be left to hope and chance. A disciplined and proactive approach to managing currency risk can protect the underlying performance of the fund's investments from unforeseen losses—and increasingly at little or no cost.

CLOSING

Risk management is at the core of every asset management discussion. As soon as PE is added to an investor's broader portfolio mix, the number and complexity of risk considerations increase significantly. Transparency and better (more complete) data sets will need to be developed in the future to further the risk management discussion and arrive at meaningful guidelines for large institutional investors looking to satisfy their constituents.

KEY LEARNING POINTS

• **Risk management in the PE context is becoming an increasingly important (and more sophisticated) function for LPs and GPs alike.**

• **The risks of investing in PE from an LP's perspective can be organized into four categories: asset class risk, portfolio risk, fund manager risk and direct investment risk. Some of these risks deal with general characteristics of PE and others with the execution of building and managing a portfolio.**

• **For GPs, risk management (beyond that related to deal execution) can be broken down into two main categories: business risks and market risks. Some of these risks impact merely performance while others threaten the existence of the PE firm itself.**

RELEVANT CASE STUDIES

from *Private Equity in Action—Case Studies from Developed and Emerging Markets*

Case #2: Going Direct: The Case of Teachers' Private Capital

Case #4: Hitting the Target: Optimizing a Private Equity Portfolio with the Partners Group

Case #18: Private Equity in Frontier Markets: Creating a Fund in Georgia

REFERENCES AND ADDITIONAL READING

Bodie, Zvi, Kane, Alex and Marcus, Alan J. (2014) *Investments*. McGraw-Hill/Irwin Series in Finance, Insurance, and Real Estate. McGraw-Hill.

Diller, C. and Jäckel, C. (2015) Risk in Private Equity: New Insights into the Risk of a Portfolio of Private Equity Funds, BVCA, http://www.bvca.co.uk/Portals/0/library/documents/Guide%20to%20Risk/Risk%20in%20Private%20Equity%20-%20Oct%202015.pdf.

Huber, C. and Imfeld, D. (2013) Operational Risk Management in Practice: Implementation, Success Factors and Pitfalls, CAIA, https://www.caia.org/sites/default/files/AIAR-2013-Vol-2-Issue-2-Managment.pdf.

Ilmanen, Antti (2011) *Expected Returns*. John Wiley & Sons.

Institutional Limited Partners Association (ILPA (2016) Quarterly Reporting Standards. https://ilpa.org/wp-content/uploads/2016/09/ILPA-Best-Practices-Quarterly-Reporting-Standards_Version-1.1.pdf.

International Private Equity and Venture Capital Valuation Guidelines (2015), http://www.privateequityvaluation.com/valuation-guidelines/4588034291.

Swensen, David (2009) *Pioneering Portfolio Management: An Unconventional Approach to Institutional Investment*. Free Press.

The private equity (PE) secondaries[1] market refers to the purchase and sale of existing stakes in PE investments, either limited partnership interests in funds or equity stakes in PE-backed companies. Secondaries offer owners of PE positions an additional path to liquidity and added flexibility in managing a portfolio of PE investments. They provide buyers access to PE investments at varying stages of maturity, and additional means of gaining exposure to specific managers and strategies. Since the late 1990s, secondaries market participants have developed a range of structures to meet an array of bespoke needs.

The secondaries market has been one of the fastest-growing subcategories in the PE asset class, with annual transaction volumes growing from a niche US$2 billion in 2002 to $40 billion globally in 2015 (Exhibit 24.1). Limited partners (LPs) are clearly reaping the benefits as liquidity constraints of the PE asset class become less of an issue. The market received a boost as, in response to regulation following the global financial crisis, large financial institutions used secondaries to substantially reduce their PE portfolios.

This chapter opens with a discussion of the primary secondaries transaction types then explores various structures employed in the marketplace. We conclude by highlighting unique elements and considerations of the secondaries transaction process.

Exhibit 24.1 PE Secondaries Annual Market Volume

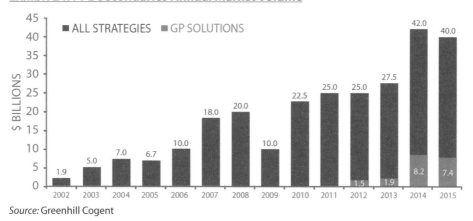

Source: Greenhill Cogent

MAIN TRANSACTION TYPES

The development of the PE secondaries market was a natural consequence of LPs' predominantly passive role in the PE industry. Indeed, LPs' ability to influence

---

1. The term "secondaries" is frequently used within the context of a secondary buyout, i.e., a sale of a portfolio company from one GP to another. We will explain the differences later in the chapter.

capital flows and achieve liquidity on demand is nonexistent given that all investment decisions in a traditional, closed-end PE fund are determined entirely by its general partner (GP). Today's secondaries market allows LPs to sell their interests in funds or equity stakes in private companies prior to fund dissolution or investment exit.

There are two main types of secondary transactions: the sale of interests in a PE fund (limited partnership secondaries) and the sale of equity stakes in PE-backed companies (direct secondaries). In both cases, these transactions represent a straight sale of an interest or equity stake between a buyer and a seller, with no residual claim or relationship maintained by the selling party. These transactions can include the sale of a single fund interest or stake in a PE-backed company or a portfolio of either.

LIMITED PARTNERSHIP SECONDARIES

LP secondaries have long been the dominant form of transaction in the secondaries market, accounting for between 72% and 96% of the total dollar value of secondaries since 2002.[2] The sale of an LP stake breaks the relationship between the selling LP and the fund and transfers all rights—mainly capital distributions—and obligations—mostly unfunded commitments—to the buying party (Exhibit 24.2).

SELLERS: LPs decide to sell interests in PE funds for either internal or external factors. Yet their decision does not necessarily reflect on the quality (or performance) of the PE investment itself. The performance of the fund will be priced into the transaction, with better performing funds attracting more buyers, leading to lower discounts against intrinsic value.

- *Internal factors:* Secondary sales can help shift a portfolio's exposure to preferred geographies, strategies and vintage years without committing capital to a new fund. Secondaries can also be employed to mitigate the "denominator effect," which occurs when falling prices in listed public markets reduce overall portfolio value and cause overexposure to private market assets that revalue more gradually.

Exhibit 24.2 Limited Partnership Secondary Transaction

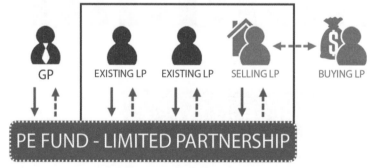

GP   EXISTING LP   EXISTING LP   SELLING LP   BUYING LP

PE FUND - LIMITED PARTNERSHIP

➡ CAPITAL ➡ DISTRIBUTIONS ◆➡ TRANSFER OF RIGHTS AND OBLIGATIONS

- *External factors:* A key driver of secondaries activity has been regulatory pressure or change—for example, the constraints imposed on banks by Basel III and the "Volcker Rule" and on insurance companies by Solvency II—that make the cost of owning stakes in alternative investments untenable. LP financial distress is also a driver of secondary activity, as could be seen following the dotcom crash in 2001 and the financial crisis in 2008, when LPs reduced their liabilities by divesting their commitments through secondaries transactions.

BUYERS: The most active buyers of LP fund interests are specialized secondary funds and fund of funds, who have a specific mandate to acquire secondary interests.[3] A primary investment thesis for these specialized investors is the discount to net asset value (NAV) at which the interests often change hands, providing an immediate arbitrage opportunity. As the market matured, however, traditional PE LPs, especially large pension plans, have emerged as additional active buyers of secondary interests.

The acquisition of LP interests can provide institutional investors with additional exposure to a given PE strategy, geography or fund vintage and increase portfolio diversification outside of a traditional primary fund commitment. Moreover, secondary purchases can be used to smooth cash flows for LPs with choppy J-curve[4] exposure given the range of fund maturities sold in secondaries markets. Buying an LP interest on the secondaries market also provides an additional avenue to access top-performing fund managers and establish a relationship for participation in future funds.

The sale of an LP interest can be combined with a commitment to invest in a GP's next fund in a transaction commonly referred to as a stapled secondary. Stapled secondaries require the buyer of the interest to have the capacity to invest in the primary market. Given the frequency of LPs' commitment to a successful GP's follow-on fund, this can solidify the sustainability of a fund manager's business.

PRICING: Pricing LP interests is arguably one of the most contentious steps of a traditional secondary transaction. Prices are typically based on a fund's NAV at a given point in time, and are quoted at a discount or premium to NAV. The two most common valuation methods are (1) the top-down valuation method, which applies comparable transaction multiples and/or trading multiples to arrive at the value of an LP interest, and (2) the bottom-up valuation method, which uses a discounted cash flow model to calculate the intrinsic value of the fund's underlying assets.

Top-down valuation employs information from comparable secondary market transactions to determine the pricing of an LP interest. A common multiple used in secondary market transactions is the ratio of the price paid and fund's NAV in a given transaction (price/NAV). Pricing can also be determined by looking at historical trading values of listed PE funds. In this method, the multiple considered is the total value of the comparable listed fund—equity market capitalization plus debt—divided by its last published NAV. In reality, however, there is often a lack of comparable transactions—given the opacity of the secondaries market—and too few listed PE funds to develop a robust valuation.

The bottom-up valuation method calculates the price of an LP secondary by discounting the projected future cash flows of the fund in question. The discount

---

3. Some of the largest funds in the secondaries market are Lexington Partners, Coller Capital, Ardian, Goldman Sachs, Partners Group, Strategic Partners, and HarbourVest.

4. Please refer to Chapter 1 Private Equity Essentials for additional information on J-curves.

rate in this scenario is based on the gross return generated from fund cash flows that the secondary buyer expects to achieve. The cash flows include expected distributions from existing portfolio investments, drawdowns for future primary and follow-on investments, and distributions generated from these future investments. Cash flow expectations for existing portfolio companies are estimated by examining the stage of the investment, its expected growth rate and investment needs, and exit valuation expectations, among other metrics. Projecting drawdowns and returns for future investments is less straightforward: estimating the timing and size of cash flows can be based only on due diligence calls with fund managers and the GP's past performance record. Exogenous market factors are also considered.

The Importance of the Discount to Maximize Return: Myth or Reality?

By Daniel Dupont, Managing Director, Northleaf Capital Partners

The PE secondary market started out as a cottage industry in the late '90s, with a few distressed sellers, a few buyers, skeptical GPs and very few intermediaries, and has grown into a full-blown investment, management and even fundraising tool. It has become a more mature, efficient and transparent market, thus increasing the pressure on pricing for buyers and impacting returns for investors.

Before the 2008/9 financial crisis, average high bids were at a record high (Exhibit 24.3). Years 2008/9 were not really representative, as the volume of transactions dropped significantly, sellers and buyers having great difficulty agreeing on prices because of the low visibility on exits caused by market turbulence. Since then, average high bids command low discounts, even at or above par for more commoditized large portfolios of buyout positions.

Pricing is obviously very important for the seller, as it will command a profit or loss on the sale of a portfolio. Other important considerations which will be relevant to the seller are speed of reaction, discretion and the willingness of the seller/buyer to help the existing managers of the positions to access fresh primary money.

Exhibit 24.3 Secondaries Market Pricing (Average High Bids)

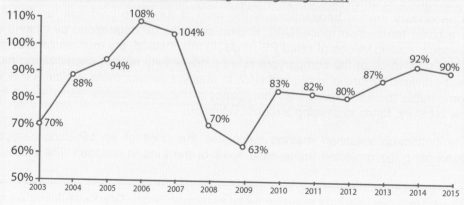

For many buyers such as Northleaf Capital, the discount (or premium) is a consequence of: a) a detailed and rigorous bottom up analysis—an exercise involving building cash flow projections by company under various scenarios, and b) an assessment of manager capabilities and alignment of interest to balance and meet the seller's expectations as well as investment returns.

Although secondary buyers occupy various market niches, finding compelling deals in a more competitive, high priced environment has become more challenging. What tools and strategies can secondary buyers employ to keep delivering good returns?

- *The mid-market segment does present an interesting niche,* because of various factors, including the large number of smaller funds and managers, underlying portfolio companies and the more private nature of financial information. Pricing is less efficient than at the larger end of the market.

- *Access to information as an investor, and close relationships:* some secondary buyers with primary dry powder have developed close relationships with certain managers through previous transactions, a distinct advantage of primary investors and funds of funds vs. pure secondary investors. Access to information and good understanding of the portfolio is particularly important as portfolios are often more concentrated in the mid-market segment.

- *Growth companies* present a better hedge over the medium term. While a high discount on a mediocre portfolio may represent a short term profit through a revaluation exercise after closing, the purchase of a portfolio including growth quality companies whose value will increase over time does represent a better risk/return proposition over the medium term.

- *Quality of deal flow:* deal flow comes from various sources: sellers, intermediaries, and more increasingly fund managers introducing secondary positions to buyers willing to build a long term relationship.

- *A well-established platform, with long-term investment experience and extensive network,* where reliable and trustworthy team members form a solid foundation to attract recurring business with various parties.

- *Tail-end and structured transactions:* plain vanilla LP position portfolio sales are very competitive. Extension of fund's life and participation in GP-led restructurings (from providing fresh capital to an existing fund against a preferential return, to a full transfer of a fund's remaining assets into a new fund structure while buying out existing investors' positions) is less competitive. It will, however, demand an intimate knowledge of the portfolio, a good relationship with the manager, and high negotiations and structuring skills.

- *Financial tools:* well-known use of certain financial tools such as deferred payments, earn outs, leverage and use of a best valuation date can also unlock certain discussions to meet sellers' expectations and buyers' investment returns.

Low discounts are definitely a reality, and are here to stay with the increasing efficiency in the secondary market. Having said that, seeing hefty discounts as the only way to superior returns is a myth. One should never fear paying the right price for a quality portfolio, even at par or premium. Neither should one lose sight of relative returns in comparing various investment options. Prudent private equity investing remains, without doubt, an excellent quality option.

DIRECT SECONDARIES

A direct secondary involves the sale of a passive equity stake or a portfolio of passive equity stakes in a PE-backed company when the lead PE investor—typically a fund—has not yet exited.[5] In most cases, the target's capital structure is not changed after the sale (Exhibit 24.4). These transactions have grown in frequency since the secondary market's infancy but significantly lag behind the more established LP secondary in terms of total transacted value.

Exhibit 24.4 Direct Secondary Transaction

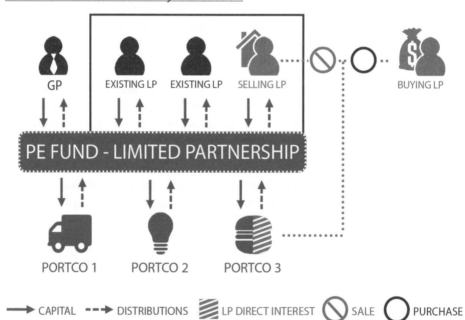

Direct secondaries should not be confused with a secondary buyout, which is the acquisition of a PE-backed company by another PE fund. Secondary buyout transactions involve a sale of a controlling stake in the company by the lead investor, i.e., the PE fund. A new holding structure is normally set up by the buying party, and existing shares and debt capital are typically refinanced.

SELLERS: Sellers of direct secondary stakes include LPs, GPs, founders, company employees, and conglomerates. Portfolios of direct interests often originate from corporate development programs, large financial institutions' direct and co-investment

---

5. Following a direct secondary transaction, the new owner may not remain passive.

programs, and PE funds. The sale of a direct interest in a PE-backed company provides investors with liquidity without impacting the continued management of the investment by the lead PE investor. The sale of a portfolio of direct interests in PE-backed companies offers the seller an opportunity to realize liquidity across several direct stakes in a single transaction rather than via several sales processes. A common trigger for the sale of a portfolio of stakes is the winding down of a fund at the end of a fund's term (tail-end transaction).

BUYERS: The leading direct secondaries buyers include traditional secondary and fund of fund investors as well as dedicated direct secondary funds that specialize in the purchase of direct interests in PE-backed companies.

Direct secondaries provide buyers with immediate access to PE-backed companies, often at attractive prices. The skills required to execute a direct secondary transaction are similar to those in direct investing. Apart from the ability to manage an investment, a buyer also needs relevant transaction skills in due diligence and valuation. Direct secondaries often provide the buyer with the opportunity to acquire a company or portfolio of orphaned assets where substantial value can be created through more active management, access to new capital or operational expertise.

APPLICATION: Typical applications of a direct secondary include spin-outs and buy-ins. In a spin-out, the buyer acquires a portfolio of captive assets, often resulting from changes in strategy or regulation governing activity at a corporate or financial institution. Buyers in these transactions often purchase and manage the spun-out assets in a newly formed investment vehicle, with the GP typically staying on. This strategy is commonly employed when a GP is spun out of a bank.

In a buy-in, a new GP is engaged to manage an existing portfolio of assets. A buy-in is often utilized when a corporation wishes to dispose of a portfolio of non-core assets or when a PE firm wishes to dispose of legacy or tail-end investments. In practice, where there is a capable existing GP, most often that GP will continue to manage the assets, otherwise a new GP will be brought in. Corporates who have no team left to manage portfolios often sell assets directly to an investor in a new structure.

PRICING: Pricing of a direct secondary transaction follows a similar process of that used to value a purchase of equity shares in a PE transaction.[6] When a portfolio of companies is acquired, the aggregate value of each equity stake represents a common starting point for pricing. These transactions are typically executed at a price near this aggregate value, with a moderate discount as a result of buying a portfolio in a single transaction, which reduces a seller's costs, number of counterparties and complexity of execution. Also, buyers in portfolio transactions typically conduct limited due diligence, as it is often unrealistic and quite expensive to assess each asset in a portfolio. The portfolio discount, therefore, represents a fair adjustment for the additional risk assumed following a due diligence-lite approach.

---

6. Please refer to Chapter 7 Target Valuation and Chapter 8 Deal Pricing Dynamics for additional information.

DEAL STRUCTURING

In addition to the two dominant transaction types, PE secondaries market players apply a range of transaction structures to address their stakeholders' specific needs. These structures provide tailored solutions and range from the partial sale of an LP interest to complex structures, including joint ventures and securitization. Most transaction structures can be applied to limited partnership secondaries, direct secondaries or a combination of the two. Each structure addresses a unique set of legal, regulatory or tax considerations for transaction participants.

In some instances, an LP may wish to maintain exposure to specific assets within a fund, while realizing liquidity from others. Structures are also employed to transfer the economic interest in a fund from one LP to another, while the original investor maintains a relationship with the GP. A seller may also be required to exit specific assets in a fund's portfolio for regulatory or strategic reasons that change over a fund's term. Structured secondaries also allow LPs to apply leverage to an LP stake to magnify returns or to receive vendor financing. Similar to a portfolio of direct secondaries, the structure may allow counterparties to limit transaction costs and process complexity. Common structures to achieve these goals are explained in more detail below.

STRUCTURED SECONDARY TRANSACTIONS

In this type of transaction, a special purpose vehicle (SPV) acquires an underlying LP interest, a direct stake in a PE-backed company, or a portfolio of these. The "buyer" purchases exposure to a specific portion of the SPV for a specific amount, the proceeds of which are transferred to the "seller." The seller typically retains exposure to a portion of the cash flow rights and obligations or exposure to specific assets in the SPV. The proportion of future capital calls and distributions or the allocation of exposure to fund interests owned by the SPV is typically formalized in a cash flow share-out agreement (see Exhibit 24.5).

Exhibit 24.5 Structured Secondary Transaction

GP   EXISTING LP   EXISTING LP   SELLING LP   SPV   BUYING LP   SELLING LP

PE FUND - LIMITED PARTNERSHIP

CAPITAL   DISTRIBUTIONS   TRANSFER OF RIGHTS AND OBLIGATIONS

FUNDING AND SPV   SPV STAKE

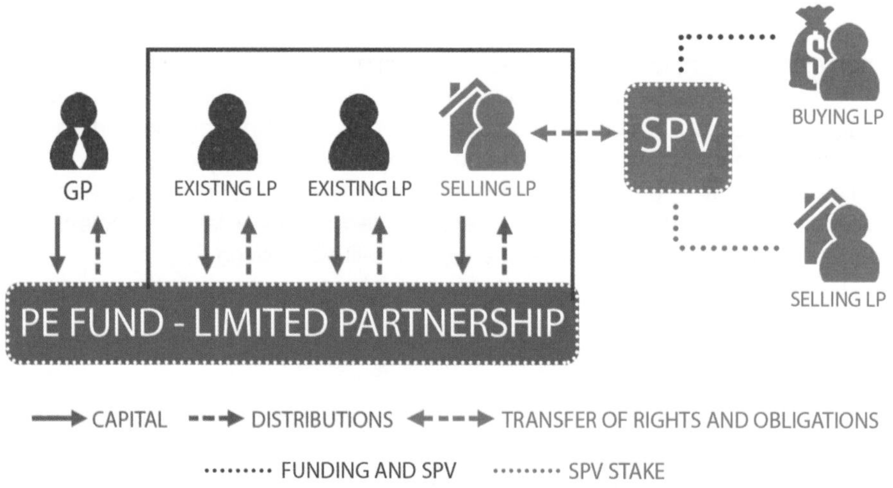

In a common application of an SPV transaction, a seller seeks to maintain its underlying position in existing fund portfolio companies, yet reduce its unfunded future commitments. In this case, a buyer will meet all future capital calls in exchange for a preferred return from the SPV that is secured against future distributions. This structure can be useful if the seller does not wish to sell its LP interest at a discount via a straight sale, but is willing to forego a portion of the returns from future fund investments.

SPV transactions are also used to securitize and sell a portfolio of underlying PE assets. Securitization is an attractive option for a selling party when there is sufficient demand from a group of buyers to yield an attractive valuation on a portfolio of assets. Following the acquisition of PE assets by an SPV, an intermediary will structure and sell tailor-made securities—or tranches—providing exposure to specific cash flows or assets of the SPV to satisfy the risk appetite and other priorities of investors. A common type of securitization is the collateralized fund obligation.

TOTAL RETURN SWAPS

Total return swaps in the secondaries market shift the exposure of an investment in a PE fund from one party to another, in exchange for a regular cash payment (see Exhibit 24.6). The party reducing its exposure to the PE fund (the seller) continues to meet all capital calls and receive all fund distributions, which are transfered on to the buying party. In return, the buying party pays the seller a regular, fixed cash payment. A total return swap allows a selling LP to maintain its interest in the fund and the relationship with the fund's GP, while mitigating the impact of unpredictable capital calls and distributions from its investment.

The counterparties in a swap exchange a "floating" payment—the distributions received from the fund—for a "fixed" payment determined by the fund's NAV and a LIBOR-based interest rate. In addition to fund distributions, the selling party also makes cash transfers to the buying party when there is an increase in the unrealized value of the PE fund (i.e., an increase in the NAV). When the unrealized value of a PE fund falls, the buying party makes a cash transfer to the selling party to offset the loss in underlying value. As a fund's NAV changes following fund distributions and changes in unrealized value, the amount of the fixed payment changes mechanically.

Exhibit 24.6 Total Return Swap Secondary Transaction

| GP | EXISTING LP | EXISTING LP | SELLING LP | BUYING LP |

PE FUND - LIMITED PARTNERSHIP

→ CAPITAL   ⇢ DISTRIBUTIONS   ⟹ TOTAL RETURN OF PE INTEREST   ⟹ LIBOR-BASED RATE ON FUND NAV

EXECUTING SECONDARIES TRANSACTIONS
UNIQUE ELEMENTS

The sales process for a secondary transaction contains several unique aspects related to the transfer of existing PE investments. In particular, specific terms are included in a fund's limited partnership agreement to protect the interests of existing fund LPs and its GP. Some of the key considerations are listed below.

GP CONSENT: In nearly all cases, an LP reducing its exposure to a fund via the straight sale of an LP interest must receive consent from the fund's GP before an LP secondary transaction can be completed. The GP consent clause provides a GP with a degree of discretion to choose a replacement LP in its fund. This clause was particularly relevant when the secondaries market was in its infancy, with the market and reputation of secondaries buyers not well defined or vetted. As the market has matured, GPs often work closely with the selling LP and the buyers to best improve the fund's investor base.

RIGHT OF FIRST REFUSAL: Fund documentation may include a right of first refusal, which grants existing LPs the right to purchase an LP interest before it can be sold to another investor. Existing LPs typically must match the terms offered by external parties. This clause can be waived by LPs to reduce the complexity of a sales process. Similar terms can protect the interests of other shareholders in a direct secondary transaction, where shareholder syndication agreements often include pre-emption rights that provide existing investors in a PE-backed company the right to acquire a selling shareholder's stake at a market-clearing price.

OTHER TRANSFER RESTRICTIONS: The LPs' ability to sell stakes in a fund may be limited by other clauses defining the terms under which interests in the fund can be transferred. These may include clauses that limit the transferability to specific dates—such as month-end or quarter-end—for accounting and administrative purposes or that require specific legal validation before proceeding. The onus rests with fund managers to ensure that a new LP does not introduce regulatory or other issues for the fund. The fund manager must ensure that the transfer will not invalidate any legal agreements or break rules or exemptions provided by financial authorities. These requirements can prolong the sales process significantly and make the transaction more complex depending on which transfer restrictions apply to the fund.[7]

CLOSING

The strong growth of the secondaries market has been driven by LPs' demand for liquidity solutions and portfolio rebalancing. Initially, secondaries consisted primarily of the sale and purchase of portfolios of interests in PE funds, yet as the market matured, direct secondaries began to make up a sizable portion of total transaction

---

7. https://apps.americanbar.org/buslaw/blt/2009-03-04/beaudoin.shtml.

volume. Regulatory changes that made positions in alternative strategies prohibitively expensive for financial firms (e.g., Volcker, Basel III) added sizable volume and impetus.

The secondaries market is of course a derivative of primary investment activity. Given the strong growth of the overall PE industry in recent years, the maturing and ballooning of LP portfolios, and the still small proportion of secondary transactions relative to the primary market, further growth seems assured.

KEY LEARNING POINTS

• Secondary transactions allow LPs to manage their PE portfolio and thereby reduce the illiquidity constraints of the asset class.

• Two distinct transaction types stand out: LP secondaries and direct (or synthetic) secondaries.

• The size of the secondaries market—over US$40 billion in transaction volume in 2015—has given LPs a chance to take control of their exposure to the asset class, to buy and sell stakes in PE funds and actively manage their portfolios.

RELEVANT CASE STUDIES

from *Private Equity in Action—Case Studies from Developed and Emerging Markets*

Case #4: Hitting the Target: Optimizing a Private Equity Portfolio with the Partners Group

REFERENCES AND ADDITIONAL READING

BVCA (2014) Guide to the Private Equity Secondaries Market, February, http://www.bvca.co.uk/Portals/0/library/documents/Secondaries%20Guide-Feb14%20web.pdf.

Coller Capital Barometer (2016) http://www.collercapital.com/Publications/Publications.aspx.

Dow Jones (2015) Guide to the Secondary Market.

Welcome to the final chapter of our book. After laying the theoretical foundations and sharing industry best practice, we shift from the arm's-length, factual style of the preceding 24 chapters to three distinct opinion pieces that address the past, present and future of private equity (PE), written in our respective voices. In addition to providing some much appreciated editorial license, our comments are designed to connect the dots, touch on some of the more controversial issues raised in both the media and public discourse and invite discussions related to the future of the PE industry.

We hope that our shared thoughts will open the door for further research and give our readers an opportunity to reflect and form their own opinions. Enjoy.

PE–HOW WE GOT HERE
BY BOWEN WHITE

Before we look ahead to the themes and trends shaping the PE industry of the future, let us first reflect on the development of the PE industry over the last several years.

In line with many other industries, a megatrend has been the rapid globalization of PE. From its emergence as professional venture and buyout investing in North America, the industry has spread first to Europe and then to all corners of the globe and is now equally entrenched in developed, emerging and frontier markets. While the largest percentage of the industry's assets under management (AUM) continues to be allocated to North American markets (55% of global AUM in 2015), both domestic and international fund managers—often US-headquartered general partners (GPs) with global ambitions—have increasingly raised and deployed capital in Europe (24% of industry AUM in 2015 versus 18% in 2000), Asia (17% versus 4%) and the rest of the world (see Exhibit 25.1).

Exhibit 25.1 PE Industry AUM by Region

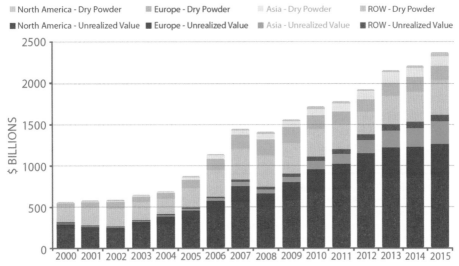

Source: Preqin

So, where will the next wave of industry growth come from? The short answer is Asia, based on its historical growth rate (a 21% 15-year compound annual growth rate of AUM in Asia, compared to 12% in Europe and 8% in North America) and the recent spate of multibillion-dollar Pan-Asian funds raised. Yet given their lower starting AUMs, it will take Asia and the rest of the world several years to match the annual increases in AUM (in dollar terms) produced in developed markets. Even assuming AUM growth in emerging markets equal to the pace set since the turn of the century—which has slowed significantly post-financial crisis—AUM in emerging markets would only match that in developed markets in 2022.

Comparing a region's AUM with GDP provides an additional view on the PE industry's past and future development. The large, sophisticated economies of North America and the scale of PE in the United States combine to form what may be considered the most "mature" PE market, and PE AUM as a percentage of GDP in North America is currently the highest among the four main regions, at 6.6% in 2015. The ratio in Europe stands at 2.8%, in Asia at 1.8% and a low 1.0% in the rest of the world.[1]

While this implies tremendous upside for the latter markets, the ability of PE activity in a region to grow also relies on its capacity of suitable target companies to absorb professionally managed capital. When a shortage of opportunities runs into a surplus of dry powder, the fallout will be in the form of higher prices paid and—likely—lower returns. In addition, structural impediments in emerging markets—including, for example, capital flow and equity ownership restrictions, opaque and variable regulation, still-developing debt capital markets, and volatile initial public offering markets—are also likely to delay the maturation of the industry in these economies.

PRIVATE EQUITY VERSUS THE OTHER EQUITY

While year-on-year growth in AUM has been an industry theme since 2000—but for a brief stumble following the global financial crisis—PE has not grown in a vacuum: over a typical 15-year period, the size of pretty much anything one measures on a regional level—population, consumer prices, the number of Starbucks—will grow, particularly in the context of financial markets and asset management. To put the growth of the PE industry in perspective, we turn to a comparison of PE with public equity markets: Exhibit 25.2 shows PE AUM as a percentage of public equity market capitalization, both globally and in the four main regions.[2]

The upward trend in this ratio over the last 15 years underscores the appetite for PE among investors; in fact, global PE AUM grew nearly three times as fast as global market capitalization over the period. The sharp jump in this ratio during 2008 underscores a theme highlighted earlier in the book: the more predictable, less volatile nature of PE performance—in this case illustrated by AUM growth—relative to public markets. The sharp increase in this ratio was caused predominantly by a

---

1. GDP data source: The World Bank. Where GDP data in 2015 for a country was missing, it was estimated by multiplying the last available GDP figure by the growth rate in the largest country by GDP in the region. Data source: The World Bank.
2. Market capitalization data source: The World Bank. Where equity market capitalization through 2015 in a country was unavailable, it was estimated by multiplying the last available figure available by the growth rate in market capitalization of the largest country (by GDP) in the region. Data for countries with no market capitalization reported were left blank.

Exhibit 25.2 PE AUM as a Percentage of Public Equity Market Capitalization

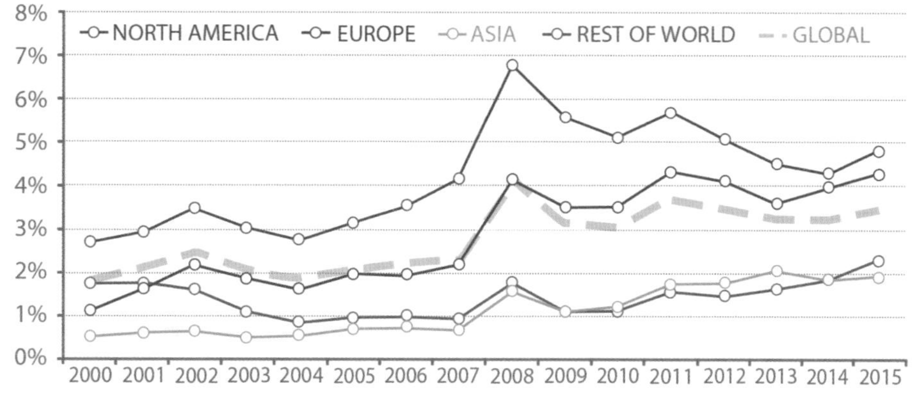

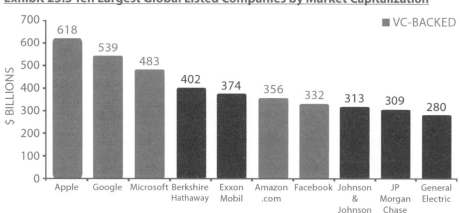

Sources: Preqin, The World Bank, author analysis

significant decrease in public equity market value during the global financial crisis (47% between 2007 and 2008), while PE AUM fell by just 3%. With evidence that PE has outperformed public equity over the long haul—and the ever-present allure of top-quartile returns—there is every suggestion that the popularity of PE relative to the "other" equity will persist.

THE IMPACT OF PRIVATE EQUITY

Beyond the metrics and data, the nature of PE—with serial, professional owners taking significant stakes in privately owned companies—often results in a high-intensity transformational period for the companies backed by PE funds. Through its impact on, and success in, backing companies from cradle to grave, the PE industry helps change, and one hopes in most cases better, businesses, sectors and economies. A clear example of the disruptive impact of venture capital (VC) can be seen in Exhibit 25.3.

Exhibit 25.3 shows that the three largest publicly listed companies in the world as of year-end 2016, and five of the top 10, were backed by VC in their early days. The innovation that these companies fostered revolutionized their respective verticals

Exhibit 25.3 Ten Largest Global Listed Companies by Market Capitalization

Source: Bloomberg

(from software at Microsoft, to internet search at Google, to ecommerce at Amazon) and underscores the role of VC funding as fuel for innovation and market disruption. While each company in this group of five hails from the United States, the VC industry is also stoking change farther afield in emerging markets, increasingly funding home-grown business models. With start-up hotbeds from Beijing to Singapore to Mumbai to Moscow, VC is fueling innovation that taps into the purchasing power of a fast-emerging middle class and the continued growth of mobile services.

The PE industry's impact through investments in mature companies is not about redefining the industries and eye-catching market disruption, but rather about strategic repositioning and the refinement of business processes. Through the rigorous application of best practice in a governance setting that enables quick decision-making and aligns economic interests, buyout investors have the ability to point an entire organization towards a single goal and drive change to the roots of a business. As leverage gives way to operational value creation as a core differentiator for PE investors, the ability to drive change takes on additional importance. In today's competitive mergers and acquisitions market, buyout firms must focus on making long-term, sustainable improvements to portfolio companies' operations to generate their returns.

Indeed, the sense of urgency and the industry's increasing focus on value creation ensure that businesses are reshaped through a process of creative destruction: resources will be concentrated on the best opportunities, enhance competitive strengths and generate investor returns. The full control offered to a buyout firm, but also the fresh perspective provided by a minority investor, makes it likely that operating segments and projects with the highest productivity or net present value will be favored. This in turn means that firms often emerge from PE ownership more profitable and better prepared for the challenges ahead. Contrary to the popular perception, the effect on employment throughout the PE holding period tends to be a net positive, although it oftentimes follows a U-shape given the restructuring frequently preceding a strategic repositioning.

The adoption of many of the guiding principles of the PE industry across businesses and by other asset managers underscores its impact on the broader economy. From increased equity-linked compensation to more active governance and monitoring, PE has impacted the way businesses are run. From corporate VC arms to increased leverage ratios on corporate balance sheets, PE has changed the way companies think about investment. From family offices with dedicated in-house PE teams to the blurred lines between PE firms and activist hedge fund managers, other asset managers borrow from PE—and PE from other asset managers—in the pursuit of a competitive edge.

PE—CAN IT REMAIN ATTRACTIVE?
BY MICHAEL PRAHL

The most fundamental question investors ask us, and with surprising frequency at that, is "should my organization invest in PE?" and "if so, how should we go about it?" While this book deals with the second question in multiple chapters and from various angles, the first question can actually be paraphrased into "are the high historical returns generated by PE sustainable?"

PE, once on the fringes of respectable investing, has undoubtedly arrived in the mainstream. With AUM of about $2.5 trillion it can now be found in the portfolios of most institutional investors. The reasons for its success are undoubtedly the returns it has delivered to investors. While not "absolute" returns, i.e., uncorrelated to public equities or financial markets at large, they have nevertheless been strong and outperformed most other asset classes over a surprisingly long period, despite the strong inflow of capital and increase in the number of PE firms. At the same time, risk has not been as high as expected. While there are fair discussions about reporting and valuation mechanisms employed in the industry underrepresenting true volatility, at the end of the day there have been fewer defaults at the portfolio company level and lower loss rates for funds and certainly for a portfolio of funds (the exception to most of this being VC) than expected at the height of the financial crisis.

In parallel with the growth of the industry, its structure changed. A large portion of PE firms have grown from small partnerships into large financial services firms. At the same time, the performance of the asset class and the scale of the investment opportunity have changed the investor mix. While PE was initially backed by risk-taking high-net worth individuals, endowments and financial institutions (pre-regulation), by now the bulk of the capital comes from pensions, sovereign wealth funds and insurance businesses. The latest trend is to even "go retail," i.e., open the asset class up to main street investors.

THE INSTITUTIONALIZATION OF PRIVATE EQUITY

These changes in size and industry structure have led to, and in turn been enabled by, a trend towards what is called the "institutionalization of PE." Institutionalization as a process integrates compliance and risk management into the fabric of the PE firm and includes policies and guidelines on how to conduct business. So now there are standards and best practices according to which firms are expected to operate.

This is useful for investors, especially institutional ones, in many ways. Standards allow for more efficient due diligence, reporting and portfolio management, and increased transparency and thereby reduced downside risk. However, in turn, information gathering has become an arduous task for GPs, with longer and more detailed investment proposals and due diligence questionnaires. Investors pour over investment processes, compliance procedures, valuation guidelines, and co-investment allocation policies, while GPs prepare different, customized sets of data for each of their investors and engage in legal negotiations about side letters. On top of this, in line with the zeitgeist, regulatory requirements have increased.

This combination of investor and regulatory demands requires a huge investment in people and infrastructure for managers, in effect creating barriers to entry for first-time funds and smaller firms. The large investors that now make up the bulk of the capital in the industry prefer to allocate to larger managers that can provide this institutional set-up (and absorb larger check sizes). So, the bigger managers are getting bigger, as shown by the amount of industry AUM now controlled by funds $1 billion and larger (56%) or even larger ones at more than $2.5 billion (37%) in Exhibit 25.4.

Exhibit 25.4 PE Industry AUM by Fund Size

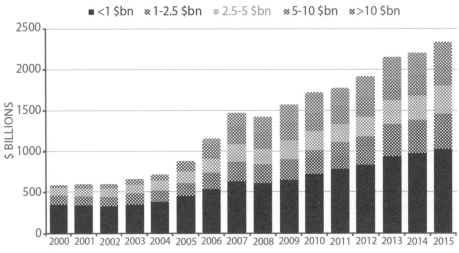

Source: Preqin

Institutionalization and standardization has other effects too. Firstly, it allows the creation of other products as offshoots of the primary PE market. Chief among them are the emergence of a relatively deep and liquid secondaries market. Some of its more recent innovations, e.g., the transfer of economic interest without the underlying legal ownership, have in turn all but paved the way to the emergence of derivatives on PE funds. Initially devised to help investors manage liquidity and risk, it is not much of a stretch to see them become investment solutions in their own rights.

Secondly, by creating more transparency around the investment process and economic model of PE, some power in the limited partner (LP)–GP relationship has moved back to the former, or at least to the larger LPs. Not only have they renegotiated fees and expense allocation practices but they have also moved aggressively into co-investments and, although from a low base, independent direct investments. In effect, PE is now experiencing the first signs of commoditization and disintermediation characteristic for a mature market with standardized products.

HOW DOES THE INDUSTRY RESPOND?

The question therefore is can the industry maintain its entrepreneurial spirit of earlier years and the returns associated with it? How will GPs react to the pressures on their business model?

Historically, the PE industry has been innovative and highly adaptable. We currently see three approaches, which are not mutually exclusive, in how GPs deal with the challenges. One is to adjust to specific LP demands, which in themselves are no longer as homogeneous as before, two is to reduce dependency on LPs and three is to retreat into highly specialized niches, which for the moment are less impacted by the trends described above.

As discussed earlier, many of the largest PE firms have been benefiting tremendously from the trend towards institutionalization. Yes, they have had to accept lower fees, some reshuffling of conditions, and extensive co-investment rights, but this is more than compensated for by the very large commitments investors write for their funds. In fact, by offering generous fee breaks and co-investment rights, they tie investors closer to their firm, elevating their relationship to a "strategic" one. GPs have also been quite willing to adjust to specific investor needs. An example is the set-up of vehicles with a substantially longer fund life, matching the investment horizon of certain investors. While again less lucrative on a percentage fee basis than the conventional structure, GPs are compensated with a quasi-permanent capital vehicle. Another popular approach has been to establish separately managed accounts for very large commitments or for investors with special needs. For smaller institutional investors, new semi-bespoke platforms are emerging, pooling their capital and offering them access to specific strategies such as co-investment or secondaries.

At the same time, PE firms are actively looking to reduce the dependency on their established LPs. Noticeable routes are the sale of a stake in the manager either to strategic investors or to the general public through a listing. Aside from solving succession issues, this is often undertaken to create permanent capital vehicles (no longer requiring fundraising), a balance sheet to invest alongside the closed-end funds or acquisition currency to diversify away from the core PE business. The increased brand recognition gained in the process of a listing might also help with opening the asset class to individual investors. And just to link back to the earlier theme, any attempt to market to retail investors will require an institutional set-up to reduce the perceived risk.

Lastly, GPs may try to conserve their model by focusing on the areas least exposed to the commoditization trend. This includes raising sector or thematic funds with the explicit promise of high industry expertise and operating value creation and a distinct, less correlated strategy. GPs may also define their niche by focusing on smaller, more complex deals, including restructuring activities or frontier market investing. Fundraising needs to be tailored to these strategies, for instance by targeting smaller investors such as high-net worth individuals and family offices, who have a higher risk tolerance and remain willing to invest in the original PE model.

Where does this leave the industry? We expect several distinct segments to emerge:

* For lower risk (e.g., infrastructure or secondary buys from PE firms) and larger bilateral transactions, we expect to see more investors attempt to deploy capital directly, to save on the layer of fees and gain more control over their exposure. Whether investors will be able to set up the independent processes and develop the teams needed, in the context of large organizations, and stomach the concentration risk associated with such a strategy, especially in a volatile environment, remains to be seen.

* For medium risk, i.e., "standard" PE transactions, LPs are going to expect to pay lower fees and gain more control over their portfolio build-out either directly through separately managed accounts and special vehicles or indirectly through an increased proportion of co-investments. Economies of scale, a brand (especially with LPs), multi-product offerings and a global reach will continue to give an advantage to larger PE firms.

* Highly specialized, higher risk–return bundles, which require specialist skills and have the potential to generate the elusive alpha, are likely to remain the exclusive domain of top PE firms for the foreseeable future. This segment will attract smaller, more sophisticated investors (including PE professionals themselves), able to absorb the risk that comes with this strategy in exchange for market-beating returns.

PRIVATE EQUITY—QUO VADIS
BY CLAUDIA ZEISBERGER

The average birthdate of this year's crop of INSEAD MBA students coincides with the 1989 publication of *Barbarians at the Gate*, a tale of greed, subversion and conspiracy that chronicled the largest leveraged buyout of its time in the early days of PE. In light of such an ignoble beginning for the industry, who would have thought that the intentions of those pioneer raiders would, over several decades, mature into a focus on value creation and the impact of their investments on the communities in which they operate and on society as a whole? Who could have envisioned today's vibrant start-up ecosystems back in the 1940s and '50s when the likes of ARDC[3] and 3i were set up by their respective governments to stimulate post-war economies?

PE is no longer a fringe asset class. It has matured and is now considered mainstream. PE funds have figured out how to embrace change and evolve, which bodes well for the coming decades. I foresee major changes on the horizon and, fully understanding that forward-looking statements have a reputation of straying significantly from future reality, wanted to share my attempt at a glimpse into the future.

SUCCESS SPAWNS IMITATORS: AND BUSINESSES HAVE STARTED TO PAY ATTENTION

Organizations frequently ask INSEAD to run in-house seminars distilling PE's recipe for success. Senior executives ask us to reveal the secret sauce that makes top-quartile funds so successful. They wish to learn about private equity's effective tools, processes and business models and bring them back to the board rooms of their own organizations. Family businesses in particular have started to pay attention. A fourth-generation European family business (the world's most profitable toy maker) recently announced a restructuring that employed a standard PE model as a guide. With greater frequency, real economy institutions regard the modern PE model as something to emulate and aspire to.

Of course, it remains to be seen if the companies of tomorrow that take a leaf or two out of the PE playbook can be as rigorous and disciplined in their execution as PE investors have been in the past. But if estimates from the United States are correct (12–17% of all companies over $100 million in value are in PE hands), a large group of senior executives currently occupy ringside seats, not just as observers but working side by side with their investors to learn the tools of the trade.

LPs—A TSUNAMI OF CAPITAL?

The rapid growth of capital flowing into the PE industry will likely continue.

---

3. American Research and Development Corporation.

The historically low interest rate environment of the last decade has influenced investor behavior and put significant pressure on portfolio managers to search for means of enhancing returns.

Institutional investors understand that ignoring the investable universe of non-listed companies and maintaining a strategy focused exclusively on public market equity is a luxury that few can afford. Some of the institutional investor holdouts—namely, Norway's pension plan and Japan's GPIF—recently announced policy changes that allow them to add PE to their investable universe, thereby joining other public and private pension plans and sovereign wealth funds in addition to family offices and high-net worth individuals in their desire to invest in funds backed by the best GPs.

Pension plans will continue to be enthusiastic allocators to PE given that they face underfunding issues (by some estimates as high as $5 trillion[4]). Existing sovereign wealth funds added US$1 trillion in investable assets between 2013 and 2015 alone[5] and new sovereign funds continue to be launched, mainly in the emerging markets. China's insurers have also started to allocate to offshore funds and their contribution to the wave of new capital looking for investable assets will likely grow. Considering the origins of these new players and the rapid growth in their participation, allocations from Europe and Asia may very well overtake those from the United States in the coming decades.

More than 15 years ago, veteran institutional investors started to expand their traditional PE model to avoid the "2+20" fee structure by circumventing PE funds and trying their hands at direct investments. Some have developed a solid reputation with excellent teams and nowadays sit across the table from traditional PE players when interesting deals come to market. This trend—the desire to "go direct"—is bound to continue on the margin but is unlikely to lead to a meaningful break with the traditional GP–LP model; it is a trend that will prove successful only for a select few of the very large investors.

Indeed, the LP community is increasingly subject to an 'access bifurcation'; a division into an investment world of "haves" and "have-nots"—those with access to top-quartile fund managers and those having to make do with less successful or unexperienced managers. Additionally, many large allocators have been trying to consolidate their GP relationships, thereby reducing the number of funds they commit to (but writing larger checks) and this just exacerbates the accessibility gap.

GPs AND THE PE MODEL

The continuous stream of LP capital in recent years led to some firms growing beyond their wildest dreams and in the process extending their product offerings beyond that of closed-end PE funds. (At times, it left their LPs wondering if the hungry dealmakers from the past had turned into asset accumulators.) The increasing pool of investible

4. Pension Task Force at the Actuarial Standards Board (ASB); underfunding for state and local government pensions in the US alone, considering adjusted valuations. http://www.forbes.com/sites/andrewbiggs/2016/07/01/are-state-and-local-government-pensions-underfunded-by-5-trillion/#7c323ce17c8f.
5. Preqin Sovereign Wealth Fund Review, June 2015.

capital has made it easier for new players to enter the scene, a trend that will impact deal making in the future. In addition to experienced PE partners spinning out to set up shop and some large LPs turning into quasi-GPs, the emerging markets are driving change and have added new players.

Chinese "outward bound" investment activities and cross-border transactions are truly becoming a reality with Middle Kingdom PE vehicles buying aggressively into overseas assets. One can expect that players in other emerging markets will soon gain the confidence and skills to explore old world investments.

Abundant investible capital plus new players entering the industry have clearly led to increased competition for deals and higher valuations. The trend towards more expensive deal making will certainly continue to test the mettle of PE investors. Old tricks may need to be complemented with new strategies to maintain the desired returns.

NOT JUST PRIVATE EQUITY—PRIVATE CAPITAL

As the PE industry has matured, the scope of investment strategies employed by "traditional" fund managers has expanded; PE is no longer just about venture, growth equity and buyouts. As the share of these "alternative strategies" under the umbrella of PE has grown rapidly since 2005, "private capital" may be a more appropriate term for the industry in the future. We took the aggregated AUM from PE (Exhibit 25.1) and added infrastructure, natural resources and real estate as well as distressed PE, secondaries, co-investment and mezzanine funds (see Exhibit 25.5) and the picture became clear: in 2015, investors had more than US$4 trillion invested in private capital and a fast-growing percentage was dedicated to these alternative strategies. Given the liquidity and diversification benefits of including those assets in a portfolio, I expect their share will continue to grow.

Exhibit 25.5 Private Capital AUM by Strategy

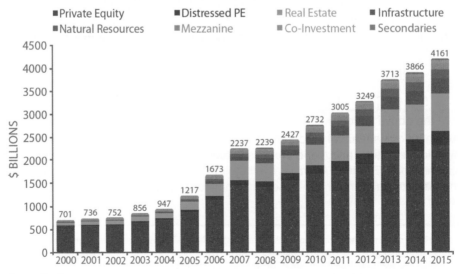

Source: Preqin

HOW MAY THIS PLAY OUT IN THE IMMEDIATE FUTURE?

Let me close with a look at the next five years and in the process help our readers to connect the dots and apply some of the theory from the earlier chapters in the book:

We are in the midst—perhaps just coming to the end—of a so-called "exit supercycle" in PE (started 2014), which is bound to have long-term consequences. A sound exit environment for global buyouts meant that even pre-crisis deals (done in 2005–2007) were able to work their way towards closure at reasonable valuations. To the delight of the investor community, post-2010 distributions from exits exceeded LP contributions (capital calls) and led to a few solid years of cash inflows and a positive sloping J-curve. Returning money endeared the industry to its LPs and of course facilitated fundraising. LPs were happy to "re-up," remembering the recent "good years" of positive cash flows. It is no surprise that 2014/15 will go down in history as a banner period for fundraising.

Nevertheless, the good times are unlikely to continue to roll post-2017. The following are some expected consequences of such "irrational exuberance"[6]:

Deal making has been slow in 2015/16. This is of course not surprising in an era where "10 is the new 8," as a partner from a large buyout fund commented at an industry conference. He was referring to the steep EBITDA entry multiples he and his peers were paying to deploy the successfully raised funds. (In certain emerging market industries entry multiples of 20–30 times EBITDA are not unheard of.) Whether deals done at such ambitious valuations will be managed to a profitable exit is anyone's guess, but three predictions can be made:

1. Fewer deals now will lead to fewer exits in the years to come, in turn returning less money to investors. In addition,
2. Slower deal activity will lead to rising dry powder and to LPs questioning the justification for their funds sitting idle on the sidelines—possibly encouraging them to look for greener pastures elsewhere.
3. Multiples at such high levels will encourage quick exits, leading to shorter holding periods (a reminder of pre-global financial crisis times). It will certainly question the industry's proposition of value creation. For other less fortunate deals, they might delay exits and prolong the wait for investee companies to create value through profit growth.

While the above concerns are well justified, the demand from companies for (private) capital and experienced partners willing to roll up their sleeves is increasing in parallel. Given the track record of the industry over the past four decades, where those promoting rumors of its demise were regularly proven wrong, I expect to see solutions (maybe even new models) emerging that will ensure that capital continues to reach deserving companies.

---

6. "Irrational exuberance" is a phrase used by the then-Federal Reserve Board chairman, Alan Greenspan, in a speech given at the American Enterprise Institute during the dot-com bubble of the 1990s. The phrase was interpreted as a warning that the market might be somewhat overvalued.

ACKNOWLEDGMENTS

To INSEAD for the opportunity to develop a PE Center, where many of the ideas that found their way into this book were proposed, tested and refined. Working with colleagues who push the boundaries of academic research and teaching provided the environment that allowed this book to come to life. INSEAD colleagues who deserve special mention include professors Balagopal Vissa, Vikas Aggarwal and Peter Joos whose sound advice kept us on the right track.

To our students (by now alumni): A special thank you goes to our MBAs, EMBAs and the senior executives, who have over the years refined and challenged our thinking, thereby helping us to arrive at the clear and concise concepts presented here.

To our guest authors, whose contributions provide a complementary viewpoint and at times inject a solid dose of reality into the chapters. Our engagement with many of you over the years helped us to understand and appreciate the different facets of the industry.

To some special contributors: Certain chapters benefited from the attention of specialists in their fields. Special thanks go to Andrew Ostrognai who went beyond the call of duty in ensuring that our fund formation chapter reflected best industry practices. Input from Josi Langhorne helped shape our chapter on deal documentation, ensuring an easy read despite the required degree of detail. Special thanks go to the team at INSEAD Alum Ventures and Vinnie Lauria at Golden Gate Ventures for providing input and ideas for our venture chapter. The chapter on responsible investment benefited greatly from Ian Potter's input; we appreciate his time and support. And thanks also to Dominik Woessner and Michael Hu who helped refine our chapter on PE secondaries.

To the staff and researchers at INSEAD: At the PE Center, special thanks go to our research assistant Alexandra Albers, who created the backbone for many of the chapters, and to Tan Sze Gar who helped compile and refine our glossary. A shout-out is in order to the world class INSEAD case team in particular Isabel Assureira, Carine Dao Panam and our tireless case administrator Claire Derouin and senior editor Hazel Hamelin; their support was invaluable for the publication of *Private Equity in Action*.

To the people with that special something: Thank you to our editor Lynn Selhat, who took on the task of coordinating the voices of three different authors and created a cohesive product. Our visual designer Harold Cheng brought our ideas to life by creating visuals that are crisp and clear and show a sense of humor.

To our publishing team at Wiley who worked with a team of first-time authors to bring two books to market; thanks to Thomas Hyrkiel for his steady hand and sound advice from conception to publication and to Samantha Hartley for translating our manuscript and design ideas into two well-designed books.

From Claudia a thank you to my academic mentors and colleagues at INSEAD, in particular my faculty colleagues in the Entrepreneurship department. A special thank you goes to Phil Anderson who was a fantastic sounding board after encouraging me for years to write this book. I would like to mention as well Herminia Ibarra and Erin Meyer, who shared their experience as authors and offered advice when needed.

From Michael to my business partner Denis Tse, who picked up the slack while I worked on the book, with deadlines more than once corresponding to the hot phases of a deal. Things that I've learned from him as we grew our business, I have liberally shared with the readers of this book.

From Bowen to my first mentor in New York City, David Officer, who brought me into the fold at Permal and provided the springboard that launched me to INSEAD and Asia. Many happy returns Permalinfo.

Finally, we would like to acknowledge with gratitude the support and love of our families; this book would not have been possible without their patience.

ABOUT THE AUTHORS

Claudia Zeisberger
Senior Affiliate Professor of Decision Sciences and Entrepreneurship & Family Enterprise
Academic Director, Global Private Equity Initiative (GPEI)
INSEAD

Claudia Zeisberger is a Senior Affiliate Professor of Decision Sciences and Entrepreneurship & Family Enterprise at INSEAD, and the Founder and Academic Director of the school's private equity centre (GPEI). Before joining INSEAD in 2005, she spent 16 years in investment banking in New York, London, Frankfurt, Tokyo and Singapore.

Professor Zeisberger is a founding investor of INSEAD Alum Ventures (IAV), the business school's first dedicated seed fund and she actively mentors early stage companies and first-time entrepreneurs. At INSEAD, she launched Managing Corporate Turnarounds, a popular MBA elective known for its intensive computer-based simulation involving an iconic car brand and its struggle with bankruptcy. As a natural extension, she teaches INSEAD's Risk management elective. She has frequently been nominated for the MBA Best Teaching Award in her PE elective and has been awarded the Dean's Commendation for Excellence in MBA Teaching annually since 2008.

Professor Zeisberger is known for her extensive research on PE in emerging markets, and her output is a function of her close working relationships with private equity firms and their investee companies, institutional investors, family offices and sovereign wealth funds.

Michael Prahl
Partner, Asia-IO Advisors
Adjunct Professor of Entrepreneurship & Family Enterprise,
Distinguished Fellow, Global Private Equity Initiative (GPEI)
INSEAD

Michael Prahl is the co-founder of Asia-IO Advisors, a private equity firm focused on implementing Asia and cross-border private equity investment programs for large institutional and corporate investor. Michael has spent almost 20 years in private equity, starting in venture capital during the dotcom boom. He worked for many years at a global PE firm, in Europe, the US and Asia, completing deals including regular buyouts, public to privates, PIPEs, minority investments and privatizations.

An INSEAD alumnus, Michael served as the first Executive Director of the school's PE Centre, with research interests in the areas of co-investment, family offices and market entry strategies & portfolio allocation for limited partners. Michael remains an INSEAD Distinguished Fellow attached to GPEI with a focus on LBOs and Asian private equity and an Adjunct Professor teaching the MBA Leveraged Buyout elective.

Bowen White
Centre Director, Global Private Equity Initiative (GPEI)
INSEAD

Bowen White currently serves as the Centre Director of INSEAD's GPEI, the business school's centre in private equity. As Centre Director, he leads its research and outreach activities and has published on topics including operational value creation, responsible investment, LP portfolio construction and minority investment in family businesses.

Bowen has spent his career working in and conducting research on the global alternative asset management industry. In the New York hedge fund industry, he researched topics from statistical arbitrage investment strategies in commodities markets to macroeconomic trends and global hedge fund performance. Having worked for both a proprietary trading firm and a fund of funds, he has seen first-hand the challenges faced by investors and allocators of capital to the hedge fund industry. An INSEAD alumnus, Bowen has also advised on a range of VC and growth equity fundraising opportunities across Southeast Asia.

GLOSSARY

Additional material to complement this book and connect it to the case book *Private Equity in Action – Case Studies from Developed and Emerging Markets* can be found on the companion website:

www.masteringprivateequity.com

Term	Definition
100-day Plan	A plan that outlines clearly the changes to be achieved by a company during the first three months post-investment.
500-day Plan	Exit plan by a private equity (PE) firm to prepare the portfolio company for sale.
Affiliate Transaction	Transaction between two funds managed by the same sponsor.
Agency Risk	Part of agency theory. Risk of management (the agent) pursuing their own interests instead of shareholders (the principal).
Alternative Investment Vehicles (AIVs)	AIVs are structured to accommodate one or more special investments made outside of the primary fund (and/or a parallel fund).
American-style Waterfall	Also known as deal-by-deal waterfall: this structure entitles a general partner (GP) to carried interest after each portfolio company's exit, provided investors have received their invested capital and any preferred return including a "make whole" payment for losses incurred on prior deals.
Amortized	For a loan: repaid on an annual basis over the life of the loan.
Anti-dilution	A clause that gives investors the right to maintain their percentage ownership in a company by buying additional, proportional shares in the company in future financing rounds. In the event of a "down-round" the conversion price of the preferred share class will be adjusted downwards to the level of the new valuation; as a result, shareholders who invested at a higher valuation will receive additional shares to maintain their ownership stake in the start-up.
Articles of Association (AOA)	A mandatory agreement entered into between the company and its shareholders and filed with a government institution post-closing. An AOA typically includes a limited amount of information that the company and its shareholders are required to disclose. Also referred to as the articles of incorporation, certificate of incorporation, and other names in different jurisdictions.
As-converted Basis	A metric to determine the total equity base by assuming that all preferred shares have been converted into common shares based on a prespecified conversion ratio.

Auction	A sales process involving multiple competing parties to maximize the price for the seller.
Back-testing	Process of applying an allocation or trading strategy to historical data to gauge the effect on portfolio or investment performance.
Bankruptcy	Legal status in which an insolvent company (which cannot fully repay its debt) is declared bankrupt, typically by court order.
Base Case Financial Scenario	Scenario based on the company's expected/most likely operating performance.
BidCo	The legal entity that executes the acquisition of a target company.
Blind Pool	A fund in which investors don't know which assets will be acquired or have any influence over investment decision-making.
Break-up Fee	Financial penalties imposed on the party terminating an agreement, referred to as break-up or break fees in the case of termination by the seller and reverse break-up fees in the case of termination by the buyer.
Bridge Loan	A short-term loan that bridges funding until the arrangement of long-term financing.
Bullet Repayment	A single, lump sum repayment of the entire principal of a loan and accrued interest at the end of its term.
Burn Rate	Rate at which a new company spends its (venture) capital before reaching positive operational cash flow. It is typically measured in $/month.
Business Plan	A document describing a company's strategic vision, key value drivers and forward-looking risks and opportunities with a multi year financial forecast.
Buyout	Acquisition of a controlling equity stake in a company. If initiated by the firm's incumbent management it's called a management buyout, if driven by an external management a management buy-in, and if by the PE firm then an institutional buyout. Buyouts that use significant amounts of debt are called leveraged buyouts (LBOs). Transactions in which a PE fund sells a company to another PE fund are called secondary buyouts.
Capital Calls	Drawdowns of limited partner (LP) commitments over the investment period of a fund. "Capital calls" fund investments and pay for a fund's fees and expenses.
Capital Structure	The way a company finances its assets and operations by using different sources of funds such as equity, debt or hybrid securities.
Carve-out	Acquisition of a corporate division, business unit or subsidiary and conversion into a standalone company.
Cash Conversion Rate	Proportion of profits converted into cash flow (typically operating cash flow/operating profit).

Cash Sweep	Requirement that any excess cash be used to repay a loan facility before dividend payments are made to shareholders.
Closed-end fund	A closed-end fund issues a fixed number of shares (and is not open to new investors.) In the context of PE, funds have a finite lifespan (term) with no redemption prior to the expiration of the fund.
Closing Mechanism	Clauses in the sale and purchase agreement (SPA) that define the manner in which the final purchase price is established.
Co-investing	Investing side by side with a PE fund directly in an operating company.
Co-investment Funds	Co-investment funds are vehicles set up by the GP to invest alongside the primary and parallel funds for a portion of a single investment. The co-investment is typically provided by one or more of a fund's LPs at lower (or no) fee and carried interest terms; at times the funds may be drawn from an external party.
Co-leading	Active co-investing. In active co-investing the LP is invited early on to join forces with a PE fund and shares in the work, cost and risk of a not yet completed transaction.
Collateralized Loan Obligations (CLOs)	Security backed by a pool of loans. Sold on to investors in various tranches with different interest rates reflecting their different riskiness.
Common Equity	Common equity is the most junior instrument in a company's capital structure and provides a residual claim on cash flows and company assets after claims of all other capital providers are satisfied.
Completion Accounts Mechanism	A pricing mechanism that adjusts the preliminary purchase price based on the difference between a company's net debt and target working capital at signing and the actual balance sheet values at closing.
Conditions Precedent (CPs)	Specific events or states of affairs that must be satisfied or waived for a transaction to proceed.
Conversion Rights	The right of preferred shareholders to convert their preferred shares to common shares; the conversion rate—at the outset usually 1:1 of preferred to common—is clearly defined.
Convertible Debt	A type of debt instrument that can be converted into equity or cash.
Covenants	Financial covenants are a promise by the borrowing company that certain activities will (affirmative covenants) or will not (negative covenants) be undertaken. They protect lenders from borrowers defaulting on their obligations. Some covenants are checked on a regular basis (maintenance covenants) while others are only tested upon the occurrence of a specific event (incurrence covenants).
Data Room	A database (physical or virtual) established by a target company and its advisors that contains all material documentation for due diligence.

Deal Flow	Investment opportunities available to a PE firm. If sourced by a PE firm directly it's called "proprietary" deal flow, if through an advisor (e.g., banks, accountants) then "intermediated" deal flow.
Deal-by-deal Structure	In a deal-by-deal fund structure, a dedicated vehicle will be created for the purposes of making an investment in a single target opportunity.
Debt Capacity	An assessment on the amount of debt a company can service and pay back over a certain period.
Debt Commitment Letter	An agreement in which a lender sets out the terms on which it is prepared to lend money to the borrower. In an LBO, this letter is typically addressed to a buyout fund's acquisition vehicle by the lead arranger of an LBO's debt financing. Securing a debt commitment letter is often required before a seller will sign an SPA to provide funding certainty for the seller.
Debt Free/Cash Free	The seller receives all cash and pays off all debt of the target at the time of sale.
Debt Multiple	A measure of a company's debt relative to a key metric, typically earnings before interest, tax, depreciation and amortization (EBITDA) (debt/EBITDA).
Debt Push-down	To transfer the debt of a "BidCo" to the target company. By executing a debt push-down, senior lenders have a direct claim on target company assets and eliminate the structural subordination of senior lenders to trade creditors.
Debt Servicing	Payment of interest and agreed mandatory repayments of debt over a certain time period.
Direct Investing	Investing directly into private companies instead of through a fund.
Distressed Debt Investing	Acquiring stakes in the debt obligations of distressed companies to generate returns through the appreciation of the debt or an eventual restructuring of the target company.
Distribution "Waterfall"	The order of priority and timing of distributions made to a fund's LPs and its GP. See also European-style Waterfall and American-style Waterfall.
Distributions	Capital returned to LPs plus LPs' share of profits.
Dividend Recapitalizations	Repayment of a portion or all of a fund's invested capital via a special dividend funded by either releveraging the portfolio company's balance sheet through the issuance of debt securities (leveraged recap) or from cash on hand in the company (non-leveraged recap).
Down-round	A round of funding raised at a lower valuation than the previous financing round.
Drag-along Provision	A drag-along provision provides the majority shareholder with the right to force minority shareholders to sell their shares in a third-party transaction at equal terms.

Dry Powder	A fund's uninvested committed capital. Also used to describe the PE industry's total uninvested capital.
Earn-out	Represents an agreement to pay a portion of the purchase price at a later date based on the performance of the business.
EBITDA Multiple	Enterprise value expressed as a multiple of EBITDA.
Economic Net Income (ENI)	Non-generally accepted accounting principles performance measure used by several listed PE firms adjusting regular net income for income taxes, non-cash charges related to vesting of equity-based compensation and amortization of intangible assets.
Employee Stock Ownership Plan (ESOP)	An ESOP sets aside a percentage of shares in a company to non-founder/owner employees in the form of stock options to attract, reward and retain talent.
Enterprise Value (EV)	A company's total value—calculated as equity value plus net debt.
Environment, Social and Governance (ESG) Management	Actively and systematically manage environmental, social and governance factors by establishing structured ESG programs with ESG policies and procedures being put in place.
Equity Commitment Letter	An agreement addressed by a PE fund in an LBO to its acquisition vehicle, which provides a limited guarantee for the equity financing detailed in an SPA. Securing these letters is often required for the PE fund to enter into an SPA and to satisfy buyer financing reps and warranties. In some instances, the PE firm may directly provide a limited guarantee on the equity component of the transaction.
European-style Waterfall	Also known as all capital first waterfall: a GP is entitled to carried interest only after all capital contributed by investors over a fund's life has been returned and any capital required to satisfy a hurdle rate or preferred return has been distributed.
Family Office	Wealth management advisory firms that manage the portfolios of high-net worth individuals or families. Usually run by professional managers.
Feeder Funds	Feeder funds aggregate commitments from one or more investors and invest directly into the primary fund as an LP.
Fiduciary Duties	Highest standard of care between a fiduciary and beneficiary.
Financial Distress	Situation when a company cannot meet or has difficulty meeting its financial obligations.
First Closing	PE firms raise capital for a fund by securing capital commitments from investors through a series of fund closings. The first closing is when an initial threshold of capital commitments has been reached and the fund can begin deploying capital.
First Lien Term Loan	Typically, senior secured loans with first priority on payment.
Free Float	Proportion of shares of a listed company that is traded in the stock market.

General Partners (GPs)	A fund's GP is wholly responsible for all aspects related to managing a fund and has a fiduciary duty to act solely in the interest of the fund's investors. A GP will issue capital calls to LPs and make all investment and divestment decisions for the fund in line with the mandate set out in the limited partnership agreement (LPA).
Global Private Equity Initiative (GPEI)	The INSEAD GPEI drives teaching, research and events in the field of PE and related alternative investments at INSEAD, a leading business school. www.insead.edu/gpei
High-yield Debt	Also known as high-yield bonds, they are bonds rated below investment grade. They offer higher interest rates than investment-grade bonds to compensate for the additional risk and low ranking in the capital structure.
Hurdle Rate	The preferred return to investors before a carried interest is permitted. The hurdle rate, frequently set at 8%, will be negotiated during fundraising.
Impact Investing	Investing in companies with the aim of achieving a social return component in addition to a financial return target.
Indemnification	Contractual obligation by one party to compensate the other party from losses incurred following a breach of contract, removing the uncertainty of pursuing a legal claim in court or arbitration.
Information Memorandum	Typically, the first formal document shared by a target that provides an up-to-date overview of its business and the investment opportunity.
In-kind Distributions	Distributions to LPs made in the form of marketable securities, typically listed shares of portfolio companies after an initial public offering (IPO).
INSEAD	One of the world's leading and largest graduate business schools with campuses in Europe (France), Asia (Singapore) and Abu Dhabi. https://www.insead.edu/
Interest Coverage Ratio	EBITDA/interest expense. Measures a company's ability to pay interest on its outstanding debt.
Investment Committee (IC)	An IC makes the binding investment and divestment decisions for the fund under delegated authority from the GP.
Investment Manager	An investment manager conducts the day-to-day activities of a PE fund; it evaluates potential investment opportunities, provides advisory services to the fund's portfolio companies, and manages the fund's audit and reporting processes.
Investment Period	The time period during which a fund can draw down LP commitments to make investments. It typically lasts for three to five years from the date of the fund's first closing.
IRR	Internal rate of return—a widely used measure of the return earned by investors from an individual investment, fund or portfolio of funds. It represents the discount rate that renders the net present value of a series of cash flows zero.

J-curve	A J-curve in PE represents an LP's cumulative net cash position in a fund over time. The curve starts with an increasingly negative net cash position as capital is drawn down during the investment periods before reversing direction as LPs start receiving distributions from a maturing portfolio.
Jump Bid	A bid in the second round of an auction that is substantially higher above perceived bids of the first round in an attempt to lock up the deal.
Letter of Intent (LOI)	An LOI functions as a bidding document and sets out key economic (e.g., bid price) and procedural terms that form the basis for further negotiations in an acquisition process. These provisions are non-binding and seen as a "good faith" representation of a bidder's intent. PE firms and sellers use LOIs to ensure that there is general alignment on key terms before incurring the expense of in-depth due diligence and negotiating a definitive sale and purchase agreement.
Leverage	The use of various debt instruments to increase the equity return of an investment. Also the amount of debt used in an LBO.
Leveraged Loan	A loan issued by one or a group of banks. In an LBO, bank(s) often sell it on (syndicate) to other banks or investors.
Limited Partners (LPs)	Investors. LPs participate in PE funds as passive investors, with no involvement in the fund's day-to-day operations, with an individual LP's liability limited to the capital committed to the fund. LPs legally commit to provide capital for investment when it is drawn down (or "called") by the PE fund and they receive distributions of invested capital—and a share of profits—upon successful exits of the underlying assets in the fund.
Limited Partnership Agreement (LPA)	A fund's LPA sets out the general terms and conditions applicable to all participants in a fund, in particular a fund's GP and LPs. It covers, among other things, their rights and responsibilities related to fundraising, capital calls and distributions, expenses and profit sharing, fund governance and reporting, and fund termination.
Liquidation Preference	Refers to the priority claim that preferred shareholders hold on the proceeds (dividends or exit including bankruptcy). These shareholders receive their investment back first (and in the case of multiple liquidation preference, several times) before other shareholders participate.
Listed Funds (LFs)	Publicly traded PE funds—also referred to as evergreen funds. Investing in an LF provides retail investors with returns through both share price appreciation and dividends.
Listed PE Firms (LGPs)	Publicly traded PE firms. Shareholders of an LGP participate in all revenues generated by the firm, including carried interest and fees.
Locked-box Mechanism	A fixed-price mechanism that fixes net debt and working capital values at a specific date (known as the locked-box date) before the signing of the SPA.

Lock-up Period	Time period in which a large shareholder cannot divest shares following an IPO, commonly lasting 3 to 12 months.
Majority Control	Control of more than 50% of a company's voting rights (typically linked to the economic interest in the company). The majority shareholder controls the board of directors and hence can dictate strategic and operational decision-making.
Management Fee	A fee charged by a PE fund's investment manager to cover day-to-day expenses of the fund, including salaries, office rent and costs related to deal sourcing and monitoring portfolio investments. It typically ranges from 1 to 2.5% depending on the size and strategy of the fund and the bargaining power of the PE firm during fundraising.
Management Fee Offset	Reduction of a fund's management fee by a percentage of the fees collected from a fund's portfolio companies.
Material Adverse Change (MAC) Clause	A legal provision that provides a buyer with the right to terminate an acquisition contract in case of an event that substantially impairs the value of the acquisition target. In an SPA, the specific definition of what constitutes a MAC at the target company varies from transaction to transaction and is formalized in the definitions of the agreement.
Mezzanine Financing	A form of junior unsecured debt or preferred equity raised in the private institutional market. Mezzanine loans may provide additional upside by including an "equity kicker" through a convertible debt feature or attached warrants.
Minority Equity Stake	A shareholding of less than 50% of a company's equity, which is not a controlling stake.
Minority Protection Rights	Rights and safeguards to mitigate the risks associated with a minority shareholding. These rights will enable the minority shareholders to monitor their investee firms, influence the proceedings, and pre-empt or mitigate potential conflicts of interest with the majority shareholder.
Multiple Expansion	An increase in the valuation multiple.
Multiple of Money Invested (MoM)	Also known as the investment multiple, it is the ratio of the realized and unrealized fund/equity value divided by the capital invested in the fund/company.
Negative Screening	Screening out investments that fall outside the "Do no harm" investment mandate. The investment mandate may mean avoiding controversial sectors, such as tobacco, gambling, fossil fuel production or defense technology.
Net Asset Value (NAV)	Value of a fund's assets minus liabilities.
Net Debt	Net debt is arrived at by subtracting the value of a company's liabilities from the value of its liquid assets. The main components of net debt are interest-bearing bank borrowings and cash. Which additional elements of debt-like liabilities and cash equivalents will be included in net debt is often the subject of intense negotiation.

Net Invested Capital	Net invested capital consists of contributed capital, minus capital returned from exits and any write-downs of investment value.
Non-disclosure Agreement (NDA)	A legal agreement, also known as a confidentiality agreement, that restricts access for third parties to information that parties share. NDAs can be structured to protect a one-way or a mutual flow of information.
Open-ended (Evergreen) Vehicles	In an open-ended (evergreen) fund structure, funds can be raised at any time during the life of the fund and the fund has an indefinite term.
Opt-in/Opt-out Funds	Investment vehicles through which investors make "soft commitments" to the fund prior to its investments being identified. Investors are given the right to "opt in" to (or "opt out" of) each investment opportunity that the manager of the fund presents.
Paid-in-kind (PIK) interest	PIK interest refers to interest on an instrument paid with additional amounts of that instrument instead of cash, i.e., PIK interest is rolled up and added to the principal amount of the loan.
Parallel Funds	Funds set up to accommodate the special legal, tax, regulatory, accounting or other needs of an individual or group of LPs participating in a fund offering. These vehicles invest and divest side by side with the primary fund.
Partial Exit	The divestment of part of a PE fund's holdings in a portfolio company.
Portfolio Company	A company that a PE fund invests in. A PE fund will invest in a limited number of companies that represent its portfolio of companies. These companies are also referred to as investee companies or, pre-investment, as target companies.
Post-money Valuation	Value of a company after injection of new capital, i.e., invested capital plus "pre-money" valuation.
Preferred Shares	A senior form of equity that provides shareholders with certain preferential rights relative to common equity shareholders.
Pre-money Valuation	Valuation of a company before the injection of new capital.
Price/Earnings to Growth Multiple	Ratio of price-to-earnings divided by the expected future earnings growth rate of the company.
Private Debt	Non-bank lending from institutional investors (e.g., funds and insurance companies). Includes direct lending, mezzanine, venture debt and distressed debt.
Private Investment in Public Equity (PIPEs)	Private placement of shares of a publicly listed company to selected investors.
Privatization	Transfer of a business from public to private ownership, i.e., acquisition of a state-owned company.
Public to Private (P2P)	The acquisition of a publicly listed company and subsequent delisting. Also referred to as "going private" and a "take private."
Real Assets	Tangible, physical assets that include infrastructure, real estate and natural resources.

Real Option Pricing	A valuation technique that specifically takes flexibility of corporate decisions into account. Mostly used for capital budgeting decisions.
Redemption	Withdrawal; return of an investor's capital.
Redemption Rights	Redemption rights provide the holder of an equity stake the right (a put) to sell the equity stake back to the company.
Representations and Warranties	Statements of fact and promises that underpin specific elements of the transaction set out in an agreement. Reps and warranties are principally used to offer protection to a buyer in case a vendor's statements of fact regarding the target business prove to be false, to allocate a portion of performance risk at the target company to the seller and to provide an opportunity for a buyer to gain additional information on the target.
Return on Capital	Measures the return an investment generates for capital contributors, i.e., debt and equity holders.
Return on Investment	Measures amount of return on an investment relative to the investment cost, often expressed as a percentage and calculated as net profit/cost of investment.
Revolving Credit Facility	A line of bank credit predominantly used to fund a target's working capital needs.
Sale and Purchase Agreement (SPA)	A contract entered into between a buyer and a seller that governs the terms and conditions of the envisioned transaction and the acquisition process.
Search Fund	Investment vehicle through which investors finance an entrepreneur's efforts to locate, acquire and manage a company.
Second Lien Term Loans	Second lien loans are used as a bridge between first lien term loans and junior unsecured debt. They are secured against the same collateral as first lien loans but are only entitled to claims on it after the first lien debtholders are paid in full.
Secondary Transactions	Sale and purchase of interests in a PE fund (limited partnership secondaries) or sale and purchase of equity stakes in PE-backed companies (direct secondaries).
Security	Collateral or assets that a loan/debt is secured by.
Seniority	Order (priority) of repayment in the event of a sale or bankruptcy of the issuer.
Share Subscription Agreement (SSA)	An agreement between investors and a company specifying the purchase price for a certain amount of new shares in the company. It expands on the provisions of the term sheet and adds representations and warranties from each party.
Shareholder Loans	The most junior form of debt provided by shareholders. Shareholder loans typically roll up interest, which is repaid together with the principal on exit or in the case of a refinancing.

Shareholders' Agreement (SHA)	A private agreement that defines the relationship among shareholders and between shareholders and the portfolio company. An SHA is more flexible than an AOA and can include nearly any provision; as a private document, it often includes more sensitive agreements among shareholders.
Shareholding Structure	The various classes of shares that a company has issued and their rights.
Sovereign Wealth Funds	State-owned investment funds.
Special Purpose Vehicle (SPV)	A legal entity set up for a special purpose and to isolate financial risk.
Standstill Provisions	Terms in an agreement that restrict the seller from engaging with other potential buyers over a specified period of time to protect the interests of the winning bidder, who is going to incur substantial transaction cost (primarily in connection with finalizing legal documents) during the final phase of the process.
Stapled Secondary	A sale of an LP interest combined with a commitment to invest in a GP's next fund.
Successor Funds	PE firms will try to raise a new (successor) fund as soon as permitted by its current fund's LPA, typically after a significant portion of the current fund (e.g., 75%) has been invested, resulting in a new fund about every three to four years.
Sweet Equity	Equity (or options) issued to management at a discount to incentivize and align interests of management with shareholders.
Tag-along Provision	A tag-along provision provides minority shareholders with the right to sell their shares in conjunction with the majority shareholder in a third-party transaction.
Turnaround Investing	Acquiring majority equity stakes in mature companies under considerable operational duress with the aim of affecting change in the company to restore profitability.
Valuation Multiple	An expression of the market value of a company relative to a key statistic driving that value.
Vendor Debt	Debt provided by a target's sellers, essentially rolling a portion of seller proceeds back into the target company. Vendor debt is typically unsecured and subordinated to junior and senior debt, but senior to shareholder loans and equity.
Venture Philanthropy	Venture investments with philanthropic goals.
Vesting Schedule	Defined timeline for the process in which employees accrue rights to share incentives (i.e., options or shares).
Vintage	The year in which a fund has its first closing and can start investing.
Volatility	Statistical measure of dispersion of returns. A measure of risk.
Warrants	Options to purchase a company's shares at a predetermined price, often when certain trigger events occur (such as a change of control, a sale or an IPO).

INDEX